7th Edition

AP Calculus
AB&BC Rewritten from the Beginning
Vol.1

A Whole New Way to Understand Calculus
Hyunsung Shim (Albert Shim)

Copyright © 2025 by Mastering Math
All rights reserved. No part of this book may be reproduced in any form without permission of the publisher. In order to use it as educational material in schools or organizations, it is necessary to have a contact with the author first.

America Math Lab(Mastering Math)
One Samsone Street, Suite 3500, San Francisco, CA94104

Room 403, Sky Plaza, 322 Byeollae 3-ro, Namyangju-si, Gyeonggi-do, Republic of Korea

Email address : albertmath11@gmail.com

Why This Book Matters

A Calculus Companion Everyone Should Own — Not Just for Majors
Many students struggle with calculus not because the ideas are too complex, but because the notations and logic behind them are rarely explained clearly—especially at the beginning. Symbols like dy/dx, the definition of continuity, or the concept of a tangent line often appear suddenly, with no historical context or intuitive motivation. As a result, students simply follow procedures without grasping the underlying ideas, and often try to memorize formulas without understanding them.
This book was created to solve that problem — to make calculus understandable and approachable for anyone, regardless of background.

1. Unique Features of This Book

1) A New Way to Understand Continuity
Continuity is not just about a function having a value. It means the function value, the left-hand limit, and the right-hand limit all coincide—so closely that they appear to be one and the same point. This book provides visual and conceptual clarity that makes this idea intuitive.

2) The Hidden Truth Behind dy/dx
Leibniz introduced dy/dx centuries ago, but never explained why it behaves like a fraction. No standard textbook has offered a complete answer—until now. This book presents a world-first proof of why dy/dx can be manipulated like a fraction, even though it's not one.

3) See the Shape of a Graph Instantly
Learn how to spot relative maxima, minima, inflection points, concavity, and increasing/decreasing behavior at a glance. This book offers visual strategies and shortcuts that make graph analysis second nature.

4) What a Tangent Line Really Is

A line must pass through two points, yet a tangent line is defined at a single point on a curve. The key insight: A point on a curve is actually composed of three values: the left-hand limit, the function value, and the right-hand limit. What we thought was a single line (the tangent) is in fact made up of two lines—one connecting the left-hand limit to the function value, and the other connecting the function value to the right-hand limit. These two lines feel like one because their slopes are nearly identical. When this happens, we say the function is differentiable at that point.

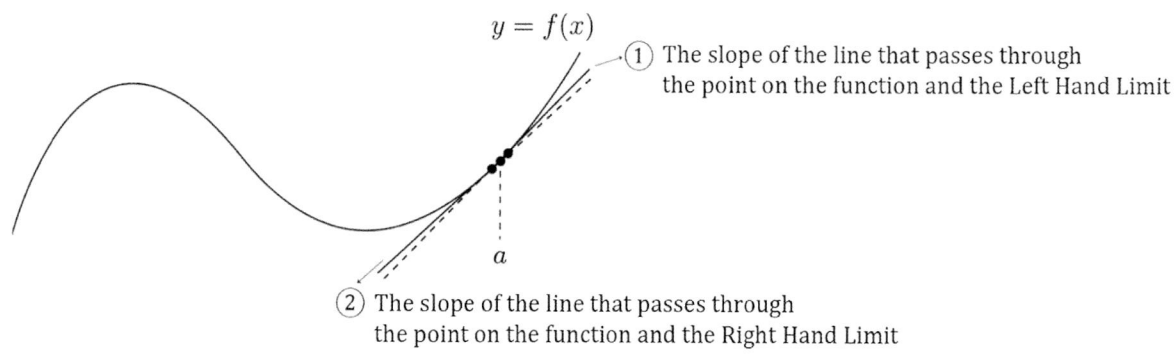

The slopes of line ① and line ② are so similar that the two lines look like one, so y = f(x) is differentiable at x = a.

5) Where the Integral Symbol Came From

Did you know that the integral sign combines the concepts of summation and integration? It's a stylized blend of S (sum) and I (integrate)—a symbol full of meaning. This book explores its origin and visual logic.

SUM + Integrate = S+I = $\int$

6) Volume Methods Demystified

Every volume formula comes down to this: Cross section area × height.

Cross-Section Method: Area of a known cross section shape × tiny height (dx or dy)

Washer Method: Don't overthink the cross section shape—it's always a circle. Just subtract one circular slice from another and integrate.

Shell Method: Visualize thin cylinders. Unroll them, and you're summing thin rectangular prisms. Simple and powerful.

7) Convergence Tests Made Visual

Instead of memorizing endless rules, learn convergence tests through comics and story-driven diagrams. Complex ideas become fun, memorable, and meaningful.

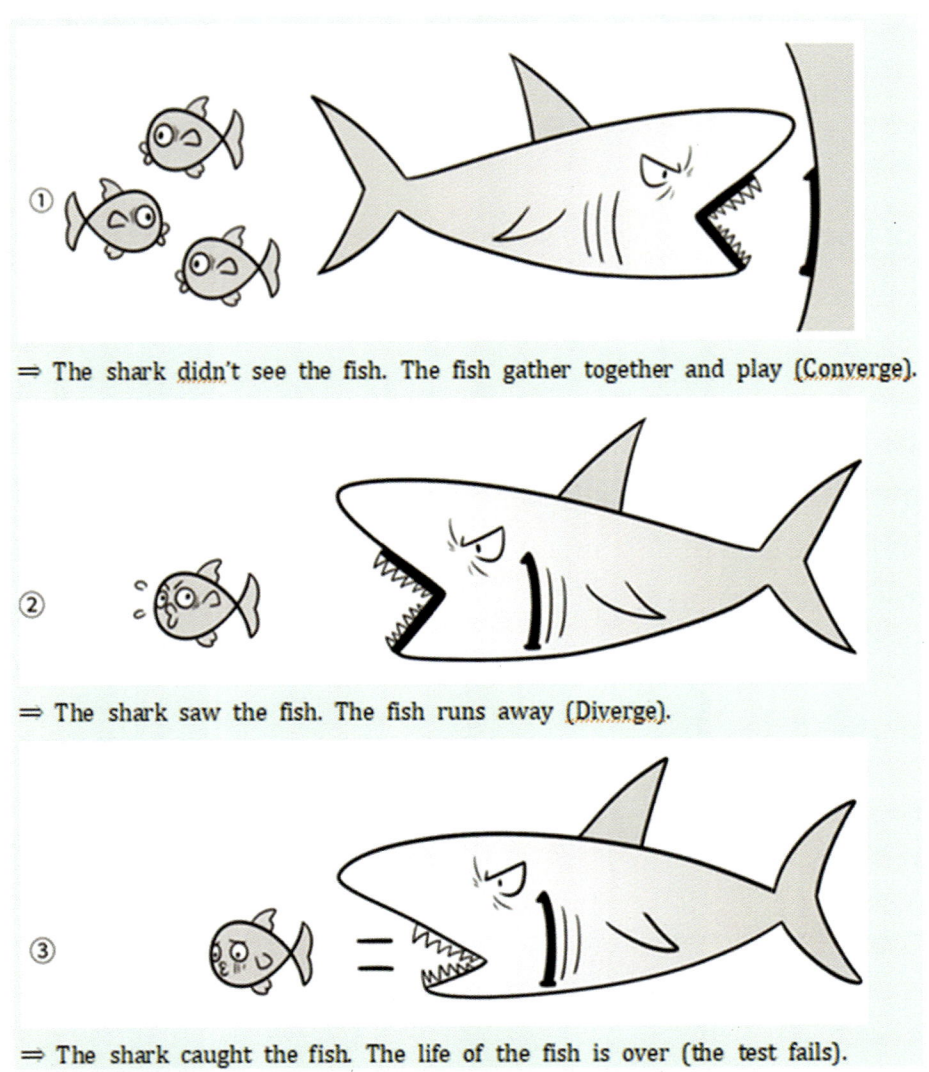

⇒ The shark didn't see the fish. The fish gather together and play (Converge).

⇒ The shark saw the fish. The fish runs away (Diverge).

⇒ The shark caught the fish. The life of the fish is over (the test fails).

2. Designed with Students in Mind
Comics and Illustrations
Visual learners will appreciate the abundant comics and diagrams that explain abstract concepts in a light and engaging way.

Why is the shape of the cross-section always a circle for "Revolutions?"

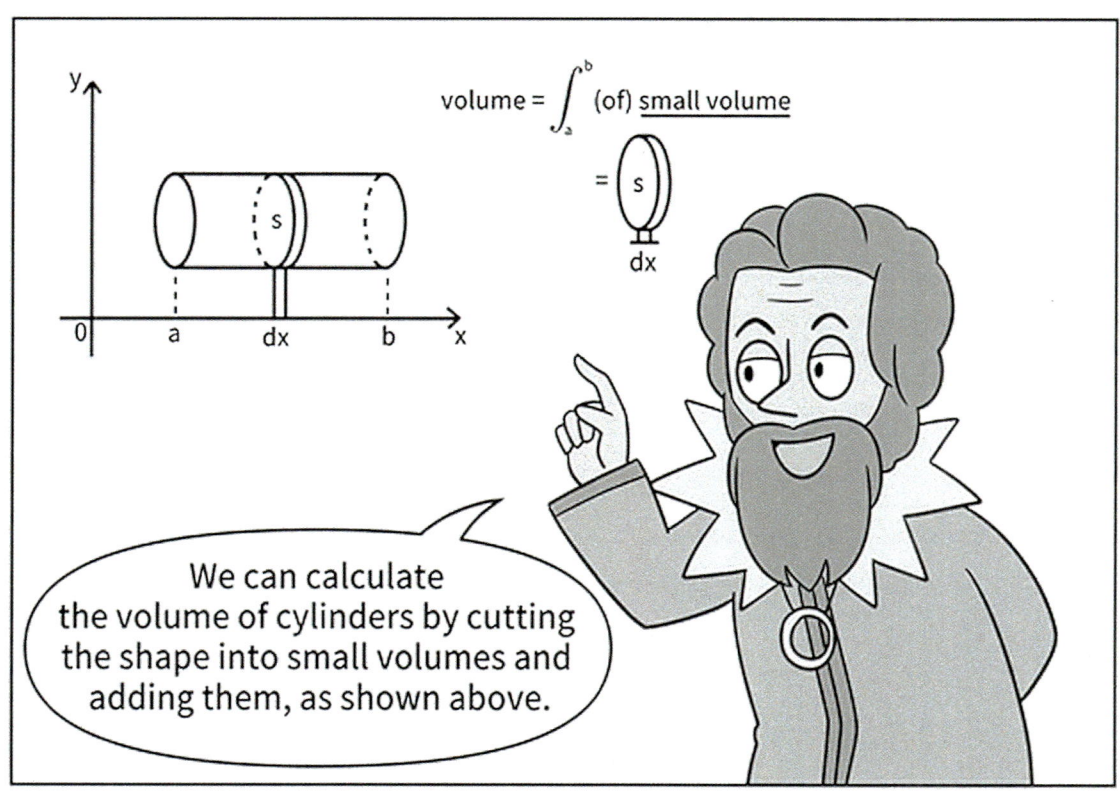

3. Smart Memorization Techniques

Instead of rote memorization, this book provides pattern-based, intuitive methods to remember essential formulas and theorems.

If the integral is of the form $\int g(x) a^{f(x)} dx$,
where g(x) is the differentiation of f(x), substitute f(x) as u.

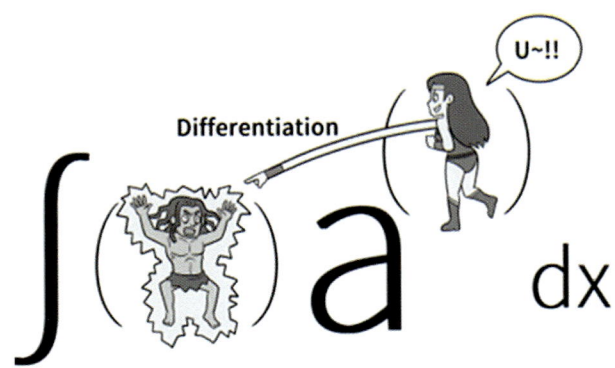

Preface

For decades, I have taught calculus and asked myself: Why do so many students find it so difficult? Over time, I realized that the real obstacle isn't the complexity of calculus itself—it's the lack of clear explanations for the notations and ideas that are completely new to beginners.

To address this, I read countless historical papers and original sources on the development of calculus. But to my surprise, I found that even the mathematicians who introduced many of the symbols and operations had not fully explained their reasoning.

So, I decided to do what no one else had done: I worked to prove and explain these ideas from the ground up. This book contains those original insights, explained with clarity and precision.

While most students own at least one calculus textbook, traditional texts are often too abstract, filled with exercises but lacking in conceptual explanation. That's where this book comes in—not to replace those texts, but to complete them.

Whether you're a beginner or an advanced student, this book is the calculus companion you didn't know you needed.

June 2025

Hyunsung Shim(Albert Shim)

Contents...

Limit — p.11

1. Limits of Sequences — p.13
2. Limits of Functions — p.55
3. Limit of Trigonometric Function — p.99
4. Asymptotes and Theorems of Continuous Function — p.106

Differentiation — p.123

1. Definition — p.125
2. Methods of Differentiation — p.142
3. T,D,M,L — p.213
   - Tangents and Normals — p.214
   - Derivative of Inverse Functions — p.221
   - Mean Value Theorem and Rolle's Theorem — p.227
   - L'Hopital's Rule — p.234
4. Analyzing Graphs — p.253
5. Related Rates — p.327
6. Applied Maximum and Minimum problems — p.345
7. Differentials Approximation — p.359

AP Calculus AB & BC Rewritten from the Beginning

Limits

AP Calculus AB & BC Rewritten from the Beginning

01 Limit

AP Calculus AB & BC Rewritten from the Beginning

Limit

01. Limits of Sequences
02. Limits of Functions
03. Limit of Trigonometric Function
04. Asymptotes and Theorems of Continuous Function

Before we begin

$\lim\limits_{x \to \infty} f(x)$ is estimation of the value of $f(x)$ as x grows infinitely large, and $\lim\limits_{x \to a} f(x)$ is estimation of the value of $f(x)$ as x approaches a certain value. That is, in this "Limit" chapter, rather than finding the exact value, the estimation is obtained.

01 Limits of Sequences

01. What is $\lim\limits_{n \to \infty} a_n$?

$\lim\limits_{x \to \infty} f(x)$ is estimation of the value of $f(x)$ as x grows infinitely large.
Let's look at the following.

① 1, 3, 5, 7, 9, $\cdots$, $(2n-1), \cdots$
$\Rightarrow$ If you list numbers infinitely like this, you get a number that is too big to know $(= \infty)$.

② 1, -1, -3, -5, -7, $\cdots$, $(-2n+3), \cdots$
$\Rightarrow$ If you list infinitely like this, you get a number that is too small to know $(= -\infty)$.

③ $1, \dfrac{1}{3}, \dfrac{1}{3^2}, \dfrac{1}{3^3}, \dfrac{1}{3^4}, \cdots, \dfrac{1}{3^n} \cdots$
$\Rightarrow$ If you list numbers infinitely like this, you get a denominator that is too big, so you get a number that is close to 0.

④ $1+\dfrac{1}{10}, 1+\dfrac{1}{10^2}, 1+\dfrac{1}{10^3}, \cdots$

What will happen if we list the numbers infinitely like this?
The answer is $1.000000\cdots010\cdots$, that is, we will get a number that is "very very close to/almost the same as/almost equal to" 1.

Dealing with such phenomena is called "the limit of a sequence".

AP Calculus AB & BC Rewritten from the Beginning

Let us look at the following.

$$1,\ 1+\frac{1}{10},\ 1+\frac{1}{10^2},\ 1+\frac{1}{10^3},\ \cdots,\ a_n,\ \cdots$$

$$\underbrace{\qquad\qquad\qquad}_{a_n} + \boxed{\begin{array}{c} n \to \infty, \\ = \lim\limits_{n\to\infty} \end{array}}$$

$$\to\ \lim_{n\to\infty} a_n$$

The following properties hold for the limits of sequences.

If two sequences $\{a_n\}$, $\{b_n\}$ converge and $\lim\limits_{n\to\infty} a_n = \alpha$, $\lim\limits_{n\to\infty} b_n = \beta$, the following properties hold.

(1) Scalar Multiplication

$$\lim_{n\to\infty} c \cdot a_n = c \cdot \lim_{n\to\infty} a_n = c\alpha \quad (c \text{ is a constant})$$

(2) Addition/Subtraction

$$\lim_{n\to\infty} (a_n \pm b_n) = \lim_{n\to\infty} a_n \pm \lim_{n\to\infty} b_n = \alpha \pm \beta$$

(3) Multiplication

$$\lim_{n\to\infty} (a_n \cdot b_n) = \lim_{n\to\infty} a_n \cdot \lim_{n\to\infty} b_n = \alpha \cdot \beta$$

(4) Division

$$\lim_{n\to\infty} \frac{b_n}{a_n} = \frac{\lim\limits_{n\to\infty} b_n}{\lim\limits_{n\to\infty} a_n} = \frac{\beta}{\alpha}, \text{ where } \alpha \neq 0$$

(5) Constant sequence

$$\lim_{n\to\infty} c = c, \text{ where } c \text{ is a constant}$$

Limits

Supplement

Be careful! Above five basic properties of limits of sequences hold only when the two sequences both converge.

Example

If the two sequences $\{a_n\}, \{b_n\}$ are

$$\{a_n\} : 1.1, 1.01, 1.001, 1.0001, \cdots$$
$$\{b_n\} : 3.1, 3.01, 3.001, 3.0001, \cdots$$

then, the two sequences $\{a_n\}, \{b_n\}$ both converge and $\lim\limits_{n\to\infty} a_n = 1$, $\lim\limits_{n\to\infty} b_n = 3$.

(1) The sequence $\{3a_n\}$ is

$$\{3a_n\} : 3.3, 3.03, 3.003, 3.0003, \cdots$$

so $\lim\limits_{n\to\infty} 3a_n = 3$, and $3\lim\limits_{n\to\infty} a_n = 3 \times 1 = 3$. Thus, $\lim\limits_{n\to\infty} 3a_n = 3\lim\limits_{n\to\infty} a_n$.

(2) The sequence $\{a_n + b_n\}$ is

$$\{a_n + b_n\} : 4.2, 4.02, 4.002, 4.0002, \cdots$$

so $\lim\limits_{n\to\infty} (a_n + b_n) = 4$. Thus, $\lim\limits_{n\to\infty} (a_n + b_n) = \lim\limits_{n\to\infty} a_n + \lim\limits_{n\to\infty} b_n$.

(3) The sequence $\{a_n \cdot b_n\}$ is

$$\{a_n \cdot b_n\} : 3.41, 3.0401, 3.004001, 3.00040001, \cdots$$

so $\lim\limits_{n\to\infty} (a_n \cdot b_n) = 3$. Thus, $\lim\limits_{n\to\infty} (a_n \cdot b_n) = \lim\limits_{n\to\infty} a_n \cdot \lim\limits_{n\to\infty} b_n$.

(4) The sequence $\left\{\dfrac{b_n}{a_n}\right\}$ is

$$\left\{\dfrac{b_n}{a_n}\right\} : 2.8181\ldots, 2.9801\ldots, 2.9980\ldots, 2.9998\ldots, \cdots$$

So, $\lim\limits_{n\to\infty} \dfrac{b_n}{a_n} = 3$. Thus, $\lim\limits_{n\to\infty} \dfrac{b_n}{a_n} = \dfrac{\lim\limits_{n\to\infty} b_n}{\lim\limits_{n\to\infty} a_n}$.

AP Calculus AB & BC Rewritten from the Beginning

02. What is the meaning of ∞?

However, in many cases, your given sequence does not converge to any number. As an easiest example, consider

$$1, 2, 3, 4, \cdots$$

As we all know, this sequence of natural number increases infinitely and diverges. In such cases, we use the symbol "∞" and write $\lim_{n \to \infty} a_n = \infty$.

Now, what is ∞ and how can we calculate the limits (as in the box above), if α or β is ∞?

∞ is a symbol that represents the "largest" of numbers; a number that is to big to know. Is $\infty + \infty$ equal to 2∞? No. It is just ∞. There is nothing larger than ∞. In other words, since we added two numbers that are too big to know, we obviously get a number that is also too big to know.

Therefore, $\infty \times \infty = \infty$, $\infty - 10^{10} = \infty$, $\dfrac{\infty}{10^{10}} = \infty$, and $\dfrac{10^{10}}{\infty} = 0.000 \cdots 1 \approx 0$.

How about the following?

(1) $\dfrac{\infty}{\infty}$ (2) $\infty - \infty$

We do not know the values of (1) and (2) at the first glance, so we need some careful calculations.

Make Sure to Know the Following!

We need careful calculations if $\lim_{n \to \infty} a_n$ belongs to one of the following two cases.

(1) $\dfrac{\infty}{\infty}$ (2) $\infty - \infty$

Supplement

If the limit is of $\dfrac{\infty}{\infty}$ form, then we need to see which one increases faster; is it the denominator or is in the numerator?

First, observe

$$\{a_n\} = \{1, 2, 3, 4, 5, 6, \cdots, n, \cdots\}$$
$$\{b_n\} = \{1, 2, 4, 8, 16, 32, \cdots, 2^n, \cdots\}$$

Clearly, b_n increases much faster than a_n. That is, as $n \to \infty$, $\dfrac{a_n}{b_n}$ will go to zero even though $\lim\limits_{n \to \infty} a_n$ and $\lim\limits_{n \to \infty} b_n$ are both ∞.

This, we shall learn more in next chapter.

AP Calculus AB & BC Rewritten from the Beginning

03. Calculating the limits of sequences

⇒ Divide the denominator and the numerator by "the largest term" in the denominator. That is, if the given limit is of the form (polynomial)/(polynomial), divide by n^k (for largest degree k) in the denominator, and if the given limit is of the form (exponential)/(exponential), divide by a^n (for largest base a) in the denominator.

Let's look at the following examples.

①
$$\lim_{n\to\infty} \frac{2n^4+3}{n^3+2n} = \lim_{n\to\infty} \frac{2n^4+3}{\underbrace{n^3}_{\text{The largest one in the denominator}}+2n} = \lim_{n\to\infty} \frac{2n+\frac{3}{n^3}}{1+\frac{2}{n^2}} = \frac{\infty+0}{1+0} = \infty$$

②
$$\lim_{n\to\infty} \frac{3n^2+1}{n^2+2n} = \lim_{n\to\infty} \frac{3n^2+1}{\underbrace{n^2}_{\text{The largest one in the denominator}}+2n} = \lim_{n\to\infty} \frac{3+\frac{1}{n^2}}{1+\frac{2}{n}} = \frac{3+0}{1+0} = 3$$

③
$$\lim_{n\to\infty} \frac{5n^2+1}{2n^3+3n} = \lim_{n\to\infty} \frac{5n^2+1}{\underbrace{2n^3}_{\text{The largest one in the denominator}}+3n} = \lim_{n\to\infty} \frac{\frac{5}{n}+\frac{1}{n^3}}{2+\frac{3}{n^2}} = \frac{0+0}{2+0} = 0$$

The results of ①~③ above are summarized as follows.

Make Sure to Know the Following!

Case ①
[Highest Degree of the Numerator]>[Highest Degree of the Denominator] ⇒ ∞

Case ②
[Highest Degree of the Numerator]=[Highest Degree of the Denominator]
⇒ The ratio of Leading Coefficients

Case ③
[Highest Degree of the Numerator]<[Highest Degree of the Denominator] ⇒ 0

Now, we want to look at the case where exponential terms are included in $\frac{\infty}{\infty}$.

Let's look at the following.

$$\lim_{n\to\infty}\left(\frac{1}{2}\right)^n = \frac{1}{2}, \frac{1}{2^2}, \frac{1}{2^3}, \frac{1}{2^4}, \cdots, \frac{1}{2^{1000}}, \cdots \qquad \Rightarrow 0$$

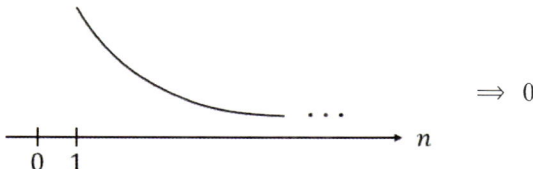

$$\lim_{n\to\infty}\left(-\frac{1}{2}\right)^n = -\frac{1}{2}, \frac{1}{2^2}, -\frac{1}{2^3}, \frac{1}{2^4}, \cdots \qquad \Rightarrow 0$$

$$\lim_{n\to\infty}(-1)^n = -1, 1, -1, 1, \cdots \qquad \Rightarrow \text{Oscillate between -1 and 1}$$

$$\lim_{n\to\infty}(2)^n = 2^1, 2^2, 2^3, \cdots \qquad \Rightarrow \infty$$

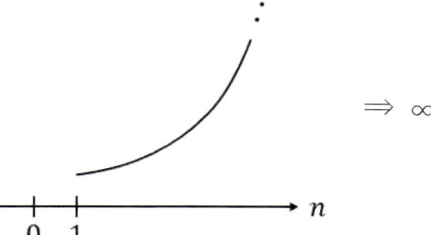

$$\lim_{n\to\infty}(-2)^n = -2, 2^2, -2^3, 2^4, \cdots \qquad \Rightarrow \text{Oscillate between } -\infty \text{ and } \infty$$

As you see above...

That is, in $\lim_{n\to\infty} r^n$

① If $r > 1 \Rightarrow \infty$
② If $r = 1 \Rightarrow 1$
③ If $-1 < r < 1 \Rightarrow 0$
④ If $r = -1 \Rightarrow$ Oscillate between -1 and 1
⑤ If $r < -1 \Rightarrow$ Oscillate between $-\infty$ and ∞

AP Calculus AB & BC Rewritten from the Beginning

Now we shall look at real examples where exponential terms are included in $\frac{\infty}{\infty}$.

①
$$\lim_{n\to\infty} \frac{3^{n+2}+2^n}{2^n+1} = \lim_{n\to\infty} \frac{9\cdot 3^n + 2^n}{\boxed{2^n}+1} = \lim_{n\to\infty} \frac{9\cdot\left(\frac{3}{2}\right)^n + 1}{1+\frac{1}{2^n}} = \frac{\infty+1}{1+0} = \infty$$

The largest one in the denominator

②
$$\lim_{n\to\infty} \frac{3^{n+2}-1}{3^{n+1}+2^n} = \lim_{n\to\infty} \frac{3^2\cdot 3^n - 1}{3\cdot\boxed{3^n}+2^n} = \lim_{n\to\infty} \frac{3^2 - \frac{1}{3^n}}{3+\left(\frac{2}{3}\right)^n} = \frac{9-0}{3+0} = 3$$

The largest one in the denominator

③
$$\lim_{n\to\infty} \frac{2^{n+1}+2}{3^n-1} = \lim_{n\to\infty} \frac{2\cdot 2^n + 2}{\boxed{3^n}-1} = \lim_{n\to\infty} \frac{2\cdot\left(\frac{2}{3}\right)^n + \frac{2}{3^n}}{1-\frac{1}{3^n}} = \frac{0+0}{1-0} = 0$$

The largest one in the denominator

The results of ①~③ above are summarized as follows.

Make Sure to Know the Following!

In forms of $\lim_{n\to\infty} \frac{a\times c^n + \cdots}{b\times d^n + \cdots}$ ($c, d > 0$, c^n and d^n are the largest terms in the numerator and the denominator, respectively.)

① $c > d \Rightarrow \infty$

② $c = d \Rightarrow \frac{a}{b}$

③ $c < d \Rightarrow 0$

Example

(1) $\lim\limits_{n\to\infty}\dfrac{9n^2+1}{3n^2+5n}=\lim\limits_{n\to\infty}\dfrac{\dfrac{9n^2+1}{n^2}}{\dfrac{3n^2+5n}{n^2}}=\lim\limits_{n\to\infty}\dfrac{9+\dfrac{1}{n^2}}{3+\dfrac{5}{n}}=\dfrac{9+0}{3+0}=3$

(2) $\lim\limits_{n\to\infty}\dfrac{9n+1}{3n^2+5n}=\lim\limits_{n\to\infty}\dfrac{\dfrac{9n+1}{n^2}}{\dfrac{3n^2+5n}{n^2}}=\lim\limits_{n\to\infty}\dfrac{\dfrac{9}{n}+\dfrac{1}{n^2}}{3+\dfrac{5}{n}}=\dfrac{0+0}{3+0}=0$

(3) $\lim\limits_{n\to\infty}\dfrac{9n^3+1}{3n^2+5n}=\lim\limits_{n\to\infty}\dfrac{\dfrac{9n^3+1}{n^2}}{\dfrac{3n^2+5n}{n^2}}=\lim\limits_{n\to\infty}\dfrac{9n+\dfrac{1}{n^2}}{3+\dfrac{5}{n}}=\dfrac{\infty+0}{3+0}=\infty$

(4) $\lim\limits_{n\to\infty}\dfrac{3^{n+1}+2^n}{3^n+1}=\lim\limits_{n\to\infty}\dfrac{\dfrac{3^{n+1}+2^n}{3^n}}{\dfrac{3^n+1}{3^n}}=\lim\limits_{n\to\infty}\dfrac{3+(\dfrac{2}{3})^n}{1+\dfrac{1}{3^n}}=\dfrac{3+0}{1+0}=3$

(5) $\lim\limits_{n\to\infty}\dfrac{2^n+1}{3^n+1}=\lim\limits_{n\to\infty}\dfrac{\dfrac{2^n+1}{3^n}}{\dfrac{3^n+1}{3^n}}=\lim\limits_{n\to\infty}\dfrac{(\dfrac{2}{3})^n+\dfrac{1}{3^n}}{1+\dfrac{1}{3^n}}=\dfrac{0+0}{1+0}=0$

(6) $\lim\limits_{n\to\infty}\dfrac{5^n+1}{3^n+1}=\lim\limits_{n\to\infty}\dfrac{\dfrac{5^n+1}{3^n}}{\dfrac{3^n+1}{3^n}}=\lim\limits_{n\to\infty}\dfrac{(\dfrac{5}{3})^n+\dfrac{1}{3^n}}{1+\dfrac{1}{3^n}}=\dfrac{\infty+0}{1+0}=\infty$

Summary

As in Examples (1) and (4), if the order of the numerator is equal to the order of the denominator (polynomial/polynomial case) or similarly, if the largest base in the numerator is the same as the largest base in the denominator (exponential/exponential case), then the limit is equal to the ratio of the coefficients of the largest terms. That is,

$$\lim_{n\to\infty} \frac{qn^k + (\text{lower order terms})}{pn^k + (\text{lower order terms})} = \frac{q}{p} \quad \text{and} \quad \lim_{n\to\infty} \frac{qa^n + (\text{terms with smaller base})}{pa^n + (\text{terms with smaller base})} = \frac{q}{p}.$$

② As in Examples (2) and (5), if the order of the denominator is greater than the order of the numerator (polynomial/polynomial case) or similarly if the largest base in the denominator is greater than the largest base in the numerator (exponential/exponential case), then the limit is 0.

③ As in Examples (3) and (6), if the order of the numerator is greater than the order of the denominator (polynomial/polynomial case) or similarly if the largest base in the numerator is greater than the largest base in the denominator (exponential/exponential case), then the limit is ∞.

04. Calculating $\infty - \infty$

Whenever you encounter the indeterminate form $\infty - \infty$, you should convert it into $\dfrac{\infty}{\infty}$ form. The way you do this is by Rationalization.

Let's look at the following example.

● ········ **Example 1**

Evaluate $\lim\limits_{n\to\infty}(\sqrt{n^2+2n}-n)$.

● ········ **Answer** 1

● ········ **Solution**

$$\lim_{n\to\infty}\frac{(\sqrt{n^2+2n}-n)}{1}=\lim_{n\to\infty}\frac{(\sqrt{n^2+2n}-n)\cdot(\sqrt{n^2+2n}+n)}{1\cdot(\sqrt{n^2+2n}+n)}=\lim_{n\to\infty}\frac{2n}{(\sqrt{n^2+2n}+n)}$$

$\Rightarrow$ The largest in the denominator is $\sqrt{n^2}=n$,

so if we divide the numerator and the denominator by n,

$$\lim_{n\to\infty}\frac{\frac{1}{n}\cdot 2n}{\frac{1}{n}(\sqrt{n^2+2n}+n)}=\lim_{n\to\infty}\frac{2}{\left(\sqrt{\frac{n^2+2n}{n^2}}+\frac{n}{n}\right)}=\lim_{n\to\infty}\frac{2}{\left(\sqrt{1+\frac{2}{n}}+1\right)}=\frac{2}{\sqrt{1+0}+1}=1$$

AP Calculus AB & BC Rewritten from the Beginning

Make Sure to Know the Following!

How do we find "the largest term" if there is a square root, as in Example 1 above? If $\sqrt{an^k + \text{(lower order terms)}}$ is the largest term within the denominator, then divide both the numerator and the denominator by $\sqrt{n^k}$. Then how do we compare if there are more than one terms in the denominator, some in the square root and some outside the square root? See the example below:

$$\frac{2n}{\sqrt{n^3 + 2n} + n + 1}.$$

The largest term in $\sqrt{n^3 + 2n}$ is $\sqrt{n^3}$. The largest term in $n+1$ is n. How do we compare $\sqrt{n^3}$ and n? $\sqrt{n^3} = n^{3/2} = n^{1.5}$ and $n = n^1$. So the largest term is $\sqrt{n^3}$. We go back to Example 1:

$$\frac{2n}{\sqrt{n^2 + 2n} + n}.$$

The largest term in $\sqrt{n^2 + 2n}$ is $\sqrt{n^2} = n^{2/2} = n^1$. The largest term in n is n. Two are the same. Therefore we just take n.

This is what we really did in Example 1.

Example 2

For the two sequences $\{a_n\}, \{b_n\}$, $\lim\limits_{n\to\infty} a_n = 5$ and $\lim\limits_{n\to\infty} b_n = -2$. Calculate the following limits.

(1) $\lim\limits_{n\to\infty} (3a_n - b_n)$

(2) $\lim\limits_{n\to\infty} \dfrac{2a_n}{5b_n}$

(3) $\lim\limits_{n\to\infty} 2a_n \cdot b_n$

Answer (1) 17   (2) -1 (3) -20

Solution

(1) $3\lim\limits_{n\to\infty} a_n - \lim\limits_{n\to\infty} b_n = 3 \times 5 - (-2) = 17$

(2) $\dfrac{2\lim\limits_{n\to\infty} a_n}{5\lim\limits_{n\to\infty} b_n} = \dfrac{2 \times 5}{5 \times (-2)} = -1$

(3) $2\lim\limits_{n\to\infty} a_n \cdot \lim\limits_{n\to\infty} b_n = 2 \times 5 \times (-2) = -20$

AP Calculus AB & BC Rewritten from the Beginning

Example 3

Investigate the following limits. If the limit exists, find it.

(1) $\displaystyle\lim_{n\to\infty} \frac{6n^3-1}{2n^3+2n}$

(2) $\displaystyle\lim_{n\to\infty} \frac{3n}{\sqrt{n^2+1}-\sqrt{n}}$

(3) $\displaystyle\lim_{n\to\infty} \frac{5^{n+2}-3}{5^n+3^n}$

(4) $\displaystyle\lim_{n\to\infty} \{\log(10n+1)-\log(n+5)\}$

(5) $\displaystyle\lim_{n\to\infty} \frac{5^n+2^n}{3^n+1}$

(6) $\displaystyle\lim_{n\to\infty} \frac{1+2+3+\cdots+n}{4n^2}$

(7) $\displaystyle\lim_{n\to\infty} \left\{\left(1-\frac{1}{2}\right)\cdot\left(1-\frac{1}{3}\right)\cdot\ \cdots\ \cdot\left(1-\frac{1}{n}\right)\right\}\cdot(1+2+3+\cdots+n)$

(8) $\displaystyle\lim_{n\to\infty} \frac{10}{5+\dfrac{1}{3^n}}$

(9) $\displaystyle\lim_{n\to\infty} \left(\sqrt{n^2+5n}-\sqrt{n^2+1}\right)$

(10) $\displaystyle\lim_{n\to\infty} \sqrt{n}\left(\sqrt{n+2}-\sqrt{n-2}\right)$

Limits

● ⋯⋯ **Answer**   (1) 3   (2) 3   (3) 25   (4) 1   (5) ∞   (6) $\frac{1}{8}$

(7) ∞   (8) 2   (9) $\frac{5}{2}$ (10) 2

● ⋯⋯ **Solution**

(1) $\lim\limits_{n \to \infty} \dfrac{6n^3 - 1}{2n^3 + 2n} = \lim\limits_{n \to \infty} \dfrac{\dfrac{6n^3 - 1}{n^3}}{\dfrac{2n^3 + 2n}{n^3}} = \lim\limits_{n \to \infty} \dfrac{6 - \dfrac{1}{n^3}}{2 + \dfrac{2}{n^2}} = \dfrac{6}{2} = 3$

(2) Here, the given limit is of the form $\dfrac{\infty}{\infty - \infty}$ NOT the usual $\dfrac{\infty}{\infty}$. Therefore, before dividing numerator and denominator by the largest term in the denominator, we must first get rid of the minus in the denominator and change it into $\dfrac{\infty}{\infty}$ instead of $\dfrac{\infty}{\infty - \infty}$! We do so by rationalization.

$\lim\limits_{n \to \infty} \dfrac{3n(\sqrt{n^2+1} + \sqrt{n})}{(\sqrt{n^2+1} - \sqrt{n})(\sqrt{n^2+1} + \sqrt{n})} = \lim\limits_{n \to \infty} \dfrac{3n(\sqrt{n^2+1} + \sqrt{n})}{n^2 - n + 1}$

$= \lim\limits_{n \to \infty} \dfrac{3 \cdot \dfrac{\sqrt{n^2+1} + \sqrt{n}}{n}}{\dfrac{n^2 - n + 1}{n^2}} = 3 \lim\limits_{n \to \infty} \dfrac{\sqrt{\dfrac{n^2+1}{n^2}} + \sqrt{\dfrac{1}{n}}}{1 - \dfrac{1}{n} + \dfrac{1}{n^2}} = 3 \lim\limits_{n \to \infty} \dfrac{\sqrt{1 + \dfrac{1}{n^2}} + \sqrt{\dfrac{1}{n}}}{1 - \dfrac{1}{n} + \dfrac{1}{n^2}} = 3 \cdot \dfrac{1}{1} = 3$

(3) $\lim\limits_{n \to \infty} \dfrac{5^{n+2} - 3}{5^n + 3^n} = \lim\limits_{n \to \infty} \dfrac{\dfrac{5^{n+2} - 3}{5^n}}{\dfrac{5^n + 3^n}{5^n}} = \lim\limits_{n \to \infty} \dfrac{5^2 - \dfrac{3}{5^n}}{1 + (\dfrac{3}{5})^n} = 25$

(4) $\lim\limits_{n \to \infty} \log\left(\dfrac{10n+1}{n+5}\right) = \lim\limits_{n \to \infty} \log\left(\dfrac{\dfrac{10n+1}{n}}{\dfrac{n+5}{n}}\right) = \lim\limits_{n \to \infty} \log\left(\dfrac{10 + \dfrac{1}{n}}{1 + \dfrac{5}{n}}\right) = \log 10 = 1$

(5) $\lim\limits_{n \to \infty} \dfrac{5^n + 2^n}{3^n + 1} = \lim\limits_{n \to \infty} \dfrac{\dfrac{5^n + 2^n}{3^n}}{\dfrac{3^n + 1}{3^n}} = \lim\limits_{n \to \infty} \dfrac{(\dfrac{5}{3})^n + (\dfrac{2}{3})^n}{1 + \dfrac{1}{3^n}} = \infty$ (Diverge)

27

AP Calculus AB & BC Rewritten from the Beginning

Solution

(6) $\lim\limits_{n\to\infty}\dfrac{\frac{n(n+1)}{2}}{4n^2}=\lim\limits_{n\to\infty}\dfrac{n^2+n}{8n^2}=\lim\limits_{n\to\infty}\dfrac{\frac{n^2+n}{n^2}}{\frac{8n^2}{n^2}}=\lim\limits_{n\to\infty}\dfrac{1+\frac{1}{n}}{8}=\dfrac{1}{8}$

(7) $\lim\limits_{n\to\infty}\left(\dfrac{1}{2}\times\dfrac{2}{3}\times\dfrac{3}{4}\times\cdots\times\dfrac{n-1}{n}\right)\times\dfrac{n(n+1)}{2}=\lim\limits_{n\to\infty}\dfrac{1}{n}\times\dfrac{n(n+1)}{2}=\lim\limits_{n\to\infty}\dfrac{n+1}{2}=\infty$ This limit diverges.

(8) $\lim\limits_{n\to\infty}\dfrac{10}{5+\frac{1}{3^n}}=\dfrac{10}{5+0}=2$

(9) $\lim\limits_{n\to\infty}\dfrac{(\sqrt{n^2+5n}-\sqrt{n^2+1})(\sqrt{n^2+5n}+\sqrt{n^2+1})}{\sqrt{n^2+5n}+\sqrt{n^2+1}}=\lim\limits_{n\to\infty}\dfrac{5n-1}{(\sqrt{n^2+5n}+\sqrt{n^2+1})}$

$=\lim\limits_{n\to\infty}\dfrac{\frac{5n-1}{\sqrt{n^2}}}{\frac{\sqrt{n^2+5n}+\sqrt{n^2+1}}{\sqrt{n^2}}}=\lim\limits_{n\to\infty}\dfrac{\frac{5n-1}{n}}{\sqrt{\frac{n^2+5n}{n^2}}+\sqrt{\frac{n^2+1}{n^2}}}=\lim\limits_{n\to\infty}\dfrac{5-\frac{1}{n}}{\sqrt{1+\frac{5}{n}}+\sqrt{1+\frac{1}{n^2}}}$

$=\dfrac{5}{\sqrt{1}+\sqrt{1}}=\dfrac{5}{2}$

(10) By rationalization, we change $\infty-\infty$ into $\dfrac{\infty}{\infty}$.

$$\lim_{n\to\infty}\sqrt{n}\cdot\left\{\dfrac{(\sqrt{n+2}-\sqrt{n-2})(\sqrt{n+2}+\sqrt{n-2})}{\sqrt{n+2}+\sqrt{n-2}}\right\}$$

$$=\lim_{n\to\infty}\sqrt{n}\cdot\left\{\dfrac{4}{\sqrt{n+2}+\sqrt{n-2}}\right\}=\lim_{n\to\infty}\dfrac{4\sqrt{n}}{\sqrt{n+2}+\sqrt{n-2}}$$

The "largest term" in the denominator $\sqrt{n+2}+\sqrt{n-2}$ is $\sqrt{n+2}$ and so we divide both the numerator and the denominator by $\sqrt{n+2}$:

$$\lim_{n\to\infty}\dfrac{4\sqrt{n}}{\sqrt{n+2}+\sqrt{n-2}}=\lim_{n\to\infty}\dfrac{\frac{4\sqrt{n}}{\sqrt{n+2}}}{\frac{\sqrt{n+2}+\sqrt{n-2}}{\sqrt{n+2}}}$$

$$=\lim_{n\to\infty}\dfrac{4\sqrt{\frac{n}{n+2}}}{1+\sqrt{\frac{n-2}{n+2}}}=\lim_{n\to\infty}\dfrac{4\sqrt{1-\frac{2}{n+2}}}{1+\sqrt{1-\frac{4}{n+2}}}=\dfrac{4\sqrt{1}}{1+\sqrt{1}}=2$$

Example 4

(1) Given that $\lim\limits_{n\to\infty} \dfrac{an^2+bn+2}{5n+1} = 4$ for constants a, b, find the value of $a+b$.

(2) Given that $\lim\limits_{n\to\infty} \left(\sqrt{n^2+an} - \sqrt{n^2+2}\right) = 4$, find the value of constant a.

(3) Given that the sequence $\{a_n\}$ satisfies the inequality $12n^2 < (n^2+2)a_n < 12n^2+6$ for all positive integers n, find $\lim\limits_{n\to\infty} a_n$.

Solution

(1) In $\lim\limits_{n\to\infty} \dfrac{an^2+bn+2}{5n+1}$, if $a \neq 0$, the limit diverges (the order of the numerator is greater than the order of the denominator). Thus, $a = 0$.

Therefore, $\lim\limits_{n\to\infty} \dfrac{bn+2}{5n+1} = \lim\limits_{n\to\infty} \dfrac{b+\dfrac{2}{n}}{5+\dfrac{1}{n}} = \dfrac{b}{5} = 4$ and so $b = 20$. The answer is $a+b = 20$.

(2) $\lim\limits_{n\to\infty} \left(\sqrt{n^2+an} - \sqrt{n^2+2}\right) = \lim\limits_{n\to\infty} \dfrac{\left(\sqrt{n^2+an} - \sqrt{n^2+2}\right)\left(\sqrt{n^2+an} + \sqrt{n^2+2}\right)}{\sqrt{n^2+an} + \sqrt{n^2+2}}$

$= \lim\limits_{n\to\infty} \dfrac{an-2}{\sqrt{n^2+an} + \sqrt{n^2+2}} = \lim\limits_{n\to\infty} \dfrac{a-\dfrac{2}{n}}{\sqrt{1+\dfrac{a}{n}} + \sqrt{1+\dfrac{2}{n^2}}} = \dfrac{a}{2}$

Therefore, $a = 8$.

(3) Dividing each side by (n^2+2) gives $\dfrac{12n^2}{n^2+2} < a_n < \dfrac{12n^2+6}{n^2+2}$. Taking $\lim\limits_{n\to\infty}$ of each side gives $\lim\limits_{n\to\infty} \dfrac{12n^2}{n^2+2} \leq \lim\limits_{n\to\infty} a_n \leq \lim\limits_{n\to\infty} \dfrac{12n^2+6}{n^2+2}$. Here, $\lim\limits_{n\to\infty} \dfrac{12n^2}{n^2+2} = \lim\limits_{n\to\infty} \dfrac{12n^2+6}{n^2+2} = 12$, and so $\lim\limits_{n\to\infty} a_n = 12$.

Supplement For (3)

Is there a constant a for which $2 < a < 2$ holds? Obviously not. However, in this problem, $\lim\limits_{n\to\infty} \dfrac{12n^2}{n^2+2}$ is not exactly 12 but a value "very very close to" 12. Therefore, when taking limits, inequality $\dfrac{12n^2}{n^2+2} < a_n$ (which does not include equality) becomes $\lim\limits_{n\to\infty} \dfrac{12n^2}{n^2+2} \leq \lim\limits_{n\to\infty} a_n$, allowing equality. Similarly, taking limit on $a_n < \dfrac{12n^2+6}{n^2+2}$ gives $\lim\limits_{n\to\infty} a_n \leq \lim\limits_{n\to\infty} \dfrac{12n^2+6}{n^2+2}$. As such, whenever you take a limit on both sides of a sequence of inequalities $a_n < b_n$, you get $\lim\limits_{n\to\infty} a_n \leq \lim\limits_{n\to\infty} b_n$ instead of $\lim\limits_{n\to\infty} a_n < \lim\limits_{n\to\infty} b_n$. This is because you can think of the limit value of a sequence as an approximation rather than an exact value.

Problem 1

Find the limits.

(1) $\displaystyle\lim_{n\to\infty}\frac{(2n-1)(n+1)}{n^2}$

(2) $\displaystyle\lim_{n\to\infty}\frac{\sqrt{n}}{n+1}$

(3) $\displaystyle\lim_{n\to\infty}n^2(1+n^2)$

(4) $\displaystyle\lim_{n\to\infty}\log_2\sqrt{\frac{8n+3}{n}}$

(5) $\displaystyle\lim_{n\to\infty}(\sqrt{n^2-1}-n)$

(6) $\displaystyle\lim_{n\to\infty}\sin\frac{n\pi}{2n+1}$

(7) $\displaystyle\lim_{n\to\infty}\frac{\cos 2\pi n}{n}$

(8) $\displaystyle\lim_{n\to\infty}\frac{2^{-n}}{2^n}$

(9) $\displaystyle\lim_{n\to-\infty}\frac{2^{-n}}{2^n}$

(10) $\displaystyle\lim_{m\to\infty}\frac{3^{m+2}+1}{3^{m+1}+2^m}$

(11) $\displaystyle\lim_{m\to\infty}\frac{2m-1}{\sqrt{m^2+3}}$

(12) $\displaystyle\lim_{n\to\infty}\frac{3^{-n}}{2^n}$

AP Calculus AB & BC Rewritten from the Beginning

Solution

(1) 2

(2) 0

(3) ∞

(4) $\lim\limits_{n\to\infty}\sqrt{\dfrac{8n+3}{n}} = \lim\limits_{n\to\infty}\sqrt{\dfrac{8+3\times\dfrac{1}{n}}{1}} = \sqrt{8}$, so $\log_2\sqrt{8} = \log_2 2^{\frac{3}{2}} = \dfrac{3}{2}$

(5) $\lim\limits_{n\to\infty}\dfrac{(\sqrt{n^2-1}-n)(\sqrt{n^2-1}+n)}{\sqrt{n^2-1}+n} = \lim\limits_{n\to\infty}\dfrac{-1}{\sqrt{n^2-1}+n} = 0$

(6) $\lim\limits_{n\to\infty}\dfrac{n\pi}{2n+1} = \lim\limits_{n\to\infty}\dfrac{\pi}{2+\dfrac{1}{n}} = \dfrac{\pi}{2}$, so $\sin\dfrac{\pi}{2} = 1$

(7) $\lim\limits_{n\to\infty}\dfrac{\cos 2n}{n} = \dfrac{-1\sim 1}{\infty} = 0$

(8) $\lim\limits_{n\to\infty}\dfrac{\dfrac{1}{2^n}}{2^n} = \dfrac{0}{\infty} = 0$

(9) $\lim\limits_{n\to-\infty}\dfrac{\dfrac{1}{2^n}}{2^n} = \dfrac{\dfrac{1}{2^{-\infty}}}{2^{-\infty}} = \dfrac{2^\infty}{\dfrac{1}{2^\infty}} = \dfrac{\infty}{0}$

(※ $\dfrac{1}{2^\infty}$ is a value near 0. i.e. $0.000\cdots 1$, so) $= \dfrac{\infty}{0.000\cdots 1} = \infty$

(10) $\lim\limits_{m\to\infty}\dfrac{3^2\times 3^m+1}{3\times 3^m+2^m} = \lim\limits_{m\to\infty}\dfrac{3^2+\dfrac{1}{3^m}}{3+\dfrac{2^m}{3^m}} = \dfrac{3^2+0}{3+0} = 3$

(11) $\lim\limits_{m\to\infty}\dfrac{2m-1}{\sqrt{m^2+3}} = \lim\limits_{m\to\infty}\dfrac{\dfrac{1}{m}\times(2m-1)}{\dfrac{1}{m}\times\sqrt{m^2+3}} = \lim\limits_{m\to\infty}\dfrac{2-\dfrac{1}{m}}{\sqrt{1+3\times\dfrac{1}{m^2}}} = \dfrac{2}{1} = 2$

(12) $\lim\limits_{n\to\infty}\dfrac{\dfrac{1}{3^n}}{2^n} = \dfrac{0}{\infty} = 0$

Problem 2

(1) If $\lim\limits_{n\to\infty} a_n = -3$ and $\lim\limits_{n\to\infty} b_n = -2$, then evaluate $\lim\limits_{n\to\infty} \dfrac{3a_n b_n + 7}{a_n + b_n}$.

(2) If $\lim\limits_{n\to\infty} \dfrac{\cos n\theta}{n} = a$ and $\lim\limits_{n\to\infty} \dfrac{2n^2 + 1}{n^2 + n + 3} = b$, then find $a + b$.

(3) If $2n^2 - 1 < n^2 a_n < 2n^2 + 2$, then $\lim\limits_{n\to\infty} a_n$ is

ⓐ 1   ⓑ 2   ⓒ 3   ⓓ 4

Answer
(1) -5 (2) 2   (3) ⓑ

Solution

(1) $\dfrac{3(-3)(-2) + 7}{(-3) + (-2)} = \dfrac{25}{-5} = -5$

(2) $a = \dfrac{-1 \sim 1}{\infty} = 0$ and $b = 2$, so $a + b = 2$.

(3) Dividing each side by n^2, we get $2 - \dfrac{1}{n^2} < a_n < 2 + \dfrac{2}{n^2}$, and if we take the $\lim\limits_{n\to\infty}$,

$\lim\limits_{n\to\infty}\left(2 - \dfrac{1}{n^2}\right) \leq \lim\limits_{n\to\infty} a_n \leq \lim\limits_{n\to\infty}\left(2 + \dfrac{2}{n^2}\right)$, so $\lim\limits_{n\to\infty} a_n = 2$. Hence, the answer is ⓑ.

01 Exercise

01~12 Evaluate the following limits.

01 $\lim\limits_{n \to \infty} 5$

02 $\lim\limits_{n \to \infty} \dfrac{3n^3 + 8n}{2n^2 + 3n - 1}$

03 $\lim\limits_{n \to \infty} \dfrac{9n^2 - 10}{3n^2 + 8n}$

04 $\lim\limits_{n \to \infty} \dfrac{5n^2 + 7n}{2n^3 + 2n - 1}$

05 $\displaystyle\lim_{n\to\infty}\frac{9^{-n}}{9^n}$

06 $\displaystyle\lim_{n\to\infty}\frac{1.5^{-n}}{1.5^n}$

07 $\displaystyle\lim_{n\to\infty}\frac{\sin n}{2n}$

08 $\displaystyle\lim_{n\to\infty}\frac{3n+1}{\sqrt{2n^2+1}}$

09 $\displaystyle\lim_{n\to\infty}(\sqrt{n^2+5n}-n)$

10 $\lim\limits_{n\to\infty}\dfrac{3^{n-1}+1}{2^n+1}$

11 $\lim\limits_{n\to\infty}\dfrac{3^{n+3}+2^n}{3^{n+1}-1}$

12 $\lim\limits_{n\to\infty}\dfrac{2^{n+1}+2}{3^n-1}$

13 Which of the following is not true?

ⓐ $\lim\limits_{n\to\infty}(\dfrac{1}{n}-\dfrac{3}{n^3})=0$ 　　　ⓑ $\lim\limits_{m\to\infty}(\dfrac{1}{m^2+1}-\dfrac{2}{2-m})=0$

ⓒ $\lim\limits_{n\to\infty}\dfrac{\dfrac{1}{n}+1}{1+\dfrac{1}{n}}=1$ 　　　ⓓ $\lim\limits_{m\to\infty}\dfrac{\dfrac{3}{m}}{1+\dfrac{1}{m^3}}=3$

14 If $\lim\limits_{n\to\infty} a_n = 2$ and $\lim\limits_{n\to\infty} b_n = -3$, then evaluate $\lim\limits_{n\to\infty} \dfrac{2a_n b_n + 5}{a_n + b_n}$.

15 If $\lim\limits_{n\to\infty} \dfrac{8n^3 + 2n^2 - 1}{n(2n^2 + 1)} = A$, $\lim\limits_{n\to\infty} \dfrac{1+2+3+\cdots+n}{n^2} = B$, what is the value of AB?

ⓐ 1   ⓑ 2   ⓒ 3   ⓓ 4

16 If $\lim\limits_{n\to\infty} \dfrac{1}{n^2} \cdot \cos(n\theta) = a$ and $\lim\limits_{n\to\infty} \dfrac{3\sin(n\theta)}{2 + n^2} = b$, then $a+b$ is

ⓐ $-\infty$ ⓑ -1   ⓒ 0   ⓓ 1

17 If $3n^2 + 1 < (n^2 + 1)a_n < 3n^2 + 5$, then $\lim\limits_{n\to\infty} a_n$ is

ⓐ 1   ⓑ 2   ⓒ 3   ⓓ 4

18 Given that $\lim\limits_{n\to\infty} \dfrac{bn + 8}{an^2 + 4n + 2} = 4$ for constants a, b, find the value of $a+b$.

AP Calculus AB & BC Rewritten from the Beginning

19 Given that $\displaystyle\lim_{n\to\infty}\frac{\sqrt{n^2+4}+an}{n}=20$, find the value of constant a.

20 Given that $\displaystyle\lim_{n\to\infty}\left(\sqrt{n^2+an+1}-\sqrt{bn^2+4n+6}\right)=2$ for constants a, b, find the value of $a+b$.

21 Given that the sequence $\{a_n\}$ satisfies $\displaystyle\lim_{n\to\infty}\frac{2a_n-6}{a_n-2}=4$, find the value of $\displaystyle\lim_{n\to\infty} a_n$.

22 Given that the sequence $\{a_n\}$ satisfies $\displaystyle\lim_{n\to\infty} n\cdot a_n=3$, find the value of $\displaystyle\lim_{n\to\infty}\frac{8n^2+5n}{n^3\cdot a_n}$.

23 Given that the sequence $\{a_n\}$ satisfies the inequality $4n^2 < (n^2+3)a_n < 4n^2+5$ for all positive integers n, find the value of $\lim_{n\to\infty} \dfrac{6a_n-1}{2a_n+1}$.

24 Calculate $\lim_{n\to\infty} \{\log_2(4n-1)+\log_2(16n+1)-2\log_2(n+3)\}$.

25 For two converging sequences $\{a_n\}$ and $\{b_n\}$, $\lim_{n\to\infty}(a_n+b_n)=6$ and $\lim_{n\to\infty} a_n \cdot b_n = 2$ hold. Find the value of $\lim_{n\to\infty}(a_n^2+b_n^2)$.

26 Calculate $\lim_{n\to\infty}\left(5+\dfrac{\sin(n\theta)}{n}\right)$. ($\theta$ is a constant)

27 Calculate $\displaystyle\lim_{n\to\infty}\frac{\sin(n\theta)-8n^2}{4n^2+n}$. ($\theta$ is a constant)

28 For each positive integer n, let a_n and b_n each represent the integer and decimal parts of $\sqrt{4n^2+6n+2}$, respectively. Find the value of $\displaystyle\lim_{n\to\infty}\frac{a_n+nb_n}{n}$

01 | Answers & Solutions

01 5

$\lim\limits_{n \to \infty} 5 = 5$

02 ∞

In the form $\dfrac{\infty}{\infty}$, the degree of the numerator is bigger: numerator grows faster than the denominator and hence the solution is ∞.

03 3

$\lim\limits_{n \to \infty} \dfrac{9n^2 - 10}{3n^2 + 8n}$ is in form $\dfrac{\infty}{\infty}$. Degree of the numerator and the denominator are the same. So dividing the numerator and the denominator by "the largest term" n^2 gives

$\lim\limits_{n \to \infty} \dfrac{9n^2 - 10}{3n^2 + 8n} = \lim\limits_{n \to \infty} \dfrac{9 - \dfrac{10}{n^2}}{3 + \dfrac{8}{n}} = \dfrac{9 - 0}{3 + 0} = 3$.

04 0

In the form $\dfrac{\infty}{\infty}$, the highest degree in the denominator is bigger: denomirator grows faster than the numerator and so, the result is 0.

05 0

$9^{-n} = \dfrac{1}{9^n}$. Thus, the limit is in the form $\lim\limits_{n \to \infty} \dfrac{1}{9^n} \dfrac{1}{9^n} = \lim\limits_{x \to \infty} \dfrac{1}{9^{2n}} = \dfrac{1}{\infty}$ and so, the result is 0.

AP Calculus AB & BC Rewritten from the Beginning

06 0

$1.5^{-n} = \dfrac{1}{1.5^n}$, so $\lim\limits_{n\to\infty} \dfrac{1}{1.5^n} \dfrac{1}{1.5^n} = \lim\limits_{n\to\infty} \dfrac{1}{1.5^{2n}} = 0$

07 0

$\sin n$ has a value between -1 and 1. That is, $-1 \le \sin n \le 1$.

$\lim\limits_{n\to\infty} \dfrac{\sin n}{2n} = \dfrac{-1 \sim 1}{\infty} = 0$

08 $\dfrac{3\sqrt{2}}{2}$

The limit has $\lim\limits_{n\to\infty} \dfrac{3n+1}{\sqrt{2n^2+1}} = \dfrac{\infty}{\infty}$ form.

The highest degree of the numerator and the denominator are the same as $n = \sqrt{n^2}$.

$\lim\limits_{n\to\infty} \dfrac{3n+1}{\sqrt{2n^2+1}} = \lim\limits_{n\to\infty} \dfrac{\dfrac{1}{n}\times(3n+1)}{\dfrac{1}{n}\times\sqrt{2n^2+1}} = \lim\limits_{n\to\infty} \dfrac{3+\dfrac{1}{n}}{\sqrt{2+\dfrac{1}{n^2}}} = \dfrac{3+0}{\sqrt{2+0}} = \dfrac{3}{\sqrt{2}}.$

09 $\dfrac{5}{2}$

Change the form of $\lim\limits_{n\to\infty}(\sqrt{n^2+5n}-n) = \infty - \infty$ to $\dfrac{\infty}{\infty}$ by rationalization.

$\lim\limits_{n\to\infty} \dfrac{(\sqrt{n^2+5n}-n)(\sqrt{n^2+5n}+n)}{(\sqrt{n^2+5n}+n)} = \lim\limits_{n\to\infty} \dfrac{5n}{\sqrt{n^2+5n}+n}.$

The largest term in the numerator $5n$ is n. The largest term in the term $\sqrt{n^2+5n}$ is $\sqrt{n^2} = n$, the largest term in the term n is n and so the largest term in the denominator is n. The highest degree of the numerator and the denominator are the same, so we only need to look at the coefficients. Thus, $\dfrac{5}{\sqrt{1}+1} = \dfrac{5}{2}.$

Limits

10 ∞

Since $\lim\limits_{n\to\infty} 2^n = \infty$, and $\lim\limits_{n\to\infty} 3^{n-1} = \infty$, it is of the form $\dfrac{\infty}{\infty}$. More specifically, this has the form of $\lim\limits_{n\to\infty} \dfrac{a \times c^n + \cdots}{b \times d^n + \cdots} = \lim\limits_{n\to\infty} \dfrac{\frac{1}{3} \times 3^n + \cdots}{1 \times 2^n + \cdots}$. Since $c > d$, the answer is ∞.

11 9

This has the form $\lim\limits_{n\to\infty} \dfrac{a \times c^n + \cdots}{b \times d^n + \cdots}$. Since $c = d(=3)$, $\lim\limits_{n\to\infty} \dfrac{3^3 \times 3^n + 2^n}{3 \times 3^n - 1} = \dfrac{3^3}{3} = 9$.

12 0

This has the form $\lim\limits_{x\to\infty} \dfrac{a \times c^x + \cdots}{b \times d^x + \cdots}$. Since $c < d$, the answer is 0.

13 ⓓ

ⓐ $\dfrac{1}{\infty} - \dfrac{3}{\infty} = 0 - 0 = 0$

ⓑ $\dfrac{1}{\infty} - \dfrac{2}{-\infty} = 0 + 0 = 0$

ⓒ $\dfrac{0+1}{1+0} = 1$

ⓓ $\dfrac{0}{1+0} = 0$

14 7

$\lim\limits_{n\to\infty} \dfrac{2a_n b_n + 5}{a_n + b_n} = \dfrac{2(2)(-3) + 5}{2 - 3} = \dfrac{-7}{-1} = 7$

AP Calculus AB & BC Rewritten from the Beginning

15 ⓑ

From $\lim\limits_{n\to\infty} \dfrac{8n^3+2n^2-1}{n(2n^2+1)} = A$, $A = \dfrac{8}{2} = 4$.

Since $1+2+3+\cdots+n = \dfrac{n(n+1)}{2}$, from $\lim\limits_{n\to\infty} \dfrac{n(n+1)}{2n^2} = B$, we get $B = \dfrac{1}{2}$. Thus, $AB = 2$.

16 ⓒ

Since $\lim\limits_{n\to\infty} \dfrac{\cos n\theta}{n^2} = \dfrac{-1 \sim 1}{\infty} = 0$, $a = 0$.

Since $\lim\limits_{n\to\infty} \dfrac{3\sin n\theta}{2+n^2} = \dfrac{-3 \sim 3}{\infty} = 0$, $b = 0$.

Thus, $a+b = 0$.

17 ⓒ

Dividing each side by (n^2+1) gives $\dfrac{3n^2+1}{n^2+1} < a_n < \dfrac{3n^2+5}{n^2+1}$. If we take $\lim\limits_{n\to\infty}$ to each side, we get

$$\lim_{n\to\infty} \dfrac{3n^2+1}{n^2+1} \leq \lim_{n\to\infty} a_n \leq \lim_{n\to\infty} \dfrac{3n^2+5}{n^2+1}, \text{ so } \lim_{n\to\infty} a_n = 3.$$

18 16

Since the limit converges to a value that is not 0, the order of the numerator and the denominator must be the same; $a = 0$. Thus, $\lim\limits_{n\to\infty} \dfrac{bn+8}{4n+2} = \lim\limits_{n\to\infty} \dfrac{b+\dfrac{8}{n}}{4+\dfrac{2}{n}} = \dfrac{b}{4} = 4$ and so $b = 16$. Therefore, $a+b = 16$.

19 19

This limit is in $\frac{\infty}{\infty}$ form, so we divide the denominator and the numerator by n.

$$\lim_{n\to\infty}\frac{\sqrt{n^2+4}+an}{n}=\lim_{n\to\infty}\frac{\frac{\sqrt{n^2+4}+an}{n}}{\frac{n}{n}}=\lim_{n\to\infty}\frac{\sqrt{\frac{n^2+4}{n^2}}+a}{1}=\lim_{n\to\infty}\frac{\sqrt{1+\frac{4}{n^2}}+a}{1}=1+a=20,$$

so $a=19$.

20 9

By rationalization, we change $\infty-\infty$ into $\frac{\infty}{\infty}$:

$$\lim_{n\to\infty}\frac{(\sqrt{n^2+an+1})^2-(\sqrt{bn^2+4n+6})^2}{\sqrt{n^2+an+1}+\sqrt{bn^2+4n+6}}=\lim_{n\to\infty}\frac{(1-b)n^2+(a-4)n-5}{\sqrt{n^2+an+1}+\sqrt{bn^2+4n+6}}.$$

Divide both the numerator and denominator by $\sqrt{n^2}\,(=n)$ to get

$$\lim_{n\to\infty}\frac{(1-b)n+(a-4)-\frac{5}{n}}{\sqrt{1+\frac{a}{n}+\frac{1}{n^2}}+\sqrt{1+\frac{4}{n}+\frac{6}{n^2}}}$$

If $1-b\neq 0$, then the limit is $\frac{\infty}{2}$, so it cannot be 2. Therefore, $1-b=0$, which gives $b=1$. Since $b=1$,

$$\lim_{n\to\infty}\frac{(1-b)n+(a-4)-\frac{5}{n}}{\sqrt{1+\frac{a}{n}+\frac{1}{n^2}}+\sqrt{1+\frac{4}{n}+\frac{6}{n^2}}}=\lim_{n\to\infty}\frac{(a-4)-\frac{5}{n}}{\sqrt{1+\frac{a}{n}+\frac{1}{n^2}}+\sqrt{1+\frac{4}{n}+\frac{6}{n^2}}}=\frac{a-4}{\sqrt{1}+\sqrt{1}}=\frac{a-4}{2}$$

Thus, $\frac{a-4}{2}=2$ implies $a=8$ and therefore, $a+b=9$.

21 1

Let $\frac{2a_n-6}{a_n-2}=b_n$. Then, $2a_n-6=b_n(a_n-2)$ gives $a_n=\frac{6-2b_n}{2-b_n}$.

Since $\lim_{n\to\infty}b_n=4$, we get $\lim_{n\to\infty}a_n=\lim_{n\to\infty}\frac{6-2b_n}{2-b_n}=\frac{6-8}{2-4}=1$.

AP Calculus AB & BC Rewritten from the Beginning

22 $\dfrac{8}{3}$

Let $na_n = b_n$. Then, $a_n = \dfrac{b_n}{n}$ and $\lim\limits_{n\to\infty} b_n = 3$. Thus,

$$\lim_{n\to\infty} \frac{8n^2+5n}{n^3 \cdot a_n} = \lim_{n\to\infty} \frac{8n^2+5n}{n^3 \cdot \dfrac{b_n}{n}} = \lim_{n\to\infty} \frac{8n^2+5n}{n^2 \cdot b_n} = \lim_{n\to\infty} \frac{\dfrac{8n^2+5n}{n^2}}{\dfrac{n^2 \cdot b_n}{n^2}} = \lim_{n\to\infty} \frac{8+\dfrac{5}{n}}{b_n} = \frac{8}{3}.$$

23 $\dfrac{23}{9}$

Dividing all sides of the given inequality by (n^2+3) and taking $\lim\limits_{n\to\infty}$ gives

$$\lim_{n\to\infty} \frac{4n^2}{n^2+3} \leq \lim_{n\to\infty} a_n \leq \lim_{n\to\infty} \frac{4n^2+5}{n^2+3}.$$

Here, $\lim\limits_{n\to\infty} \dfrac{4n^2}{n^2+3} = \lim\limits_{n\to\infty} \dfrac{\dfrac{4n^2}{n^2}}{\dfrac{n^2+3}{n^2}} = \lim\limits_{n\to\infty} \dfrac{4}{1+\dfrac{3}{n^2}} = \dfrac{4}{1+0} = 4$

and $\lim\limits_{n\to\infty} \dfrac{4n^2+5}{n^2+3} = \lim\limits_{n\to\infty} \dfrac{\dfrac{4n^2+5}{n^2}}{\dfrac{n^2+3}{n^2}} = \lim\limits_{n\to\infty} \dfrac{4+\dfrac{5}{n^2}}{1+\dfrac{3}{n^2}} = \dfrac{4+0}{1+0} = 4$, so $\lim\limits_{n\to\infty} a_n = 4$.

Therefore, $\lim\limits_{n\to\infty} \dfrac{6a_n-1}{2a_n+1} = \dfrac{6\times 4-1}{2\times 4+1} = \dfrac{23}{9}$.

24 6

$\log_2(4n-1) + \log_2(16n+1) - 2\log_2(n+3) = \log_2 \dfrac{(4n-1)(16n+1)}{(n+3)^2}$.

Therefore,

$\lim\limits_{n\to\infty}\left\{\log_2 \dfrac{(4n-1)(16n+1)}{(n+3)^2}\right\} = \lim\limits_{n\to\infty}\left\{\log_2\left(\dfrac{64n^2-12n-1}{n^2+6n+9}\right)\right\}$

$= \lim\limits_{n\to\infty}\left\{\log_2\left(\dfrac{\dfrac{64n^2-12n-1}{n^2}}{\dfrac{n^2+6n+9}{n^2}}\right)\right\} = \lim\limits_{n\to\infty}\left\{\log_2\left(\dfrac{64-\dfrac{12}{n}-\dfrac{1}{n^2}}{1+\dfrac{6}{n}+\dfrac{9}{n^2}}\right)\right\} = \log_2\left(\dfrac{64+0+0}{1+0+0}\right)$

$= \log_2 64 = \log_2 2^6 = 6$

25 32

$a_n^2 + b_n^2 = (a_n + b_n)^2 - 2a_n b_n.$

Therefore,

$\lim_{n\to\infty}(a_n^2 + b_n^2) = \lim_{n\to\infty}\{(a_n + b_n)^2 - 2a_n b_n\} = \lim_{n\to\infty}(a_n + b_n)^2 - 2 \cdot \lim_{n\to\infty}(a_n \cdot b_n) = 6^2 - 2 \cdot 2 = 32.$

26 5

$-1 \leq \sin(n\theta) \leq 1$ for any positive integer n.

Therefore, $-\dfrac{1}{n} \leq \dfrac{\sin n\theta}{n} \leq \dfrac{1}{n}.$

Taking limits and we get $\lim_{n\to\infty}\left(-\dfrac{1}{n}\right) \leq \lim_{n\to\infty}\left(\dfrac{\sin n\theta}{n}\right) \leq \lim_{n\to\infty}\left(\dfrac{1}{n}\right).$

Here, $\lim_{n\to\infty}\left(-\dfrac{1}{n}\right) = \lim_{n\to\infty}\left(\dfrac{1}{n}\right) = 0,$ so $\lim_{n\to\infty}\left(\dfrac{\sin n\theta}{n}\right) = 0$ and $\lim_{n\to\infty}\left(5 + \dfrac{\sin n\theta}{n}\right) = 5.$

27 −2

$-1 \leq \sin(n\theta) \leq 1$ for any positive integer n.

Therefore, $-8n^2 - 1 \leq \sin(n\theta) - 8n^2 \leq -8n^2 + 1$, which gives

$\dfrac{-8n^2 - 1}{4n^2 + n} \leq \dfrac{\sin n\theta - 8n^2}{4n^2 + n} \leq \dfrac{-8n^2 + 1}{4n^2 + n}.$

Taking limits to get

$$\lim_{n\to\infty}\dfrac{-8n^2 - 1}{4n^2 + n} \leq \lim_{n\to\infty}\dfrac{\sin n\theta - 8n^2}{4n^2 + n} \leq \lim_{n\to\infty}\dfrac{-8n^2 + 1}{4n^2 + n}.$$

Since $\lim_{n\to\infty}\dfrac{-8n^2 - 1}{4n^2 + n} = \lim_{n\to\infty}\dfrac{\dfrac{-8n^2 - 1}{n^2}}{\dfrac{4n^2 + n}{n^2}} = \lim_{n\to\infty}\dfrac{-8 - \dfrac{1}{n^2}}{4 + \dfrac{1}{n}} = \dfrac{-8 - 0}{4 + 0} = -2$

and $\lim_{n\to\infty}\dfrac{-8n^2 + 1}{4n^2 + n} = \lim_{n\to\infty}\dfrac{\dfrac{-8n^2 + 1}{n^2}}{\dfrac{4n^2 + n}{n^2}} = \lim_{n\to\infty}\dfrac{-8 + \dfrac{1}{n^2}}{4 + \dfrac{1}{n}} = \dfrac{-8 + 0}{4 + 0} = -2,$

we get $\lim_{n\to\infty}\dfrac{\sin n\theta - 8n^2}{4n^2 + n} = -2.$

28 $\dfrac{5}{2}$

$\sqrt{4n^2+4n+1} < \sqrt{4n^2+6n+2} < \sqrt{4n^2+8n+4}$.

That is, $\sqrt{(2n+1)^2} < \sqrt{4n^2+6n+2} < \sqrt{(2n+2)^2}$, so $2n+1 < \sqrt{4n^2+6n+2} < 2n+2$.

Therefore, the integer part of $\sqrt{4n^2+6n+2}$ is $2n+1$,

so $a_n = 2n+1$, $b_n = \sqrt{4n^2+6n+2} - (2n+1)$.

$\displaystyle\lim_{n\to\infty} \dfrac{(2n+1) + n\{\sqrt{4n^2+6n+2} - (2n+1)\}}{n}$

$= \displaystyle\lim_{n\to\infty} \dfrac{2n+1}{n} + \lim_{n\to\infty}\{\sqrt{4n^2+6n+2} - (2n+1)\}$

$\displaystyle\lim_{n\to\infty}\dfrac{2n+1}{n} = \lim_{n\to\infty}\dfrac{\frac{2n+1}{n}}{\frac{n}{n}} = \lim_{n\to\infty}\dfrac{2+\frac{1}{n}}{1} = \dfrac{2+0}{1} = 2.$

For $\displaystyle\lim_{n\to\infty}\{\sqrt{4n^2+6n+2} - (2n+1)\}$ we change $\infty - \infty$ into $\dfrac{\infty}{\infty}$, by rationalization:

$\displaystyle\lim_{n\to\infty}\{\sqrt{4n^2+6n+2} - (2n+1)\} = \lim_{n\to\infty}\dfrac{2n+1}{\sqrt{4n^2+6n+2} + (2n+1)}.$

Divide both the numerator and denominator by $\sqrt{n^2} = n$.

$\displaystyle\lim_{n\to\infty}\dfrac{2n+1}{\sqrt{4n^2+6n+2}+(2n+1)} = \lim_{n\to\infty}\dfrac{\frac{2n+1}{n}}{\frac{\sqrt{4n^2+6n+2}+(2n+1)}{n}}$

$= \displaystyle\lim_{n\to\infty}\dfrac{2+\frac{1}{n}}{\sqrt{\frac{4n^2+6n+2}{n^2}} + 2 + \frac{1}{n}} = \lim_{n\to\infty}\dfrac{2+\frac{1}{n}}{\sqrt{4+\frac{6}{n}+\frac{2}{n^2}} + 2 + \frac{1}{n}}$

$= \dfrac{2+0}{\sqrt{4+0+0} + 2 + 0} = \dfrac{2}{\sqrt{4}+2} = \dfrac{2}{4} = \dfrac{1}{2}.$

Therefore, the answer is $2 + \dfrac{1}{2} = \dfrac{5}{2}.$

AP Calculus AB & BC Rewritten from the Beginning

Limits

AP Calculus AB & BC Rewritten from the Beginning

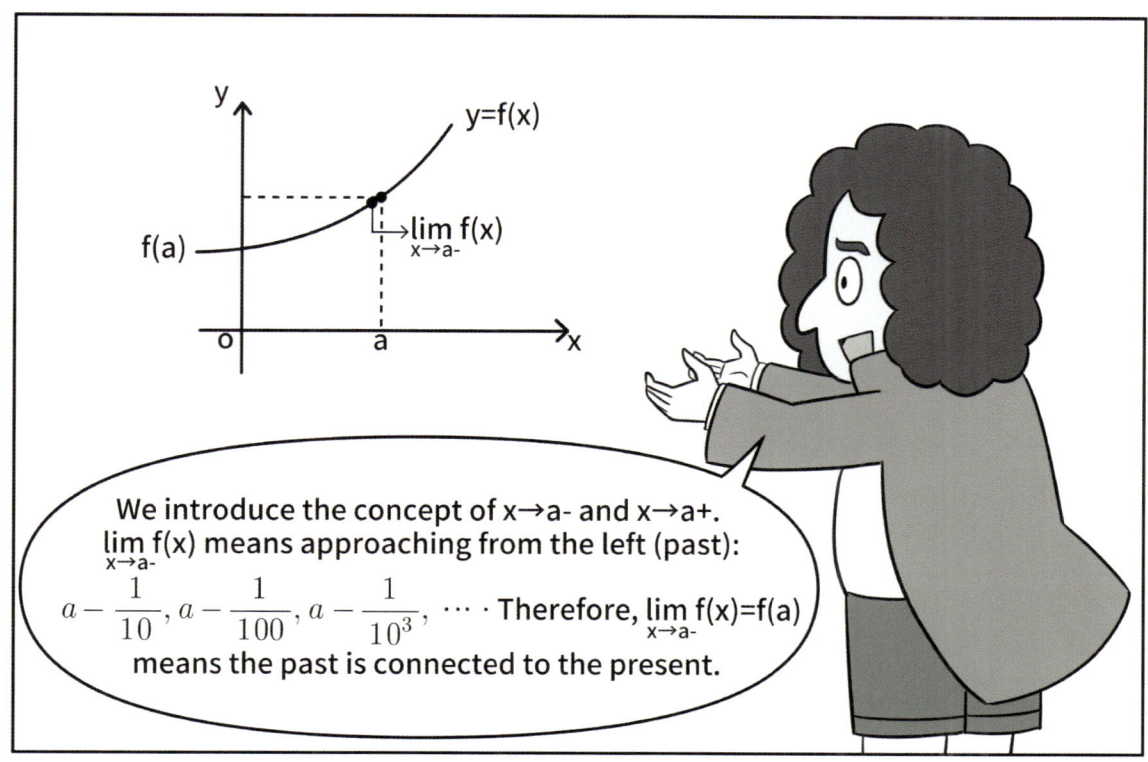

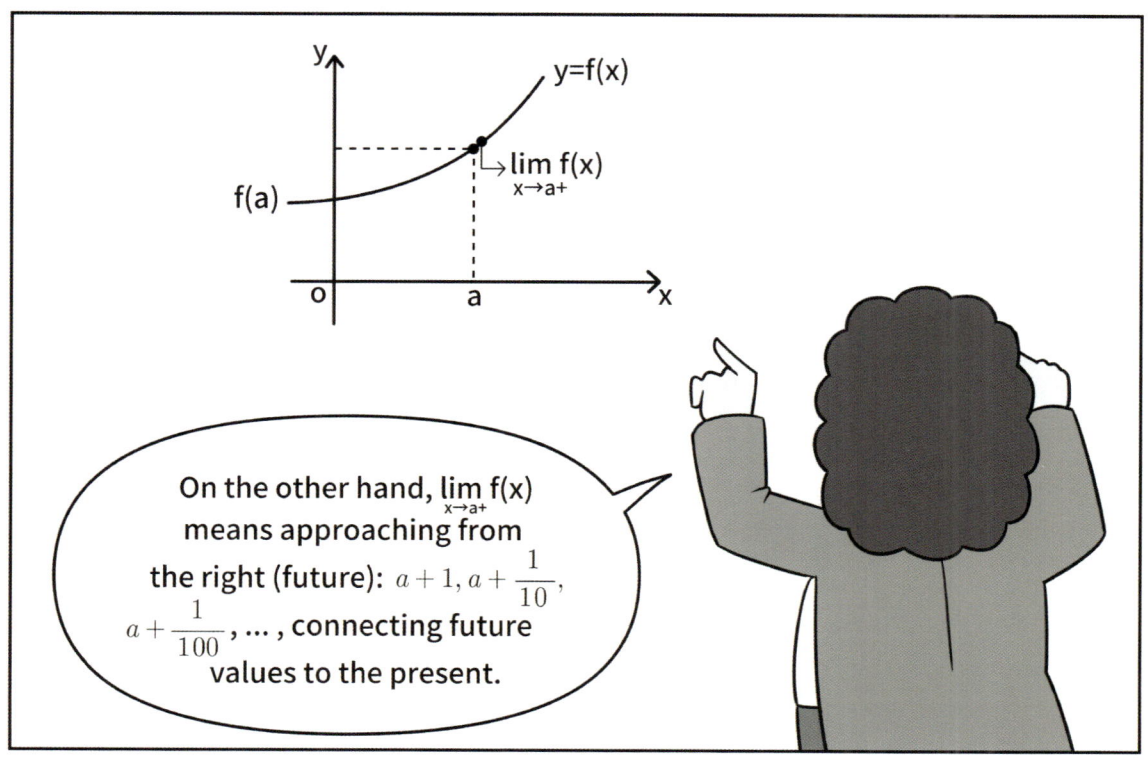

AP Calculus AB & BC Rewritten from the Beginning

02 Limits of Functions

01. The Meaning of Limits as x Approaches a Value

The expression

$$\lim_{x \to \infty} f(x)$$

refers to the value of $f(x)$ as x grows infinitely large, and $\lim_{x \to a} f(x)$ is estimation of the value of $f(x)$ as x approaches a certain value a.

Let's look at the following.

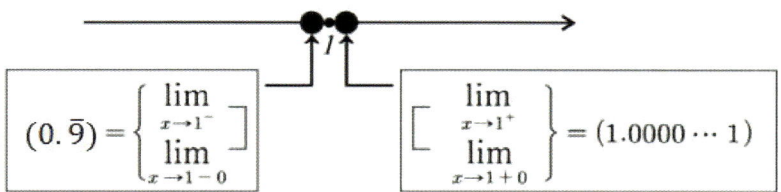

When we zoom in on a graph on a 2-dimensional plane, we can detect small gap around a point.

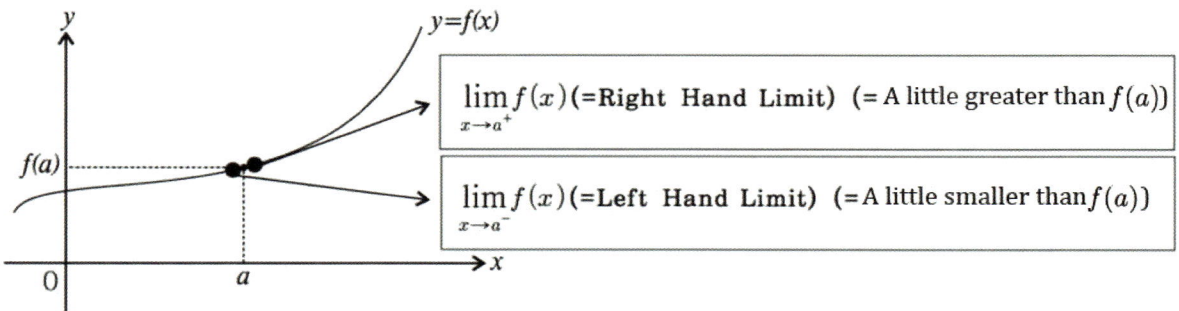

But when we zoom out—viewing the same graph from a great distance—it may appear as if everything converges into a single, smooth point.

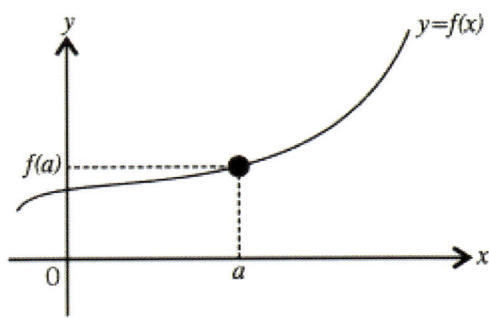

Why does this happen?

$\lim_{x \to a^+} f(x)$ is located extremely close to $f(a)$ from the right and $\lim_{x \to a^-} f(x)$ is located extremely close to $f(a)$ from the left. Thus, it looks like a single point to the human eye. **We call such case as continuous!**

If $\lim_{x \to a^+} f(x) = \lim_{x \to a^-} f(x)$, we simply call it as $\lim_{x \to a} f(x)$. You need to be careful not to confuse the value of $\lim_{x \to a} f(x)$ with $f(a)$. $\lim_{x \to a} f(x)$ is simply extremely close to $f(a)$ from the right and the left. That is, $f(a)$ is $f(a)$, and $\lim_{x \to a} f(x)$ is $\lim_{x \to a} f(x)$. $f(a)$ not existing does not mean that $\lim_{x \to a} f(x)$ does not exist, nor that it does.

Limits

02. Continuity

When $\lim_{x \to a^-} f(x)$, $f(x)$, and $\lim_{x \to a^+} f(x)$ are extremely close so that **they look like a single point to the human eye, we call this as continuous.**

In other words, if $\lim_{x \to a^-} f(x) = f(a) = \lim_{x \to a^+} f(x)$, we say that $f(x)$ is continuous at a.

Make Sure to Know the Following!

The Definition of Continuity! $\lim_{x \to a^-} f(x) = \lim_{x \to a^+} f(x) = f(a)$. That is, $\lim_{x \to a} f(x) = f(a)$.

$$\underbrace{\lim_{x \to a^-} f(x) = \lim_{x \to a^+} f(x)}_{\lim_{x \to a} f(x)}$$

Example 5

In the following, mark the graphs that are continuous at $x = a$ with ○ and those that aren't as ✕.

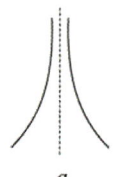
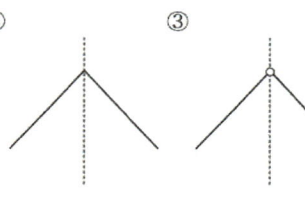
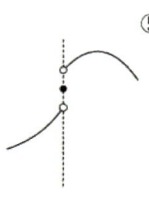
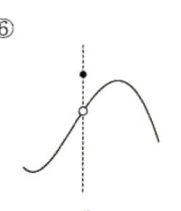

Solution

① (✕)   ② (○)   ③ (✕)   ④ (✕)   ⑤ (○)   ⑥ (✕)

AP Calculus AB & BC Rewritten from the Beginning

03. When does $\lim\limits_{x \to a} f(x)$ exist?

There are two different ways to approach the point $x = a$: from the left and from the right. If both the Left Hand Limit ($\lim\limits_{x \to a^-} f(x)$) and the Right Hand Limit ($\lim\limits_{x \to a^+} f(x)$) exist, and if these two values are "so close that they look almost the same", we say that $\lim\limits_{x \to a} f(x)$ exists.

Let's remember this as follows.

Special Lecture

Does $\lim\limits_{x \to a} f(x)$ exist?

When the left hand limit and the right hand limit at $x = a$ are so close that $\lim\limits_{x \to a^-} f(x)$ and $\lim\limits_{x \to a^+} f(x)$ appears the same, $\lim\limits_{x \to a} f(x)$ exists!

Let us look at the following example.

Example 6

Determine whether $\lim\limits_{x \to a} f(x)$ exists.

(1) (2) (3)

Solution

(1) In this example, $\lim\limits_{x \to a} f(x)$ exists. This is because the values of $\lim\limits_{x \to a-} f(x)$ and $\lim\limits_{x \to a+} f(x)$ are "so close that they look almost the same".

(2) In this example, $\lim\limits_{x \to a} f(x)$ does not exist. This is because the values of $\lim\limits_{x \to a-} f(x)$ and $\lim\limits_{x \to a+} f(x)$ are completely different.

(3) In this example, $\lim\limits_{x \to a} f(x)$ exists. This is because the values of $\lim\limits_{x \to a-} f(x)$ and $\lim\limits_{x \to a+} f(x)$ are "so close that they look almost the same".

As seen above, if a graph is continuous at $x = a$, $\lim\limits_{x \to a} f(x)$ exists, but if it is discontinuous at $x = a$, $\lim\limits_{x \to a} f(x)$ may or may not exist.

AP Calculus AB & BC Rewritten from the Beginning

Supplement

About the Existence of $\lim_{x \to a} f(x)$ and its calculation

1. $\lim_{x \to a} f(x)$ exists when the values of the Left Hand Limit ($\lim_{x \to a^-} f(x)$) and the Right Hand Limit ($\lim_{x \to a^+} f(x)$) are "so close that they look the same".

2. When calculating $\lim_{x \to a} f(x)$, both the Left Hand Limit and the Right Hand Limit must be calculated

※ $\lim_{x \to a^+} f(x)$ is also denoted as $\lim_{x \to a+0} f(x)$, which means that "x is '0' greater than a." Similarly, $\lim_{x \to a^-} f(x)$ is also denoted as $\lim_{x \to a-0} f(x)$, which means that "x is '0' smaller than a."

04. Calculating $\lim\limits_{x \to a} f(x)$

Now we move on to actual computations.

Let's say, we want to calculate $\lim\limits_{x \to 1}(x+1)$. Easy way would be to just input 1 in the place of x and compute $(x+1) = 1+1 = 2$. However, this is NOT the correct way. We should remember that $\lim\limits_{x \to 1}(x+1)$ exists when $\lim\limits_{x \to 1-}(x+1)$ and $\lim\limits_{x \to 1+}(x+1)$ both exists and their value are the same. Here,

$\lim\limits_{x \to 1-}(x+1) = 0.999\cdots + 1 = 1.999\cdots = 2$

$\lim\limits_{x \to 1+}(x+1) = 1.000\cdots 1 + 1 = 2.000\cdots 1 = 2$

and so $\lim\limits_{x \to 1}(x+1) = 2$.

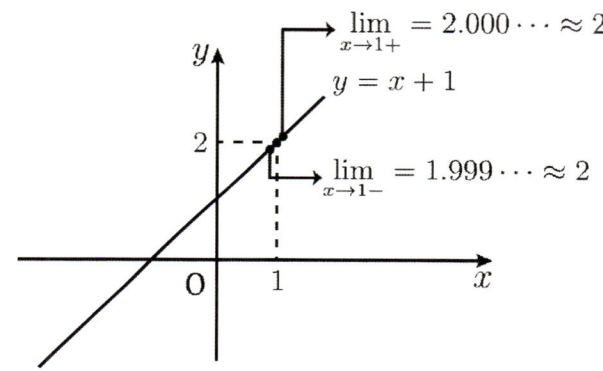

We should always keep in mind that limit was defined as left and right limits. The reason why $(x+1) = 1+1 = 2$ gives the same answer is because $\lim\limits_{x \to 1} f(x) = f(1)$ here. But this need NOT be true in general. We see another example below.

Think about $\lim\limits_{x \to 1}\dfrac{(x-1)(x+1)}{x-1}$. One might think, reduce $x-1$ both from numerator and denominator; $\dfrac{(x-1)(x+1)}{x-1} = x+1$, and so these are not the same? The answer is NO. Reduction can only happen when the number is NOT zero. $f(x) = x+1$ has a value $f(1) = 2$ at $x = 1$. But $f(x) = \dfrac{(x-1)(x+1)}{(x-1)}$ does not have a value at $x=1$ since it is $\dfrac{0}{0}$. $f(x) = \dfrac{(x-1)(x+1)}{(x-1)}$ is NOT defined at $x=1$.

61

AP Calculus AB & BC Rewritten from the Beginning

However, $\lim\limits_{x \to 1} \dfrac{(x-1)(x+1)}{x-1}$ is the same as $\lim\limits_{x \to 1}(x+1)$:

$$\lim_{x \to 1-} \dfrac{(x-1)(x+1)}{(x-1)} = \dfrac{(-0.000\cdots 1)(1.999\cdots)}{(-0.000\cdots 1)} = 1.999\cdots = 2$$

$$\lim_{x \to 1+} \dfrac{(x-1)(x+1)}{(x-1)} = \dfrac{(0.000\cdots 1)(2.000\cdots 1)}{(0.000\cdots 1)} = 2.000\cdots 1 = 2$$

$\lim\limits_{x \to 1+} \dfrac{(x-1)(x+1)}{x-1} = 2.000\cdots \approx 2$

$y = \dfrac{(x-1)(x+1)}{x-1}$

$f(1)$ does not exist

$\lim\limits_{x \to 1-} \dfrac{(x-1)(x+1)}{x-1} = 1.999\cdots \approx 2$

What can we see from this? Why can we cancel out $(-0.000\cdots 1)$ and $(0.000\cdots 1)$ here? Aren't they something "almost" zero? The answer is, even though they are "almost" zero, they are not actual zero.

Here, we learn one important thing. When calculating $\lim\limits_{x \to 1-}$, $\lim\limits_{x \to 1+}$, and $\lim\limits_{x \to 1}$, even though x is close to 1, x is never 1. That is, "$\lim\limits_{x \to 1}$" means that "$x \neq 1$". Remember the "Special Lecture" below.

Special Lecture

$\lim\limits_{x \to 1-}$, $\lim\limits_{x \to 1+}$, and $\lim\limits_{x \to 1}$ means that $x \neq 1$!

$$\lim_{x \to 1-} \dfrac{(x-1)(x+1)}{(x-1)} = \dfrac{(-0.000\cdots 1)(1.999\cdots)}{(-0.000\cdots 1)} = 1.999\cdots = 2$$

$$\lim_{x \to 1+} \dfrac{(x-1)(x+1)}{(x-1)} = \dfrac{(0.000\cdots 1)(2.000\cdots 1)}{(0.000\cdots 1)} = 2.000\cdots 1 = 2$$

Because $x \neq 1$, we can simplify:

$$\lim_{x \to 1-} \dfrac{(\cancel{x-1})(x+1)}{(\cancel{x-1})} = \lim_{x \to 1-}(x+1) = 1.999\cdots = 2$$

$$\lim_{x \to 1+} \dfrac{(\cancel{x-1})(x+1)}{(\cancel{x-1})} = \lim_{x \to 1+}(x+1) = 2.000\cdots = 2$$

Limits

Example 7

Calculate $\lim_{x \to 1} [x]$.

Read the Following!

※ $[x]$ is the greatest integer less than or equal to x (Left Integer on the vertical line). For example,

$[-1.001] = $  $= -2$

$[0.\dot{9}] = $ ──────────── $= 0$

$[1.5] = $ ──────────── $= 1$

Answer
Does Not Exist (DNE)

Solution

Here, we see another reason why simply plugging in 1 into $f(x) (= [x])$ and saying $\lim_{x \to 1} [x] = [1] = 1$ is a wrong way to solve it.

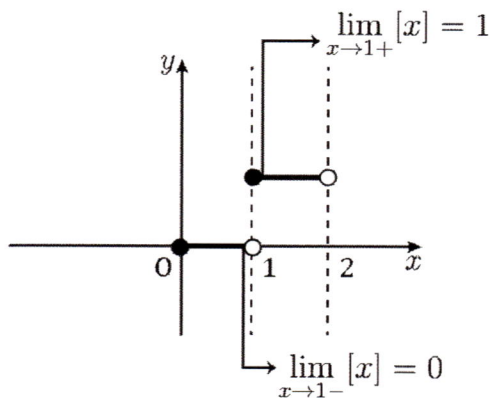

From the above graph, we know
$\lim_{x \to 1-} [x] = [0.999 \cdots] = 0$, $\lim_{x \to 1+} [x] = [1.000 \cdots 1] = 1$.

Left Hand Limit $\lim_{x \to 1-} [x] = 0$ and Right Hand Limit $\lim_{x \to 1+} [x] = 1$ are different and so the limit $\lim_{x \to 1} [x]$ does NOT exist!

63

AP Calculus AB & BC Rewritten from the Beginning

> ### Make Sure to Know the Following!
>
> When calculating $\lim\limits_{x \to a} f(x)$, plugging in $x = a$ and computing $f(a)$ is NOT the right way.
>
> Always keep in mind of BOTH $\lim\limits_{x \to a-} f(x)$ and $\lim\limits_{x \to a+} f(x)$ and compute.
>
> Be aware that they can be different!

●········ **Example 8**

If $f(x) = \begin{cases} \dfrac{x^2-4}{x-2}, & \text{if } x \neq 2 \\ a, & \text{if } x = 2 \end{cases}$ and if $f(x)$ is continuous at $x = 2$, find a.

●········ **Answer** $\quad a = 4$

●········ **Solution**

Since it is continuous at $x = 2$, the three points $(\lim\limits_{x \to a^-} f(x),\ f(x),\ \lim\limits_{x \to a^-} f(x))$ look like a single point, so "$\lim\limits_{x \to 2^-} f(x) = f(2) = \lim\limits_{x \to 2^-} f(x)$". The meaning of $x \neq 2$ is $\lim\limits_{x \to 2}$, and the meaning of $\dfrac{x^2-4}{x-2}$ when $x \neq 2$ is $\lim\limits_{x \to 2^-}\dfrac{x^2-4}{x-2}$. That is, $\lim\limits_{x \to 2^-}\dfrac{x^2-4}{x-2} = \lim\limits_{x \to 2^-}\dfrac{x^2-4}{x-2} = \lim\limits_{x \to 2^-}\dfrac{x^2-4}{x-2} = f(2) = a$

$\qquad\qquad\qquad\qquad\qquad\qquad$ If it is continuous, the limit exists as one.

$\Rightarrow \lim\limits_{x \to 2}\dfrac{(x-2)(x+2)}{(x-2)} = f(x) = a$, so from $\lim\limits_{x \to 2}(x+2) = a$, $a = 4$

The meaning of $\dfrac{x^2-4}{x-2}$ when $x \neq 2$ is $\lim\limits_{x \to 2^+}\dfrac{x^2-4}{x-2}$.

$\Rightarrow$ The meaning of $\dfrac{x^2-4}{x-2}$ when $x \neq 2$ is $\lim\limits_{x \to 2}\dfrac{x^2-4}{x-2}$.

Special Lecture

Continued from the previous example let's look at the meaning of

" $f(x) = \begin{cases} \dfrac{x^2-4}{x-2} & \text{if } x \neq 2 \\ a & \text{if } x = 2 \end{cases}$ " in a figure.

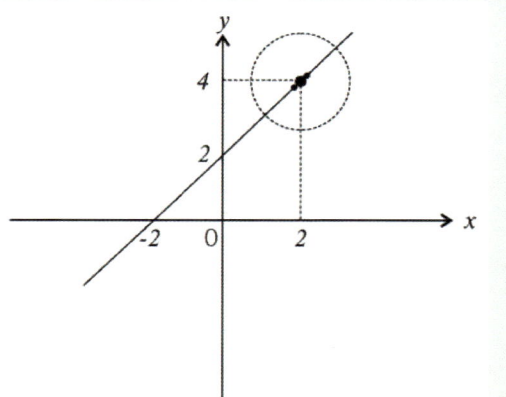

⇒

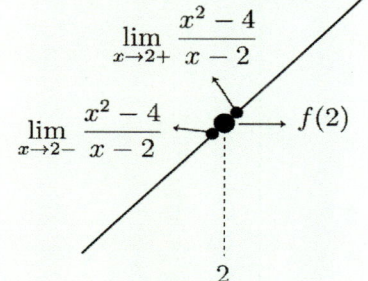

The expression when $x \neq 2$.

That is, $\lim\limits_{x \to 2} \dfrac{x^2-4}{x-2}$.

$\lim\limits_{x \to 2+} \dfrac{x^2-4}{x-2}$

$\lim\limits_{x \to 2-} \dfrac{x^2-4}{x-2}$ → $f(2)$

Thus, $f(x) = \dfrac{x^2-4}{x-2}$ $(x \neq 2)$ is $\lim\limits_{x \to 2} \dfrac{x^2-4}{x-2}$,

and since it is continuous at $x \neq 2$, it is " $\lim\limits_{x \to 2} \dfrac{x^2-4}{x-2} = f(2)$ ".

05. Kinds Of Discontinuity

There are three kinds of discontinuities.

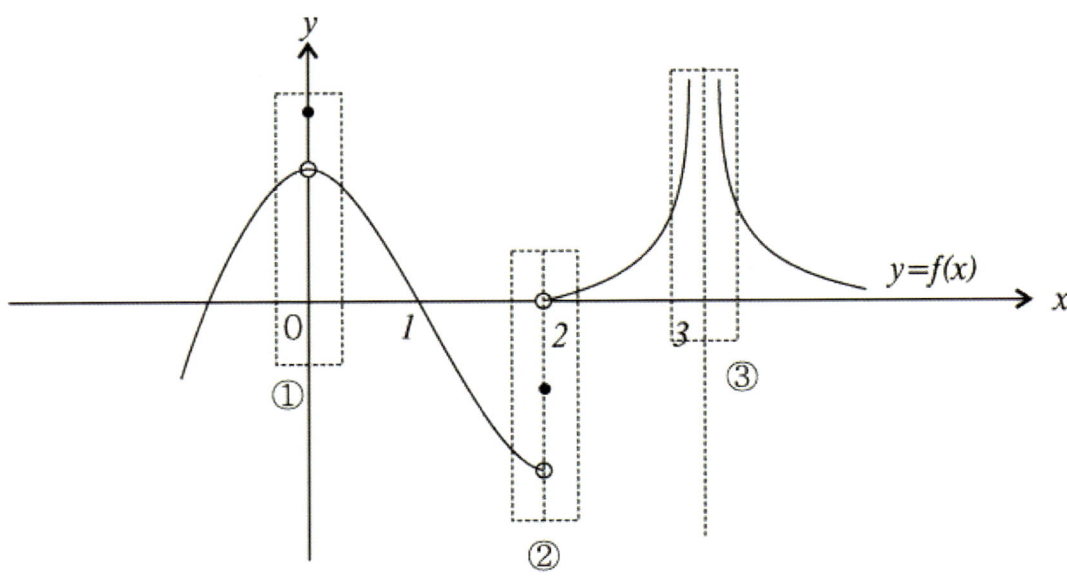

① **Removable Discontinuity (Limit exists, but function value differs)**

: "When the limit exists, but it is different from the value of the function…"

That is, $\lim_{x \to a^+} f(x) = \lim_{x \to a^-} f(x) \neq f(a)$. For example, look at $x = 0$ of the above graph.

(※ $\lim_{x \to a} f(x)$ exists)

② **Jump Discontinuity (Limit does not exist)**

: "When the left hand limit and the right hand limit both exist but are different …"

That is, $\lim_{x \to a^+} f(x) \neq \lim_{x \to a^-} f(x) \neq f(a)$. For example, look at $x = 2$ of the above graph.

(※ $\lim_{x \to a} f(x)$ does not exist)

③ **Infinite Discontinuity**

: Vertical Asymptote

An infinite discontinuity occurs when the function approaches positive or negative infinity as x approaches to a (either left or right direction).

06. Differentiability

This will be explained in detail in the Differentiation chapter, but I will explain differentiability briefly here.

A function is differentiable when the slope of the two lines; line ① (the line that passes through "the point on the function" and "the Left Hand Limit") and line ② (the line that passes through "the point on the function" and "the Right Hand Limit"); are so similar that the two lines look like a single line.

(1)

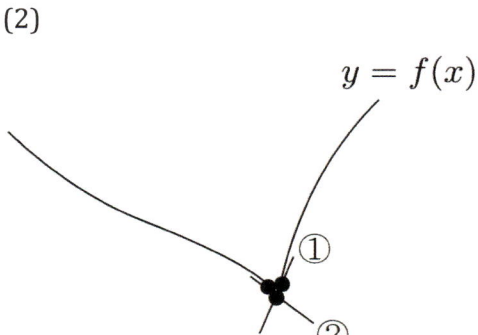

① The slope of the line that passes through the point on the function and the Left Hand Limit

② The slope of the line that passes through the point on the function and the Right Hand Limit

The slopes of line ① and line ② are so similar that the two lines look like one, so $y = f(x)$ is differentiable at $x = a$.

(2)

The slopes of line ① and line ② are completely different. So, two lines are different lines. Therefore, $y = f(x)$ is not differentiable at $x = a$.

AP Calculus AB & BC Rewritten from the Beginning

Example 9

Evaluate the following limits.

1. $\lim\limits_{x \to 2} \dfrac{x+2}{x^2-4}$

2. $\lim\limits_{x \to 3} \dfrac{x^2-9}{x+5}$

3. $\lim\limits_{x \to 0} \dfrac{|x|}{x}$

4. $\lim\limits_{x \to 1} [x-1]$

5. $\lim\limits_{x \to 4} \dfrac{x^2-16}{x-4}$

Limits

 **Answer**

1. Does not exist 2. 0 3. Does not exist
4. Does not exist 5. 8

Solution

1. Look at both the left hand limit and the right hand limit.

$$\lim_{x \to 2-} \frac{x+2}{x^2-4} = \frac{3.999\ldots}{-0.00\ldots1} = -\infty$$

$$\lim_{x \to 2+} \frac{x+2}{x^2-4} = \frac{4.000\ldots}{0.00\ldots1} = \infty$$

Thus, $\lim_{x \to 2-} \frac{x+2}{x^2-4} \neq \lim_{x \to 2+} \frac{x+2}{x^2-4}$, so limit does not exist.

2. Look at both the left hand limit and the right hand limit.

$$\lim_{x \to 3+} \frac{x^2-9}{x+5} = \frac{0.000\ldots1}{8.00\ldots1} = 0 \, , \, \lim_{x \to 3-} \frac{x^2-9}{x+5} = \frac{-0.000\cdots1}{7.999\cdots} = 0. \text{ Thus, } \lim_{x \to 3} \frac{x^2-9}{x+5} = 0.$$

3. Look at both the left hand limit and the right hand limit.

$$\lim_{x \to 0+} \frac{|x|}{x} = 1, \, \lim_{x \to 0-} \frac{|x|}{x} = -1. \text{ Thus, } \lim_{x \to 0+} \frac{|x|}{x} \neq \lim_{x \to 0-} \frac{|x|}{x}, \text{ so limit does not exist.}$$

4. Look at both the left hand limit and the right hand limit.

$$\lim_{x \to 1-} [x-1] = -1, \, \lim_{x \to 1+} [x-1] = 0. \text{ Thus, } \lim_{x \to 1-} [x-1] \neq \lim_{x \to 1+} [x-1], \text{ so limit does not exist.}$$

5. Look at both the left hand limit and the right hand limit.

$$\lim_{x \to 4+} \frac{(x-4)(x+4)}{x-4} = \lim_{x \to 4+} (x+4) = 8, \, \lim_{x \to 4-} \frac{(x-4)(x+4)}{x-4} = \lim_{x \to 4-} (x+4) = 8.$$

Thus, $\lim_{x \to 4} \frac{x^2-16}{x-4} = 8$

AP Calculus AB & BC Rewritten from the Beginning

Look at the following example.

● ········ **Example 10**

Look at the graph below and fill in the table with O and X.

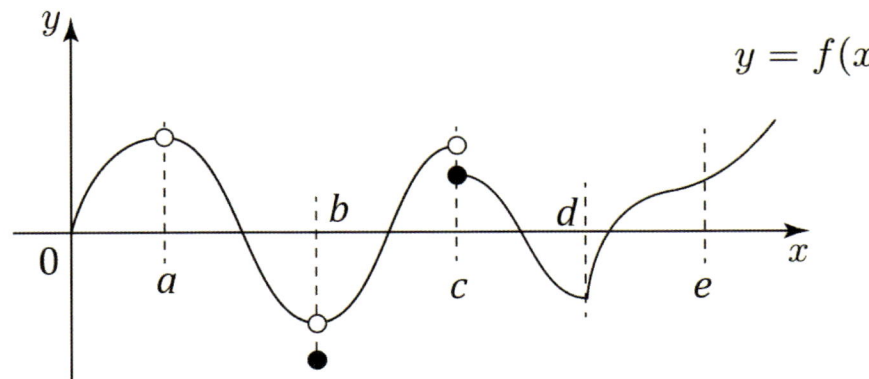

	a	b	c	d	e
Function exists?					
Does the limit exist?					
Continuous?					
Differentiable?					

● ········ **Solution**

	a	b	c	d	e
Function exists?	X	O	O	O	O
Does the limit exist?	O	O	X	O	O
Continuous?	X	X	X	O	O
Differentiable?	X	X	X	X	O

From the example above, we can learn the following. These are essential takeaways often emphasized in class. Students frequently confuse the following foundational ideas, so it is critical to clarify them explicitly.

Make Sure to Know the Following!

1. Continuity Implies Both the Function and the Limit Exist, But Not Necessarily Differentiability.

If a function is continuous at a certain point (see points d and e in the above example) then, ① the limit at that point always exists, and ② the function also exists at the point. However, the function may or may not be differentiable. In other words, continuity does not guarantee that the function is differentiable.

Supplement

If a function is continuous, then all of the three points (the Left Hand Limit, the point on the function, and the Right Hand Limit) 1) exists and moreover, 2) are very very close to one another so that they look the same.

i) the "point on the function" exists → the function exists at that point.

ii) the Left Hand Limit and the Right Hand Limit look the same → the limit exists. Therefore, "**continuous** → **function exists & limit exists**".

In terms of equations, we can also say as the following. If function f is continuous at $x=p$, then $\lim\limits_{x \to p} f(x) = f(p)$. The equation "$\lim\limits_{x \to p} f(x) = f(p)$" implicitly means that both $\lim\limits_{x \to p} f(x)$ and $f(p)$ **exists**, and are the same. That is, if function f is continuous at $x=p$, then the limit at $x=p$ (i.e. $\lim\limits_{x \to p} f(x)$) exists and the function at $x=p$ (i.e. $f(p)$) also exists.

Make Sure to Know the Following!

2. A Limit Can Exist Even If the Function Is Not Continuous

The fact that the limit exist at a point does not guarantee any of the following: the function exists / is continuous / differentiable (at that point).

(See points $a, b, d,$ and e in the Example 10. Especially $x=a$ and $x=e$ show two extremes. At point $x=a$, $\lim\limits_{x \to a} f(x)$ exists but $f(a)$ does not exist, the function is not continuous at $x=a$, and the function is not differentiable at $x=a$. On the other hand, at point $x=e$, $\lim\limits_{x \to e} f(x)$ exists, $f(e)$ exists, the function is continuous at $x=e$, and also the function is differentiable at $x=e$.)

Supplement

If $\lim\limits_{x \to p} f(x)$ exists, for instance if $\lim\limits_{x \to p} f(x) = k$, then $\lim\limits_{x \to p^-} f(x)$ and $\lim\limits_{x \to p^+} f(x)$ are equal as k. However, it does not gurantee that $f(p)$ is also equal to k. Indeed, we cannot even know for sure whether $f(p)$ exists or not. If $f(p)$ exists and its value is equal to k (as in points d and e in the above example), then the function is continuous, but if $f(p)$ does not exist (as in point a) or $f(p) \neq k$ (as in point b), then $f(p)$ is not continuous at point $x=p$.

Make Sure to Know the Following!

3. Differentiability Implies Continuity and More

If a function $y=f(x)$ is differentiable at a certain point (as in point e in the example above), $y=f(x)$ is always continuous, has a limit, and the function exists at that point.

4. Types of Discontinuity

At a point, if the function $y=f(x)$ has limits but is not continuous at (as in points a and b in the example above), then we say that the function has a "removable discontinuity" at that point. On the other hand, at a point if the function $y=f(x)$ does not have a limit (and thus, is not continuous) **but has both the left hand limit and the right hand limit** (as in point c in the example above), then we say that the function has a "jump discontinuity" at that point.

Limits

● ······· **Problem 1**

Evaluate the following limits.

(1) $\lim_{x \to 10} \log x$

(2) $\lim_{x \to 2} \dfrac{x^2 - 3x + 2}{x - 2}$

(3) $\lim_{x \to 0^+} \ln x$

(4) $\lim_{x \to 1} \dfrac{\sqrt{x} - 1}{x - 1}$

(5) $\lim_{x \to 2} \dfrac{\sqrt{2x+1} - \sqrt{x+3}}{x - 2}$

AP Calculus AB & BC Rewritten from the Beginning

● **Answer** (1) 1 (2) 1 (3) $-\infty$ (4) $\dfrac{1}{2}$ (5) $\dfrac{\sqrt{5}}{10}$

● **Solution**

(1) $\lim\limits_{x \to 10+} \log x = \lim\limits_{x \to 10-} \log x = 1$

(2) $\lim\limits_{x \to 2+} \dfrac{(x-1)(x-2)}{x-2} = \lim\limits_{x \to 2+} (x-1) = 1$, $\lim\limits_{x \to 2-} \dfrac{(x-1)(x-2)}{x-2} = \lim\limits_{x \to 2-} (x-1) = 1$.

Thus, $\lim\limits_{x \to 2} \dfrac{(x-1)(x-2)}{x-2} = 1$

(3)

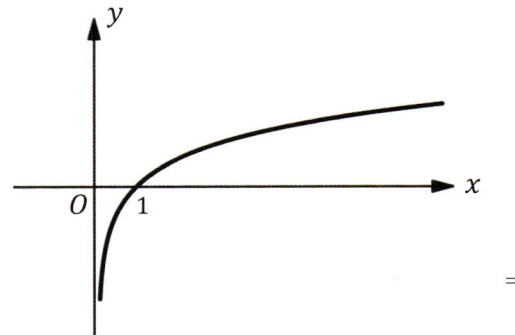

$\Rightarrow \lim\limits_{x \to 0^+} \ln x = -\infty$

(4) $\lim\limits_{x \to 1+} \dfrac{(\sqrt{x}-1)(\sqrt{x}+1)}{(x-1)(\sqrt{x}+1)} = \lim\limits_{x \to 1+} \dfrac{x-1}{(x-1)(\sqrt{x}+1)} = \lim\limits_{x \to 1+} \dfrac{1}{\sqrt{x}+1} = \dfrac{1}{2}$

$\lim\limits_{x \to 1-} \dfrac{(\sqrt{x}-1)(\sqrt{x}+1)}{(x-1)(\sqrt{x}+1)} = \lim\limits_{x \to 1-} \dfrac{x-1}{(x-1)(\sqrt{x}+1)} = \lim\limits_{x \to 1-} \dfrac{1}{\sqrt{x}+1} = \dfrac{1}{2}$

Thus, $\lim\limits_{x \to 1} \dfrac{\sqrt{x}-1}{x-1} = \dfrac{1}{2}$

(5) $\lim\limits_{x \to 2+} \dfrac{(\sqrt{2x+1}-\sqrt{x+3})(\sqrt{2x+1}+\sqrt{x+3})}{(x-2)(\sqrt{2x+1}+\sqrt{x+3})} = \lim\limits_{x \to 2+} \dfrac{x-2}{(x-2)(\sqrt{2x+1}+\sqrt{x+3})}$

$= \lim\limits_{x \to 2+} \dfrac{1}{\sqrt{2x+1}+\sqrt{x+3}} = \dfrac{1}{2\sqrt{5}} = \dfrac{\sqrt{5}}{10}$

$\lim\limits_{x \to 2-} \dfrac{(\sqrt{2x+1}-\sqrt{x+3})(\sqrt{2x+1}+\sqrt{x+3})}{(x-2)(\sqrt{2x+1}+\sqrt{x+3})} = \lim\limits_{x \to 2-} \dfrac{x-2}{(x-2)(\sqrt{2x+1}+\sqrt{x+3})}$

$= \lim\limits_{x \to 2-} \dfrac{1}{\sqrt{2x+1}+\sqrt{x+3}} = \dfrac{1}{2\sqrt{5}} = \dfrac{\sqrt{5}}{10}$

Thus, $\lim\limits_{x \to 2} \dfrac{\sqrt{2x+1}-\sqrt{x+3}}{x-2} = \dfrac{\sqrt{5}}{10}$

Problem 2

Evaluate the following limits.

(1) $\lim\limits_{x \to 1} \dfrac{1}{1-|x|}$

(2) $\lim\limits_{x \to 4} \dfrac{x-4}{\sqrt{x}-2}$

(3) $\lim\limits_{x \to 1+} \ln x$

(4) $\lim\limits_{x \to 0} \dfrac{x}{|x|}$

(5) $\lim\limits_{x \to 3} \dfrac{\sqrt{2x+1}-\sqrt{x+4}}{x-3}$

(6) $\lim\limits_{x \to 3} [x]$ ($[x]$ is the greatest integer less than or equal to x)

AP Calculus AB & BC Rewritten from the Beginning

● **Answer**
(1) Does not exist (2) 4 (3) 0
(4) Does not exist (5) $\dfrac{\sqrt{7}}{14}$ (6) Does not exist

● **Solution**

(1) $\lim\limits_{x\to 1+}\dfrac{1}{1-|x|} = \lim\limits_{x\to 1+}\dfrac{1}{1-x} = \dfrac{1}{1-(1+)} = \dfrac{1}{0-} = -\infty$

and $\lim\limits_{x\to 1-}\dfrac{1}{1-|x|} = \lim\limits_{x\to 1-}\dfrac{1}{1-x} = \dfrac{1}{1-(1-)} = \dfrac{1}{0+} = +\infty$

Since the left hand limit and the right hand limit are different
(i.e. $\lim\limits_{x\to 1+}\dfrac{1}{1-|x|} \neq \lim\limits_{x\to 1-}\dfrac{1}{1-|x|}$), the limit does not exist.

Another approach:
If calculation by equation is difficult, you can also solve by drawing the graph.
How do we draw the graph of $y = \dfrac{1}{1-|x|}$. We don't like the absolute value sign $|x|$ part. However, note that we are only interested in $\lim\limits_{x\to 1}$ which means,

① $x \neq 1$ ② but x is really really close to 1.

If x is really really close to 1, at least x is going to be positive. So $|x| = x$.
All we need to draw is the graph of $y = \dfrac{1}{1-x}$ and then observe near by $x = 1$.

Graph of $y = \dfrac{1}{1-x}$, we can draw. $\lim\limits_{x\to 1+}\dfrac{1}{1-x} = -\infty$ and $\lim\limits_{x\to 1-}\dfrac{1}{1-x} = +\infty$.

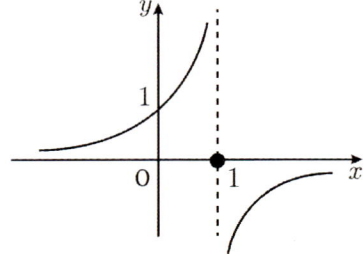

(2) $\lim\limits_{x\to 4+}\dfrac{(x-4)}{(\sqrt{x}-2)} = \lim\limits_{x\to 4+}\dfrac{(x-4)(\sqrt{x}+2)}{(\sqrt{x}-2)(\sqrt{x}+2)} = \lim\limits_{x\to 4+}\dfrac{(x-4)(\sqrt{x}+2)}{x-4} = \lim\limits_{x\to 4+}(\sqrt{x}+2) = 4$

$\lim\limits_{x\to 4-}\dfrac{(x-4)}{(\sqrt{x}-2)} = \lim\limits_{x\to 4-}\dfrac{(x-4)(\sqrt{x}+2)}{(\sqrt{x}-2)(\sqrt{x}+2)} = \lim\limits_{x\to 4-}\dfrac{(x-4)(\sqrt{x}+2)}{x-4} = \lim\limits_{x\to 4-}(\sqrt{x}+2) = 4$

Thus, $\lim\limits_{x\to 4}\dfrac{x-4}{\sqrt{x}-2} = 4$

Solution

(3) $\lim\limits_{x \to 1+} \ln x = 0$

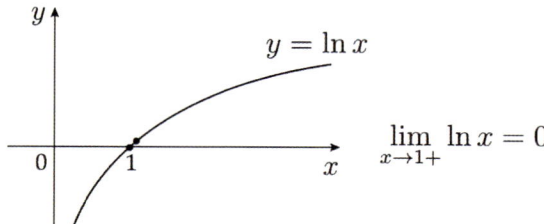

(4) $\lim\limits_{x \to 0-} \dfrac{x}{|x|} = \lim\limits_{x \to 0-} \dfrac{x}{-x} = -1$ and $\lim\limits_{x \to 0+} \dfrac{x}{|x|} = \lim\limits_{x \to 0+} \dfrac{x}{x} = 1$.

Since the left hand limit and the right hand limit are different

(i.e. $\lim\limits_{x \to 0-} \dfrac{x}{|x|} \neq \lim\limits_{x \to 0+} \dfrac{x}{|x|}$), the limit does not exist.

(5) $\lim\limits_{x \to 3+} \dfrac{(\sqrt{2x+1} - \sqrt{x+4})(\sqrt{2x+1} + \sqrt{x+4})}{(x-3)(\sqrt{2x+1} + \sqrt{x+4})}$

$= \lim\limits_{x \to 3+} \dfrac{x-3}{(x-3)(\sqrt{2x+1} + \sqrt{x+4})}$

$= \lim\limits_{x \to 3+} \dfrac{1}{\sqrt{2x+1} + \sqrt{x+4}} = \dfrac{1}{2\sqrt{7}} = \dfrac{\sqrt{7}}{14}$

$\lim\limits_{x \to 3-} \dfrac{(\sqrt{2x+1} - \sqrt{x+4})(\sqrt{2x+1} + \sqrt{x+4})}{(x-3)(\sqrt{2x+1} + \sqrt{x+4})}$

$= \lim\limits_{x \to 3-} \dfrac{x-3}{(x-3)(\sqrt{2x+1} + \sqrt{x+4})}$

$= \lim\limits_{x \to 3-} \dfrac{1}{\sqrt{2x+1} + \sqrt{x+4}} = \dfrac{1}{2\sqrt{7}} = \dfrac{\sqrt{7}}{14}$

Thus, $\lim\limits_{x \to 3} \dfrac{\sqrt{2x+1} - \sqrt{x+4}}{x-3} = \dfrac{\sqrt{7}}{14}$.

Solution

(6) Draw the graph of $y = [x]$ for $2 \leq x < 4$.

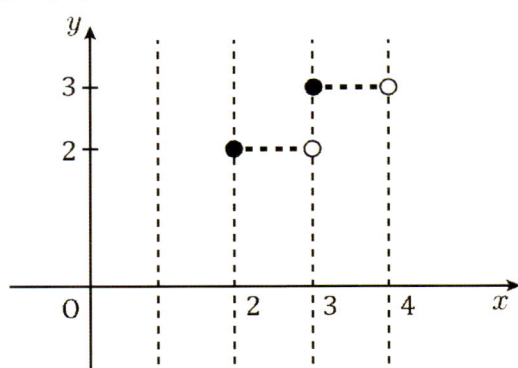

$\lim\limits_{x \to 3^-} [x] = 2$, $\lim\limits_{x \to 3^+} [x] = 3$.

Since the left hand limit and the right hand limit are different (i.e. $\lim\limits_{x \to 3^-} [x] \neq \lim\limits_{x \to 3^+} [x]$), the limit does not exist.

Problem 3

(1) If $f(x) = \begin{cases} x^2 + 1 & \text{for } x \leq 1 \\ e^x & \text{for } x > 1 \end{cases}$, then $\lim_{x \to 1} f(x)$ is

ⓐ Nonexistent　　ⓑ 2　　ⓒ e　　ⓓ e^2

(2) If $f(x) = \begin{cases} \dfrac{x^2 - 4x + 3}{x - 1} & (x \neq 1) \\ k & (x = 1) \end{cases}$, and f is continuous at $x = 1$, then $k =$

ⓐ -2　　ⓑ -1　　ⓒ 0　　ⓓ 1

Answer　　(1) ⓐ　　(2) ⓐ

Solution

(1) Left hand limit : $\lim_{x \to 1^-} (x^2 + 1) = 2$

　　Right hand limit : $\lim_{x \to 1^+} e^x = e$

$\lim_{x \to 1^-} f(x) \neq \lim_{x \to 1^+} f(x)$, so Nonexistent.

(2) It is continuous at $x = 1$, so from $\lim_{x \to 1^+} \dfrac{(x-1)(x-3)}{(x-1)} = \lim_{x \to 1^-} \dfrac{(x-1)(x-3)}{(x-1)} = k$,

$-2 = k$.

AP Calculus AB & BC Rewritten from the Beginning

Problem 4

If $\lim\limits_{x \to 2} f(x) = 3$, which of the following must be true?

I. $\lim\limits_{x \to 2^-} f(x) = \lim\limits_{x \to 2^+} f(x)$.

II. f is continuous at $x = 2$.

III. f is differentiable at $x = 2$.

IV. $f(2) = 3$.

ⓐ I only   ⓑ I and II   ⓒ I, II, and III   ⓓ I, III, and IV

Answer
ⓐ

Solution

$\lim\limits_{x \to 2} f(x) = 3$ means that $\lim\limits_{x \to 2} f(x)$ exists. That is, $\lim\limits_{x \to 2^-} f(x) = \lim\limits_{x \to 2^+} f(x) = 3$

$\lim\limits_{x \to 2} f(x)$ existing does not mean that the function must be continuous or differentiable, or that $f(2) = 3$. Thus, the answer is ⓐ.

※ $\lim\limits_{x \to 2} f(x) = f(2)$ means that it is continuous at $x = 2$, and in this case $f(2)$ exists.

Limits

Problem 5

(1) $\lim\limits_{x \to 3} \dfrac{1}{2x-6}$ is

ⓐ 1   ⓑ 2   ⓒ 3   ⓓ Nonexistent

(2) $\lim\limits_{x \to 2} [x]$ is ($[x]$ is the greatest integer less than or equal to x)

ⓐ 1   ⓑ 2   ⓒ 3   ⓓ Nonexistent

Answer   (1) ⓓ   (2) ⓓ

Solution

(1) It is in $\dfrac{c}{0}$ form, so look at both the left hand limit and the right hand limit.

$$\lim_{x \to 3^-} \dfrac{1}{2x-6} = \dfrac{1}{-0.000\cdots 1} = -\infty$$

$$\lim_{x \to 3^+} \dfrac{1}{2x-6} = \dfrac{1}{0.000\cdots 1} = \infty \qquad \text{Thus, it is nonexistent.}$$

(2) Look at both the left hand limit and the right hand limit.

$\lim\limits_{x \to 2+} [x] = 2$, $\lim\limits_{x \to 2-} [x] = 1$.

$\lim\limits_{x \to 2+} [x] \neq \lim\limits_{x \to 2-} [x]$, so $\lim\limits_{x \to 2} [x]$ does not exist.

AP Calculus AB & BC Rewritten from the Beginning

Problem 6

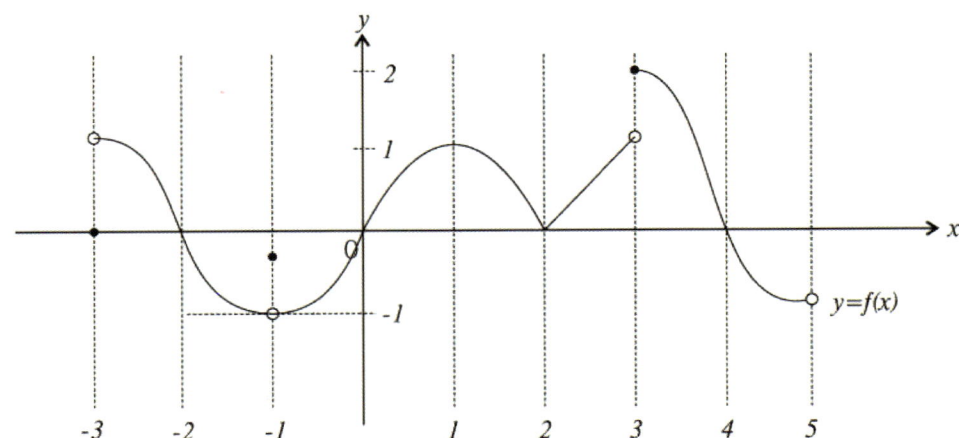

In the graph above, find the following limits.

(1) $\lim_{x \to -3+0} f(x)$ (2) $\lim_{x \to -1} f(x)$ (3) $\lim_{x \to 1} f(x)$

(4) $\lim_{x \to 2} f(x)$ (5) $\lim_{x \to 3} f(x)$ (6) $\lim_{x \to 4} f(x)$

Answer (1) 1 (2) -1 (3) 1 (4) 0 (5) DNE (6) 0

Solution

(1) $\lim_{x \to -3+0} f(x) = 1$

(2) $\lim_{x \to -1} f(x) = -1$

(3) $\lim_{x \to 1} f(x) = 1$

(4) $\lim_{x \to 2} f(x) = 0$

(5) $\lim_{x \to 3} f(x) =$ Does Not Exist (DNE)

(6) $\lim_{x \to 4} f(x) = 0$

Problem 7

(1) The function $f(x) = \begin{cases} e^x & (x \leq 1) \\ \ln x & (x > 1) \end{cases}$

ⓐ is continuous everywhere.
ⓑ is differentiable at $x = 1$.
ⓒ is continuous but not differentiable at $x = 1$.
ⓓ has a jump discontinuity at $x = 1$.

(2) The function $f(x) = \begin{cases} \dfrac{x^2 - 8x + 15}{x - 3} & (x \neq 3) \\ 2 & (x = 3) \end{cases}$

ⓐ is continuous everywhere.
ⓑ is differentiable at $x = 3$.
ⓒ is continuous but not differentiable at $x = 1$.
ⓓ has a removable discontinuity at $x = 3$.

Answer

(1) ⓓ   (2) ⓓ

Solution

(1) $f(1) = e$, $\lim\limits_{x \to 1^-} f(x) = e$, and $\lim\limits_{x \to 1^+} f(x) = 0$,

so $\lim\limits_{x \to 1^-} f(x) \neq \lim\limits_{x \to 1^+} f(x)$

Thus, at $x = 1$,
there is a jump discontinuity.

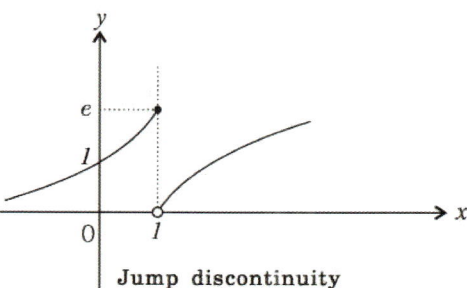
Jump discontinuity

(2) $\lim\limits_{x \to 3} \dfrac{(x-3)(x-5)}{x-3} = \lim\limits_{x \to 3}(x-5) = -2$ and

$f(3) = 2$, so $\lim\limits_{x \to 3} f(x) \neq f(3)$.

Thus, at $x = 3$,
there is a removable discontinuity.

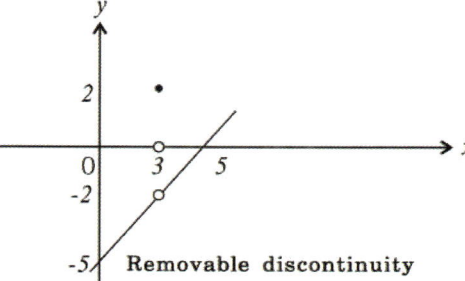
Removable discontinuity

02 Exercise

01 Determine ○ or ✕.

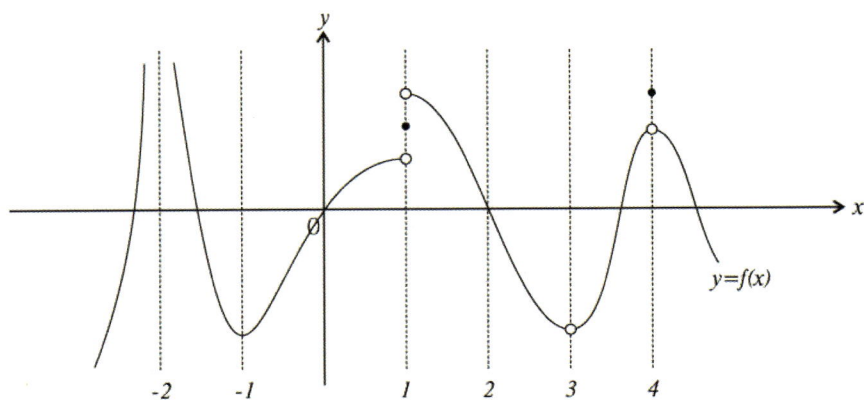

a	−2	−1	1	2	3	4
Continuous						
Does $\lim_{x \to a} f(x)$ exist?						
Does $f(a)$ exist?						

※ Does $\lim_{x \to 1^-} f(x)$ exist?

02 Find the limit $\lim_{x \to 3} \dfrac{x-3}{x^2 - 2x - 3}$.

03 Find the limit $\lim_{x \to 2} \dfrac{x^3 - 8}{x - 2}$.

04 Find the limit $\lim_{x \to 0} \dfrac{|x|}{x}$.

05 Find the limit $\lim_{x \to 0} (2x - 3)\cos x$.

06 Find the limit $\lim_{x \to \frac{\pi}{2}} 3\sin x$.

07 Find the limit $\lim\limits_{x \to 0^+} \dfrac{|x|}{x}$.

08 Find the limit $\lim\limits_{x \to 1^+} \dfrac{3}{x^2 - 1}$.

09 Find the limit $\lim\limits_{x \to 4} \dfrac{\sqrt{x} - 2}{x - 4}$.

10 Find the limit $\lim\limits_{x \to 0.3} [x]$. ($[x]$ is the greatest integer less than or equal to x)

11 Find the limit $\lim_{x \to 3}[x]$. ($[x]$ is the greatest integer less than or equal to x)

12 Find the limit $\lim_{x \to \frac{\pi}{2}} \dfrac{\sin x}{x - \dfrac{\pi}{2}}$.

13 Let $f(x) = \begin{cases} \dfrac{x^2 - 9}{x - 3} &, \text{if } x \neq 3 \\ 5 &, \text{if } x = 3 \end{cases}$.

Which of the following statements is (are) true?

> I. $\lim_{x \to 3} f(x)$ exist.   II. $f(3)$ exists.   III. f is continuous at $x = 3$

ⓐ I   ⓑ II   ⓒ I and II   ⓓ All of them.

14 If $f(x) = \begin{cases} \dfrac{x^2 + x}{5x} &, \text{for } x \neq 0 \\ a &, \text{for } x = 0 \end{cases}$ and f is continuous at $x = 0$, then $a =$

ⓐ $-\dfrac{1}{5}$ ⓑ $\dfrac{1}{5}$ ⓒ 0   ⓓ 1

15 Suppose $f(x) = \begin{cases} \dfrac{5x(x-1)}{x^2-5x+4}, & \text{for } x \neq 1, 4 \\ -\dfrac{5}{3}, & \text{for } x = 1 \\ 0, & \text{for } x = 4 \end{cases}$. Then, $f(x)$ is continuous

ⓐ except at $x = 1$
ⓑ except at $x = 4$
ⓒ except at $x = 1$ or $x = 4$
ⓓ at each real number

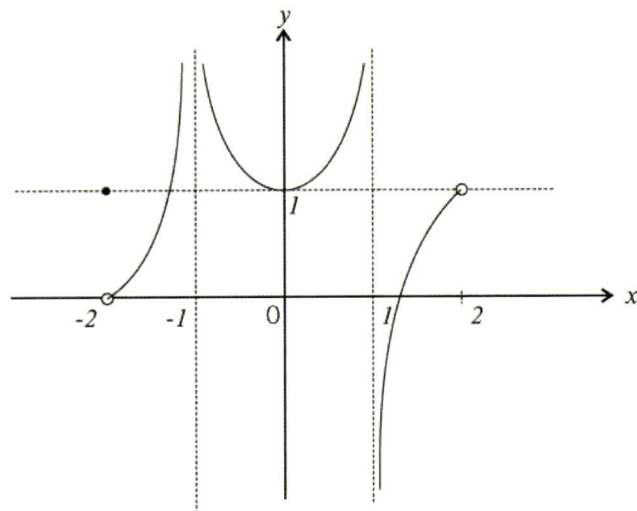

16 Use the above graph to find the following limits.

(1) $\lim\limits_{x \to 2^-} f(x)$

(2) $\lim\limits_{x \to -1} f(x)$

(3) $\lim\limits_{x \to 1} f(x)$

(4) $\lim\limits_{x \to 0} f(x)$

17 Evaluate the following limits.

(1) $\lim\limits_{x \to 3^+} \dfrac{x+1}{x-3}$

(2) $\lim\limits_{x \to \frac{\pi}{2}^+} \tan x$

(3) $\lim\limits_{x \to 1^+} (\ln x)$

(4) $\lim\limits_{x \to 3} \sqrt{4-x}$

(5) $\lim\limits_{x \to \infty} \tan^{-1} x$

(6) $\lim\limits_{x \to 2^-} \dfrac{-4}{x-2}$

18 Find the limits indicated below.

(1) $\lim\limits_{x \to 0^-} \dfrac{|x|}{x}$

(2) $\lim\limits_{x \to -4^-} [x]$, where $[x]$ is the greatest integer less than or equal to x.

(3) $\lim\limits_{x \to 3} \dfrac{\sqrt{x+1}-2}{x-3}$

(4) $\lim\limits_{x \to 2} [x]$, where $[x]$ is the greatest integer less than or equal to x.

19 What value must be assigned to k to make $f(x)=\begin{cases} kx+3, x \neq 1 \\ x^2, x=1 \end{cases}$ continuous?

20 The function $f(x)=\begin{cases} [x-1], (x \neq 1) \\ 3, (x=1) \end{cases}$ (※ $[x]$ is the greatest integer less than or equal to x)

ⓐ is continuous everywhere.
ⓑ is continuous except at $x=1$.
ⓒ has a jump discontinuity at $x=1$.
ⓓ has a removable discontinuity at $x=1$.

21 The function $f(x)=\begin{cases} x+1, (x \neq 1) \\ -2, (x=1) \end{cases}$

ⓐ is continuous everywhere.
ⓑ is continuous except at $x=1$.
ⓒ has a jump discontinuity at $x=1$.
ⓓ has a removable discontinuity at $x=1$.

For problem 22 and 23, refer to the following graph of the function $y = f(x)$.

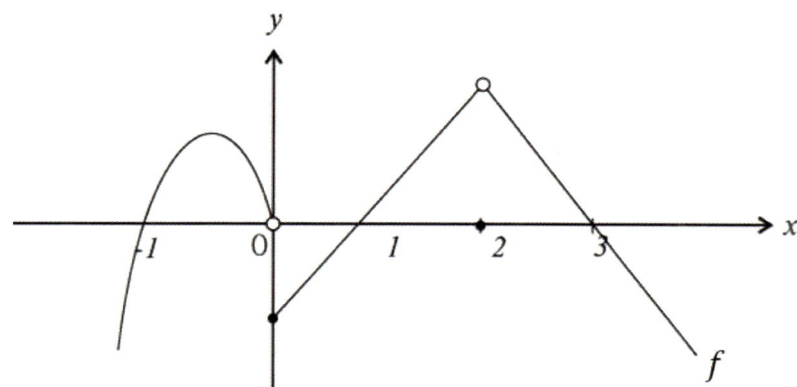

22 The function $y = f(x)$ has a jump discontinuity at

ⓐ $x = -1$ ⓑ $x = 0$ ⓒ $x = 1$ ⓓ $x = 2$

23 The function $y = f(x)$ has a removable discontinuity at

ⓐ $x = -1$ ⓑ $x = 0$ ⓒ $x = 1$ ⓓ $x = 2$

24 If $\lim_{x \to 1} f(x) = 2$, which of the following must be true?

ⓐ $f'(1)$ exists.
ⓑ $f(x)$ is continuous at $x = 1$.
ⓒ $f(x)$ is differentiable at $x = 1$.
ⓓ None of these.

AP Calculus AB & BC Rewritten from the Beginning

02   Answers & Solutions

01   5

x	−2	−1	1	2	3	4
Continuous	X	O	X	O	X	X
Does $\lim_{x \to a} f(x)$ exist?	O	O	X	O	O	O
Does $f(a)$ exist?	X	O	O	O	X	O

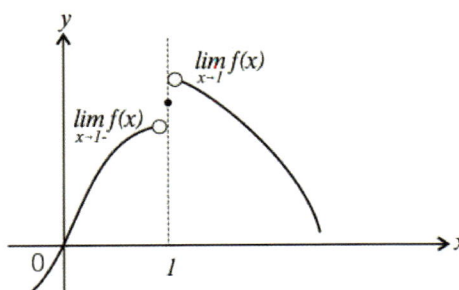

※ Does $\lim_{x \to 1-} f(x)$ exist?

$\Rightarrow$ Yes, $\lim_{x \to 1-} f(x)$ exists.

As seen in the figure, $\lim_{x \to 1+} f(x)$ also exists.

02 $\frac{1}{4}$

$\lim_{x \to 3+} \dfrac{x-3}{x^2-2x-3} = \lim_{x \to 3+} \dfrac{(x-3)}{(x-3)(x+1)} = \lim_{x \to 3+} \dfrac{1}{x+1} = \dfrac{1}{4}$,

$\lim_{x \to 3-} \dfrac{x-3}{x^2-2x-3} = \lim_{x \to 3-} \dfrac{(x-3)}{(x-3)(x+1)} = \lim_{x \to 3-} \dfrac{1}{x+1} = \dfrac{1}{4}$. Thus, $\lim_{x \to 3} \dfrac{x-3}{x^2-2x-3} = \dfrac{1}{4}$.

03   12

$\lim_{x \to 2+} \dfrac{(x-2)(x^2+2x+4)}{x-2} = \lim_{x \to 2+} (x^2+2x+4) = 12$,

$\lim_{x \to 2-} \dfrac{(x-2)(x^2+2x+4)}{x-2} = \lim_{x \to 2-} (x^2+2x+4) = 12$. Thus, $\lim_{x \to 2} \dfrac{(x-2)(x^2+2x+4)}{x-2} = 12$.

04 DNE

$|x| = \begin{cases} x \geq 0 : x \\ x < 0 : -x \end{cases}$, so from $\begin{cases} \lim\limits_{x \to 0+} \dfrac{|x|}{x} = \lim\limits_{x \to 0+} \dfrac{x}{x} = 1 \\ \lim\limits_{x \to 0-} \dfrac{|x|}{x} = \lim\limits_{x \to 0-} \dfrac{-x}{x} = -1 \end{cases}$, $(\lim\limits_{x \to 0+} \dfrac{|x|}{x} = 1) \neq (\lim\limits_{x \to 0-} \dfrac{|x|}{x} = -1)$

Therefore, limit Does Not Exist. (DNE)

05 −3

$\lim\limits_{x \to 0+} (2x-3)\cos x = -3$, $\lim\limits_{x \to 0-} (2x-3)\cos x = -3$. Thus, $\lim\limits_{x \to 0} (2x-3)\cos x = -3$.

06 3

$\lim\limits_{x \to \frac{\pi}{2}+} 3\sin x = 3\sin\dfrac{\pi}{2} = 3$, $\lim\limits_{x \to \frac{\pi}{2}-} 3\sin x = 3\sin\dfrac{\pi}{2} = 3$. Thus, $\lim\limits_{x \to \frac{\pi}{2}} 3\sin x = 3$.

07 1

$\lim\limits_{x \to 0+} \dfrac{|x|}{x} = \lim\limits_{x \to 0+} \dfrac{x}{x} = \lim\limits_{x \to 0+} 1 = 1$

08 ∞

$\lim\limits_{x \to 1+} \dfrac{3}{x^2 - 1}$ ⇒ Substituting a number slightly greater than 1 for x, approximately $1.0000 \cdots 1$, $\dfrac{3}{0.000 \cdots 1} = \infty$.

09 $\dfrac{1}{4}$

$\lim\limits_{x \to 4+} \dfrac{(\sqrt{x}-2)(\sqrt{x}+2)}{(x-4)(\sqrt{x}+2)} = \lim\limits_{x \to 4+} \dfrac{x-4}{(x-4)(\sqrt{x}+2)} = \lim\limits_{x \to 4+} \dfrac{1}{\sqrt{x}+2} = \dfrac{1}{4}$,

$\lim\limits_{x \to 4-} \dfrac{(\sqrt{x}-2)(\sqrt{x}+2)}{(x-4)(\sqrt{x}+2)} = \lim\limits_{x \to 4-} \dfrac{x-4}{(x-4)(\sqrt{x}+2)} = \lim\limits_{x \to 4-} \dfrac{1}{\sqrt{x}+2} = \dfrac{1}{4}$.

Thus, $\lim\limits_{x \to 4} \dfrac{(\sqrt{x}-2)(\sqrt{x}+2)}{(x-4)(\sqrt{x}+2)} = \dfrac{1}{4}$.

10 0

$\lim\limits_{x \to 0.3+} [x] = [0.3000 \cdots 1] = 0$ and $\lim\limits_{x \to 0.3-} [x] = [0.2999 \cdots] = 0$

Thus, $\lim\limits_{x \to 0.3} [x] = 0$.

11 DNE

$\lim\limits_{x \to 3}[x] = \lim\limits_{x \to 3+} [x] = [3.0000 \cdots 1] = 3$

$\qquad\qquad \lim\limits_{x \to 3-} [x] = [2.9999 \cdots] = 2$

Thus, $\lim\limits_{x \to 3+} [x] \neq \lim\limits_{x \to 3-} [x]$, so the limit Does Not Exist. (DNE)

12 DNE

$\lim\limits_{x \to \frac{\pi}{2}} \dfrac{\sin x}{x - \frac{\pi}{2}} = \begin{vmatrix} \lim\limits_{x \to \frac{\pi}{2}+} \dfrac{\sin x}{x - \frac{\pi}{2}} = \dfrac{1}{0.000 \cdots 1} = \infty \\ \lim\limits_{x \to \frac{\pi}{2}-} \dfrac{\sin x}{x - \frac{\pi}{2}} = \dfrac{1}{-0.000 \cdots 1} = -\infty \end{vmatrix}$

Thus, $\lim\limits_{x \to \frac{\pi}{2}+} \dfrac{\sin x}{x - \frac{\pi}{2}} \neq \lim\limits_{x \to \frac{\pi}{2}-} \dfrac{\sin x}{x - \frac{\pi}{2}}$, so the limit Does Not Exist. (DNE)

13 ⓒ

From $f(x) = \begin{cases} \dfrac{x^2 - 9}{x - 3}, & \text{If } x \neq 3 \\ 5, & \text{If } x = 3 \end{cases}$

I. $x \neq 3$ means $\lim\limits_{x \to 3}$, and for $\lim\limits_{x \to 3} f(x)$ to exist, $\lim\limits_{x \to 3+} f(x) = \lim\limits_{x \to 3-} f(x)$ must hold.

$\lim\limits_{x \to 3+} \dfrac{(x-3)(x+3)}{(x-3)} = \lim\limits_{x \to 3+} (x+3) = 6$, and

$\lim\limits_{x \to 3-} \dfrac{(x-3)(x+3)}{(x-3)} = \lim\limits_{x \to 3-} (x+3) = 6$

So, $\lim\limits_{x \to 3} f(x)$ exists.

II. $f(3)=5$, so $f(3)$ exists.

III. $\lim\limits_{x \to 3} f(x) \neq f(3)$, so discontinuous.

Thus, the answer is ⓒ.

14 ⓑ

It is continuous at $x=0$. So $\lim\limits_{x \to 0-} f(x) = \lim\limits_{x \to 0+} f(x) = f(0)$.

Thus, $\lim\limits_{x \to 0} f(x) = f(0)$.

On the other hand, $\lim\limits_{x \to 0} \dfrac{x^2 + x}{5x} = a \Rightarrow \lim\limits_{x \to 0} \dfrac{x(x+1)}{5x} = \lim\limits_{x \to 0} \dfrac{x+1}{5} = a \Rightarrow \dfrac{1}{5} = a$.

Thus, the answer is ⓑ.

15 ⓑ

$[x \neq 1]$ $\lim\limits_{x \to 1} \dfrac{5x(x-1)}{x^2 - 5x + 4} = \lim\limits_{x \to 1} \dfrac{5x(x-1)}{(x-1)(x-4)} = \lim\limits_{x \to 1} \dfrac{5x}{x-4} = -\dfrac{5}{3}$

$[x \neq 4]$ $\lim\limits_{x \to 4} \dfrac{5x(x-1)}{x^2 - 5x + 4} = \lim\limits_{x \to 4} \dfrac{5x(x-1)}{(x-1)(x-4)}$

Looking at both the left Hand Limit and the Right Hand Limit,

$\left[\begin{array}{l} \lim\limits_{x \to 4-} \dfrac{5x(x-1)}{(x-1)(x-4)} = \dfrac{20 \times 3}{3 \times (-0.000 \cdots 1)} = -\infty \\ \lim\limits_{x \to 4+} \dfrac{5x(x-1)}{(x-1)(x-4)} = \dfrac{20 \times 3}{3 \times (+0.000 \cdots 1)} = \infty \end{array} \right.$ Thus, $\lim\limits_{x \to 4-} f(x) \neq \lim\limits_{x \to 4+} f(x)$.

So, the limit Does Not Exist. (DNE)

$f(1) = -\dfrac{5}{3}$, $f(4) = 0$, and $\lim\limits_{x \to 1} f(x) = f(1)$, $\lim\limits_{x \to 4} f(x) \neq f(4)$, so it is continuous at $x = 1$.

Thus, the answer is ⓑ.

16

(1) 1   (2) ∞   (3) DNE   (4) 1

AP Calculus AB & BC Rewritten from the Beginning

17   (1) ∞ (2) $-\infty$ (3) 0 (4) 1 (5) $\dfrac{\pi}{2}$ (6) ∞

(1) $\displaystyle\lim_{x\to 3+}\dfrac{x+1}{x-3}=\dfrac{4}{0.000\cdots 1}=\infty$

(2)

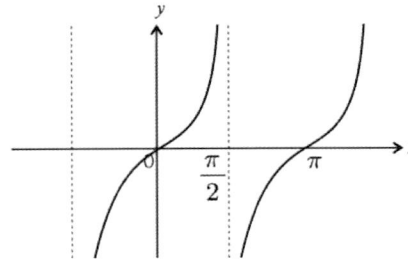

$\displaystyle\lim_{x\to\frac{\pi}{2}+}\tan x=-\infty$

(3)

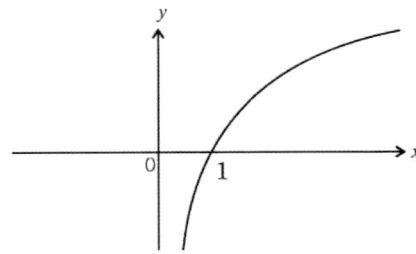

$\displaystyle\lim_{x\to 1+}\ln x=0$

(4) $\displaystyle\lim_{x\to 3+}\sqrt{4-x}=\lim_{x\to 3-}\sqrt{4-x}=1$

(5)

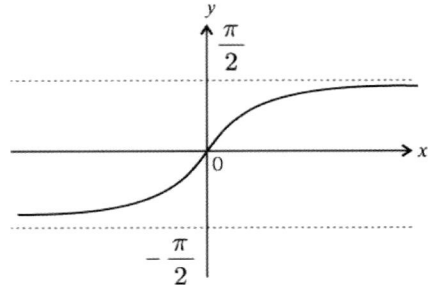

$\displaystyle\lim_{x\to\infty}\tan^{-1}x=\dfrac{\pi}{2}$

(6) $\displaystyle\lim_{x\to 2-}\dfrac{-4}{x-2}=\dfrac{-4}{-0.000\cdots 1}=\infty$

Limits

18   (1) -1 (2) -5 (3) $\dfrac{1}{4}$ (4) Nonexistent

(1) $\displaystyle\lim_{x\to 0-}\dfrac{|x|}{x}=\lim_{x\to 0-}\dfrac{-x}{x}=\lim_{x\to 0-}-1=-1$

(2) $\displaystyle\lim_{x\to -4^-}[x]=[-4.000\cdots 1]=-5$

(3) $\displaystyle\lim_{x\to 3+}\dfrac{(\sqrt{x+1}-2)(\sqrt{x+1}+2)}{(x-3)(\sqrt{x+1}+2)}=\lim_{x\to 3+}\dfrac{(x-3)}{(x-3)(\sqrt{x+1}+2)}=\lim_{x\to 3+}\dfrac{1}{\sqrt{x+1}+2}=\dfrac{1}{4}$

$\displaystyle\lim_{x\to 3-}\dfrac{(\sqrt{x+1}-2)(\sqrt{x+1}+2)}{(x-3)(\sqrt{x+1}+2)}=\lim_{x\to 3-}\dfrac{(x-3)}{(x-3)(\sqrt{x+1}+2)}=\lim_{x\to 3-}\dfrac{1}{\sqrt{x+1}+2}=\dfrac{1}{4}$

Thus, $\displaystyle\lim_{x\to 3}\dfrac{\sqrt{x+1}-2}{x-3}=\dfrac{1}{4}$

(4) $\displaystyle\lim_{x\to 2}[x]$,   Left hand limit $\displaystyle\lim_{x\to 2^-}[x]=1$

Right hand limit $\displaystyle\lim_{x\to 2^+}[x]=2$

Thus, Nonexistent.

19 -2

Since f is continuous at $x=1$, we know

$$\lim_{x\to 1}f(x)=f(1)\Rightarrow \lim_{x\to 1+}(kx+3)=\lim_{x\to 1-}(kx+3)=f(1)=1.$$

Finally, we get $k+3=1$. Thus, $k=-2$.

20 ⓒ

$\displaystyle\lim_{x\to 1}[x-1]$,   Left hand limit $\displaystyle\lim_{x\to 1^-}[x-1]=[-0.000\cdots 1]=-1$

Right hand limit $\displaystyle\lim_{x\to 1^+}[x-1]=[0.000\cdots 1]=0$

and $f(1)=3$

$\displaystyle\lim_{x\to 1^+}[x-1]\neq \lim_{x\to 1^-}[x-1]$, so at $x=1$, there is a Jump Discontinuity.

21 ⓓ

$\lim_{x \to 1^+}(x+1) = \lim_{x \to 1^-}(x+1) = 2$ and $f(1) = -2$, so $\lim_{x \to 1} f(x) \neq f(1)$

$\lim_{x \to 1} f(x) \neq f(1)$, so at $x = 1$, there is a Removable Discontinuity.

22 ⓑ

At $x = 0$, $\lim_{x \to 0^-} f(x)$ and $\lim_{x \to 0^+} f(x)$ both exist but $\lim_{x \to 0^-} f(x) \neq \lim_{x \to 0^+} f(x)$, so there is a Jump discontinuity.

23 ⓓ

At $x = 2$, $\lim_{x \to 2} f(x)$ and $f(2)$ both exist but $\lim_{x \to 2} f(x) \neq f(2)$, so there is a Removable discontinuity.

24 ⓓ

$\lim_{x \to 1} f(x) = 2$ means $\lim_{x \to 1^-} f(x) = \lim_{x \to 1^+} f(x)$. That is, $\lim_{x \to 1} f(x)$ exists. However, the existence of $\lim_{x \to 1} f(x)$ does not necessarily mean that the function is continuous or differentiable at $x = 1$ nor that $f(1)$ exists. Thus, none of the options is true.

03 Limit of Trigonometric Function

This chapter introduces several key limit formulas, especially those involving trigonometric functions near zero. Memorizing these identities is crucial for solving more advanced problems quickly and accurately.

Although we will explore the derivations, the main emphasis should be on internalizing the final forms and knowing when to apply them.
Let's begin with this intuitive inequality involving trigonometric functions:

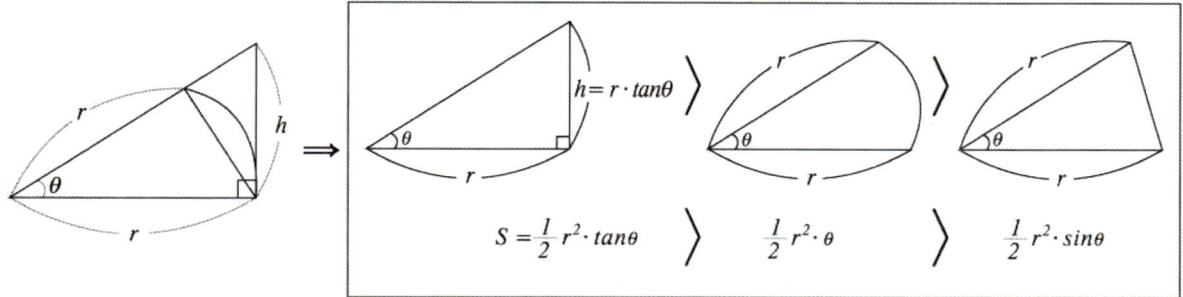

⇒ If we cancel $\frac{1}{2}r^2$ terms from each side, we get $\tan\theta > \theta > \sin\theta$. ⋯ ①

Divide each side of ① by $\tan\theta$, and we get $1 > \dfrac{\theta}{\tan\theta} > \cos\theta$. ⋯ ②

Take $\lim\limits_{\theta \to 0}$ to each side of ②, and we get $\lim\limits_{\theta \to 0} 1 \geq \lim\limits_{\theta \to 0} \dfrac{\theta}{\tan\theta} \geq \lim\limits_{\theta \to 0} \cos\theta (= 1)$,

so $\lim\limits_{\theta \to 0} \dfrac{\theta}{\tan\theta} = 1$ and $\lim\limits_{\theta \to 0} \dfrac{\tan\theta}{\theta} = 1$.

Now, divide each side of ① by $\sin\theta$, and get $\dfrac{1}{\cos\theta} = \dfrac{\tan\theta}{\sin\theta} > \dfrac{\theta}{\sin\theta} > 1$. ⋯ ③

Take the $\lim\limits_{\theta \to 0}$ of each side of ③, and we get $(1.000\cdots =) \lim\limits_{\theta \to 0} \dfrac{1}{\cos\theta} \geq \lim\limits_{\theta \to 0} \dfrac{\theta}{\sin\theta} \geq \lim\limits_{\theta \to 0} 1$.

Finally, we get

$$\lim_{\theta \to 0} \frac{\theta}{\sin\theta} = 1 \quad \text{and} \quad \lim_{\theta \to 0} \frac{\sin\theta}{\theta} = 1.$$

AP Calculus AB & BC Rewritten from the Beginning

Read the Following!

"Is 1 greater than 1? Does 1<1<1 hold?"

Of course, the answer is "No", but the situation is different in the case of limits.

In the ③ above, if we take $\lim_{\theta \to 0}$, in $(1.000\cdots)\lim_{\theta \to 0}\dfrac{1}{\cos\theta} > \lim_{\theta \to 0}\dfrac{\theta}{\sin\theta} > \lim_{\theta \to 0} 1$, $\lim_{\theta \to 0}\dfrac{\theta}{\sin\theta}$ is technically a little greater than 1, and $\lim_{\theta \to 0}\dfrac{1}{\cos\theta}$ is a bit greater than both 1 and $\lim_{\theta \to 0}\dfrac{\theta}{\sin\theta}$.

These limits look almost the same as 1, so we are just saying that it is 1.

The formulas we have proven until now are $\lim_{\theta \to 0}\dfrac{\theta}{\sin\theta}=1$, $\lim_{\theta \to 0}\dfrac{\sin\theta}{\theta}=1$, $\lim_{\theta \to 0}\dfrac{\tan\theta}{\theta}=1$, and $\lim_{\theta \to 0}\dfrac{\theta}{\tan\theta}=1$. Some examples using these formulas are,

① $\lim_{x \to 0}\dfrac{\sin x}{2x} = \lim_{x \to 0}(\dfrac{\sin x}{x} \times \dfrac{1}{2}) = 1 \times \dfrac{1}{2} = \dfrac{1}{2}$

② $\lim_{x \to 0}\dfrac{\sin 5x}{\tan 3x} = \lim_{x \to 0}(\dfrac{3x}{\tan 3x} \times \dfrac{\sin 5x}{5x} \times \dfrac{5}{3}) = 1 \times 1 \times \dfrac{5}{3} = \dfrac{5}{3}$

③ $\lim_{x \to 0}\dfrac{\sin 5x}{\sin 2x \cdot \cos 3x} = \lim_{x \to 0}(\dfrac{2x}{\sin 2x} \times \dfrac{\sin 5x}{5x} \times \dfrac{5}{2} \times \dfrac{1}{\cos 3x}) = 1 \times 1 \times \dfrac{5}{2} \times 1 = \dfrac{5}{2}$

(※ $\cos 0 = 1$, so do not pay attention to $\cos 3x$.)

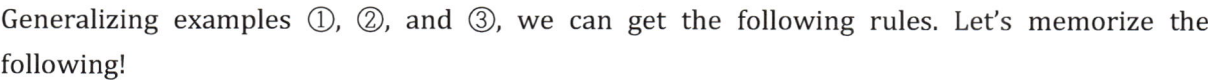

Generalizing examples ①, ②, and ③, we can get the following rules. Let's memorize the following!

Must memorize!

If $a \neq 0$, we have following variations of $\lim\limits_{\theta \to 0} \dfrac{\sin\theta}{\theta} = 1$.

- $\lim\limits_{x \to 0} \dfrac{\sin bx}{ax} = \dfrac{b}{a}$
- $\lim\limits_{x \to 0} \dfrac{bx}{\sin ax} = \dfrac{b}{a}$
- $\lim\limits_{x \to 0} \dfrac{\tan bx}{ax} = \dfrac{b}{a}$
- $\lim\limits_{x \to 0} \dfrac{bx}{\tan ax} = \dfrac{b}{a}$
- $\lim\limits_{x \to 0} \dfrac{\sin bx}{\sin ax} = \dfrac{b}{a}$
- $\lim\limits_{x \to 0} \dfrac{\tan bx}{\tan ax} = \dfrac{b}{a}$
- $\lim\limits_{x \to 0} \dfrac{\tan bx}{\sin ax} = \dfrac{b}{a}$
- $\lim\limits_{x \to 0} \dfrac{\sin bx}{\tan ax} = \dfrac{b}{a}$
- $\lim\limits_{x \to 0} \dfrac{\tan bx \cdot \cos bx}{\sin ax} = \dfrac{b}{a}$
- $\lim\limits_{x \to 0} \dfrac{\tan bx}{\sin ax \cdot \cos bx} = \dfrac{b}{a}$

⇒ It is important to note that x is approaching 0, and not ∞ or a number other than 0. For example, $\lim\limits_{x \to 0} \dfrac{\sin x}{x} = 1$ holds, but neither $\lim\limits_{x \to a} \dfrac{\sin x}{x} = 1$ nor $\lim\limits_{x \to \infty} \dfrac{\sin x}{x} = 1$ holds.

AP Calculus AB & BC Rewritten from the Beginning

● ········ **Problem 1**

Find the limits.

(1) $\displaystyle\lim_{x\to 0}\frac{\sin x \cos x}{5x}$

(2) $\displaystyle\lim_{x\to 0}\frac{\tan 5x}{\sin 2x}$

(3) $\displaystyle\lim_{x\to \infty}\left(x\tan\frac{1}{x}\right)$

(4) $\displaystyle\lim_{x\to 0}\frac{\sin^2 9x}{\sec^2 3x - 1}$

(5) $\displaystyle\lim_{x\to 0}\frac{\sin(\tan 5x)}{x}$

● ········ **Answer** (1) $\frac{1}{5}$ (2) $\frac{5}{2}$ (3) 1 (4) 9 (5) 5

● ········ **Solution**

(1) $\cos 0 = 1$, so $\displaystyle\lim_{x\to 0}\frac{\sin x}{5x} = \lim_{x\to 0}\left(\frac{\sin x}{x}\times\frac{1}{5}\right) = \frac{1}{5}$.

(2) $\displaystyle\lim_{x\to 0}\frac{\tan 5x}{\sin 2x} = \frac{5}{2}$

(3) If we let $\frac{1}{x} = k$, then if $x\to\infty$, $k\to 0$, so $\displaystyle\lim_{x\to\infty}\left(x\tan\frac{1}{x}\right) = \lim_{k\to 0}\frac{\tan k}{k} = 1$.

(4) $\sec^2 3x - 1 = \tan^2 3x$, so $\displaystyle\lim_{x\to 0}\left(\frac{\sin 9x}{\tan 3x}\times\frac{\sin 9x}{\tan 3x}\right) = \frac{9}{3}\times\frac{9}{3} = 9$

(5) $\displaystyle\lim_{x\to 0}\left(\frac{\sin(\tan 5x)}{\tan 5x}\times\frac{\tan 5x}{x}\right) = 1\times 5 = 5$

03 Exercise

01~06 Find the limits.

01 $\lim\limits_{x \to 0} \dfrac{\sin 7x}{x^2 + 10x}$

02 $\lim\limits_{x \to \infty} \left(x \sin \dfrac{1}{x} \right)$

03 $\lim\limits_{x \to 0} \dfrac{\sin^2(2x)}{\tan^2(3x)}$

04 $\lim\limits_{x \to 0} \dfrac{\sin(5x)}{\sin(3x)\cos(x)}$

05 $\lim\limits_{x \to 0} \dfrac{x \sin x}{1 - \cos^2 x}$

06 $\lim\limits_{t \to 0} \dfrac{\tan(\sin(3t))}{t}$

03 Answers & Solutions

01 $\dfrac{7}{10}$

$\lim\limits_{x\to 0}\dfrac{\sin 7x}{x(x+10)}=\lim\limits_{x\to 0}(\dfrac{\sin 7x}{x}\times\dfrac{1}{x+10})=\dfrac{7}{10}$

02 1

Substituting $\dfrac{1}{x}=t$, if $x\to\infty$, then $t\to 0$. so $\lim\limits_{x\to\infty}x\sin\dfrac{1}{x}=\lim\limits_{t\to 0}\dfrac{\sin t}{t}=1$.

03 $\dfrac{4}{9}$

$\lim\limits_{x\to 0}\left(\dfrac{\sin 2x}{\tan 3x}\times\dfrac{\sin 2x}{\tan 3x}\right)=\dfrac{2}{3}\times\dfrac{2}{3}=\dfrac{4}{9}$

04 $\dfrac{5}{3}$

$\lim\limits_{x\to 0}\left(\dfrac{\sin 5x}{\sin 3x}\times\dfrac{1}{\cos x}\right)=\dfrac{5}{3}$

05 1

$\lim\limits_{x\to 0}\dfrac{x\sin x}{1-\cos^2 x}=\lim\limits_{x\to 0}\dfrac{x\sin x}{\sin^2 x}=\lim\limits_{x\to 0}\left(\dfrac{x}{\sin x}\times\dfrac{\sin x}{\sin x}\right)=1$

06 3

$\lim\limits_{t\to 0}\dfrac{\tan(\sin 3t)}{t}=\lim\limits_{t\to 0}\left(\dfrac{\tan(\sin 3t)}{\sin 3t}\times\dfrac{\sin 3t}{3t}\times 3\right)=1\times 1\times 3=3$

04 Asymptotes and Theorems of Continuous Functions

Let's look at the following figure.

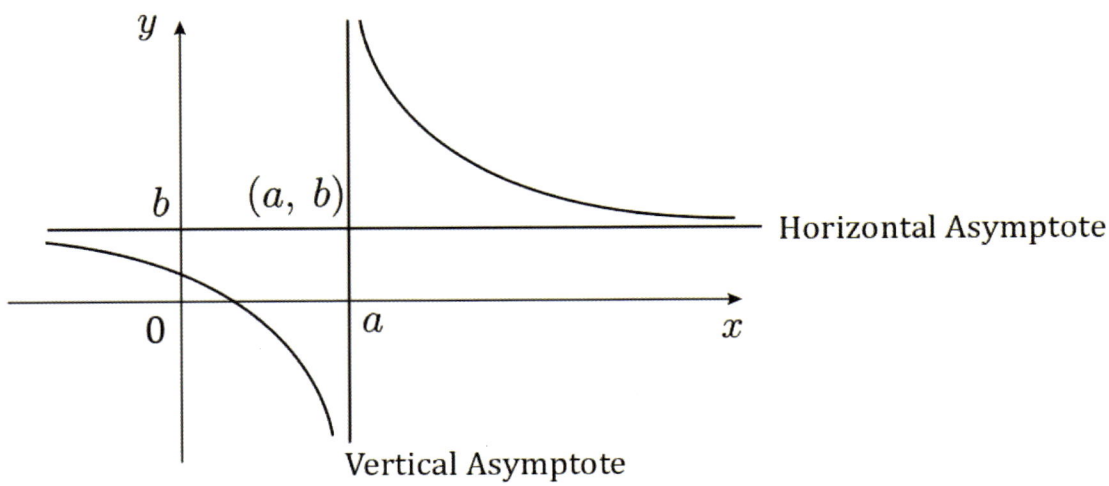

For a graph of a fractional function $y = \dfrac{g(x)}{f(x)}$,

(1) Vertical Asymptotes are values of x such that $f(x) = 0$ and $g(x) \neq 0$:

e.g., $x = a$ in the figure above.

(2) Horizontal Asymptotes are values of y that is equal to $\displaystyle\lim_{x \to \infty} \dfrac{g(x)}{f(x)}$ or $\displaystyle\lim_{x \to -\infty} \dfrac{g(x)}{f(x)}$:

e.g., $y = b$ in the figure above.

Limits

01. Finding the Asymptote

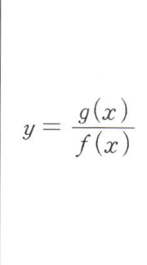

① Vertical Asymptote ⇒ The value of x that makes the denominator, $f(x)$, to be equal to 0, while the numerator is not equal to 0. That is, if $f(a) = 0$ and $g(a) \neq 0$, then the vertical asymptote is $x = a$.

$y = \dfrac{g(x)}{f(x)}$

② Horizontal Asymptote ⇒ If $\lim\limits_{x \to \infty} \dfrac{g(x)}{f(x)} = b$ and $\lim\limits_{x \to -\infty} \dfrac{g(x)}{f(x)} = c$, $y = b$ and $y = c$ are the horizontal asymptotes. In the above graph, $b = c$ and thus $y = b$ is the only horizontal asymptote. But in general, b and c need not be the same.

※ $f(x)$ and $g(x)$ does not have to be polynomials. See examples below.

● ········ **Problem 1**

(1) Find the vertical and horizontal asymptotes of $f(x) = \dfrac{4x+1}{2x-2}$.

(2) Find the horizontal asymptotes of $f(x) = \dfrac{3^{x+1} - 2}{3^x + 1}$.

● ········ **Answer**   (1) $x = 1$, $y = 2$ (2) $y = -2, 3$

● ········ **Solution**

(1) • Vertical asymptote : Make the denominator equal to zero.

Thus, from $2x - 2 = 0$, $x = 1$

Note that numerator is NOT zero at $x = 1$: $4x + 1 = 5$.

• Horizontal asymptote : From $\lim\limits_{x \to \infty} \dfrac{4x+1}{2x-2} = 2$, $y = 2$

(2) $\lim\limits_{x \to \infty} \dfrac{3 \cdot 3^x - 2}{3^x + 1} = \dfrac{\dfrac{3 \cdot 3^x}{3^x} - \dfrac{2}{3^x}}{\dfrac{3^x}{3^x} + \dfrac{1}{3^x}} = \dfrac{3 \cdot 1 - 0}{1 + 0} = 3$,

$\lim\limits_{x \to -\infty} \dfrac{3 \cdot 3^x - 2}{3^x + 1} = \dfrac{3 \cdot \dfrac{1}{3^\infty} - 2}{\dfrac{1}{3^\infty} + 1} = \dfrac{3 \cdot 0 - 2}{0 + 1} = -2$

Thus, the Horizontal asymptotes are $y = -2$ and $y = 3$.

02. Theorems of Continuous Functions

There are two important theorems regarding Continuous Functions.

Theorems of Continuous Function
- I. The Extreme Value Theorem
- II. The Intermediate Value Theorem(IVT)

These theorems will be explained briefly in this chapter. They will be explained in detail in the "Differentiation" chapter later on.

I. The Extreme Value Theorem

If a function $y=f(x)$ is continuous on a closed interval $[a,b]$, then the function $y=f(x)$ must have a maximum and minimum value within the given interval $[a,b]$.

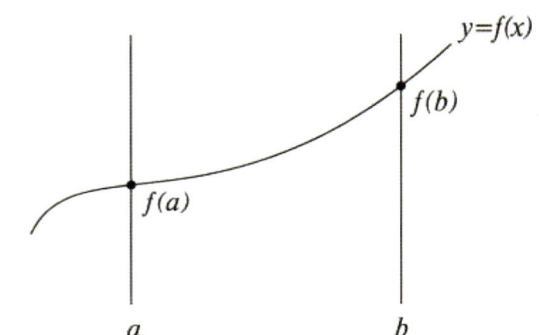

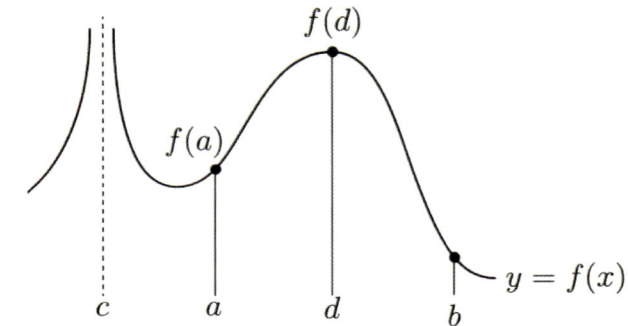

Maximum Value : $f(b)$

($f(b) \geq f(x)$ for all $a \leq x \leq b$)

Minimum Value : $f(a)$

($f(a) \leq f(x)$ for all $a \leq x \leq b$)

Maximum Value : $f(d)$

Minimum Value : $f(b)$

$\Rightarrow$ Function $y=f(x)$ is not continuous on all real numbers but is continuous on the close interval $[a,b]$.

II. The Intermediate Value Theorem (IVT)

If a function $y = f(x)$ is continuous on a closed interval $[a,b]$, and if $f(a)$ and $f(b)$ have opposite signs (one is positive and the other one is negative), then there exists at least one $c \in (a,b)$ such that $f(c) = 0$.

This theorem is to determine whether a function that is continuous on some interval has at least one root in the given interval. The important thing is, even if the function is not continuous on all real numbers, **it must be continuous on the given interval!**

Let's compare the following two figures.

ⓐ

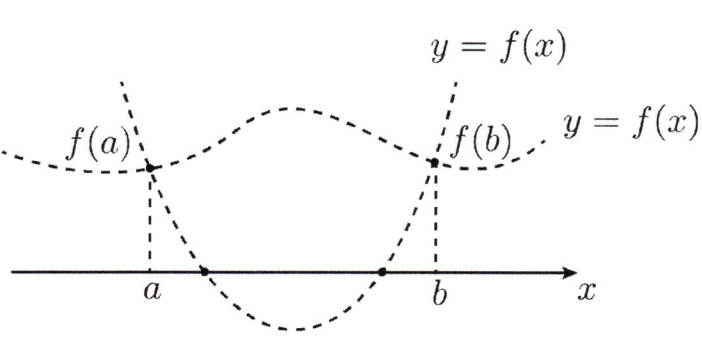

ⓑ

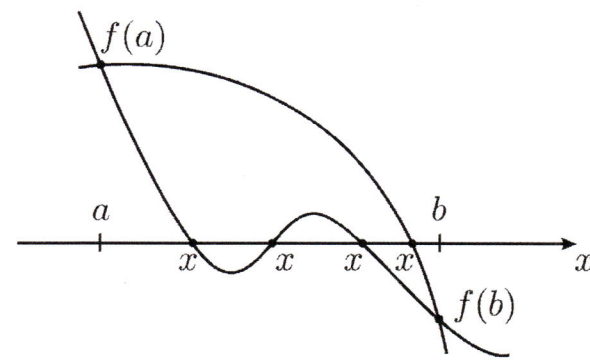

Suppose that we only know about two points $f(a)$ and $f(b)$ and we want to talk about function $y = f(x)$. Suppose that we know that $y = f(x)$ is at least continuous (on $[a,b]$). What can you tell? If $f(a)$ and $f(b)$ are as in ⓐ, it might be that $y = f(x)$ has no root (no intersection with the x-axis). However, if $f(a)$ and $f(b)$ are as in ⓑ, then no matter how you connect the two points, as long as you connect them "continuously" there must be an intersection with the x-axis.

That is, a function $y = f(x)$ that is continuous on interval $[a, b]$ must have a root in the interval $[a, b]$ if $f(a)f(b) < 0$ ($f(a)$, $f(b)$ have different signs).

AP Calculus AB & BC Rewritten from the Beginning

●······· **Problem 2**

Which of the following lines is(are) asymptote(s) of the graph of $f(x) = \dfrac{x^2 - 3x - 2}{x^2 - 4}$?

> I. $y = 1$ II. $x = \pm 2$ III. $x = -1$ IV. $x = -2$ **and -1**

ⓐ I only   ⓑ II only   ⓒ I and II only   ⓓ II and IV only

●······· **Answer** ⓒ

●······· **Solution**

- To make the denominator to zero, we need $x^2 - 4 = 0$, $x = \pm 2$ (that is, $x = 2$ and $x = -2$) are the Vertical Asymptotes.

- From $\lim\limits_{x \to \pm \infty} \dfrac{x^2 - 3x - 2}{x^2 - 4}$, $y = 1$ is the Horizontal Asymptote.

●······· **Problem 3**

The vertical line $x = 3$ is an asymptote for the graph of the function f. Which of the following must not be true?

ⓐ $f(3)$ is not defined   ⓑ $\lim\limits_{x \to \infty} f(x) = 3$ ⓒ $\lim\limits_{x \to \infty} f(x) = \infty$ ⓓ $\lim\limits_{x \to 3} f(x) = 0$

●······· **Answer** ⓓ

●······· **Solution**

Here, be careful that f is the entire function, not the denominator. Let $f(x) = \dfrac{g(x)}{h(x)}$. Since $x = 3$ is a Vertical Asymptote, so $h(3) = 0$ and $g(3) \neq 0$: $f(3)$ is not defined. ⓐ must be true. Remember that at the Vertical Asymptote, the function is not defined. Now, if $\lim\limits_{x \to 3} f(x) = \lim\limits_{x \to 3} \dfrac{g(x)}{h(x)}$ exists then it must be $\pm \infty$: ⓓ must not be true. The problem only gives the Vertical Line, so we cannot know about the Horizontal Asymptote. That is, we do not know about ⓑ and ⓒ.

110

Problem 4

If a vertical asymptote does not exist in the expression $\dfrac{5x+20}{x+k}$, what is the value of k?

ⓐ 1 ⓑ 2 ⓒ 3 ⓓ 4

Answer
ⓓ

Solution

If there is no vertical asymptote, we know the numerator must be zero if the denominator is zero. Since the numerator is zero when $x=-4$, if we substitute -4 into the denominator it also need to be zero. Therefore, we get $-4+k=0$ and we have $k=4$.

Problem 5

1. Find the horizontal asymptotes of $f(x)=\dfrac{2^{x+2}+6}{2^x+2}$.

2. Find the horizontal asymptotes of $f(x)=\dfrac{2x-1}{\sqrt{x^2+2x}}$.

Answer
1) $y=3$ and $y=4$ 2) $y=-2$ and $y=2$

Solution

1. $\displaystyle\lim_{x\to\infty}\dfrac{2^x\times 2^2+6}{2^x+2}=\lim_{x\to\infty}\dfrac{2^2+\dfrac{6}{2^x}}{1+\dfrac{2}{2^x}}=\dfrac{4+0}{1+0}=4$

$\displaystyle\lim_{x\to-\infty}\dfrac{2^x\times 2^2+6}{2^x+2}=\dfrac{2^{-\infty}\times 2^2+6}{2^{-\infty}+2}=\dfrac{0+6}{0+2}=3$

Therefore, horizontal asymptotes are $y=3$ and $y=4$.

2. $\displaystyle\lim_{x\to\infty}\dfrac{2x-1}{\sqrt{x^2+2x}}=\lim_{x\to\infty}\dfrac{\dfrac{1}{x}\times(2x-1)}{\dfrac{1}{x}\times\sqrt{x^2+2x}}=\lim_{x\to\infty}\dfrac{2-\dfrac{1}{x}}{\sqrt{\dfrac{x^2+2x}{x^2}}}=\lim_{x\to\infty}\dfrac{2-\dfrac{1}{x}}{\sqrt{1+\dfrac{2}{x}}}=\dfrac{2-0}{\sqrt{1+0}}=2$

$\displaystyle\lim_{x\to-\infty}\dfrac{2x-1}{\sqrt{x^2+2x}}=\lim_{t\to\infty}\dfrac{2(-t)-1}{\sqrt{(-t)^2+2(-t)}}=\lim_{t\to\infty}\dfrac{-2t-1}{\sqrt{t^2-2t}}$

$=\displaystyle\lim_{t\to\infty}\dfrac{\dfrac{1}{t}\times(-2t-1)}{\dfrac{1}{t}\times\sqrt{t^2-2t}}=\lim_{t\to\infty}\dfrac{-2-\dfrac{1}{t}}{\sqrt{1-\dfrac{2}{t}}}=\dfrac{-2-0}{\sqrt{1+0}}=-2$

Therefore, horizontal asymptotes are $y=-2$ and $y=2$.

AP Calculus AB & BC Rewritten from the Beginning

Supplement

Let's go back to Problem 5-(2) above. The following is another approach.

$$\lim_{x \to -\infty} \frac{2x-1}{\sqrt{x^2+2x}} = \lim_{x \to -\infty} \frac{\frac{1}{x} \times (2x-1)}{\frac{1}{x} \times \sqrt{x^2+2x}} = \lim_{x \to -\infty} \frac{\frac{2x-1}{x}}{\sqrt{\frac{x^2+2x}{x^2}}} = \lim_{x \to -\infty} \frac{2-\frac{1}{x}}{\sqrt{1+\frac{2}{x}}} = \frac{2-0}{\sqrt{1+0}} = 2$$

This solution gives different answer: limit is 2.

What is wrong with this solution?

The answer is, $\frac{1}{x} \times \sqrt{x^2+2x} \neq \sqrt{\frac{x^2+2x}{x^2}}$!

More explicitly, $\frac{1}{x} \neq \sqrt{\frac{1}{x^2}}$. Note that right hand side is positive, since square root is always positive. BUT see that left hand side is negative since $x \to -\infty$ means x is negative. So, the correct equation is, $\frac{1}{x} = -\sqrt{\frac{1}{x^2}}$. However, taking care of this positive-negative sign issue is burdensome. So instead of doing this, whenever you see $x \to -\infty$, have a habit to substitute $t = -x$ and make it into $t \to \infty$ as shown above.

04   Exercise

01   If $f(x) = \dfrac{3x^2 + 1}{x^2 - 3x + 2}$, find the horizontal and vertical asymptote(s).

02   If $f(x) = \dfrac{3x + 6}{-x^2 + 4x - 3}$, find the horizontal and vertical asymptote(s).

03   If the vertical asymptote does not exist for function $\dfrac{6x - k}{2x - 1}$, what is the value of k?

ⓐ 1   ⓑ 2   ⓒ 3   ⓓ 4

04   Find the horizontal asymptotes of $f(x) = \dfrac{3^{x+1} + 2}{3^x + 1}$.

05   Find the horizontal asymptotes of $f(x) = \dfrac{3x}{\sqrt{x^2 + 1}}$.

06   Let f be a function continuous on the closed interval $[0, 4]$. Prove that $f(x) = \dfrac{x^2 - 3}{x + 1}$ has at least one zero in $[0, 4]$.

04 Answers & Solutions

01 Horizontal Asymptote: $y=3$, Vertical asymptote: $x=1, 2$

Horizontal Asymptote : $\lim\limits_{x \to \infty} \dfrac{3x^2+1}{x^2-3x+2} = \lim\limits_{x \to -\infty} \dfrac{3x^2+1}{x^2-3x+2} = 3$ and thus $y=3$.

Vertical Asymptote : Set the denominator equal to zero $\Rightarrow x^2-3x+2=0$, so $x=1, 2$. See that at both $x=1, 2$, the numerator is non-zero.

02 Horizontal Asymptote $y=0$, Vertical asymptote $x=1, 3$

Horizontal Asymptote : $\lim\limits_{x \to \infty} \dfrac{3x+6}{-x^2+4x-3} = \lim\limits_{x \to -\infty} \dfrac{3x+6}{-x^2+4x-3} = 0$ and thus $y=0$.

Vertical Asymptote : roots of $-x^2+4x-3=0$, so $x=1, 3$. See that at both $x=1, 3$, the numerator is non-zero.

03 ⓒ

If vertical asymptote does not exist, then we know the denominator is zero implies that numerator is also zero. Denominator $2x-1$ is equal to zero if $x=\dfrac{1}{2}$. So at $x=\dfrac{1}{2}$, numerator should be also zero. $6 \times \dfrac{1}{2} - k = 0$ and so $k=3$.

04 $y=2$ and $y=3$

$\lim\limits_{x \to \infty} \dfrac{3 \times 3^x + 2}{3^x+1} = \lim\limits_{x \to \infty} \dfrac{3+\dfrac{2}{3^x}}{1+\dfrac{1}{3^x}} = \dfrac{3+0}{1+0} = 3 \qquad \lim\limits_{x \to -\infty} \dfrac{3 \times 3^x + 2}{3^x+1} = \dfrac{3 \times 3^{-\infty}+2}{3^{-\infty}+1} = \dfrac{0+2}{0+1} = 2$

05 $y = \pm 3$

$$\lim_{x \to \infty} \frac{3x}{\sqrt{x^2+1}} = \lim_{x \to \infty} \frac{\frac{3x}{\sqrt{x^2}}}{\sqrt{\frac{x^2(1+\frac{1}{x^2})}{x^2}}} = \lim_{x \to \infty} \frac{3}{\sqrt{1+\frac{1}{x^2}}} = \frac{3}{\sqrt{1+0}} = 3$$

$$\lim_{x \to -\infty} \frac{3x}{\sqrt{x^2+1}} = \lim_{t \to \infty} \frac{3(-t)}{\sqrt{(-t)^2+1}} = \lim_{t \to \infty} \frac{-3t}{\sqrt{t^2+1}} = -\lim_{t \to \infty} \frac{3t}{\sqrt{t^2+1}} = -3$$

(by above equation)

※Always remember! Whenever you see $x \to -\infty$, have a habit to substitute $t = -x$ and make it into $t \to \infty$ as shown above.

06 $f(0) = -3$, $f(4) = \frac{13}{5}$ that is, $f(0) < 0$, $f(4) > 0$, and $f(x)$ is continuous on the closed interval $[0, 4]$, so $f(x) = \frac{x^2-3}{x+1}$ must have at least one real root on $[0, 4]$. (Intermediate Value Theorem)

AP Calculus AB & BC Rewritten from the Beginning

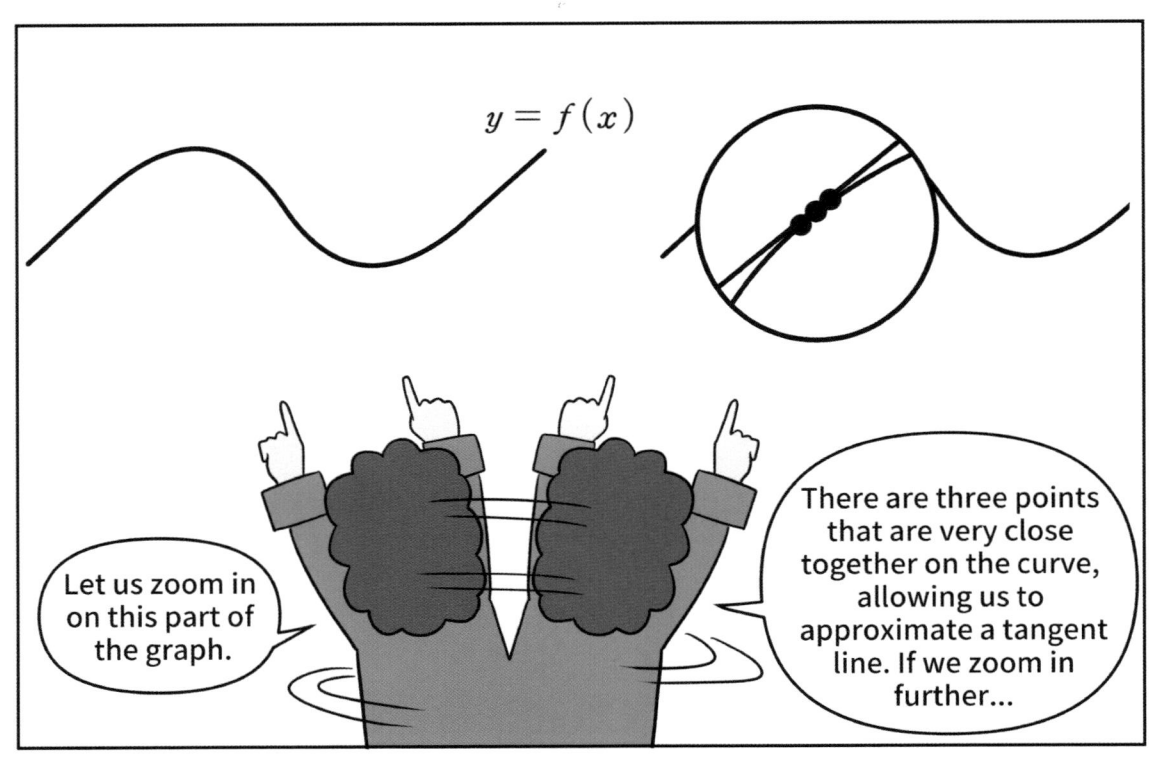

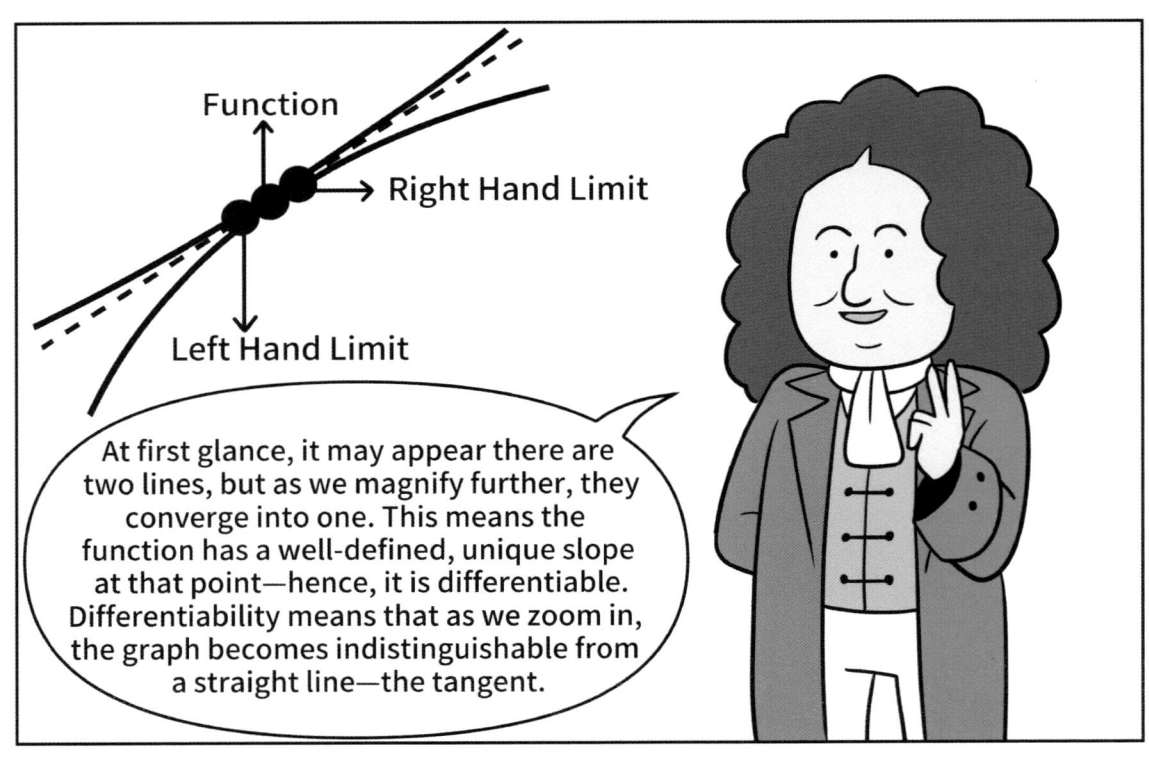

Differentiation

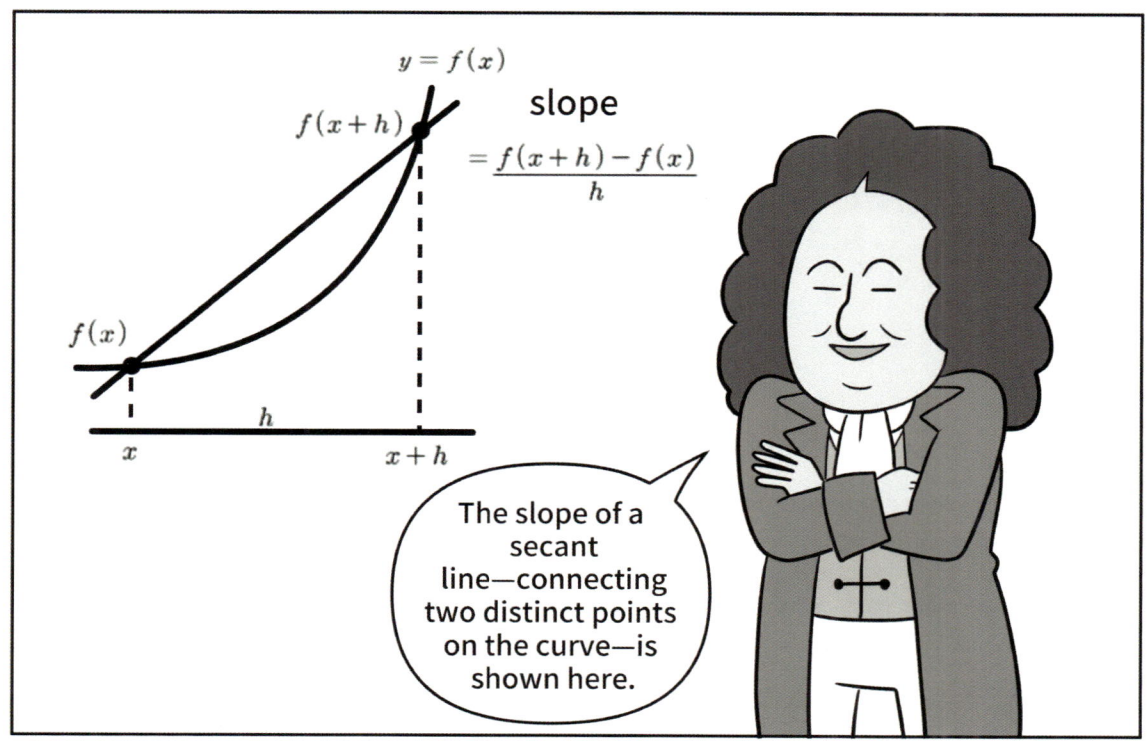

AP Calculus AB & BC Rewritten from the Beginning

Differentiation

Differentiation

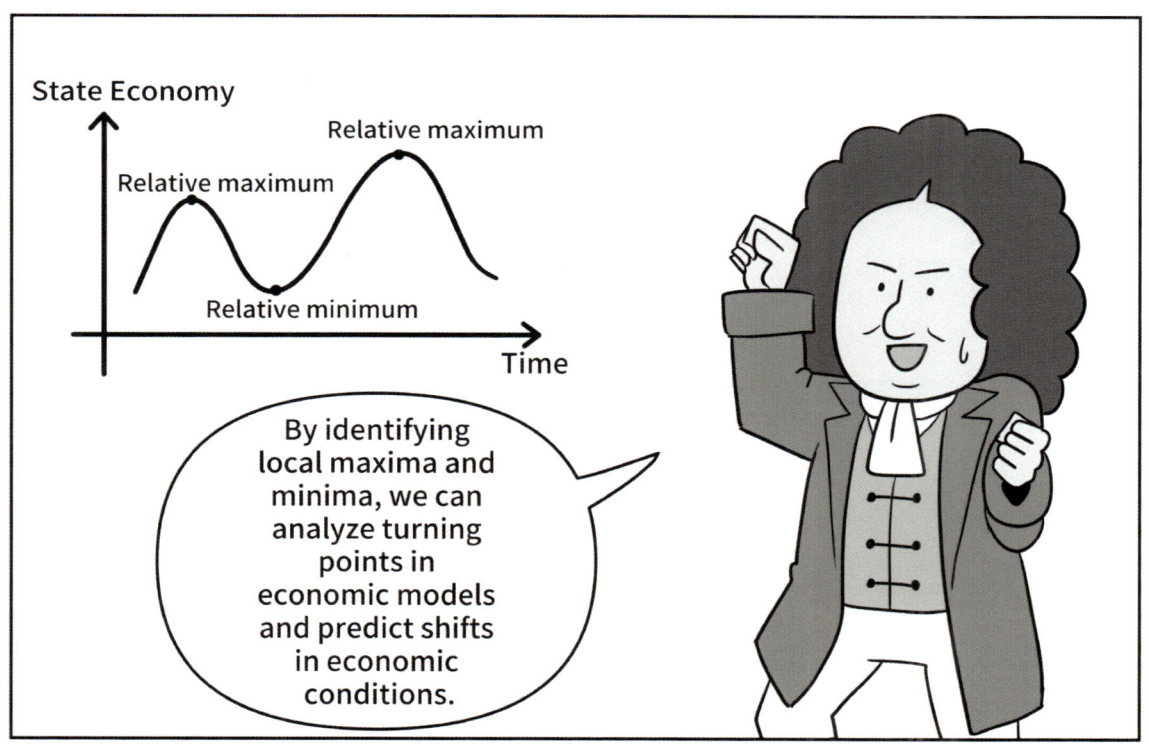

AP Calculus AB & BC Rewritten from the Beginning

02 Differentiation

Differentiation

01. Definition
02. Methods of Differentiation
03. T,D,M,L
    - Tangents and Normals
    - Derivative of the Inverse of a Function
    - Mean Value Theorem, Rolle's Theorem
    - L'Hopital's Rule
04. Analyzing Graphs
05. Related Rates
06. Applied Maximum and Minimum problems
07. Differentials Approximation

01 Definition

Before we begin

In this chapter, we will study the definition of Derivatives. This is about using the slope of the tangent line to get information about the shape of graphs. It is important to fully understand the principles and memorize it.

AP Calculus AB & BC Rewritten from the Beginning

01. Definition

Derivative?

= "The slope of the tangent line"

Derivatives helps us to analyze functions easily by using the slope of the tangent line. As you can see, if we know the slope of the tangent line at each point, we can **estimate the shape of the original graph.**

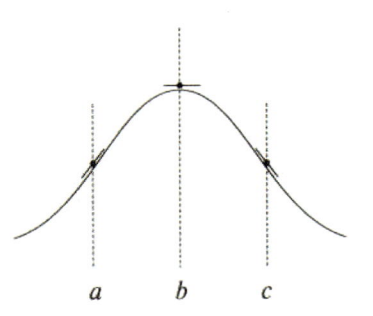

1. At $x = a$, the slope of the tangent line is positive.
   $\Rightarrow y = f(x)$ is increasing.
2. At $x = b$, the slope of the tangent line is 0.
   $\Rightarrow y = f(x)$ has a turning point at $x = b$.
3. At $x = c$ the slope of the tangent line is negative.
   $\Rightarrow y = f(x)$ is decreasing.

When the slope of the tangent line changes from positive to negative, $y = f(x)$ is concave downward.

Look at the following.

Slope $= \dfrac{\Delta y}{\Delta x}$

$= \dfrac{f(x+h) - f(x)}{h}$

That is, Slope = The average rate of change.

If two points are placed far away, it will look like as in the left figure. But if the two points reach each other very closely, that is, if the distance between the points become nearly 0 $(= \lim\limits_{h \to 0} \cdots)$, we get the figure below.

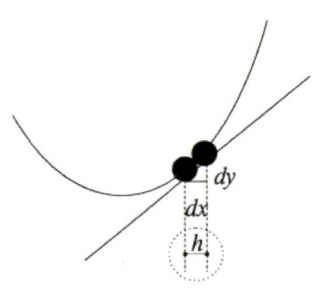

The instantaneous rate of change

$\Rightarrow \lim\limits_{h \to 0} \dfrac{f(x+h) - f(x)}{h} = \dfrac{dy}{dx} = y' = f'(x).$

This is the famous definition of derivatives.

$\Rightarrow$ The distance between two points approaches 0. $(= \lim\limits_{h \to 0} \cdots)$

Differentiation

Must memorize!

The Definition of the derivative

$$\lim_{h \to 0} \frac{f(x+h)-f(x)}{h} = \frac{dy}{dx} = y' = f'(x)$$

Special Lecture

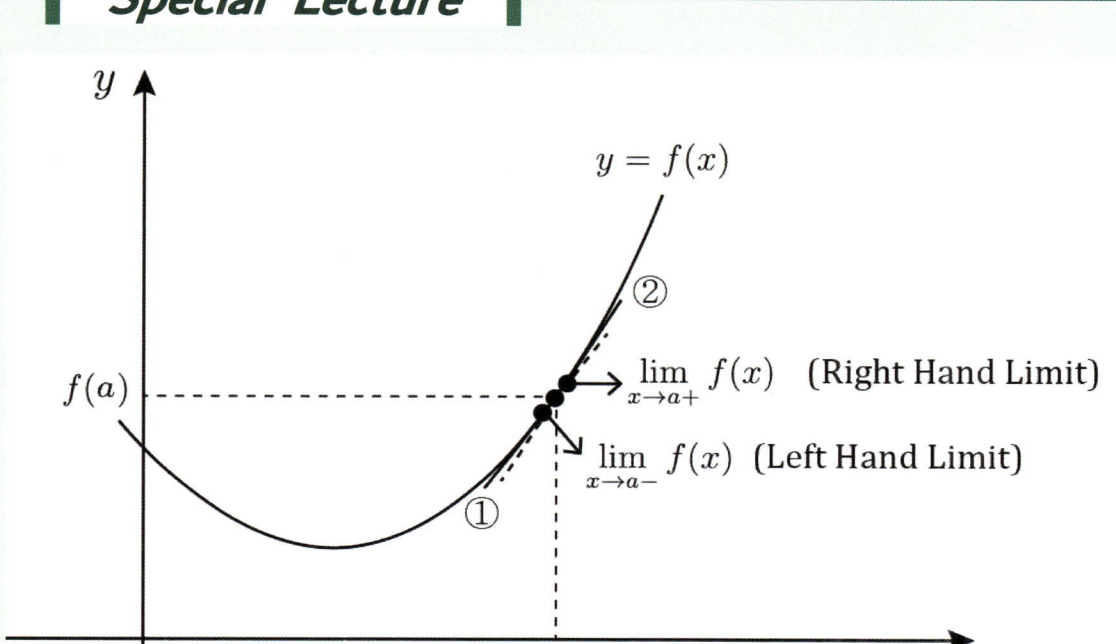

In the figure above, line ① crosses the function $(f(a))$ and $\lim_{x \to a-} f(x)$, and line ② crosses the function $(f(a))$ and $\lim_{x \to a+} f(x)$. Differentiability is when the slopes of lines ① and ② are almost the same that they look like one single line. In such case, the line that crosses the function and $\lim_{x \to a} f(x)$ is called the tangent line. Finding the slopes of such tangent lines is called the derivative.

Since the slopes of lines ① and ② are almost the same, let us take a look at the slope of line ②.

Special Lecture

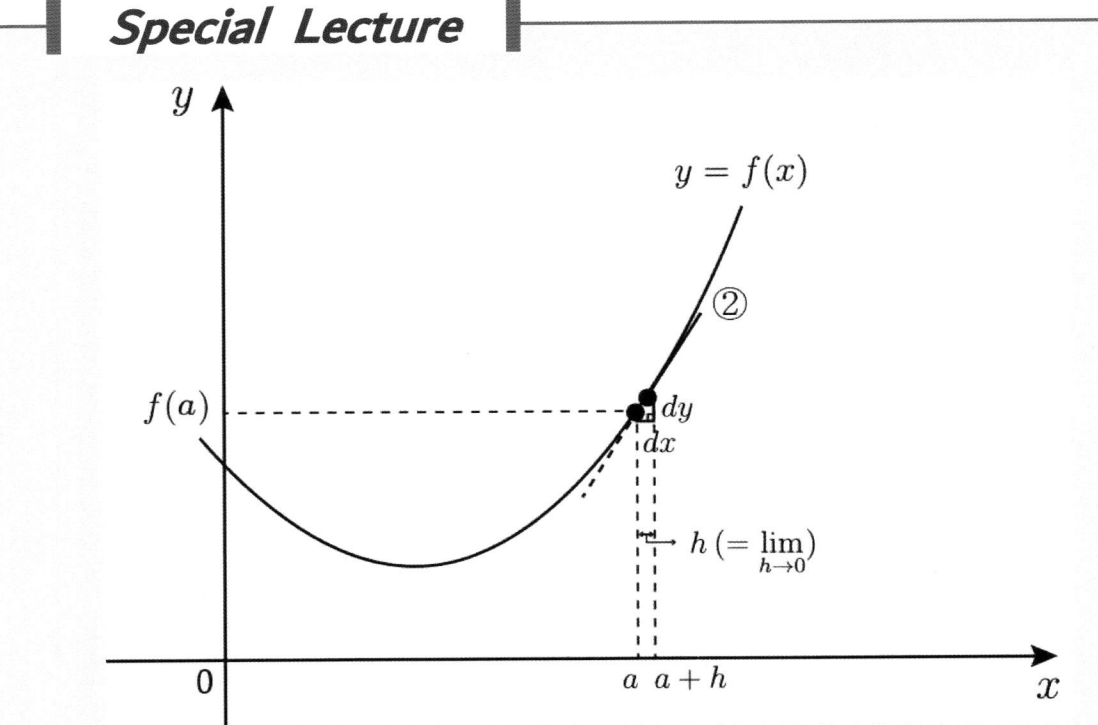

Let the distance between the x-values of the function $f(a)$ and $\lim_{x \to a+} f(x)$ be h. Then, h is extremely close to 0, so it can be expressed as $\lim_{h \to 0}$, and this has the same meaning as dx.

(※ dx represents an infinitesimal change in x)

Now, let us take a look at the slope of the tangent line from an arbitrary point x on $y = f(x)$.

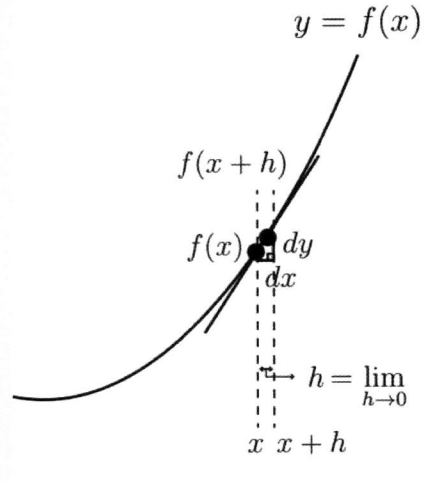

The slope of the line that crosses the two adjacent points is $\dfrac{f(x+h) - f(x)}{h}$ and h is almost 0, so

$$\lim_{h \to 0} \dfrac{f(x+h) - f(x)}{h} = \dfrac{dy}{dx} = f'(x)$$

and this is called "the instantaneous rate of change".

Differentiation

● Example 1

Find $f'(x)$, using the definition of the derivative, where $f(x)=x^2+x+3$.

● Answer $2x+1$

● Solution

Substituting the terms $f(x+h)$ and $f(x)$ in $\lim_{h\to 0}\dfrac{f(x+h)-f(x)}{h}$

gives $\lim_{h\to 0}\dfrac{(x+h)^2+(x+h)+3-(x^2+x+3)}{h} = \lim_{h\to 0}\dfrac{2xh+h^2+h}{h}$.

$\lim_{h\to 0+}(2x+h+1) = \lim_{h\to 0-}(2x+h+1) = 2x+1$.

※ Here, the meaning of $2x+1$ is the slope of the tangent line at any specific point (x, y) on the graph of the function $f(x)=x^2+x+3$. (For example, at a point $(1, 5)$, where the x coordinate is 1, the slope of the tangent line is $2\times 1+1=3$.)

AP Calculus AB & BC Rewritten from the Beginning

● ······· **Example 2**

Find $f'(x)$, using the definition of the derivative, where $f(x)=\sin x$.

● ······· **Answer** $\cos x$

● ······· **Solution**

Substituting the given equation in $\lim_{h\to 0}\dfrac{f(x+h)-f(x)}{h}$

gives $\lim_{h\to 0}\dfrac{\sin(x+h)-\sin x}{h}$.

⇒ | Remember? Sum and Difference formula
$\sin(\alpha+\beta)=\sin\alpha\cos\beta+\cos\alpha\sin\beta$

$=\lim_{h\to 0}\dfrac{\sin x\cos h+\cos x\sin h-\sin x}{h}=\lim_{h\to 0}\dfrac{\sin x\cos h-\sin x+\cos x\sin h}{h}$

$=\lim_{h\to 0}(\dfrac{\sin x(\cos h-1)}{h}+\cos x\dfrac{(\sin h)}{h})=\lim_{h\to 0}(\dfrac{\sin x(\cos h-1)(\cos h+1)}{h(\cos h+1)}+\cos x\dfrac{\sin h}{h})$

$=\lim_{h\to 0}(\dfrac{\sin x(\cos^2 h-1)}{h(\cos h+1)})+\lim_{h\to 0}\cos x\dfrac{\sin h}{h}$

⇒ | You know that $\sin^2 h+\cos^2 h=1$, right? Thus, $\cos^2 h-1=-\sin^2 h$.
Also, we know that $\lim_{h\to 0}cf(h)$ is equal to $c\lim_{h\to 0}f(h)$. Thus,
$\lim_{h\to 0}\cos x\dfrac{\sin h}{h}=\cos x\lim_{h\to 0}\dfrac{\sin h}{h}$

$=\sin x\lim_{h\to 0}\dfrac{-\sin^2 h}{(\cos h+1)h}+\cos x\lim_{h\to 0}\dfrac{\sin h}{h}=0+\cos x=\cos x$

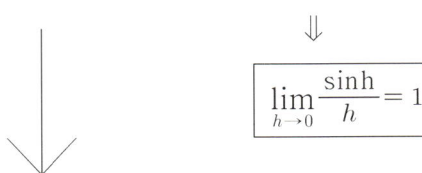

⇓

$\lim_{h\to 0}\dfrac{\sin h}{h}=1$

$\sin x\cdot\lim_{h\to 0}\dfrac{\sin h}{h}\cdot\dfrac{(-\sin h)}{(\cos h+1)}=\sin x\times 1\times 0=0$

130

Differentiation

In addition to the method described above, the slope of the tangent line at a specific point can also be obtained as follows.

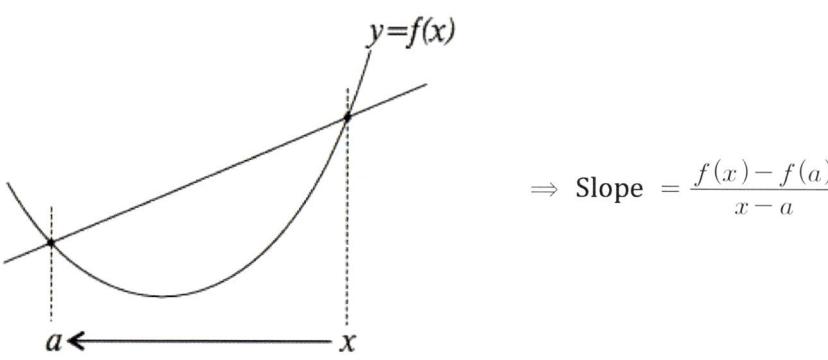

$\Rightarrow$ Slope $= \dfrac{f(x)-f(a)}{x-a}$

$\Rightarrow$ Here, when x approaches a $(=\lim\limits_{x \to a})$ it becomes the following.

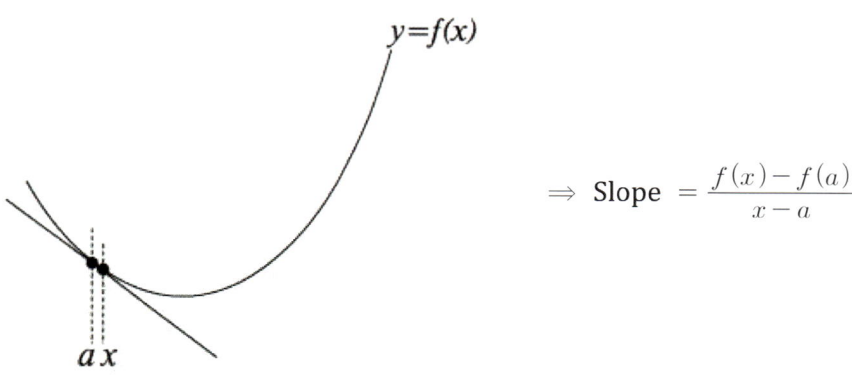

$\Rightarrow$ Slope $= \dfrac{f(x)-f(a)}{x-a}$

$\Downarrow$

| x and a are put very close together $= \lim\limits_{x \to a}$ |

$\Rightarrow$ Thus, $\lim\limits_{x \to a} \dfrac{f(x)-f(a)}{x-a} = f'(a)$

AP Calculus AB & BC Rewritten from the Beginning

● ········ **Example 3**

If $f(x) = 5x^2 - 3$, find $f'(1)$.

● ········ **Answer**   10

● ········ **Solution**

Using the definition of the derivative, we can get the following.

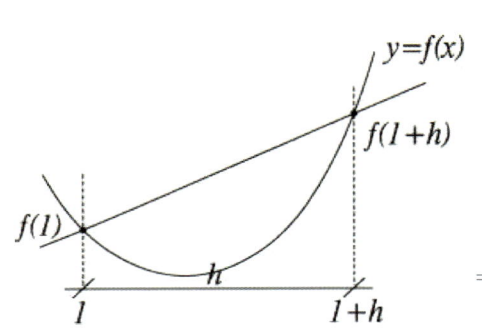

$$\lim_{h \to 0} \frac{f(1+h) - f(1)}{h}$$

$$\lim_{h \to 0} \frac{\{5(1+h)^2 - 3\} - (5(1)^2 - 3)}{h}$$

$$= \lim_{h \to 0} \frac{5 + 10h + 5h^2 - 3 - 2}{h}$$

$$= \lim_{h \to 0} \frac{10h + 5h^2}{h} = \lim_{h \to 0} (10 + 5h)$$

$$\lim_{h \to 0^+} (10 + 5h) = \lim_{h \to 0^-} (10 + 5h) = 10$$

Alternatively, we can get it like this.

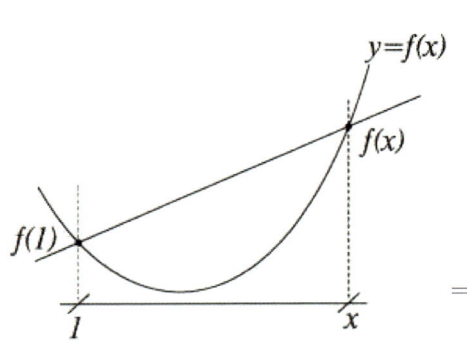

$$\lim_{x \to 1} \frac{f(x) - f(1)}{x - 1}$$

$$\lim_{x \to 1} \frac{5x^2 - 3 - (5(1)^2 - 3)}{x - 1} = \lim_{x \to 1} \frac{5x^2 - 5}{x - 1}$$

$$= \lim_{x \to 1} \frac{5(x^2 - 1)}{x - 1}$$

$$= \lim_{x \to 1} \frac{5(x - 1)(x + 1)}{x - 1}.$$

$$\lim_{x \to 1^+} 5(x + 1) = \lim_{x \to 1^-} 5(x + 1) = 10$$

Differentiation

Let's look at the following.

$$\lim_{h \to 0} \frac{f(x+h) - f(x)}{h} = f'(x) \qquad \text{We can get } f'(x) \text{ and } f'(a).$$

$$\lim_{x \to a} \frac{f(x) - f(a)}{x - a} = f'(a) \qquad \text{We can only get } f'(a).$$

If we calculate $f'(x)$ or $f'(a)$ using this equation every time, it would be very inconvenient.

In the next chapter, the results of the calculation are summarized into formulas. You must memorize them.

AP Calculus AB & BC Rewritten from the Beginning

Problem 1

1. Let f be the function defined by $f(x) = x^2 + x$.
Find the average rate of change of f over $[-1, 3]$.

2. Find the instantaneous rate of change at $x = 1$ of the function f given by $f(x) = 3x^2 + 2x$.

Answer (1) 3   (2) 8

Solution

1. $\dfrac{f(3) - f(-1)}{3 - (-1)} = \dfrac{12 - 0}{4} = 3$

2.

① $\lim\limits_{h \to 0} \dfrac{f(x+h) - f(x)}{h} = \lim\limits_{h \to 0} \dfrac{3(x+h)^2 + 2(x+h) - 3x^2 - 2x}{h}$

$= \lim\limits_{h \to 0} \dfrac{3x^2 + 6xh + 3h^2 + 2x + 2h - 3x^2 - 2x}{h}$

$= \lim\limits_{h \to 0} \dfrac{6xh + 3h^2 + 2h}{h}$

$= \lim\limits_{h \to 0} (6x + 3h + 2) = 6x + 2$

Thus, from $f'(x) = 6x + 2$, $f'(1) = 6 \times 1 + 2 = 8$.

② $\lim\limits_{x \to 1} \dfrac{f(x) - f(1)}{x - 1} = \dfrac{3x^2 + 2x - [3(1)^2 + 2(1)]}{x - 1} = \lim\limits_{x \to 1} \dfrac{3x^2 + 2x - 5}{x - 1} = \lim\limits_{x \to 1} \dfrac{(3x + 5)(x - 1)}{x - 1}.$

$\lim\limits_{x \to 1+} (3x + 5) = \lim\limits_{x \to 1-} (3x + 5) = 3 + 5 = 8$

Differentiation

● ······· **Problem 2**

If f is a differentiable function such that $f(1)=3$ and $f'(1)=2$, which of the following statements could be false?

ⓐ $\lim\limits_{x \to 1}\dfrac{f(x)-3}{x-1}=2$

ⓑ $\lim\limits_{h \to 0}\dfrac{f(1+h)-3}{h}=2$

ⓒ $\lim\limits_{x \to 1}f'(x)=2$

ⓓ f is continuous at $x=1$

● ······· **Answer** ⓒ

● ······· **Solution**

ⓐ $f(1)=3$, so $\lim\limits_{x \to 1}\dfrac{f(x)-3}{x-1}=\lim\limits_{x \to 1}\dfrac{f(x)-f(1)}{x-1}=f'(1)=2$: True

ⓑ $f(1)=3$, so $\lim\limits_{h \to 0}\dfrac{f(1+h)-3}{h}=\lim\limits_{h \to 0}\dfrac{f(1+h)-f(1)}{h}=f'(1)=2$: True

ⓓ $f'(1)=2$, That is, at $x=1$, f is differentiable.
Thus, at $x=1$, it is continuous and $\lim\limits_{x \to 1}f(x)$ exists. : True

ⓒ From $\lim\limits_{x \to 1}f(x)$, $\lim\limits_{x \to 1^-}f(x)=\lim\limits_{x \to 1^+}f(x)=f(1)=3$. However, we do not know whether $\lim\limits_{x \to 1}f'(x)=2$ or not. : Possibly False

Many students often ask the following question regarding this problem.

Q: If $f'(1)=2$, it doesn't mean that $\lim\limits_{x \to 1}f'(x)=2$ as well?

I would like to explain the following in regards to this question.

─┤ **Make Sure to Know the Following!** ├─

$\lim\limits_{x \to 1}f'(x) = f'(1) = 2$ means that $f'(x)$ is continuous at $x=1$.

But $f(x)$ is differentiable does NOT mean that $f'(x)$ is continuous.

Always remember that $f'(a)=C$ is different from $\lim\limits_{x \to a}f'(x)=C$.

AP Calculus AB & BC Rewritten from the Beginning

Problem 3

1. $\lim\limits_{h \to 0} \dfrac{\log(100+h) - 2}{h}$ is

   ⓐ $f'(2)$, where $f(x) = \log(100+x)$ ⓑ $f'(100)$, where $f(x) = \log x$
   ⓒ $f'(0)$, where $f(x) = \log(100+x)$ ⓓ $f'(2)$, where $f(x) = \log x$

2. $\lim\limits_{x \to 0} \dfrac{\cos x - 1}{x}$ is

   ⓐ $f'(0)$, where $f(x) = \sin x$ ⓑ $f'(1)$, where $f(x) = \cos x$
   ⓒ $f'(0)$, where $f(x) = \cos x$ ⓓ $f'(1)$, where $f(x) = \cos(x+1)$

3. $\lim\limits_{h \to 0} \dfrac{5(\frac{1}{3}+h)^7 - 5(\frac{1}{3})^7}{h}$ is

   ⓐ $f'(\frac{1}{3})$, where $f(x) = \frac{1}{3}x$ ⓑ $f'(0)$, where $f(x) = 5x^7$
   ⓒ $f'(0)$, where $f(x) = x^7$ ⓓ $f'(\frac{1}{3})$, where $f(x) = 5x^7$

Answer
(1) ⓑ   (2) ⓒ   (3) ⓓ

Solution

1 From $\lim\limits_{h \to 0} \dfrac{f(x+h) - f(x)}{h} = f'(x)$, we have that $\lim\limits_{h \to 0} \dfrac{\log(100+h) - 2}{h} = f'(100)$, where $f(x) = \log x$ and $\log 100 = 2$.

2 From $\lim\limits_{x \to a} \dfrac{f(x) - f(a)}{x - a} = f'(a)$, we have that $\lim\limits_{x \to 0} \dfrac{\cos x - 1}{x} = f'(0)$, where $f(x) = \cos x$ and $f(0) = 1$.

3 From $\lim\limits_{h \to 0} \dfrac{f(x+h) - f(x)}{h} = f'(x)$, we have that $\lim\limits_{h \to 0} \dfrac{5(\frac{1}{3}+h)^7 - 5(\frac{1}{3})^7}{h} = f'(\frac{1}{3})$, where $f(x) = 5x^7$ and $f(\frac{1}{3}) = 5(\frac{1}{3})^7$.

Differentiation

Problem 4

1. Find $f'(x)$, using the definition of the derivative, where $f(x) = e^x$.

   ($\ast \lim_{x \to 0} \dfrac{e^x - 1}{x} = 1$)

2. Find $f'(2)$, using the definition of the derivative, where $f(x) = 3x^2 + 5x + 1$.

Answer   (1) e^x (2) 17

Solution

1 From $\lim_{h \to 0} \dfrac{f(x+h) - f(x)}{h} = f'(x)$, we have that if $f(x) = e^x$, then

$$f'(x) = \lim_{h \to 0} \dfrac{e^{x+h} - e^x}{h} = \lim_{h \to 0} \dfrac{e^x(e^h - 1)}{h} = e^x \lim_{h \to 0} \dfrac{e^h - 1}{h} = e^x$$

2 From $\lim_{h \to 0} \dfrac{f(x+h) - f(x)}{h} = f'(x)$, we have that if $f(x) = 3x^2 + 5x + 1$, then

$$f'(2) = \lim_{h \to 0} \dfrac{3(2+h)^2 + 5(2+h) + 1 - 23}{h} = \lim_{h \to 0} \dfrac{17h + 3h^2}{h} = \lim_{h \to 0} 17 + 3h = 17$$

05 Exercise

01 Let f be the function defined by $f(x) = 2x^2 + 3$. Find the average rate of change of f over [1, 2].

02 Find the instantaneous rate of change at $x = 0$ of the function f given by $f(x) = 5x^2 + 10x + 1$.

03 If f is a differentiable function such that $f(5) = 7$ and $f'(5) = 9$, which of the following statements could be false?

ⓐ $\lim\limits_{x \to 5} f(x)$ exists ⓑ $\lim\limits_{x \to 5} f'(x) = 9$

ⓒ $\lim\limits_{h \to 0} \dfrac{f(h+5) - 7}{h} = 9$ ⓓ f is continuous at $x = 5$

04 $\lim\limits_{x \to 0} \dfrac{e^x - 1}{x}$ is

ⓐ $f'(0)$, where $f(x) = \dfrac{e^x}{x}$ ⓑ $f'(1)$, where $f(x) = \ln(x)$

ⓒ $f'(0)$, where $f(x) = e^x - 1$ ⓓ $f'(0)$ where $f(x) = e^x$

05 $\lim\limits_{h \to 0} \dfrac{2(\frac{1}{4}+h)^4 - 2(\frac{1}{4})^4}{h}$ is

ⓐ $f'(\frac{1}{4})$, where $f(x) = 2x^4$ ⓑ $f'(\frac{1}{4})$, where $f(x) = x^4$

ⓒ $f'(\frac{1}{4})$, where $f(x) = 2x$ ⓓ $f'(2)$, where $f(x) = 2x^4$

06 Find the derivative of $f(x) = \cos x$.

07 Find the derivative of $f(x) = (3x+1)^2$.

AP Calculus AB & BC Rewritten from the Beginning

05   Answers & Solutions

01   6

$$\frac{f(2)-f(1)}{2-1} = \frac{(2(2)^2+3)-(2(1)^2+3)}{1} = \frac{11-5}{1} = 6$$

02   10

Method 1: $\lim\limits_{x \to 0}\dfrac{f(x)-f(0)}{x-0} = \lim\limits_{x \to 0}\dfrac{(5x^2+10x+1)-1}{x} = \lim\limits_{x \to 0}\dfrac{x(5x+10)}{x}.$

$\lim\limits_{x \to 0^+} 5x+10 = \lim\limits_{x \to 0^-} 5x+10 = 10$

Method 2:

$f'(x) = \lim\limits_{h \to 0}\dfrac{f(x+h)-f(x)}{h} = \lim\limits_{h \to 0}\dfrac{5(x+h)^2+10(x+h)+1-(5x^2+10x+1)}{h}$

$= \lim\limits_{h \to 0}\dfrac{5x^2+10xh+5h^2+10x+10h+1-5x^2-10x-1}{h} = \lim\limits_{h \to 0}\dfrac{10xh+5h^2+10h}{h}.$

$\lim\limits_{h \to 0^+}(10x+5h+10) = \lim\limits_{h \to 0^-}(10x+5h+10) = 10x+10$

Thus, at $x=0$, we have $10(0)+10 = 10$.

03   ⓑ

$f'(5)=9$, so f is differentiable at $x=5$.
Thus, f is continuous at $x=5$ and $\lim\limits_{x \to 5}f(x)$ exists, so ⓐ and ⓓ are true.
Since $f'(5)=9$ and $f(5)=7$, we have that
$\lim\limits_{h \to 0}\dfrac{f(5+h)-f(5)}{h} = \lim\limits_{h \to 0}\dfrac{f(5+h)-7}{h} = f'(5) = 9$, so ⓒ is true.
We do not know whether f' is continuous at $x=5$ or not, hence cannot say about the existence of $\lim\limits_{x \to 5}f'(x)$.

04   ⓓ

From $\lim\limits_{x \to a}\dfrac{f(x)-f(a)}{x-a} = f'(a)$, we have that $\lim\limits_{x \to 0}\dfrac{e^x-1}{x} = \lim\limits_{x \to 0}\dfrac{f(x)-f(0)}{x} = f'(0)$, where $f(x)=e^x$, $f(0)=1$.

Differentiation

05 ⓐ

From $\lim_{x \to 0} \dfrac{f(x+h)-f(x)}{h} = f'(x)$, we have that

$\lim_{h \to 0} \dfrac{f(x+h)-f(x)}{h} = \lim_{h \to 0} \dfrac{2(\frac{1}{4}+h)^4 - 2(\frac{1}{4})^4}{h} = f'(\frac{1}{4})$, where $f(x) = 2x^4$, $f\left(\dfrac{1}{4}\right) = 2\left(\dfrac{1}{4}\right)^4$.

06 $-\sin x$

$\dfrac{f(x+h)-f(x)}{h}$ becomes $\dfrac{\cos(x+h)-\cos x}{h}$ ⇐ $\begin{array}{l}\cos(\alpha+\beta) = \cos\alpha\cos\beta - \sin\alpha\sin\beta \\ \cos(\alpha-\beta) = \cos\alpha\cos\beta + \sin\alpha\sin\beta\end{array}$

$= \lim_{h \to 0} \dfrac{\cos x \cos h - \sin x \sin h - \cos x}{h} = \lim_{h \to 0} \dfrac{\cos x(\cos h - 1) - \sin x \sin h}{h}$

$= \lim_{h \to 0} \dfrac{\cos x(\cos h - 1)(\cos h + 1)}{h(\cos h + 1)} - \sin x \lim_{h \to 0} \dfrac{\sin h}{h}$

$= \cos x \lim_{h \to 0} \dfrac{\cos^2 h - 1}{h(\cos h + 1)} - \sin x \lim_{h \to 0} \dfrac{\sin h}{h}$ ($\ast \cos^2 h - 1 = -\sin^2 h$)

$= \cos x \lim_{h \to 0} \dfrac{\sin h}{h} \dfrac{(-\sin h)}{\cos h + 1} - \sin x \lim_{h \to 0} \dfrac{\sin h}{h} = -\sin x$

($\lim_{h \to 0} \dfrac{-\sin h}{\cos h + 1} = 0$). Also, recall that $\lim_{h \to 0} \dfrac{\sin h}{h} = 1$.

07 $6(3x+1)$

$\lim_{h \to 0} \dfrac{f(x+h)-f(x)}{h}$ becomes

$\lim_{h \to 0} \dfrac{(3(x+h)+1)^2 - (3x+1)^2}{h} = \lim_{h \to 0} \dfrac{\{9(x^2+2xh+h^2)+6(x+h)+1\} - (9x^2+6x+1)}{h} =$

$\lim_{h \to 0} \dfrac{18xh + 9h^2 + 6h}{h}$.

$\lim_{h \to 0+} (18x + 9h + 6) = \lim_{h \to 0-} (18x + 9h + 6) = 18x + 6$

Thus, $6(3x+1)$.

02 Method of Differentiation

01. Differentiation Formula (Basic Formula)
02. Differentiation Formula
   (The Derivative of a Composite Function & Chain Rule)
03. Implicit Differentiation and Higher-Order Differentiation
04. Derivatives of Parametrically Defined Functions

Before we begin

As we saw in the previous chapter, solving every problem using the definition of the derivative takes too much effort.

Thus, in this chapter, we will look at formulas that help getting $f'(x)$ or $\frac{dy}{dx}$ or y' easily. If you don't know the multiplication table, you cannot do the calculations that appear later. Likewise, if you do not know the calculations in this chapter, learning the later chapters of CALCULUS will be very hard. I've used some puns to help readers understand, so I hope you bear with me.

Differentiation

01. Differentiation Formula (Basic Formula)

Must memorize!

Formula (1)

$$y = x^n \Rightarrow y' = nx^{n-1}$$

$$y = f(x)g(x) \Rightarrow y' = f'(x)g(x) + f(x)g'(x)$$
(Called Differentiation of Products)

$$y = f(x) \pm g(x) \Rightarrow y' = f'(x) \pm g'(x)$$

$$y = cf(x) \Rightarrow y' = cf'(x) \ (c \neq 0)$$

$$y = \frac{g(x)}{f(x)} \Rightarrow y' = \frac{g'(x)f(x) - g(x)f'(x)}{(f(x))^2} \quad (f(x) \neq 0)$$
(Called Differentiation of Quotients)

$$y = c \Rightarrow y' = 0$$

All the formulas above can be derived from the honest definition $\lim_{h \to 0} \frac{f(x+h) - f(x)}{h} = f'(x)$. If you want to try, you can challenge yourself. However, the formulas above are really the "multiplication table" for Calculus. In order to proceed into deeper Math of Calculus, you MUST memorize all of them.

After learning the above formulas, let's solve the following examples.

Example 4

Find $f'(x)$, using the formula (1).

(1) $f(x) = 5$

(2) $f(x) = x^2 + 2x$

(3) $f(x) = 3x^{100} - 26x^2 + 1$

(4) $f(x) = 15x^3(7x^3 - 3)$

(5) $f(x) = \dfrac{5x^3 - 3x^2}{2x + 5}$

Differentiation

● ⋯⋯⋯ **Answer**   (1) 0   (2) $2x+2$ (3) $300x^{99} - 52x$

(4) $630x^5 - 135x^2$ (5) $\dfrac{20x^3 + 69x^2 - 30x}{(2x+5)^2}$

● ⋯⋯⋯ **Solution**

(1) $f'(x) = 0$

5 is a constant and the differentiation of a constant is 0.

(2) $f'(x) = 2x + 2$
$f'(x) = (2 \times 1)x^{2-1} + (2 \times 1)x^{1-1} = 2x^1 + 2x^0 = 2x + 2$
(*A variable without any "visible" number coefficient or exponent has "1" as its coefficient or exponent. So, x^2 is technically $1x^2$ and $2x$ is technically $2x^1$. So, we applied the first formula in formula (1). Also, the zeroth-exponent equals 1. So, $2 \times x^0 = 2 \times 1 = 2$.)

(3) $f'(x) = 300x^{99} - 52x$
$f'(x) = 100 \times 3x^{100-1} - 2 \times 26x^{2-1} + 0 = 300x^{99} - 52x^1 = 300x^{99} - 52x$

(4) $f'(x) = 630x^5 - 135x^2$
Let $g(x) = 15x^3$, then $g'(x) = 3 \times 15x^{3-1} = 45x^2$.
Let $h(x) = 7x^3 - 3$, then $h'(x) = 3 \times 7x^{3-1} - 0 = 21x^2$.
From the second formula in formula (1), if $f(x) = g(x)h(x)$, then
$f'(x) = g'(x)h(x) + g(x)h'(x) = 45x^2(7x^3 - 3) + 15x^3(21x^2) = 315x^5 - 135x^2 + 315x^5$
$= 630x^5 - 135x^2$

(5) $f'(x) = \dfrac{20x^3 + 69x^2 - 30x}{(2x+5)^2}$
Let $g(x) = 5x^3 - 3x^2$, then $g'(x) = 3 \times 5x^{3-1} - 2 \times 3x^{2-1} = 15x^2 - 6x$.
Let $h(x) = 2x + 5$, then $h'(x) = 1 \times 2x^{1-1} + 0 = 2x^0 = 2$.
From the fifth formula in formula (1), if $f(x) = \dfrac{g(x)}{h(x)}$, then
$f'(x) = \dfrac{g'(x)h(x) - g(x)h'(x)}{(h(x))^2} = \dfrac{(15x^2 - 6x)(2x+5) - (5x^3 - 3x^2)2}{(2x+5)^2}$
$= \dfrac{30x^3 + 75x^2 - 12x^2 - 30x - (10x^3 - 6x^2)}{(2x+5)^2} = \dfrac{20x^3 + 69x^2 - 30x}{(2x+5)^2}.$

AP Calculus AB & BC Rewritten from the Beginning

Must memorize!

Formula (2)

① **Derivatives of trigonometric functions**

> If starting with c (excluding $\cos x$) → $-\csc$,
> including $t \to (\ )^2$.

- $\sin x \to \cos x$
- $\cos x \to -\sin x$ (※ $\sin x$ and $\cos x$ are interchanged)
- $\tan x \to \sec^2 x$ (including $t \to (\ )^2$)
- $\sec x \to \sec x \tan x$
- $\cot x \to -\csc^2 x$
- $\csc x \to -\csc x \cot x$

② **Derivatives of inverse trigonometric functions**

> If starting with c, then Negative!
> Memorize $\sin^{-1} x$, $\tan^{-1} x$, and $\sec^{-1} x$. Then, $\cos^{-1} x$, $\cot^{-1} x$, and $\csc^{-1} x$ only adds a $-$ sign in front of those.

- $\sin^{-1} x \to \dfrac{1}{\sqrt{1-x^2}}$ $(-1 < x < 1)$
- $\cos^{-1} x \to -\dfrac{1}{\sqrt{1-x^2}}$ $(-1 < x < 1)$
- $\sec^{-1} x \to \dfrac{1}{|x|\sqrt{x^2-1}}$ $(|x| > 1)$
- $\csc^{-1} x \to -\dfrac{1}{|x|\sqrt{x^2-1}}$ $(|x| > 1)$
- $\tan^{-1} x \to \dfrac{1}{1+x^2}$
- $\cot^{-1} x \to -\dfrac{1}{1+x^2}$

③ **Other formulas**

- $\log_a x \to \dfrac{1}{x \ln a}$
- $a^x \to a^x \ln a$
- $\ln x \to \dfrac{1}{x}$
- $e^x \to e^x$

Again, all the formulas from Formula (2) above can be also deduced from the honest definition $\lim\limits_{h \to 0} \dfrac{f(x+h) - f(x)}{h} = f'(x)$. If you want to try, you can challenge yourself. However, if you really try you will soon find out that the calculations are long and burdensome. (In fact in previous chapter we have seen together how difficult it is to deduce $\sin' x = \cos x$.) Not memorizing the formula and repeating the calculation every time would be a burdensome thing. You MUST memorize the formulas above.

Example 5

Differentiate the following functions.

(1) $y = x^2 \cdot e^x$

(2) $y = \sec x \cdot \ln x$

(3) $y = x^{-2} \cdot \log_3 x$

(4) $y = \dfrac{x^3}{3^x}$

(5) $y = \dfrac{x^2}{\ln x}$

(6) $y = \sin^{-1} x \cdot \sin x$

AP Calculus AB & BC Rewritten from the Beginning

Answer

(1) $e^x(x^2+2x)$

(2) $secx \cdot tanx \cdot lnx + \dfrac{secx}{x}$

(3) $-\dfrac{2\log_3 x}{x^3} + \dfrac{1}{x^3 \ln 3}$

(4) $\dfrac{3x^2 - x^3 \cdot \ln 3}{3^x}$

(5) $\dfrac{x(2\ln x - 1)}{(\ln x)^2}$

(6) $\dfrac{sinx}{\sqrt{1-x^2}} + \sin^{-1}x \cdot cosx$

Solution

(1) $y' = (x^2)' \cdot e^x + x^2 \cdot (e^x)'$

$= 2x \cdot e^x + x^2 \cdot e^x = e^x(x^2 + 2x)$

(2) $y' = (secx)' \cdot lnx + secx \cdot (lnx)'$

$= secx \cdot tanx \cdot lnx + \dfrac{secx}{x}$

(3) $y' = (x^{-2})' \cdot \log_3 x + x^{-2} \cdot (\log_3 x)'$

$= -2x^{-3} \cdot \log_3 x + x^{-2} \cdot \dfrac{1}{x \ln 3} = -\dfrac{2\log_3 x}{x^3} + \dfrac{1}{x^3 \ln 3}$

(4) $y' = \dfrac{(x^3)' \cdot 3^x - x^3 \cdot (3^x)'}{(3^x)^2}$

$= \dfrac{3x^2 \cdot 3^x - x^3 \cdot 3^x \cdot \ln 3}{3^{2x}} = \dfrac{3^x(3x^2 - x^3 \cdot \ln 3)}{3^{2x}} = \dfrac{3x^2 - x^3 \cdot \ln 3}{3^x}$

(5) $y' = \dfrac{(x^2)' \cdot lnx - x^2 \cdot (lnx)'}{(\ln x)^2}$

$= \dfrac{2x \cdot lnx - x^2 \cdot \dfrac{1}{x}}{(\ln x)^2} = \dfrac{x(2\ln x - 1)}{(\ln x)^2}$

(6) $y' = (\sin^{-1}x)' \cdot sinx + \sin^{-1}x \cdot (sinx)'$

$= \dfrac{sinx}{\sqrt{1-x^2}} + \sin^{-1}x \cdot cosx$

Differentiation

Supplement

The content from pages 149 to 162 presents a proof originally developed by the author. Until now, there has been no clear explanation as to why $\frac{dy}{dx}$ behaves like a fraction. Therefore, I provided a proof, which has since been published separately as a research paper. The version included in this book has been adapted from that paper to match the explanatory style of this text.

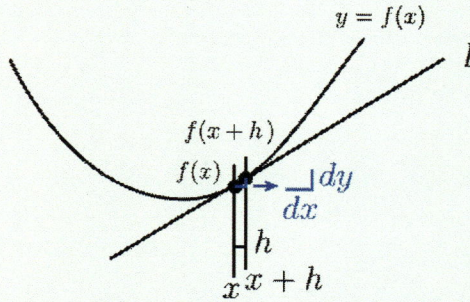

As shown in the above figure, the slope of line l tangents to graph $y = f(x)$ can be calculated as

$$\frac{dy}{dx} = y' = f'(x) = \lim_{h \to 0} \frac{f(x+h) - f(x)}{h}.$$

So far, we only calculated the slope of tangent lines using y' and $f'(x)$.

$$\lim_{h \to 0} \frac{f(x+h) - f(x)}{h} = \boxed{f'(x) = y'} = \boxed{\frac{dy}{dx}}$$
$$\qquad\qquad\qquad\qquad\qquad \text{Newton} \qquad\quad \text{Leibniz}$$

y' and $\frac{dy}{dx}$ are among the many notations used by Newton, and were adopted primarily for the convenience of notation. What we will be learning in the upcoming chapters is the fraction-like notation $\frac{dy}{dx}$ used by Leibniz, which has significant mathematical utility, particularly in the differentiation of composite and inverse functions.

AP Calculus AB & BC Rewritten from the Beginning

Supplement

However, $\frac{dy}{dx}$ only has the appearance of a fraction; it is not actually a fraction in the same way that $\frac{1}{3}, \frac{2}{5}, \cdots$ are. Nevertheless, in the next chapter, $\frac{dy}{dx}$ will be used as if it were a fraction in terms of operations.

For instance, while it's valid to say $\frac{3}{5} = \frac{2}{5} \times \frac{3}{2}$, is it equally valid to write $\frac{dy}{dx} = \frac{dy}{du} \cdot \frac{du}{dx}$?

Strictly speaking, $\frac{dy}{dx}$ is not a fraction in itself, so it should not be treated as an ordinary fraction during calculations. However, visually and symbolically, we often handle $\frac{dy}{dx}$ as though it were a normal fraction.

Even Leibniz, who first used this notation, did not provide an explanation for why it can be manipulated like a regular fraction. Instead, he simply used it that way.

As a result, there is no clear or commonly available explanation for why $\frac{dy}{dx}$ behaves like a fraction in operations. Therefore, the author intends to provide a subjective interpretation of this phenomenon.

Differentiation

Supplement

1. $\dfrac{dy}{du} \cdot \dfrac{du}{dx} = \dfrac{dy}{dx}$?

If $\dfrac{dy}{du} \cdot \dfrac{du}{dx} = \dfrac{dy}{dx}$ holds, can we consider $\dfrac{dy}{dx}$ to be a fraction?

Strictly speaking, $\dfrac{dy}{dx}$ cannot be considered a fraction in and of itself. However, it may be described as a "limit of a fraction." In other words, it is fundamentally different from ordinary fractions such as $\dfrac{8}{5} \cdot \dfrac{4}{8} = \dfrac{4}{5}$, where arithmetic operations are directly applicable.

Still, why does the expression $\dfrac{dy}{du} \cdot \dfrac{du}{dx} = \dfrac{dy}{dx}$ behave as though it were operating with ordinary fractions?

There is no definitive explanation for this. Even Leibniz, the German mathematician who first introduced the notation $\dfrac{dy}{dx}$, used it as if it were an ordinary fraction, but did not clarify the justification for doing so. The author intends to offer a subjective interpretation of this issue.

Let $y = f(x)$ be a differentiable function.
In the following figure, the slope of line l is $\dfrac{f(x_2) - f(x_1)}{x_2 - x_1} = \dfrac{y_2 - y_1}{x_2 - x_1} = \dfrac{\Delta y}{\Delta x}$

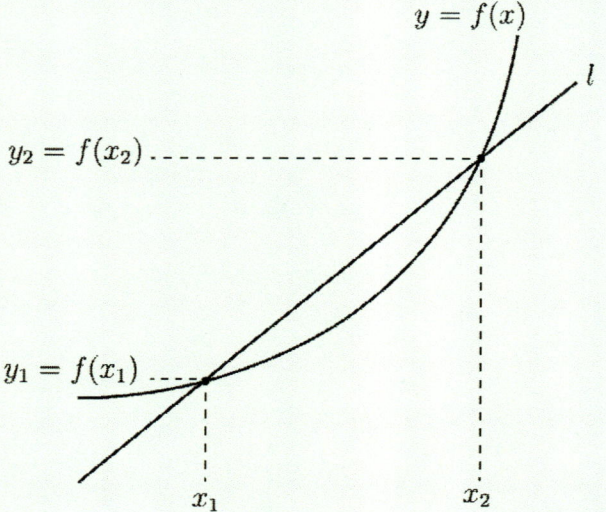

AP Calculus AB & BC Rewritten from the Beginning

Supplement

In the following figure, the slope of line l is

$$\lim_{x_2 \to x_1} \frac{f(x_2) - f(x_1)}{x_2 - x_1} = \lim_{x_2 \to x_1} \frac{y_2 - y_1}{x_2 - x_1} = \lim_{x_2 \to x_1} \frac{\Delta y}{\Delta x} = \frac{dy}{dx}$$

$y = f(x)$

$y_1 = f(x_1)$ ---- $y_2 = f(x_2)$ ---- $\frac{dy}{dx}$

$x_1\ x_2$

l

In other words, $\frac{dy}{dx}$ is not a fraction in itself, but $\frac{\Delta y}{\Delta x}$ is a proper fraction.

$\frac{dy}{dx}$ is the limit of the fraction $\frac{\Delta y}{\Delta x}$.

In the case of $\frac{\Delta y}{\Delta x}$, for example, as in $\frac{9-5}{3-2}$, the slope can be computed directly. Such expressions can clearly be regarded as fractions. However, in the case of $\frac{dy}{dx}$, where both Δx and Δy are extremely small (almost zero), it becomes difficult to treat it as an actual fraction.

The following thoughts are the author's subjective interpretation. Many students ask questions about why $\frac{dy}{du} \cdot \frac{du}{dx} = \frac{dy}{dx}$ holds, because they are taught how to compute it without fully understanding the underlying concept.

Differentiation

Supplement

Let us now subjectively interpret why $\dfrac{dy}{du} \cdot \dfrac{du}{dx} = \dfrac{dy}{dx}$ holds.

Quantities such as Δx, Δu, and Δy are concrete values that we can directly observe or calculate. Therefore, expressions like $\dfrac{\Delta y}{\Delta x}$, $\dfrac{\Delta y}{\Delta u}$, and $\dfrac{\Delta u}{\Delta x}$ can all be regarded as actual fractions.

Accordingly, the identity $\dfrac{\Delta y}{\Delta x} = \dfrac{\Delta y}{\Delta u} \cdot \dfrac{\Delta u}{\Delta x}$ holds. What happens if we take the limit on both sides?

$$\boxed{\lim_{\blacksquare} \dfrac{\Delta y}{\Delta x}} = \boxed{\lim_{\blacksquare} \dfrac{\Delta y}{\Delta u}} \cdot \boxed{\lim_{\blacksquare} \dfrac{\Delta u}{\Delta x}}$$

$$\dfrac{dy}{dx} \qquad\qquad \dfrac{dy}{du} \cdot \dfrac{du}{dx}$$

What should we put in three blue blanks? In the first limit, we should fill in with $x_2 \to x_1$. What happens if we replace all blue blanks with $x_2 \to x_1$?

(A)

$$\lim_{\boxed{x_2 \to x_1}} \dfrac{\Delta y}{\Delta x} = \lim_{\boxed{x_2 \to x_1}} \dfrac{\Delta y}{\Delta u} \cdot \lim_{\boxed{x_2 \to x_1}} \dfrac{\Delta u}{\Delta x}$$

Both are x Not equal   Both are x

(?)

(B) $\lim\limits_{x_2 \to x_1} \dfrac{\Delta y}{\Delta u} = \lim\limits_{u_2 \to u_1} \dfrac{\Delta y}{\Delta u} = \dfrac{dy}{du}$

Consider the above situation (B) as follows.

AP Calculus AB & BC Rewritten from the Beginning

Supplement

Assume that the graph of $u = g(x)$ is differentiable as the following figure.

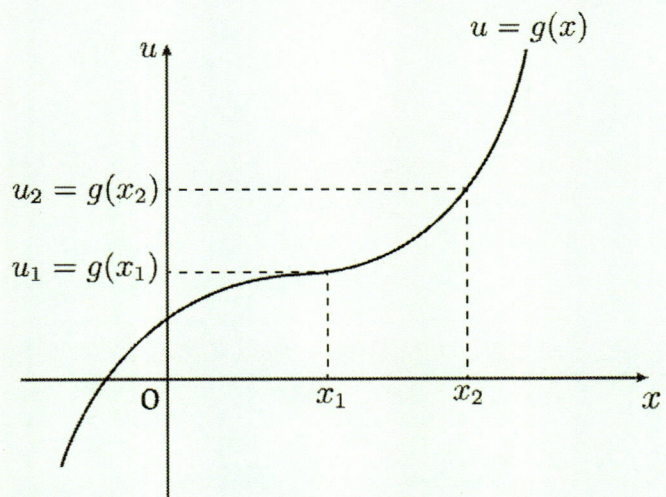

If $x_2 \to x_1$, then $g(x_2) \to g(x_1)$.

If $x_2 \to x_1$, then $u_2 \to u_1$.

We again consider (A), we know:

$$\lim_{x_2 \to x_1} \frac{\Delta y}{\Delta x} = \lim_{\boxed{x_2 \to x_1}} \frac{\Delta y}{\Delta u} \cdot \lim_{x_2 \to x_1} \frac{\Delta u}{\Delta x}$$

As $x_2 \to x_1$, we have $u_2 \to u_1$

$$\frac{dy}{dx} = \frac{dy}{du} \cdot \frac{du}{dx}$$

As a result, it appears as though du gets canceled out, just like in ordinary fraction arithmetic.

$$\frac{dy}{dx} = \frac{dy}{\cancel{du}} \cdot \frac{\cancel{du}}{dx}$$

Differentiation

Supplement

Let us approach this from a different perspective through an example. We already know that the following identity holds:

$$\frac{\Delta y}{\Delta x} = \frac{\Delta y}{\Delta u} \cdot \frac{\Delta u}{\Delta x}.$$

> **Recall**
> $u = g(x)$, $y = f(u) = f(g(x))$, we have
> $$x \to u = g(x) \to y = f(g(x)).$$

For instance, when $g(x) = x^2$ and $f(x) = e^x$, we have $f(g(x)) = f(x^2) = e^{x^2}$. Assume $x_1 = 2.0$ and $x_2 = 2.1$.

$x_1 = 2.0 \xrightarrow{g} \underbrace{g(x_1) = 2.0^2 = 4.00}_{u_1} \xrightarrow{f} \underbrace{f(g(x_1)) = e^{4.00} \approx 54.60}_{f(u_1) = y_1}$

$\updownarrow \Delta x = 0.1 \qquad\qquad \updownarrow \Delta u = 0.41 \qquad\qquad \updownarrow \Delta y = 27.67$

$x_2 = 2.1 \xrightarrow{g} \underbrace{g(x_2) = 2.1^2 = 4.41}_{u_2} \xrightarrow{f} \underbrace{f(g(x_2)) = e^{4.41} \approx 82.27}_{f(u_2) = y_2}$

The following situations (A), (B) and (C) are all the same!

(A) $\dfrac{\Delta y}{\Delta x} = \dfrac{\Delta y}{\Delta u} \cdot \dfrac{\Delta u}{\Delta x}$

$$\frac{27.67}{0.1} = \frac{27.67}{0.41} \cdot \frac{0.41}{0.1}$$

(B) $\dfrac{y_2 - y_1}{x_2 - x_1} = \dfrac{y_2 - y_1}{u_2 - u_1} \cdot \dfrac{u_2 - u_1}{x_2 - x_1}$

$$\frac{82.27 - 54.60}{2.1 - 2.0} = \frac{82.27 - 54.60}{4.41 - 4.00} \cdot \frac{4.41 - 4.00}{2.1 - 2.0}$$

(C) $\dfrac{f(g(x_2)) - f(g(x_1))}{x_2 - x_1} = \dfrac{f(g(x_2)) - f(g(x_1))}{g(x_2) - g(x_1)} \cdot \dfrac{g(x_2) - g(x_1)}{x_2 - x_1}$

$$\frac{e^{2.1^2} - e^{2.0^2}}{2.1 - 2.0} = \frac{e^{2.1^2} - e^{2.0^2}}{2.1^2 - 2.0^2} \cdot \frac{2.1^2 - 2.0^2}{2.1 - 2.0}$$

Supplement

To summarize the discussion, we can state the following:

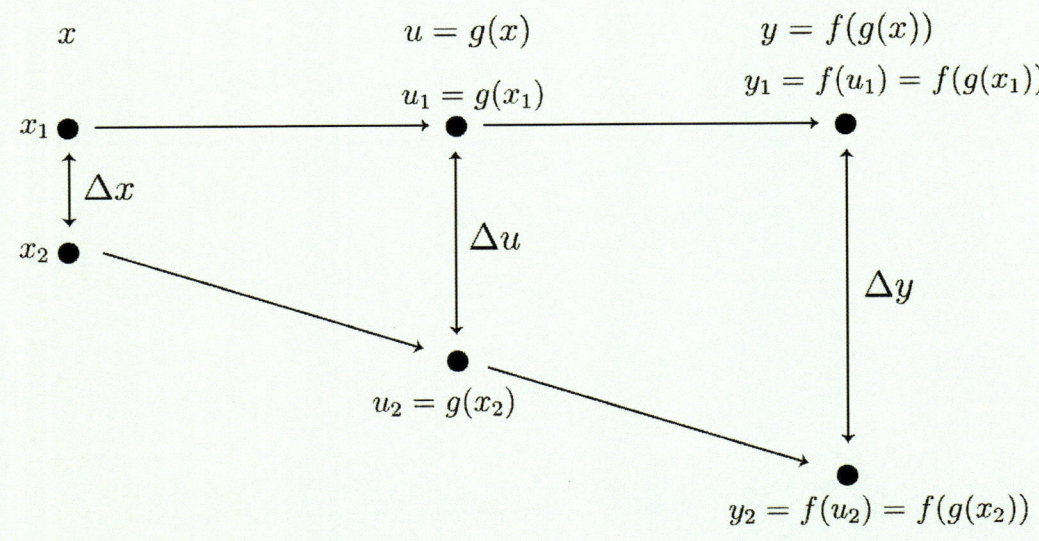

$$\underset{y_2}{\underbrace{f(g(x_2))}} - \underset{y_1}{\underbrace{f(g(x_1))}} \over x_2 - x_1 = \underset{u_2}{\underbrace{f(g(x_2))}} - \underset{u_1}{\underbrace{f(g(x_1))}} \over \underset{u_2}{\underbrace{g(x_2)}} - \underset{u_1}{\underbrace{g(x_1)}} \cdot \underset{u_2}{\underbrace{g(x_2)}} - \underset{u_1}{\underbrace{g(x_1)}} \over x_2 - x_1$$

Differentiation

Supplement

What happens if x_2 approaches x_1 infinitely closely?

Since we can reason in this way only when the function is continuous and differentiable, the function $g(x)$ introduced below is assumed to be continuous and differentiable as well.

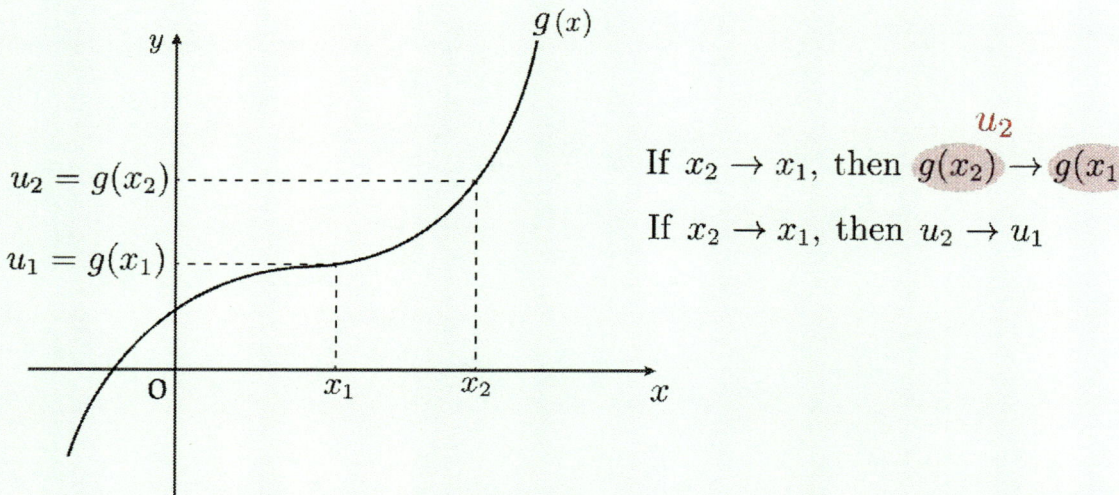

If $x_2 \to x_1$, then $g(x_2) \to g(x_1)$

If $x_2 \to x_1$, then $u_2 \to u_1$

Let us revisit what we discussed earlier.

$$x_1 = 2.0 \to u_1 = g(x_1) = x_1^2 = 2.0^2 = 4.00,$$
$$x_2 = 2.1 \to u_2 = g(x_2) = x_2^2 = 2.1^2 = 4.41.$$

What is the meaning of $x_2 \to x_1$?

$$x_2 = 2.1 \to x_2 = 2.01 \to x_2 = 2.001 \to \ldots \to 2.0 = x_1.$$

The value of x_2 approaches to the value of x_1.

The value of x_2	The value of $u_2 = x_2^2$
2.1	4.41
2.01	4.0401
2.001	4.004001
Converges to $x_1 = 2.0$	Converges to $u_1 = x_1^2 = 4.00$

As $x_2 \to x_1$, we have $u_2 \to u_1$!

$$\frac{y_2 - y_1}{x_2 - x_1} = \frac{y_2 - y_1}{u_2 - u_1} \cdot \frac{u_2 - u_1}{x_2 - x_1}.$$

AP Calculus AB & BC Rewritten from the Beginning

Supplement

By taking the limit $x_2 \to x_1$, we have

$$\lim_{x_2 \to x_1} \frac{y_2 - y_1}{x_2 - x_1} = \lim_{x_2 \to x_1} \frac{y_2 - y_1}{u_2 - u_1} \cdot \lim_{x_2 \to x_1} \frac{u_2 - u_1}{x_2 - x_1}.$$

Since $x_2 \to x_1$ implies $u_2 \to u_1$, we can replace the $x_2 \to x_1$ in the first limit of the right hand side by $u_2 \to u_1$ as follows.

$$\lim_{x_2 \to x_1} \frac{y_2 - y_1}{x_2 - x_1} = \lim_{u_2 \to u_1} \frac{y_2 - y_1}{u_2 - u_1} \cdot \lim_{x_2 \to x_1} \frac{u_2 - u_1}{x_2 - x_1}$$

and it is equivalent to

$$\frac{dy}{dx} = \frac{dy}{du} \cdot \frac{du}{dx}.$$

$\frac{dy}{dx}$ is the limit of a fraction, not an ordinary fraction. However, we can observe that treating it like an ordinary fraction still leads to the correct result.

To summarize, by taking $\lim_{x_2 \to x_1}$ to the following equalities:

$$\frac{\Delta y}{\Delta x} = \frac{\Delta y}{\Delta u} \cdot \frac{\Delta u}{\Delta x}$$

$$\frac{e^{2.1^2} - e^{2.0^2}}{2.1 - 2.0} = \frac{e^{2.1^2} - e^{2.0^2}}{2.1^2 - 2.0^2} \cdot \frac{2.1^2 - 2.0^2}{2.1 - 2.0}$$

we get

$$\frac{e^{2.0\cdots01^2} - e^{2.0^2}}{2.0\cdots01 - 2.0} = \frac{e^{2.0\cdots01^2} - e^{2.0^2}}{2.0\cdots01^2 - 2.0^2} \cdot \frac{2.0\cdots01^2 - 2.0^2}{2.0\cdots01 - 2.0}$$

$$(f \circ g)'(2.0) = f'(4.00) \cdot g'(2.0)$$
$$(f \circ g)'(x_1) = f'(u_1) \cdot g'(x_1)$$
$$= f'(g(x_1)) \cdot g'(x_1)$$

Supplement

2. (dy/dx) = (1/(dx/dy))

Consider a differentiable function $y = f(x)$ and draw its graph as follows.

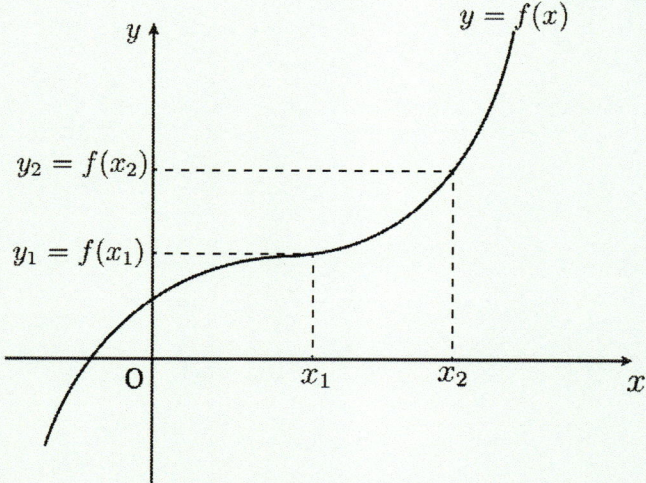

Since $\Delta x = x_2 - x_1$ and $\Delta y = y_2 - y_1$ are real numbers, we can consider the following equality:

$$\frac{y_2 - y_1}{x_2 - x_1} = \frac{1}{\frac{x_2 - x_1}{y_2 - y_1}} \quad \text{or equivalently} \quad \frac{\Delta y}{\Delta x} = \frac{1}{\frac{\Delta x}{\Delta y}}.$$

By taking $\lim_{x_2 \to x_1}$ to the both sides, we get

$$\lim_{x_2 \to x_1} \frac{y_2 - y_1}{x_2 - x_1} = \frac{1}{\lim_{x_2 \to x_1} \frac{x_2 - x_1}{y_2 - y_1}} \quad \text{or equivalently} \quad \lim_{x_2 \to x_1} \frac{\Delta y}{\Delta x} = \frac{1}{\lim_{x_2 \to x_1} \frac{\Delta x}{\Delta y}}.$$

Since $y = f(x)$ is differentiable and continuous, we know $x_2 \to x_1$ implies $y_2 \to y_1$. Therefore, $\lim_{x_2 \to x_1}$ and $\lim_{y_2 \to y_1}$ and we have

$$\frac{dy}{dx} = \lim_{x_2 \to x_1} \frac{y_2 - y_1}{x_2 - x_1} = \frac{1}{\lim_{x_2 \to x_1} \frac{x_2 - x_1}{y_2 - y_1}} = \frac{1}{\lim_{y_2 \to y_1} \frac{x_2 - x_1}{y_2 - y_1}} = \frac{1}{\frac{dx}{dy}}.$$

AP Calculus AB & BC Rewritten from the Beginning

Supplement

For example, we can write $\frac{3}{5} = \frac{1}{\frac{5}{3}}$, since 3 and 5 are real numbers and $\frac{3}{5}$ is an ordinary fraction. However, $\frac{dy}{dx}$ is a "limit of a fraction," and thus not an actual fraction. Surprisingly, performing operations with $\frac{dy}{dx}$ as if it were a regular fraction still yields correct results.

Is this merely a coincidence?

Strangely enough, although $\frac{dy}{dx}$ is only a limit of a fraction, it behaves just like an ordinary fraction in computations.

Supplement

3. $\dfrac{dy}{dx} = \dfrac{\dfrac{dy}{dt}}{\dfrac{dx}{dt}}$

Consider two continuous and differentiable functions $x = x(t)$ and $y = y(t)$.

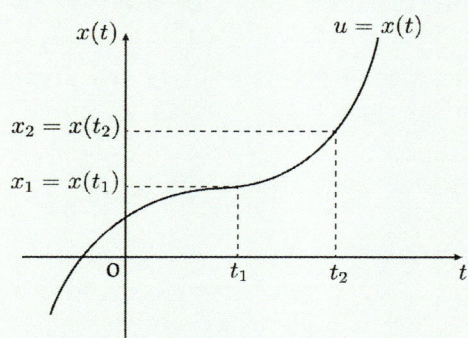

Since $\Delta t = t_2 - t_1$, $\Delta x = x_2 - x_1$, and $\Delta y = y_2 - y_1$ are real numbers, we have

$$\dfrac{y_2 - y_1}{x_2 - x_1} = \dfrac{\dfrac{y_2 - y_1}{t_2 - t_1}}{\dfrac{x_2 - x_1}{t_2 - t_1}} \quad \text{or equivalently} \quad \dfrac{\Delta y}{\Delta x} = \dfrac{\dfrac{\Delta y}{\Delta t}}{\dfrac{\Delta x}{\Delta t}}.$$

By taking $\lim\limits_{t_2 \to t_1}$ to the both sides to get

$$\lim_{t_2 \to t_1} \dfrac{y_2 - y_1}{x_2 - x_1} = \dfrac{\lim\limits_{t_2 \to t_1} \dfrac{y_2 - y_1}{t_2 - t_1}}{\lim\limits_{t_2 \to t_1} \dfrac{x_2 - x_1}{t_2 - t_1}} \quad \text{or equivalently} \quad \lim_{t_2 \to t_1} \dfrac{\Delta y}{\Delta x} = \dfrac{\lim\limits_{t_2 \to t_1} \dfrac{\Delta y}{\Delta t}}{\lim\limits_{t_2 \to t_1} \dfrac{\Delta x}{\Delta t}}.$$

Since $x = x(t)$ is continuous, $t_2 \to t_1$ implies $x_2 \to x_1$ ($x(t_2) \to x(t_1)$). Therefore, the limit at the left hand side $\lim\limits_{t_2 \to t_1}$ can be replaced into $\lim\limits_{x_2 \to x_1}$.

Finally, we have

$$\dfrac{dy}{dx} = \lim_{x_2 \to x_1} \dfrac{y_2 - y_1}{x_2 - x_1} = \lim_{t_2 \to t_1} \dfrac{y_2 - y_1}{x_2 - x_1} = \dfrac{\lim\limits_{t_2 \to t_1} \dfrac{y_2 - y_1}{t_2 - t_1}}{\lim\limits_{t_2 \to t_1} \dfrac{x_2 - x_1}{t_2 - t_1}} = \dfrac{\dfrac{dy}{dt}}{\dfrac{dx}{dt}}.$$

AP Calculus AB & BC Rewritten from the Beginning

Supplement

For example, we can write $\dfrac{3}{5} = \dfrac{\frac{3}{2}}{\frac{5}{2}}$, since 2, 3, and 5 are numerical values, and $\dfrac{3}{5}$, $\dfrac{5}{2}$, and $\dfrac{3}{2}$ are all valid fractions. However, expressions such as $\dfrac{dy}{dx}$, $\dfrac{dx}{dt}$, and $\dfrac{dy}{dt}$ are not actual fractions, but rather "limits of fractions." Even so, it turns out that $\dfrac{dy}{dx}$ behaves in computations just like an ordinary fraction.

Is this merely a coincidence?

Strangely enough, although $\dfrac{dy}{dx}$ is only a limit of a fraction, it still produces correct results when treated like a regular fraction.

So far, we have explored the use of $\dfrac{dy}{dx}$. Although $\dfrac{dy}{dx}$ is not a fraction in the traditional sense, we have seen that performing calculations as if it were a fraction still yields the correct result.

The content from pages 149 to 162 likely addresses a question that many students studying calculus have wondered about at least once:

If $\dfrac{dy}{dx}$ is not a fraction, how can it be manipulated like one?

Despite searching through numerous papers and textbooks, I could not find any that provided a proper explanation for this. According to one source, even Leibniz, who first introduced this notation, could not explain the reasoning behind it.

After much thought and reflection, I eventually came up with my own proof.
The content from pages 151 to 164 is based on a paper I published separately, and a portion of that work is included in this book.

Differentiation

02. Differentiation Formula
(The Derivative of a Composite Function & Chain Rule)

I. The Derivative of a Composite Function

Before moving on to the next step, we review what we have learned.

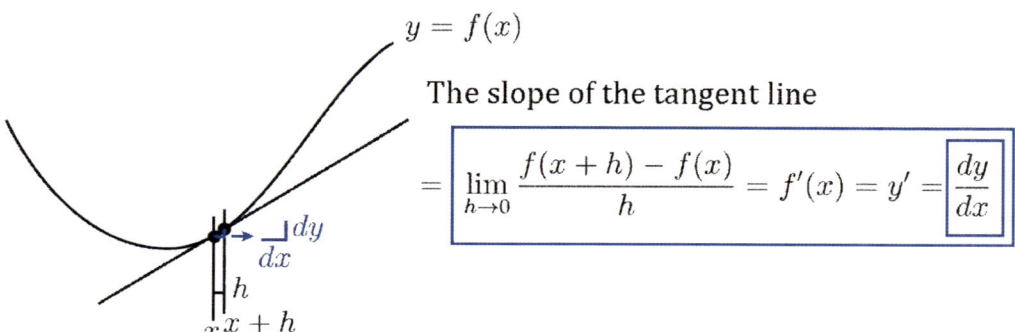

The slope of the tangent line
$$= \lim_{h \to 0} \frac{f(x+h) - f(x)}{h} = f'(x) = y' = \frac{dy}{dx}$$

We have learned that $f'(x) = y' = \frac{dy}{dx}$. For example, for $y = x^2 + 1$ we can write either $y' = 2x$ or $\frac{dy}{dx} = 2x$. In previous chapters we have used multiple times the symbols $f'(x)$ and y'. Now, then what is $\frac{dy}{dx}$, why do we need this third notation? What is its use? The true usage of $\frac{dy}{dx}$ will be later discovered in the chapter "Implicit Differentiation and Higher-Order Differentiation." However, here we shall see that $\frac{dy}{dx}$ notation also comes useful when you are computing a derivative of a composite function.

If we differentiate $y = (f \circ g)$, what will we get?

To solve this, we will take a look at what we learned in Precalculus.

Make Sure to Know the Following!

$$f \circ g = (f \circ g)(x) = f(g(x))$$

AP Calculus AB & BC Rewritten from the Beginning

Now, let $u = g(x)$ and $y = f(u)$. Suppose we want to compute $\frac{dy}{dx} = (f \circ g)'(x)$. BUT here, $\frac{dy}{dx} = (f \circ g)'(x)$ is not the only differentiation that you can do. You can also think of $\frac{dy}{du} = f'(u)$ and $\frac{du}{dx} = g'(x)$. The point is, if you multiply $\frac{dy}{du}$ and $\frac{du}{dx}$:

$$\frac{dy}{du} \cdot \frac{du}{dx},$$

then you can treat the above form as if the two forms are honest fractions and "cancel out" du!

Make Sure to Know the Following!

$$\frac{dy}{dx} = \frac{dy}{du} \cdot \frac{du}{dx}$$

$$(f \cdot g)'(x) = f'(u) \cdot g'(x) = f'(g(x)) \cdot g'(x)$$

Again, as for "why" we can do this and what is the true meaning of $\frac{dy}{dx}$, we wait until the chapter "Implicit Differentiation and Higher-Order Differentiation."

Here we see how useful this is.

Differentiation

Example 6

Compute $\dfrac{dy}{dx}$.

$$y = u^{10} \text{ and } u = 5x + 3.$$

Answer

$\dfrac{dy}{dx} = 50(5x+3)^9$

Solution

$\dfrac{dy}{du} = 10u^9,\ \dfrac{du}{dx} = 5,$

$\dfrac{dy}{dx} = \dfrac{dy}{du} \cdot \dfrac{du}{dx} = 10u^9 \cdot 5 = 50u^9.$

Don't forget that we are computing $\dfrac{dy}{dx} = (f \cdot g)'(x)$. Your answer should be written only in terms of x. Substitute $u = 5x+3$ into $\dfrac{dy}{dx} = 50u^9$:

$\dfrac{dy}{dx} = 50(5x+3)^9.$

※ Think about how you would have solved this problem if you didn't know differentiation of composite functions. You would have had to expand $(5x+3)^{10}$ using Binomial Theorem, differentiate each monomial and put them all back together. You now see why differentiation of composite functions is important. We see more examples.

Example 7

Compute $\dfrac{dy}{dx}$.

(1) $y = u^3$, $u = 2x^5 + 3x^3$

(2) $y = \tan u$, $u = 10x^3$

(3) $y = \sin^{-1} u$, $u = 5x^4$

(4) $y = e^u$, $u = x^3 + x$

(5) $y = \log_5 u$, $u = 10x^2 + x$

(6) $y = f(u)$, $u = 7x^3$

(7) $y = f(u)$, $u = ax + b$ (a, b are constants)

Solution

(1) $\dfrac{dy}{du} = 3u^2$, $\dfrac{du}{dx} = 10x^4 + 9x^2$,

$\dfrac{dy}{dx} = \dfrac{dy}{du} \cdot \dfrac{du}{dx} = 3u^2 \cdot (10x^4 + 9x^2) = (30x^4 + 27x^2)u^2.$

Substitute $u = 2x^5 + 3x^3$ into $\dfrac{dy}{dx} = (30x^4 + 27x^2)u^2$:

$\dfrac{dy}{dx} = (30x^4 + 27x^2)(2x^5 + 3x^3)^2.$

(2) $\dfrac{dy}{du} = \sec^2 u$, $\dfrac{du}{dx} = 30x^2$,

$\dfrac{dy}{dx} = \dfrac{dy}{du} \cdot \dfrac{du}{dx} = \sec^2 u \cdot 30x^2.$

Substitute $u = 10x^3$ into $\dfrac{dy}{dx} = \sec^2 u \cdot 30x^2$:

$\dfrac{dy}{dx} = 30x^2 \cdot \sec^2(10x^3).$

(3) $\dfrac{dy}{du} = \dfrac{1}{\sqrt{1-u^2}}$, $\dfrac{du}{dx} = 20x^3$,

$\dfrac{dy}{dx} = \dfrac{dy}{du} \cdot \dfrac{du}{dx} = \dfrac{1}{\sqrt{1-u^2}} \cdot 20x^3.$

Substitute $u = 5x^4$ into $\dfrac{dy}{dx} = \dfrac{1}{\sqrt{1-u^2}} \cdot 20x^3$:

$\dfrac{dy}{dx} = \dfrac{20x^3}{\sqrt{1-25x^8}}.$

(4) $\dfrac{dy}{du} = e^u$, $\dfrac{du}{dx} = 3x^2 + 1$,

$\dfrac{dy}{dx} = \dfrac{dy}{du} \cdot \dfrac{du}{dx} = e^u \cdot (3x^2 + 1).$

Substitute $u = x^3 + x$ into $\dfrac{dy}{dx} = e^u \cdot (3x^2 + 1)$:

$\dfrac{dy}{dx} = (3x^2 + 1)e^{x^3 + x}.$

Solution

(5) $\dfrac{dy}{du} = \dfrac{1}{u \cdot ln5}$, $\dfrac{du}{dx} = 20x+1$,

$\dfrac{dy}{dx} = \dfrac{dy}{du} \cdot \dfrac{du}{dx} = \dfrac{1}{u \cdot ln5} \cdot (20x+1)$.

Substitute $u = 10x^2 + x$ into $\dfrac{dy}{dx} = \dfrac{1}{u \cdot ln5} \cdot (20x+1)$:

$\dfrac{dy}{dx} = \dfrac{20x+1}{(10x^2+x) \cdot ln5}$.

(6) $\dfrac{dy}{du} = f'(u)$, $\dfrac{du}{dx} = 21x^2$,

$\dfrac{dy}{dx} = \dfrac{dy}{du} \cdot \dfrac{du}{dx} = f'(u) \cdot 21x^2$.

Substitute $u = 7x^3$ into $\dfrac{dy}{dx} = f'(u) \cdot 21x^2$:

$\dfrac{dy}{dx} = 21x^2 f'(7x^3)$.

(7) $\dfrac{dy}{du} = f'(u)$, $\dfrac{du}{dx} = a$,

$\dfrac{dy}{dx} = \dfrac{dy}{du} \cdot \dfrac{du}{dx} = f'(u) \cdot a = af'(u)$.

Substitute $u = ax+b$ into $\dfrac{dy}{dx} = af'(u)$:

$\dfrac{dy}{dx} = af'(ax+b)$.

※ After solving (7), go back to Example 6! What can you see?

The examples above were the basic templates of "differentiation of composition function" and we call it, 'Chain Rule'. However, not always your given function is kindly given to you as $y = f(u)$, $u = g(x)$, and $y = (f \circ g)(x)$. Sometimes, you have to break down your given function as two functions $y = f(u)$, $u = g(x)$ yourself, by choosing appropriate choice of u! The following Special lecture '6 Properties of the Chain Rule' gives you the formulas for finding u. Practice hard until they all feel natural to you.

II. 6 Properties of the Chain Rule

Special Lecture

ⓐ $y = (\square)^n \Rightarrow y' = n(\square)^{n-1} \cdot \square'$

(Example) $y = (3x^2 + 5x - 1)^3 \Rightarrow y' = 3(3x^2 + 5x - 1)^{3-1}(6x + 5)$

ⓑ $y = \sin \square \Rightarrow y' = \square' \cdot \cos \square$

(Example) $y = \sec(5x + 1) \Rightarrow y' = \sec(5x + 1) \tan(5x + 1) \times 5$

ⓒ $y = \sin^{-1} \square \Rightarrow y' = \dfrac{1}{\sqrt{1-\square^2}} \times \square'$

(Example) $y = \tan^{-1}(5x^2) \Rightarrow y' = \dfrac{1}{1+(5x^2)^2} \times 10x$

ⓓ $y = a^\square \Rightarrow y' = (a^\square \cdot \ln a) \times \square'$, $y = e^\square \Rightarrow y' = e^\square \times \square'$

(Example) $y = 3^{5x^3+7x} \Rightarrow y' = (3^{5x^3+7x} \cdot \ln 3) \times (15x^2 + 7)$

ⓔ $y = \log_a \square \Rightarrow y' = \dfrac{1}{\square \cdot \ln a} \times \square'$, $y = \ln \square \Rightarrow y' = \dfrac{1}{\square} \times \square'$

(Example) $y = \log_3(2x^5) \Rightarrow y' = \dfrac{1}{2x^5 \cdot \ln 3} \times 10x^4$

ⓕ $y = f(\square) \Rightarrow y' = f'(\square) \cdot \square'$

(Example) $y = f(10x) \Rightarrow y' = 10 f'(10x)$

AP Calculus AB & BC Rewritten from the Beginning

Make Sure to Know the Following!

Many students struggled with the following concepts. However, mastering the differentiation techniques below significantly simplifies the process. Ensure you understand each one thoroughly.

Make sure to know this.

① $f(x) = e^{\ln g(x)} = g(x)^{\ln e} = g(x)$ (EX) $f(x) = e^{\ln(x^2+x)} \Rightarrow f(x) = x^2 + x$

② Use $f(x) = \sqrt[m]{(\ )^n} = (\ )^{\frac{n}{m}}$ to find $f'(x)$ of radical functions.

(EX) $f(x) = \sqrt[3]{(x^2+1)^2} \Rightarrow f(x) = (x^2+1)^{\frac{2}{3}}$

Thus, $f'(x) = \frac{2}{3}(x^2+1)^{\frac{2}{3}-1} \times 2x = \frac{4x}{3\sqrt[3]{x^2+1}}$

③ Use $f(x) = \frac{a}{(\ )^n} = a(\ )^{-n}$ to find $f'(x)$ of rational functions with constant numerator. (a is a constant)

(EX) $f(x) = \frac{2}{(x^2+1)^3} \Rightarrow f(x) = 2(x^2+1)^{-3}$

Thus, $f'(x) = -3 \times 2(x^2+1)^{-3-1} \times 2x = -12x(x^2+1)^{-4} = \frac{-12x}{(x^2+1)^4}$.

④ Change $\sin^n f(x)$ to $[\sin f(x)]^n$ and find $\frac{dy}{dx}$. (EX) $\sin^2(5x) \Rightarrow [\sin(5x)]^2$

Thus, $\frac{dy}{dx} = 2\sin 5x \times \cos 5x \times 5 = 10\sin 5x \cos 5x$

⑤ If exponents are ambiguous, take ln. (EX) $e^y = x^2 \Rightarrow \ln e^y = \ln x^2 \Rightarrow y = 2\ln x$

Thus, $\frac{dy}{dx} = 2\frac{1}{x} = \frac{2}{x}$

Make Sure to Know the Following!

Let's look at the following three cases.

A formula exists.
- ⑥ $y = x^n$ $(ex) y = x^2 \Rightarrow y' = 2x$
- ⑦ $y = a^x$ $(ex) y = 2^x \Rightarrow y' = 2^x \ln 2$

A formula does not exist.
⑧ In the case of $y = x^x$, take the ln of both sides.

$\ln y = \ln x^x$ is $\ln y = x \ln x$, so $\dfrac{1}{y} y' = x' \ln x + x \dfrac{1}{x}$,

which gives $y' = y(\ln x + 1)$ because $x' = 1$, and $y = x^x$,

so $y' = x^x (\ln x + 1)$.

In ⑥, ⑦, and ⑧ above, if there is a constant in the base or the exponent, a formula can be used unconditionally. However, if both the base and the exponent contains variable, take the ln of both sides.

AP Calculus AB & BC Rewritten from the Beginning

After learning the contents so far, let's solve the following examples.

● ········ **Example 8**

Find y'.

(1) $y = (2x-1)^5$

(2) $y = \tan(13x^3)$

(3) $y = \cos^{-1}(10x)$

(4) $y = \cot^2(2x^2)$

(5) $y = 5^{\sin x}$

(6) $y = \ln(3x)$

(7) $y = e^{5x^5}$

(8) $\tan^{-1} 3x = e^{2y}$

● ········ **Answer** (1) $10(2x-1)^4$ (2) $39x^2 \sec^2(13x^3)$ (3) $-\dfrac{10}{\sqrt{1-100x^2}}$

(4) $-8x\cot(2x^2)\csc^2(2x^2)$ (5) $5^{\sin x} \times \ln 5 \times \cos x$ (6) $\dfrac{1}{x}$

(7) $25x^4 e^{5x^5}$ (8) $\dfrac{3}{2(\tan^{-1} 3x)(1+9x^2)}$

● ········ **Solution**

(1) $y' = 5 \times (2x-1)^{5-1} \times 2 = 10(2x-1)^4$

(2) $y' = \sec^2(13x^3) \times 39x^2 = 39x^2 \sec^2(13x^3)$

(3) $y' = -\dfrac{1}{\sqrt{1-(10x)^2}} \times 10 = -\dfrac{10}{\sqrt{1-(10x)^2}} = -\dfrac{10}{\sqrt{1-100x^2}}$

(4) $y = \{\cot(2x^2)\}^2 \Rightarrow y' = 2\{\cot(2x^2)\}^{2-1} \times \{-\csc^2(2x^2)\} \times 4x$,

so $y' = -8x\cot(2x^2)\csc^2(2x^2)$

(5) $y' = 5^{\sin x} \times \ln 5 \times (\sin x)' = 5^{\sin x} \times \ln 5 \times \cos x$

(6) $y' = \dfrac{1}{3x} \times 3 = \dfrac{1}{x}$

(7) $y' = e^{5x^5} \times 25x^4 = 25x^4 e^{5x^5}$

(8) Taking the ln of both sides gives $2y = \ln|\tan^{-1} 3x|$, which means $y = \dfrac{1}{2}\ln|\tan^{-1} 3x|$,

Thus, $y' = \dfrac{1}{2} \times \dfrac{1}{\tan^{-1} 3x} \times \dfrac{1}{1+(3x)^2} \times 3 = \dfrac{3}{2(\tan^{-1} 3x)(1+9x^2)}$

Differentiation

Problem 1

Find $f'(x)$.

① $f(x) = x\sqrt{3x^2+5}$ ② $f(x) = \dfrac{3}{\sqrt[3]{x^2+2x}}$ ③ $f(x) = \dfrac{e^{3x}}{x^2}$

④ $f(x) = \sec(e^{-2x})$ ⑤ $f(x) = e^{5\ln(x^3)}$

Answer

(1) $\dfrac{6x^2+5}{\sqrt{3x^2+5}}$ (2) $-\dfrac{2(x+1)}{\sqrt[3]{(x^2+2x)^4}}$ (3) $\dfrac{e^{3x}(3x-2)}{x^3}$

(4) $-2e^{-2x}\sec(e^{-2x})\tan(e^{-2x})$ (5) $15x^{14}$

Solution

- Use $f(x) = e^{\ln f(x)} = \{f(x)\}^{\ln e} = f(x)$ to find $f'(x)$.
- Use $f(x) = \sqrt[m]{(\ )^n} = (\ )^{\frac{n}{m}}$ to find $f'(x)$.
- Use $f(x) = \dfrac{a}{(\ )^n} = a(\ )^{-n}$ to find $f'(x)$.

(1) $f(x) = x\sqrt{3x^2+5} = \sqrt{3x^4+5x^2} = (3x^4+5x^2)^{\frac{1}{2}}$, so

$f'(x) = \dfrac{1}{2}(3x^4+5x^2)^{-\frac{1}{2}}(12x^3+10x) = \dfrac{12x^3+10x}{2\sqrt{3x^4+5x^2}} = \dfrac{6x^3+5x}{\sqrt{3x^4+5x^2}} = \dfrac{6x^2+5}{\sqrt{3x^2+5}}$

(2) $f(x) = 3(x^2+2x)^{-\frac{1}{3}}$, so $f'(x) = 3(-\dfrac{1}{3})(x^2+2x)^{-\frac{4}{3}}(2x+2) = -\dfrac{2(x+1)}{\sqrt[3]{(x^2+2x)^4}}$

(3) $f'(x) = \dfrac{3e^{3x}x^2 - e^{3x}2x}{x^4} = \dfrac{xe^{3x}(3x-2)}{x^4} = \dfrac{e^{3x}(3x-2)}{x^3}$

(4) $f'(x) = -2e^{-2x}\sec(e^{-2x})\tan(e^{-2x})$

(5) $f(x) = e^{\ln(x^3)^5} = e^{\ln(x^{15})} = (x^{15})^{\ln e} = x^{15}$, so $f'(x) = 15x^{14}$

AP Calculus AB & BC Rewritten from the Beginning

Problem 2

1. If $f(x) = \ln(x^2 + 5 + e^{-2x})$, find $f'(0)$.

2. If $f(x) = (2x+1)^{\frac{2}{3}} + e^{2x^3}$, find $f'(0)$.

3. If $f(x) = \ln(x^3)$, find the slope of the tangent line at $x = e$.

Answer (1) $-\dfrac{1}{3}$ (2) $\dfrac{4}{3}$ (3) $\dfrac{3}{e}$

Solution

(1) $f'(x) = \dfrac{1}{x^2 + 5 + e^{-2x}}(2x - 2e^{-2x}) = \dfrac{2x - 2e^{-2x}}{x^2 + 5 + e^{-2x}}$,

so $f'(0) = \dfrac{2(0) - 2e^{-2(0)}}{0^2 + 5 + e^{-2(0)}} = \dfrac{-2}{5+1} = -\dfrac{1}{3}$.

(2) $f'(x) = \dfrac{4}{3}(2x+1)^{-\frac{1}{3}} + 6x^2 e^{2x^3}$, so $f'(0) = \dfrac{4}{3}(2(0)+1)^{-\frac{1}{3}} = \dfrac{4}{3}$.

(3) The slope of the tangent line at $x = e$ is $f'(e)$

$f'(x) = \dfrac{3x^2}{x^3} = \dfrac{3}{x}$, so $f'(e) = \dfrac{3e^2}{e^3} = \dfrac{3}{e}$.

Differentiation

● **Problem 3**

x	$f(x)$	$f'(x)$	$g(x)$	$g'(x)$
−2	2	4	3	5
1	1	−2	−1	7
5	3	5	−2	2

The table above gives values of f, f', g', and g at selected values of x. If $h(x) = (f \circ g)(x)$, then $h'(5) =$

● **Answer** 8

● **Solution**

$h(x) = f(g(x))$, so $h'(x) = f'(g(x))g'(x)$

$h'(5) = f'(g(5))g'(5) = f'(-2)g'(5) = 4 \times 2 = 8$

03. Implicit Differentiation and Higher-Order Differentiation

Let's look at the following figure.

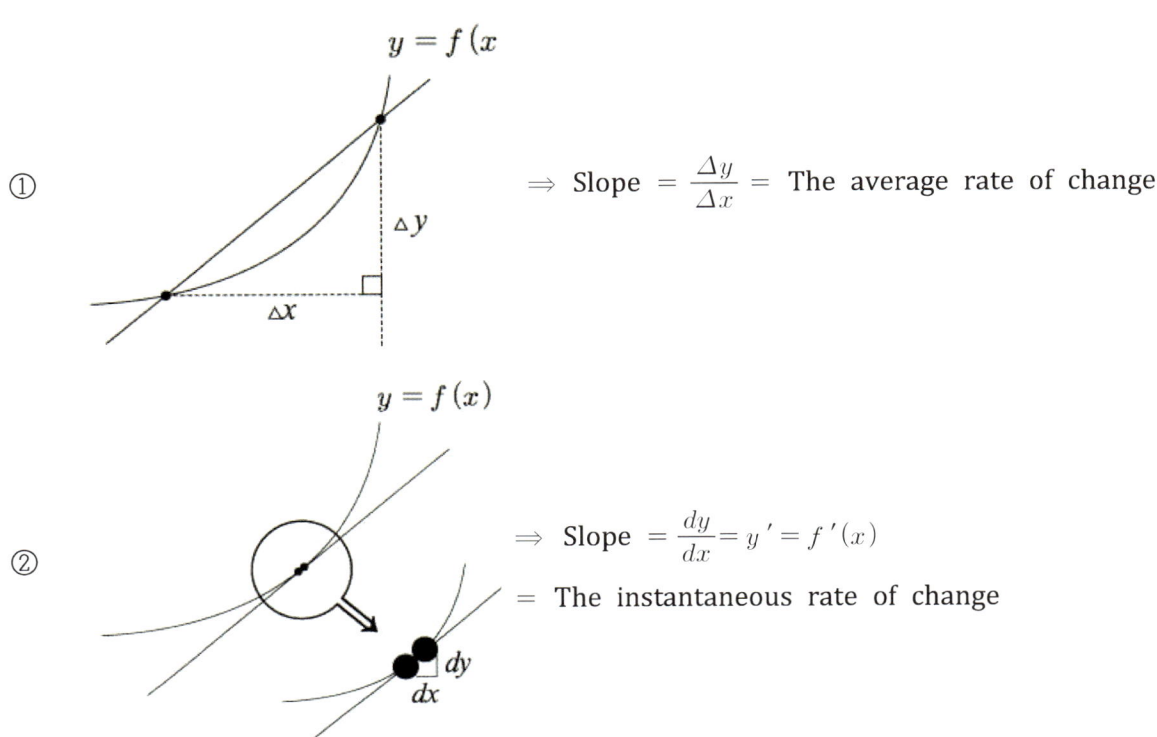

In the figure above,

Case ① is finding the slope of a line passing through two points that are distinct and separated,

and Case ② is finding the slope of a line passing through two points that are adjacent to each other.

That is, the slope of a tangent line can be expressed as $\dfrac{dy}{dx}$, and it is the same as $f'(x)$ and y'.

Differentiation

I. Implicit Differentiation $\dfrac{dy}{dx}$

Let's look at the following examples.

ⓐ $\dfrac{d}{dx}(x^2) = 2x$,　ⓑ $\dfrac{d}{d\theta}(2\theta) = 2$,　ⓒ $\dfrac{d}{dy}(y) = 1$,　ⓓ $\dfrac{d}{dr}(r^2+1) = 2r$, ….

As we can see, these expressions are directly differentiable because the variable inside the expression matches the variable in the denominator of the derivative operator.

So, what do you do in the following cases?

$$\dfrac{d}{dx}(y) \cdots, \text{ where } y \text{ is a function of } x$$

The variable in the denominator is different from the variable in the expression that we want to differentiate.

In this case, it becomes $\dfrac{d}{dy}(y)\dfrac{dy}{dx} = 1 \times \dfrac{dy}{dx} = \dfrac{dy}{dx}$.

Then, let's look at the following examples.

ⓐ $\dfrac{d}{dx}(y^2) = \dfrac{d}{dy}y^2 \dfrac{dy}{dx} = 2y\dfrac{dy}{dx}$　　　　ⓑ $\dfrac{d}{dx}(3r) = \dfrac{d}{dr}(3r)\dfrac{dr}{dx} = 3\dfrac{dr}{dx}$

ⓒ $\dfrac{d}{dx}(3\theta^5) = \dfrac{d}{d\theta}(3\theta^5)\dfrac{d\theta}{dx} = 15\theta^4\dfrac{d\theta}{dx}$ …

As in the cases of ⓐ, ⓑ, and ⓒ above, we can solve simply as follows.

If the variable in the denominator is different from the variable in the expression, just find the derivative and multiply $\dfrac{dy}{dx}$, $\dfrac{dr}{dx}$, $\dfrac{d\theta}{dx}$, etc. to it.

Let's look at the following examples.

ⓐ In $y = x^2$, if we differentiate y (the left-hand side), we get 1. Since we differentiated something other than x, we need to multiply $\dfrac{dy}{dx}$. Thus, $\dfrac{dy}{dx} = 2x$.

ⓑ In $r = 3\sin\theta$, if we want to find $\dfrac{dr}{d\theta}$, differentiating r gives 1, and when we multiply $\dfrac{dr}{d\theta}$, it becomes $\dfrac{dr}{d\theta} = 3\cos\theta$. It is convenient to know this method.

AP Calculus AB & BC Rewritten from the Beginning

Special Lecture

Many students find $\frac{d}{dx}$ unfamiliar.

You may think that it is some complex symbol, but, in fact, it is simply a compact way of saying

$$\text{"differentiate with respect to } x\text{"} = \frac{d}{dx}$$

That is, $\frac{d}{dx}$ means "differentiate what comes on the right, in terms of x!"

How about thinking of $\frac{d}{dx}$ in the following way? This is just my personal opinion and suggestion.

"define the derivative of $x = \frac{d}{dx}$"

<u>define the</u> / <u>derivative of</u> <u>x</u>
= d   dx

= d/dx

I would like to provide the following additional explanation regarding the Special Lecture above. For example, I aim to explain why the two methods for calculating the slope of a tangent—such as in the following situation—yield the same result.

The slope of the tangent can be found in two ways, as follows: (1) and (2)

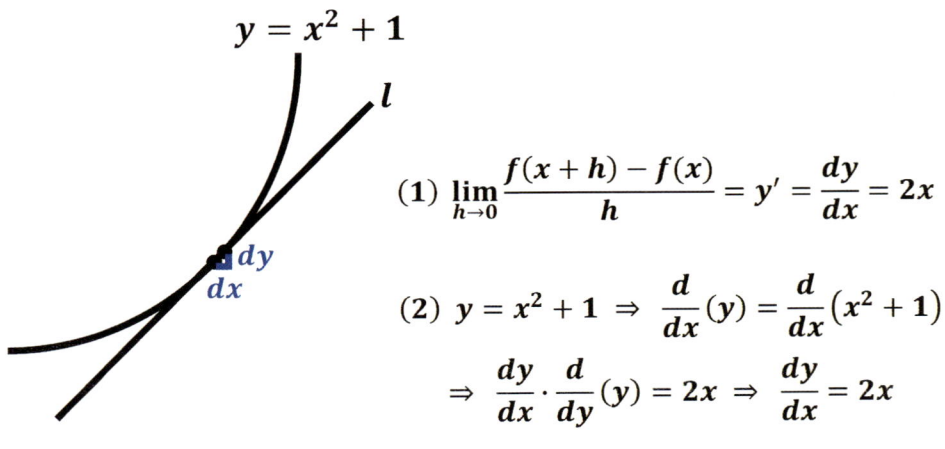

(1) $\lim\limits_{h \to 0} \dfrac{f(x+h) - f(x)}{h} = y' = \dfrac{dy}{dx} = 2x$

(2) $y = x^2 + 1 \Rightarrow \dfrac{d}{dx}(y) = \dfrac{d}{dx}(x^2 + 1)$

$\Rightarrow \dfrac{dy}{dx} \cdot \dfrac{d}{dy}(y) = 2x \Rightarrow \dfrac{dy}{dx} = 2x$

Differentiation

d/dx is a Function!!

What is the meaning of $\frac{d}{dx}y$ and why can you take $\frac{d}{dx}$ on both sides of your equation and still expect the equality to consist?

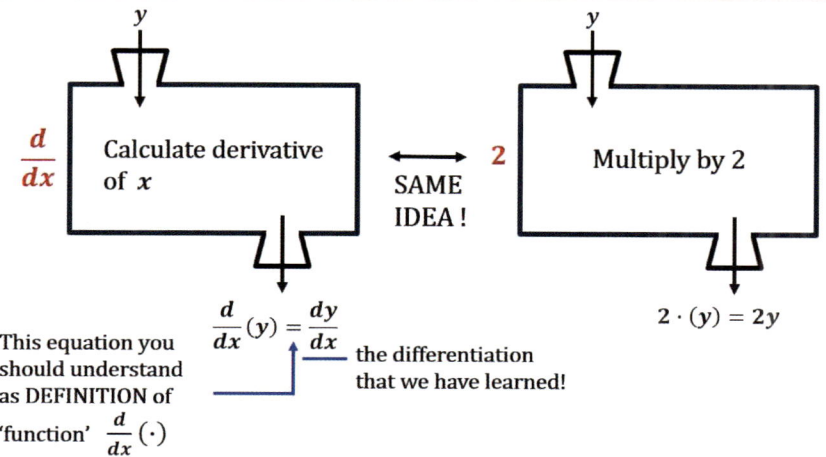

Here is the answer. Given equation $y = x^2$, no one doubts that one can multiply 2 on both hand sides of the equation and say '$2y = 2x^2$' is true. Now we shall describe this in a slightly different way. Let f be a function that sends $z \mapsto 2z$ i.e. $f(z) = 2z$. Then, the process of $y = x^2 \mapsto 2y = 2x^2$ can now be understood as

$$y = x^2 \mapsto f(y) = f(x^2) \quad \ldots (\star)$$

Now, forget that f was the simple function $f(z) = 2z$. No matter how complicated f is, $(\star)$ holds for ANY function f: doing the SAME thing(f) on the SAME object (Left Hand Side = Right Hand Side), you get the SAME result!

Taking $\frac{d}{dx}$ is nothing else but one another variation of $(\star)$ above, it is just that your function f is now just a little more complicated. As mentioned in the previous Special Lecture, $\frac{d}{dx}$ is a command for 'define the derivative of x'. If f was $f(z) = 2z$ then $f(y) = 2y$. If $f = \frac{d}{dx}$, then $f(y) = \frac{d}{dx}(y) = \frac{dy}{dx}$. It is as simple as it is. Some might have had the question, why $\frac{d}{dx}y = \frac{dy}{dx}$. But the answer to that question is simple; it is just definition. No one asks why $f(y) = 2y$ and $f(x) = 2x^2$ if $f : z \mapsto 2z$. Writing 2 to the left of your given term, we have 'promised' that it

AP Calculus AB & BC Rewritten from the Beginning

should mean: multiply your input by 2. Same thing. $\frac{d}{dx}$ is a function (or an operation) which spits out the derivative of its input, where the derivation of x is taken.

Special Lecture

$$\frac{dy}{dx} \text{ and } f'(x)$$

Previously, we learned that $\lim\limits_{h \to 0} \frac{f(x+h) - f(x)}{h} = f'(x) = \frac{dy}{dx}$. If two things, $f'(x)$ and $\frac{dy}{dx}$ are the same thing, why should we have two different notations? The answer is, if your given curve (the curve that you want to find the tangent line) can be written as a function $y = f(x)$ then the two things are exactly the same. You can just do $f'(x)$ calculation. However, not all curves are functions! Think of one of the most simple curves, a circle.

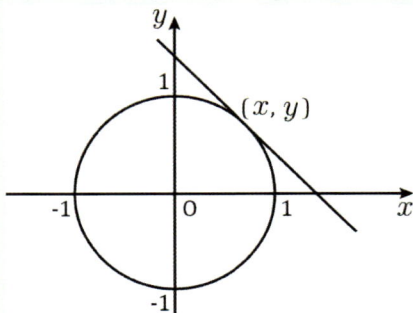

A circle can be written on a xy-plane as $x^2 + y^2 = 1$. For a single value of $x = 0$, there are two corresponding points $y = 1$ and $y = -1$: it is not a function $y = f(x)$. Function must have exactly one value of x for each value of y. However, we still want to understand the tangent line of a circle, at a given point! In such cases, we use $\frac{dy}{dx}$ method.

Let's look at the following two cases.

(Case 1) Function: $\qquad y = x^2 \Rightarrow y' = \frac{dy}{dx} = 2x$

(Case 2) Not a Function: $\qquad x^2 + y^2 = 1 \Rightarrow 2x + 2y \frac{dy}{dx} = 0 \Rightarrow \frac{dy}{dx} = -\frac{x}{y}$

The slope of the tangent line of circle $x^2 + y^2 = 1$ at a point (x, y) is $-\frac{x}{y}$. For example, at a point $\left(\frac{1}{2}, \frac{\sqrt{3}}{2}\right)$ the slope is $-\frac{1/2}{\sqrt{3}/2} = -\frac{1}{\sqrt{3}}$.

Differentiation

Example 9

1. If $y = \sin x$, find $\dfrac{dy}{dx}$.

2. If $(x^2y + y)^3 = 8x$, find the value of $\dfrac{dy}{dx}$ at the point $(x, y) = (1, 1)$.

3. If $\sin(x^2 y) = y^2$, find $\dfrac{dy}{dx}$.

Answer

(1) $\cos x$ (2) $-\dfrac{2}{3}$ (3) $\dfrac{2xy\cos(x^2y)}{2y - x^2\cos(x^2y)}$

Solution

(1) This is a function, so finding $\dfrac{dy}{dx}$ is easy. $y' = \dfrac{dy}{dx} = \cos x$.

(2) Let $\dfrac{dy}{dx} = y'$, and use the Chain Rule thoroughly.

$3(x^2y + y)^{3-1} \times (x^2y + y)' = 8x'$

$\Rightarrow 3(x^2y + y)^2(2xx'y + x^2y' + y') = 8x' \Rightarrow x' = 1$, so $3(x^2y + y)^2(2xy + x^2y' + y') = 8$

$\Rightarrow x = y = 1$, so from $3(2)^2(2 + y' + y') = 8$, we get $12(2 + 2y') = 8$

Thus, from $24 + 24y' = 8$, we get $y' = -\dfrac{16}{24}$ $\therefore \dfrac{dy}{dx} = -\dfrac{2}{3}$.

(3) Let $\dfrac{dy}{dx} = y'$, and use the Chain Rule thoroughly.

$\cos(x^2y) \times (x^2y)' = (y^2)'$

$\Rightarrow \cos(x^2y)(2xx'y + x^2y') = 2yy' \Rightarrow \cos(x^2y)(2xy + x^2y') = 2yy'$

$\Rightarrow 2xy\cos(x^2y) + x^2\cos(x^2y)y' = 2yy' \Rightarrow (2y - x^2\cos(x^2y))y' = 2xy\cos(x^2y)$

$\Rightarrow \dfrac{dy}{dx} = y' = \dfrac{2xy\cos(x^2y)}{2y - x^2\cos(x^2y)}$

AP Calculus AB & BC Rewritten from the Beginning

II. Higher-Order Differentiation $\dfrac{d^2y}{dx^2}, \cdots, \dfrac{d^ny}{dx^n}$

Know that $\dfrac{d^2y}{dx^2} = \boxed{\underset{②}{\dfrac{d}{dx}} \Big| \underset{①}{\dfrac{dy}{dx}}}$. This, we have briefly seen in the 'differential of composite functions' chapter too. That is, find ① $\dfrac{dy}{dx}$ first, and apply ② $\dfrac{d}{dx}$ second.

Also, know that we write $\dfrac{d^2y}{dx^2} = f''(x) = y''$ and it simply means "differentiate two times".

Let's look at the following examples.

● ········ **Example 10**

Find $\dfrac{d^2y}{dx^2}$.

(1) $x^2 + 2y^2 = 3$

(2) $x^2 - 10x = 5y + 2$

(3) $y = \ln x^3$

Differentiation

● ······· **Answer** (1) $-\dfrac{2y^2+x^2}{4y^3}$ (2) $\dfrac{2}{5}$ (3) $-\dfrac{3}{x^2}$

● ······· **Solution**

(1) Differentiating both sides gives $2x+4y\dfrac{dy}{dx}=0$, making $\dfrac{dy}{dx}$ the subject of the formula, we have $\dfrac{dy}{dx}=-\dfrac{x}{2y}$. Now, differentiating both sides the second time gives $\dfrac{d}{dx}\dfrac{dy}{dx}=\dfrac{d}{dx}(-\dfrac{x}{2y})$. We can solve the right-hand side using the formula for the differentiation of quotients we learned earlier.

Thus, $\dfrac{d}{dx}\left(x\times\left(-\dfrac{1}{2y}\right)\right) = \left(\dfrac{d}{dx}(x)\right)\left(-\dfrac{1}{2y}\right)+x\dfrac{d}{dx}\left(-\dfrac{1}{2y}\right) = -\dfrac{1}{2y}+x\dfrac{d}{dy}\left(-\dfrac{1}{2y}\right)\dfrac{dy}{dx}$

$= -\dfrac{1}{2y}+x\left(\dfrac{2}{4y^2}\right)\dfrac{dy}{dx} = \dfrac{-2y+2x\dfrac{dy}{dx}}{4y^2}$. Substituting $\dfrac{dy}{dx}=-\dfrac{x}{2y}$,

we get $\dfrac{-2y-\dfrac{x^2}{y}}{4y^2} = \dfrac{\dfrac{-2y^2-x^2}{y}}{4y^2} = \dfrac{-2y^2-x^2}{4y^3}$. Therefore, $\dfrac{d^2y}{dx^2}=-\dfrac{2y^2+x^2}{4y^3}$.

(2) Differentiating both sides $2x-10=5\dfrac{dy}{dx}$, making $\dfrac{dy}{dx}$ the subject of the formula, we have $\dfrac{dy}{dx}=\dfrac{2(x-5)}{5}=\dfrac{2}{5}(x-5)$. Now, differentiating both sides the second time gives $\dfrac{d^2y}{dx^2}=\dfrac{2}{5}$.

(3) $y=\ln x^3 \Rightarrow y=3\ln x$,

Differentiating $\dfrac{dy}{dx}=3\dfrac{1}{x}=\dfrac{3}{x}$.

Now, differentiating the second time gives $\dfrac{d^2y}{dx^2}=\dfrac{d}{dx}\left(\dfrac{3}{x}\right)$.

Thus, $\dfrac{d^2y}{dx^2}=\dfrac{d}{dx}(3x^{-1})=-3x^{-2}=-\dfrac{3}{x^2}$.

AP Calculus AB & BC Rewritten from the Beginning

Problem 4

1. $\dfrac{d}{dx}(\sin^3(2x^5)) =$

2. $\dfrac{d}{dx}(3xe^{\ln x^3}) =$

3. $\dfrac{d}{dx}(\arctan(5x)) =$

Answer (1) $30x^4\sin^2(2x^5)\cos(2x^5)$ (2) $12x^3$ (3) $\dfrac{5}{1+25x^2}$

Solution

> Use $e^{\ln f(x)} \Rightarrow (f(x))^{\ln e} = f(x)$ and find $\dfrac{dy}{dx}$.
>
> Use $\sin^n f(x) \Rightarrow (\sin(f(x)))^n$ and find $\dfrac{dy}{dx}$.

(1) $30x^4\sin^2(2x^5)\cos(2x^5)$

$\dfrac{d}{dx}(\sin(2x^5))^3 = 3(\sin(2x^5))^2\cos(2x^5)(10x^4) = 30x^4\sin^2(2x^5)\cos(2x^5)$

(2) $12x^3$

$3xe^{\ln x^3} = 3x(x^3)^{\ln e} = 3x^4$, so $\dfrac{d}{dx}(3xe^{\ln x^3}) = \dfrac{d}{dx}(3x^4) = 12x^3$.

(3) $\dfrac{5}{1+25x^2}$

$\dfrac{d}{dx}(\tan^{-1}(5x)) = \dfrac{1}{1+(5x)^2} \times 5 = \dfrac{5}{1+25x^2}$

Differentiation

Problem 5

1. If $x^2 + x^3 y = 1$, then when $x = 1$, $\dfrac{dy}{dx}$ is

   ⓐ −4 ⓑ −2 ⓒ 0 ⓓ 1

2. If $y = xy + y^2 + 5$, then when $y = 1$, $\dfrac{dy}{dx}$ is

   ⓐ $\dfrac{1}{4}$ ⓑ $\dfrac{1}{2}$ ⓒ 1 ⓓ 2

3. If $\sin(xy) = x^2$, then $\dfrac{dy}{dx}$ is

   ⓐ $\dfrac{y}{x} - 2\sec(xy)$ ⓑ $1 - \sin(xy)$ ⓒ $2\sec(xy) - \dfrac{y}{x}$ ⓓ $2\tan(xy) - \dfrac{y}{x}$

4. If $y = \arcsin(\cos x)$ and x is an acute angle, then $\dfrac{dy}{dx}$ is

   ⓐ $-\tan x$ ⓑ $\tan x$ ⓒ $\cot x$ ⓓ −1

5. If $y = \dfrac{\ln(3x)}{x^2}$, then $\dfrac{dy}{dx} =$

   ⓐ $\dfrac{3x + 2\ln(3x)}{x^3}$ ⓑ $\dfrac{\dfrac{1}{3}x - 2\ln(3x)}{x^3}$ ⓒ $\dfrac{3x - 2\ln(3x)}{x^3}$ ⓓ $\dfrac{1 - 2\ln(3x)}{x^3}$

AP Calculus AB & BC Rewritten from the Beginning

● .... **Answer** (1) ⓑ (2) ⓐ (3) ⓒ (4) ⓓ (5) ⓓ

● .... **Solution**

(1) ⓑ

When $x=1$, $1^2+1^3y=1 \Rightarrow y=1-1=0$.

Differentiating both sides gives $2x+3x^2y+(x^3)\dfrac{dy}{dx}=0 \Rightarrow \dfrac{dy}{dx}=\dfrac{2x+3x^2y}{-x^3}$, and when $x=1$, $y=0$, so $\dfrac{dy}{dx}=-2$.

(2) ⓐ

When $y=1$, $1=x+1+5$, so $x=-5$, and $\dfrac{dy}{dx}=y+x\dfrac{dy}{dx}+(2y)\dfrac{dy}{dx}$. Therefore, $\dfrac{dy}{dx}=1-5\dfrac{dy}{dx}+2\dfrac{dy}{dx}$, so $4\dfrac{dy}{dx}=1$. Thus, $\dfrac{dy}{dx}=\dfrac{1}{4}$.

(3) ⓒ

Differentiating both sides, we have $\cos(xy)\left\{y+x\dfrac{dy}{dx}\right\}=2x$,

so $y\cos(xy)+x\cos(xy)\dfrac{dy}{dx}=2x$, and $\dfrac{dy}{dx}=\dfrac{2x-y\cos(xy)}{x\cos(xy)}=\dfrac{2}{\cos(xy)}-\dfrac{y}{x}=2\sec(xy)-\dfrac{y}{x}$.

(4) ⓓ

$y=\sin^{-1}(\cos x)$, so $\dfrac{dy}{dx}=\dfrac{1}{\sqrt{1-\cos^2 x}}(-\sin x)$, $\dfrac{dy}{dx}=\dfrac{-\sin x}{\sqrt{\sin^2 x}}=\dfrac{-\sin x}{\sin x}=-1$.

(5) ⓓ

$\dfrac{dy}{dx}=\dfrac{\dfrac{3}{3x}x^2-2x\ln(3x)}{x^4}=\dfrac{x-2x\ln(3x)}{x^4}=\dfrac{1-2\ln(3x)}{x^3}$

Problem 6

1. If $y = 3\sin(2x)$, find $\dfrac{d^2y}{dx^2}$

2. If $x^2 + y^2 = 5$, what is the value of $\dfrac{d^2y}{dx^2}$ at the point (2, 1)?

   ⓐ −5　　ⓑ −3　　ⓒ 0　　ⓓ $\dfrac{1}{4}$

3. If $\dfrac{dy}{dx} = \sqrt{y^2 + 2}$, find $\dfrac{d^2y}{dx^2}$.

AP Calculus AB & BC Rewritten from the Beginning

Answer   (1) $-12\sin(2x)$ (2) ⓐ   (3) y

Solution

- $\dfrac{d^2y}{dx^2} = \dfrac{d}{dx}\dfrac{dy}{dx}$
- $\dfrac{d}{dx} = \dfrac{dy}{dx}\dfrac{d}{dy}$, $\dfrac{d}{dy} = \dfrac{dx}{dy}\dfrac{d}{dx}$ ...

(1) $-12\sin(2x)$

$\dfrac{dy}{dx} = 6\cos(2x)$, so $\dfrac{d^2y}{dx^2} = \dfrac{d}{dx}\dfrac{dy}{dx} = \dfrac{d}{dx}(6\cos(2x)) = -12\sin(2x)$.

(2) ⓐ

$2x + (2y)\dfrac{dy}{dx} = 0$, so $\dfrac{dy}{dx} = -\dfrac{x}{y}$,

$\dfrac{d^2y}{dx^2} = \dfrac{d}{dx}\dfrac{dy}{dx} = \dfrac{d}{dx}\left(-\dfrac{x}{y}\right) = \left(\dfrac{d}{dx}(x)\right)\left(-\dfrac{1}{y}\right) + x\dfrac{d}{dx}\left(-\dfrac{1}{y}\right) = -\dfrac{1}{y} + x\dfrac{d}{dy}\left(-\dfrac{1}{y}\right)\dfrac{dy}{dx}$

$= -\dfrac{1}{y} + x\left(\dfrac{1}{y^2}\right)\dfrac{dy}{dx} = \dfrac{-y + x\dfrac{dy}{dx}}{y^2}$.

If we substitute $\dfrac{dy}{dx} = -\dfrac{x}{y}$, we get $-\dfrac{y + \dfrac{x^2}{y}}{y^2}$.

Substituting $x = 2, y = 1$ gives $-\dfrac{1+4}{1} = -5$.

(3) y

$\dfrac{d^2y}{dx^2} = \dfrac{d}{dx}\dfrac{dy}{dx} = \dfrac{d}{dx}\sqrt{y^2+2}$ (※ $\dfrac{dy}{dx}\dfrac{d}{dy} = \dfrac{d}{dx}$) $= \dfrac{dy}{dx}\dfrac{d}{dy}(y^2+2)^{\frac{1}{2}} = \dfrac{dy}{dx}(\dfrac{1}{2}(y^2+2)^{-\frac{1}{2}}2y)$

$= \dfrac{dy}{dx}\dfrac{y}{\sqrt{y^2+2}}$ (※ $\dfrac{dy}{dx} = \sqrt{y^2+2}$) $= \sqrt{y^2+2} \cdot \dfrac{y}{\sqrt{y^2+2}} = y$

Problem 7

1. If $y = 3^x$, find y'.

2. If $y = (2x+1)^x$, find y'.

3. If $f(x) = (3x^3 + 2x)^{(2x+1)}$, find $f'(1)$.

4. If $f(x) = (\cos x)^x$ and x is an acute angle, find $f'(0)$.

5. If $e^y = \cos x$, $0 < x < \dfrac{\pi}{2}$, find $\dfrac{dy}{dx}$.

AP Calculus AB & BC Rewritten from the Beginning

Answer (1) $y' = 3^x \ln 3$ (2) $(2x+1)^x \left\{ \ln(2x+1) + \dfrac{2x}{2x+1} \right\}$

(3) $125 \left\{ \ln 25 + \dfrac{33}{5} \right\}$ (4) 0 (5) $-\tan x$

Solution

① $y = 3^x \Rightarrow y' = 3^x \ln 3$

② $y = x^3 \Rightarrow y' = 3x^2$

③ $y = x^x \Rightarrow \ln y = x \ln x$

(1) $y' = 3^x \ln 3$

You can of course use the differentiation formula for exponentials and immediately get $y = 3^x \Rightarrow y' = 3^x \ln 3$. However, here we show you another way, using implicit differentiation. Take the ln of both sides gives $\ln y = \ln 3^x$, and differentiating both sides gives $\dfrac{1}{y} \dfrac{dy}{dx} = \ln 3 \Rightarrow \dfrac{dy}{dx} = y \ln 3 = 3^x \ln 3$.

(Note that $\ln 3$ is a constant, thus the derivative of $x \ln 3$ is $\ln 3$.)

(2) $y' = (2x+1)^x \left\{ \ln(2x+1) + \dfrac{2x}{2x+1} \right\}$

Taking the ln of both sides gives $\ln y = x \ln(2x+1)$,

so $\dfrac{y'}{y} = \ln(2x+1) + \dfrac{2x}{2x+1}$.

$y' = y \left\{ \ln(2x+1) + \dfrac{2x}{2x+1} \right\}$ and $y = (2x+1)^x$, so $y' = (2x+1)^x \left\{ \ln(2x+1) + \dfrac{2x}{2x+1} \right\}$

(3) $5^3 \left(\ln 25 + \dfrac{33}{5} \right)$

Taking the ln of both sides gives

$\ln(f(x)) = (2x+1) \ln(3x^3 + 2x)$,

so $\dfrac{f'(x)}{f(x)} = 2\ln(3x^3 + 2x) + (2x+1) \dfrac{(9x^2 + 2)}{3x^3 + 2x}$

$f(x) = (3x^3 + 2x)^{(2x+1)}$, so $f'(x) = (3x^3 + 2x)^{(2x+1)} \left\{ 2\ln(3x^3 + 2x) + (2x+1) \dfrac{(9x^2 + 2)}{3x^3 + 2x} \right\}$

and $f'(1) = 5^3 \left\{ 2\ln 5 + (3)(\dfrac{11}{5}) \right\} = 125 \left\{ \ln 25 + \dfrac{33}{5} \right\}$.

Solution

(4) 0

Taking the ln of both sides gives $\ln(f(x)) = x\ln(\cos x)$,

so $\dfrac{f'(x)}{f(x)} = \ln(\cos x) + x\dfrac{-\sin x}{\cos x}$.

$f(x) = (\cos x)^x$, so $f'(x) = (\cos x)^x \{\ln(\cos x) - x\tan x\}$, $f'(0) = 0$.

(5) $-\tan x$

Taking the ln of both sides gives $y = \ln(\cos x)$, so $\dfrac{dy}{dx} = \dfrac{-\sin x}{\cos x} = -\tan x$.

04. Derivatives of Parametrically Defined Functions(BC)

A parameter is a concept that appears in CALCULUS BC. In short, when x and y are both written in terms of a third common variable t, we can get the slope $\dfrac{dy}{dx}$ in the following way.

When $x = f(t)$ and $y = g(t)$, and they are both differentiable, we can use

$$\dfrac{dy}{dx} = \dfrac{\dfrac{dy}{dt}}{\dfrac{dx}{dt}}$$ to find the slope.

Let's look at the following examples.

Example 11

Find $\dfrac{dy}{dx}$.

(1) $x = 3\cos\theta,\ y = 5\sin\theta$

(2) $x = 3 + \sin t,\ y = 5 + \cos t$

(3) $x = e^{2t} + 2,\ y = 3e^{t} - 1$

(4) $x = \sin^{3}\theta,\ y = -\cos^{3}\theta$

Answer

(1) $-\dfrac{5}{3}\cot\theta$ (2) $-\tan t$ (3) $\dfrac{3}{2e^{t}}$ (4) $\cot\theta$

Solution

(1) $\dfrac{dy}{dx} = \dfrac{\dfrac{dy}{d\theta}}{\dfrac{dx}{d\theta}} = \dfrac{5\cos\theta}{-3\sin\theta} = -\dfrac{5}{3}\cot\theta$

(2) $\dfrac{dy}{dx} = \dfrac{\dfrac{dy}{dt}}{\dfrac{dx}{dt}} = \dfrac{-\sin t}{\cos t} = -\tan t$

(3) $\dfrac{dy}{dx} = \dfrac{\dfrac{dy}{dt}}{\dfrac{dx}{dt}} = \dfrac{3e^{t}}{2e^{2t}} = \dfrac{3}{2e^{t}}$

(4) $\dfrac{dy}{dx} = \dfrac{\dfrac{dy}{d\theta}}{\dfrac{dx}{d\theta}} = \dfrac{-3\cos^{2}\theta(-\sin\theta)}{3\sin^{2}\theta\cos\theta} = \dfrac{3\cos^{2}\theta\sin\theta}{3\sin^{2}\theta\cos\theta} = \cot\theta$

Let's look at the following example.

Example 12

If $x = t^2 + 1$ and $y = t^4 + 2t^2$, then $\dfrac{d^2y}{dx^2}$ is

ⓐ 1　　　　ⓑ 2　　　　ⓒ 3　　　　ⓓ 4

Answer　ⓑ

Solution

$$\frac{dy}{dx} = \frac{\dfrac{dy}{dt}}{\dfrac{dx}{dt}} = \frac{4t^3 + 4t}{2t} = 2t^2 + 2 \ (t \neq 0)$$

From $\dfrac{d}{dx}\dfrac{dy}{dx} = \dfrac{d}{dx}(2t^2 + 2) = \dfrac{d}{dt}(2t^2 + 2)\dfrac{dt}{dx} = 4t\dfrac{dt}{dx}$. Since $\dfrac{dx}{dt} = 2t$, $\dfrac{dt}{dx} = \dfrac{1}{2t}$.

Therefore, $\dfrac{d^2y}{dx^2} = 4t\dfrac{1}{2t} = 2$.

Supplement

If we differentiate $y = (f \circ g)$, what will we get?

$f \circ g = (f \circ g)(x) = f(g(x))$

$y = f \circ g = f(g(x))$, so $y' = f'(g(x))g'(x)$. (We use chain rule)

Example 13

If $f(x) = x^2 + 2x$ and $g(x) = \sin x$, then $(g \circ f)'$ is

ⓐ $-2\sin(x^2 + 2x)$
ⓑ $-2(x+1)\cos(2x+2)$
ⓒ $2(x+1)\cos(x^2 + 2x)$
ⓓ $\cos(x^2 + 2x)$

Answer ⓒ

Solution

$g \circ f = g(f(x)) = \sin(x^2 + 2x)$, so $(g \circ f)' = (2x+2)\cos(x^2 + 2x) = 2(x+1)\cos(x^2 + 2x)$

Make Sure to Know the Following!

A vector-valued can be expressed as
- $f(t) = (x(t), y(t)) = x(t)i + y(t)j \Rightarrow f'(t) = (x'(t), y'(t)) \Rightarrow f''(t) = (x''(t), y''(t))$

Example 14

If f is a vector-valued function defined by $f(t) = (e^t, t^3 - 2t^2)$, then $f'(t) =$

ⓐ $(e^t, 3t^2 - 4t)$ ⓑ $(e^t, 6t - 4)$ ⓒ $(e^{2t}, 3t^2 - 4t)$ ⓓ $(e^t, 6)$

Answer ⓐ

Solution

$f'(t) = (e^t, 3t^2 - 4t)$

Differentiation

Problem 8

1. If $x=e^t$ and $y=\tan(3t)$, find $\dfrac{dy}{dx}$.

2. If $x(t)=t^2+1$ and $y(t)=t^4-1$, for $t>0$, then in terms of t, $\dfrac{d^2y}{dx^2}=$
   ⓐ t^2　　ⓑ 1　　ⓒ 2　　ⓓ $-t^2$

3. If f is a vector-valued function defined by $f(t)=(\sin(3t), e^{2t})$, then $f'(t)=$
   ⓐ $(\cos(3t), e^{3t})$
   ⓑ $(3\cos(3t), 2e^{2t})$
   ⓒ $(\cos(3t), 2e^{2t})$
   ⓓ $(-3\cos(3t), 2e^{2t})$

Answer
(1) $\dfrac{3\sec^2(3t)}{e^t}$　　(2) ⓒ　　(3) ⓑ

Solution

(1) $\dfrac{3\sec^2(3t)}{e^t}$

$\dfrac{dy}{dx}=\dfrac{\frac{dy}{dt}}{\frac{dx}{dt}}=\dfrac{3\sec^2(3t)}{e^t}$

(2) $\dfrac{dy}{dx}=\dfrac{\frac{dy}{dt}}{\frac{dx}{dt}}=\dfrac{4t^3}{2t}=2t^2$

$\dfrac{d^2y}{dx^2}=\dfrac{d}{dx}\dfrac{dy}{dx}=\dfrac{d}{dx}(2t^2) \Rightarrow \dfrac{dt}{dx}\dfrac{d}{dt}(2t^2) \Rightarrow \dfrac{dt}{dx}(4t). \dfrac{dx}{dt}=2t$, so $\dfrac{dt}{dx}=\dfrac{1}{2t}$.

Therefore, $(\dfrac{1}{2t})(4t)=2.$

(3) $f'(t)=(3\cos(3t), 2e^{2t})$

06 Exercise

01~36. Find $f'(x)$.

01 $f(x) = (3x^2 - 2)\cos x$

02 $f(x) = (5x^3 + 10x + 2)^3$

03 $f(x) = \sqrt{2x^3 - 7x}$

04 $f(x) = \dfrac{3x}{x^2 + 1}$

05 $f(x) = g(3x^2 + 5x)$ (find the answer in terms of $g(x)$)

06 $f(x) = \sqrt{\sin 5x}$

07 $f(x) = \cos^2(10x^2 + 2x)$

08 $f(x) = \sin(1 + \tan x)$

09 $f(x) = 3^{5x^2 + 10x}$

10 $f(x) = \log_2(\tan 2x)$

11 $f(x) = \ln(\sec x + \cot x)$ $\left(0 < x < \dfrac{\pi}{2}\right)$

12 $f(x) = 2^x + \csc 3x$

13 $f(x) = \sqrt{3 - 2x}$

14 $f(x) = \dfrac{2}{(5x+2)^2}$

15 $f(x) = \ln(\sin 3x) \quad (0 < x < \frac{\pi}{3})$

16 $f(x) = e^x \sin 3x$

17 $f(x) = \cos^{-1} 2x - \sqrt{1-x^2}$

18 $f(x) = \tan^{-1} 5x$

19 $f(x) = \sec 5x$

20 $f(x) = \sqrt{\cot^{-1}(3x^2)}$

21 Find $\dfrac{dy}{dx}$ for $x^2 - y^2 = 3$.

22 Find the derivative of $x^2 + 3y^2 + y = 2$ at $(\sqrt{2}, 0)$.

23 Find $\dfrac{d^2y}{dx^2}$ of $3y^2 - y = 5x^2 + 3x$ at $(0, 0)$.

24 Find $\dfrac{dy}{dx}$ of $x^3y^2 = 3$ at $(1, \sqrt{3})$.

25 Find $\dfrac{dy}{dx}$ of $x^3 + y^2 = 5xy$.

26 Find $\dfrac{d^2y}{dx^2}$ of $y^2 = 5x^2 + 2x$.

27 Find $\dfrac{d^2y}{dx^2}$ for $\cos x + 3 = \sin y$ at $(0, 0)$.

28 If $x = e^t + 1$ and $y = t^2 + 2$, then find $\dfrac{dy}{dx}$.

29 If $f(x) = 3^x$ and $g(x) = \cos x$, then find $(f \circ g)'$.

x	$f(x)$	$f'(x)$	$g(x)$	$g'(x)$
1	−2	5	−3	1
2	3	2	−2	−5
3	1	4	2	2

30 The table above gives values of f, f', g, and g' at selected values of x. If $h(x) = (f \circ g)(x)$, then $h'(3) =$

ⓐ −4   ⓑ 1   ⓒ 4   ⓓ 8

Differentiation

31 Which of the following is false?

ⓐ $\dfrac{d}{dx}(\tan^2(3x)) = 6\tan(3x)\sec^2(3x)$

ⓑ $\dfrac{d}{dx}(x^3 e^{\ln(3x)}) = 12x^3$

ⓒ $\dfrac{d}{dx}(\arcsin(3x)) = \dfrac{3}{\sqrt{1-9x^2}}$

ⓓ $\dfrac{d}{dx}(\sqrt[3]{x^5+2x^2}) = \dfrac{1}{3\sqrt[3]{x^5+2x^2}}$

32 If $x^2 - y^2 = 3$, what is the value of $\dfrac{d^2y}{dx^2}$ at the point $(2, 1)$?

ⓐ -6 ⓑ -3 ⓒ 0 ⓓ 1

33 If $\dfrac{dy}{dx} = \sqrt{3y^4 + y^2}$, find $\dfrac{d^2y}{dx^2}$.

34

(1) If $f(x) = (\sin 2x)^{3x}$ and x is an acute angle, find $f'(\dfrac{\pi}{4})$.

(2) If $\tan x = e^{2y}$, $0 < x < \dfrac{\pi}{2}$, find $\dfrac{dy}{dx}$.

35 $\dfrac{d}{dx}(x^{(x^2-2x)}) =$

ⓐ $x^{(x^2-2x)}(2x-2)\ln(x-2)$
ⓑ $x^{(x^2-2x)}\{\ln x + (x-2)\}$
ⓒ $(2x-2)\ln x + (x-2)$
ⓓ $x^{(x^2-2x)}\{(2x-2)\ln x + (x-2)\}$

36(BC) If f is a vector-valued function defined by $f(t) = (\cos(2t), e^{5t})$, then $f''(t) =$

ⓐ $(4\cos(2t), 25e^{5t})$
ⓑ $(4\cos(2t), 5e^{5t})$
ⓒ $(-4\cos(2t), 25e^{5t})$
ⓓ $(-2\sin(2t), 5e^{5t})$

Differentiation

06 Answers & Solutions

01 $-3x^2\sin x + 6x\cos x + 2\sin x$

$f'(x) = 6x\cos x + (3x^2 - 2)(-\sin x) = 6x\cos x - (3x^2 - 2)\sin x$

02 $15(5x^3 + 10x + 2)^2(3x^2 + 2)$

$f'(x) = 3(5x^3 + 10x + 2)^{3-1}(15x^2 + 10) = 3(5x^3 + 10x + 2)^2(15x^2 + 10)$
$= 3(5x^3 + 10x + 2)^2 \times 5(3x^2 + 2)$

03 $\dfrac{6x^2 - 7}{2\sqrt{2x^3 - 7x}}$

$f'(x) = \dfrac{1}{2}(2x^3 - 7x)^{-\frac{1}{2}}(6x^2 - 7)$

04 $\dfrac{-3(x^2 - 1)}{(x^2 + 1)^2}$

$f'(x) = \dfrac{3(x^2 + 1) - 3x \times 2x}{(x^2 + 1)^2} = \dfrac{3x^2 + 3 - 6x^2}{(x^2 + 1)^2} = \dfrac{-3(x^2 - 1)}{(x^2 + 1)^2}$

05 $(6x + 5)g'(3x^2 + 5x)$

$f'(x) = (6x + 5)g'(3x^2 + 5x)$

06 $\dfrac{5\cos 5x}{2\sqrt{\sin 5x}}$

$f'(x) = \dfrac{1}{2}(\sin 5x)^{-\frac{1}{2}}\cos(5x)5 = \dfrac{5\cos 5x}{2\sqrt{\sin 5x}}$

07 $-2(10x + 1)\sin(20x^2 + 4x)$

$f'(x) = 2\cos(10x^2 + 2x)(-\sin(10x^2 + 2x))(20x + 2)$
$= -4(10x + 1)\cos(10x^2 + 2x)\sin(10x^2 + 2x) = -2(10x + 1)\sin 2(10x^2 + 2x)$

- $\sin 2x = 2\sin x \cos x$

08 $\sec^2 x \cos(1+\tan x)$

$f'(x) = \cos(1+\tan x) \times \sec^2 x = \sec^2 x \cos(1+\tan x)$

09 $10(x+1)3^{5x^2+10x}\ln 3$

$f'(x) = 3^{5x^2+10x}\ln 3 \times (10x+10) = 10(x+1)3^{5x^2+10x}\ln 3$

10 $\dfrac{2\sec^2 2x}{(\tan 2x)\ln 2}$

$y = f(x) = \log_2(\tan 2x) \Rightarrow 2^y = 2^{\log_2(\tan 2x)} = \tan 2x$

Differentiating both sides, we have $2^y \ln 2 \dfrac{dy}{dx} = \sec^2 2x \times 2 \Rightarrow f'(x) = \dfrac{2\sec^2 2x}{(\tan 2x)\ln 2}$

11 $\dfrac{\sec x \tan x - \csc^2 x}{\sec x + \cot x}$

$f'(x) = \dfrac{1}{\sec x + \cot x}(\sec x \tan x - \csc^2 x) = \dfrac{\sec x \tan x - \csc^2 x}{\sec x + \cot x}$

12 $2^x \ln 2 - 3\csc 3x \cot 3x$

$f'(x) = 2^x \ln 2 - 3\csc 3x \cot 3x$

13 $-\dfrac{1}{\sqrt{3-2x}}$

$f'(x) = \dfrac{1}{2}(3-2x)^{-\frac{1}{2}}(-2) = -\dfrac{1}{\sqrt{3-2x}}$

14 $\dfrac{-20}{(5x+2)^3}$

$f(x) = 2(5x+2)^{-2}$, so $f'(x) = -4(5x+2)^{-3} \cdot 5$

15 $3\cot 3x$

$f'(x) = \dfrac{1}{\sin 3x} \times \cos 3x \times 3 = \dfrac{3\cos 3x}{\sin 3x} = 3\cot 3x$

16 $e^x(\sin 3x + 3\cos 3x)$

$f'(x) = e^x \sin 3x + 3e^x \cos 3x$

17 $-\dfrac{2}{\sqrt{1-4x^2}}+\dfrac{x}{\sqrt{1-x^2}}$

$f'(x)=-\dfrac{1}{\sqrt{1-(2x)^2}}\times 2-\dfrac{1}{2}(1-x^2)^{-\frac{1}{2}}\times(-2x)=-\dfrac{2}{\sqrt{1-4x^2}}+\dfrac{x}{\sqrt{1-x^2}}$

18 $\dfrac{5}{1+25x^2}$

$f'(x)=\dfrac{5}{1+(5x)^2}=\dfrac{5}{1+25x^2}$

19 $5\sec 5x\tan 5x$

$f'(x)=5\sec 5x\tan 5x$

20 $\dfrac{-3x}{\sqrt{\cot^{-1}(3x^2)}\,(1+9x^4)}$

$f(x)=\{\cot^{-1}(3x^2)\}^{\frac{1}{2}}$,

so $f'(x)=\dfrac{1}{2}\{\cot^{-1}(3x^2)\}^{-\frac{1}{2}}\dfrac{-6x}{1+(3x^2)^2}=\dfrac{-3x}{\sqrt{\cot^{-1}(3x^2)}\,(1+9x^4)}$.

21 $\dfrac{x}{y}$

$2x-2y\dfrac{dy}{dx}=0$,

so $\dfrac{dy}{dx}=\dfrac{x}{y}$

22 $-2\sqrt{2}$

$2x+6yy'+y'=0$.

Substituting $x=\sqrt{2}$ and $y=0$ gives $2\sqrt{2}+y'=0$, so $y'=\dfrac{dy}{dx}=-2\sqrt{2}$.

23 44

From $(6y-1)\dfrac{dy}{dx}=10x+3$, we get $\dfrac{dy}{dx}=\dfrac{10x+3}{6y-1}$, so

$$\dfrac{d}{dx}(\dfrac{dy}{dx})=\dfrac{d}{dx}(\dfrac{10x+3}{6y-1})=\dfrac{10(6y-1)-6(10x+3)\dfrac{dy}{dx}}{(6y-1)^2}.$$

Therefore, $\dfrac{d^2y}{dx^2}=\dfrac{10(6y-1)-6(10x+3)\dfrac{10x+3}{6y-1}}{(6y-1)^2}$,

and if we substitute $x=0$ and $y=0$, $\dfrac{10(-1)-6(3)\dfrac{3}{-1}}{(-1)^2}=\dfrac{-10+54}{1}=44.$

24 $-\dfrac{3\sqrt{3}}{2}$

$3x^2y^2+2x^3y\dfrac{dy}{dx}=0$, so $\dfrac{dy}{dx}=-\dfrac{3x^2y^2}{2x^3y}=-\dfrac{3y}{2x}$.

Substituting $x=1$ and $y=\sqrt{3}$ gives $-\dfrac{3\times\sqrt{3}}{2\times 1}=-\dfrac{3\sqrt{3}}{2}.$

25 $\dfrac{3x^2-5y}{5x-2y}$

$3x^2+2y\dfrac{dy}{dx}=5y+5x\dfrac{dy}{dx}$, so $(5x-2y)\dfrac{dy}{dx}=3x^2-5y$ and $\dfrac{dy}{dx}=\dfrac{3x^2-5y}{5x-2y}.$

26 $\dfrac{5y^2-(5x+1)^2}{y^3}$

$2y\dfrac{dy}{dx}=10x+2$, so $\dfrac{dy}{dx}=\dfrac{5x+1}{y}$,

$\dfrac{d}{dx}(\dfrac{dy}{dx})=\dfrac{d}{dx}(\dfrac{5x+1}{y})=\dfrac{5y-(5x+1)\dfrac{dy}{dx}}{y^2}$ and $\dfrac{dy}{dx}=\dfrac{5x+1}{y}$.

Therefore, $\dfrac{d^2y}{dx^2}=\dfrac{5y-(5x+1)\dfrac{(5x+1)}{y}}{y^2}=\dfrac{5y-\dfrac{(5x+1)^2}{y}}{y^2}=\dfrac{5y^2-(5x+1)^2}{y^3}.$

Differentiation

27 -1

$-\sin x = \cos y \dfrac{dy}{dx}$, so $\dfrac{dy}{dx} = -\dfrac{\sin x}{\cos y}$

$\dfrac{d}{dx}(\dfrac{dy}{dx}) = \dfrac{d}{dx}(\dfrac{-\sin x}{\cos y}) = \dfrac{-\cos x \cos y + \sin x(-\sin y)\dfrac{dy}{dx}}{\cos^2 y}$ and $\dfrac{dy}{dx} = -\dfrac{\sin x}{\cos y}$, so we have

$\dfrac{-\cos x \cos y + \sin x \sin y \dfrac{\sin x}{\cos y}}{\cos^2 y}$. Substituting $x=0$ and $y=0$ gives -1.

28 $\dfrac{2t}{e^t}$

$\dfrac{dx}{dt} = e^t$, $\dfrac{dy}{dt} = 2t$, so $\dfrac{dy}{dx} = \dfrac{\dfrac{dy}{dt}}{\dfrac{dx}{dt}} = \dfrac{2t}{e^t}$

29 $-\sin x (3^{\cos x})\ln 3$

$f \circ g = f(g(x))$, so $(f \circ g)' = f(g(x))' = f'(g(x))g'(x)$, $f'(x) = 3^x \ln 3$ and $g'(x) = -\sin x$, so $(f \circ g)' = f'(g(x))g'(x) = (3^{\cos x}\ln 3)(-\sin x)$ becomes $-(\sin x)(3^{\cos x})\ln 3$.

30 ⓒ

$h(x) = f(g(x))$, so $h'(x) = f'(g(x))g'(x)$.
Substituting 3 for x gives $h'(3) = f'(g(3))g'(3) = f'(2)g'(3) = 2 \times 2 = 4$.

31 ⓓ

ⓐ $\dfrac{d}{dx}(\tan(3x))^2 = 2(\tan(3x))\sec^2(3x)3 = 6\tan(3x)\sec^2(3x)$: **True**

ⓑ $\dfrac{d}{dx}(x^3 e^{\ln(3x)}) = \dfrac{d}{dx}(3x^4) = 12x^3$: **True**

ⓒ $\dfrac{d}{dx}(\sin^{-1}(3x)) = \dfrac{1}{\sqrt{1-(3x)^2}} \times 3 = \dfrac{3}{\sqrt{1-9x^2}}$: **True**

ⓓ $\dfrac{d}{dx}(x^5+2x^2)^{\frac{1}{3}} = \dfrac{1}{3}(x^5+2x^2)^{-\frac{2}{3}}(5x^4+4x) = \dfrac{(5x^4+4x)}{3\sqrt[3]{(x^5+2x^2)^2}}$: **False**

AP Calculus AB & BC Rewritten from the Beginning

32 ⓑ

$2x - (2y)\dfrac{dy}{dx} = 0$, so $\dfrac{dy}{dx} = \dfrac{x}{y}$. $\dfrac{d}{dx}\dfrac{dy}{dx} = \dfrac{d}{dx}(\dfrac{x}{y}) = \dfrac{y - (x)\dfrac{dy}{dx}}{y^2}$ and $\dfrac{dy}{dx} = \dfrac{x}{y}$, so $\dfrac{d^2y}{dx^2} = \dfrac{y - \dfrac{x^2}{y}}{y^2}$.

Substituting $x = 2$ and $y = 1$ gives $\dfrac{d^2y}{dx^2} = \dfrac{1 - \dfrac{2^2}{1}}{1^2} = -3$.

33 $6y^3 + y$

$\dfrac{d^2y}{dx^2} = \dfrac{d}{dx}\dfrac{dy}{dx} = \dfrac{d}{dx}(\sqrt{3y^4 + y^2}) = \dfrac{d}{dx}(3y^4 + y^2)^{\frac{1}{2}}$

$= \dfrac{dy}{dx}\dfrac{d}{dy}(3y^4 + y^2)^{\frac{1}{2}} = \dfrac{dy}{dx}\dfrac{1}{2}(3y^4 + y^2)^{-\frac{1}{2}}(12y^3 + 2y) = \dfrac{dy}{dx}\dfrac{12y^3 + 2y}{2\sqrt{3y^4 + y^2}}$

$\dfrac{dy}{dx} = \sqrt{3y^4 + y^2}$, so $\dfrac{d^2y}{dx^2} = \sqrt{3y^4 + y^2}\dfrac{12y^3 + 2y}{2\sqrt{3y^4 + y^2}} = 6y^3 + y$.

34

(1) 0

Taking the ln of each side gives $\ln f(x) = (3x)\ln(\sin 2x)$.

Thus, $\dfrac{f'(x)}{f(x)} = 3\ln(\sin 2x) + (3x) \times \dfrac{\cos 2x}{\sin 2x} \times 2$.

Since $f(x) = (\sin 2x)^{3x}$, $f'(x) = (\sin 2x)^{3x}\left[3\ln(\sin 2x) + 6x\dfrac{\cos 2x}{\sin 2x}\right]$.

And we have

$f'(\dfrac{\pi}{4}) = (\sin 2(\dfrac{\pi}{4}))^{3(\frac{\pi}{4})}[3\ln(\sin 2(\dfrac{\pi}{4})) + \dfrac{6(\dfrac{\pi}{4})\cos 2(\dfrac{\pi}{4})}{\sin 2(\dfrac{\pi}{4})})] = (1)^{\frac{3\pi}{4}}[3\ln 1 + \dfrac{\dfrac{3\pi}{2}(0)}{1}] = 1(0 + 0) = 0$.

(2) $\dfrac{1}{2}\sec x \csc x$ or $\csc 2x$ or $\dfrac{1}{2\sin x \cos x}$

Taking the ln of each side gives $\ln(\tan x) = 2y$.

Thus, $y = \dfrac{1}{2}\ln(\tan x)$.

$\dfrac{dy}{dx} = \dfrac{1}{2}\dfrac{1}{\tan x}\sec^2 x = \dfrac{\sec^2 x}{2\tan x} = \dfrac{1}{2}\sec x \csc x$

35 ⓓ

Let $y = x^{(x^2 - 2x)}$. Then, taking the ln of each side gives $\ln y = (x^2 - 2x)\ln x$, so $\dfrac{y'}{y} = (2x - 2)\ln x + (x^2 - 2x)\dfrac{1}{x}$. Since $y = x^{(x^2 - 2x)}$, $y' = \dfrac{dy}{dx} = x^{(x^2 - 2x)}\{(2x - 2)\ln x + (x - 2)\}$.

36 ⓒ

$f'(t) = (-2\sin(2t), 5e^{5t})$ and $f''(t) = (-4\cos(2t), 25e^{5t})$

AP Calculus AB & BC Rewritten from the Beginning

A Brief History of Calculus (Part 1)

In the 17th century, the German mathematician Gottfried Wilhelm Leibniz published a paper on "a new method for finding maxima and minima, applicable even to fractions and irrational numbers, along with a special kind of calculation for tangents". Leibniz received much praise for his work, but Isaac Newton, who found this displeasing, accused him of being a thief.

Newton had previously defined the concept of instantaneous velocity of a rotating ellipse, which essentially introduced the idea of differentiation. However, he shared this idea only with a few fellow mathematicians and delayed publishing it.

The plagiarism dispute was investigated by the Royal Society of London, the most prestigious scientific institution in Europe at the time. The Society concluded that Leibniz had plagiarized Newton's theory—but notably, the president of the Royal Society at that time was Isaac Newton himself. This controversy led to academic tensions between Britain and Germany, severely disrupting scientific exchange between the two countries.

Newton

Leibniz

Differentiation

03 (T, D, M, L)

01. Tangents and Normals
02. Derivatives of Inverse Functions
03. Mean Value Theorem and Rolle's Theorem
04. L'Hopital's Rule

Before we begin

Four topics are combined in this chapter.
Derivatives of inverse functions, the Mean Value Theorem, and Rolle's Theorem are simple, but it might get a bit tricky when solving a problem. Let's review it over and over.

01. Tangents and Normals

I. Tangents

We can get the equation of the tangent line using the following steps.

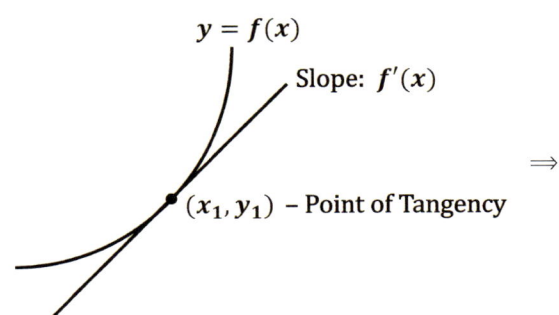

1. Find the slope $\dfrac{dy}{dx} = f'(x_1)$.

2. Using the fact that the line passes through the point of tangency (x_1, y_1), we get the equation of the tangent line as follows:

$$y - y_1 = f'(x_1)(x - x_1)$$

II. Normals

We can get the equation of the normal line using the following steps.

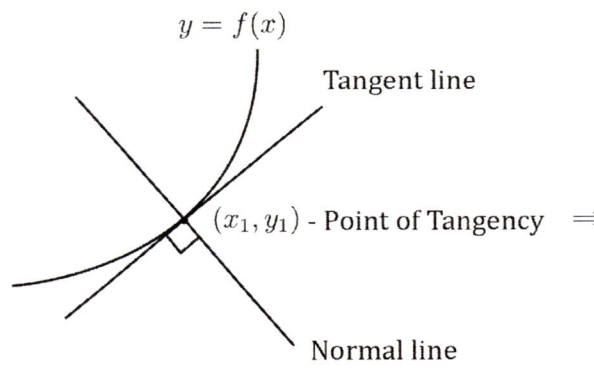

1. Find the slope of the tangent line
$\dfrac{dy}{dx} = f'(x_1)$.

2. Find the slope of the normal line
$-\dfrac{dx}{dy} = -\dfrac{1}{f'(x_1)}$.

(※ When two lines are perpendicular, the product of their slopes is -1.)

3. Using the fact that the line passes through the point of tangency (x_1, y_1), we get the equation of the tangent line as follows:

$$y - y_1 = -\dfrac{1}{f'(x_1)}(x - x_1)$$

Differentiation

III. Tangent to Parametrically Defined Curve

$$\frac{dy}{dx} = \frac{\frac{dy}{dt}}{\frac{dx}{dt}} = \frac{\frac{dy}{d\theta}}{\frac{dx}{d\theta}}$$

All are the same as before. You use third parameter (t or θ) to compute $\frac{dy}{dx}$. What is the difference? When you want to know the slope at $t = t_1$ (or $(x, y) = (x(t_1), y(t_1))$) substitute $t = t_1$ into $\frac{\frac{dy}{dt}}{\frac{dx}{dt}}$.

IV. Slope

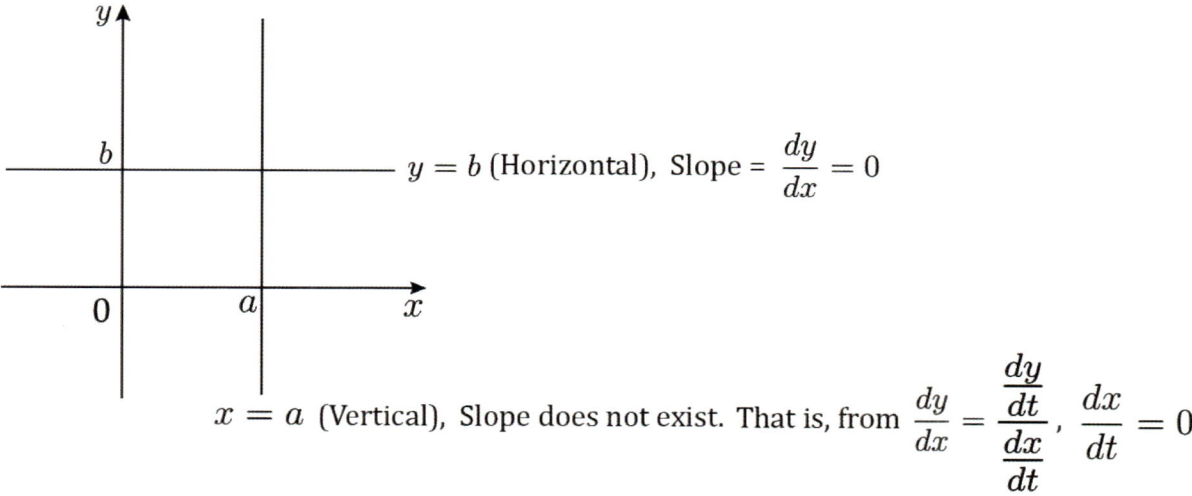

$y = b$ (Horizontal), Slope = $\frac{dy}{dx} = 0$

$x = a$ (Vertical), Slope does not exist. That is, from $\frac{dy}{dx} = \frac{\frac{dy}{dt}}{\frac{dx}{dt}}$, $\frac{dx}{dt} = 0$

AP Calculus AB & BC Rewritten from the Beginning

※ **Note that some tangent lines are special.**

① If $\dfrac{dy}{dx} = f'(x_1) = 0$ then at point (x_1, y_1) the tangent line has a slope of zero: it is parallel to the x-axis. Equation of the tangent line is $y = b$.

② On some other cases, when the given curve is NOT a function (for instance, think of $(x, y) = (x(t), y(t)) = (\cos t, \sin t)$, which is the unit circle), from $\dfrac{dy}{dx} = \dfrac{\frac{dy}{dt}}{\frac{dx}{dt}}$, if $\dfrac{dx}{dt} = 0$ then $\dfrac{dy}{dx} = \dfrac{\frac{dy}{dt}}{\frac{dx}{dt}}$ is NOT defined. What is this situation?

See $(x(0), y(0)) = (\cos 0, \sin 0) = (1, 0)$ below. At $t = 0$ and $(x(0), y(0)) = (1, 0)$, $\dfrac{dx}{dt} = -\sin t = -\sin 0 = 0.$

But geometrically, we know that the tangent line at $(x(0), y(0)) = (1, 0)$ is a vertical line!

As such, for some other cases, $\dfrac{dy}{dx} = \dfrac{\frac{dy}{dt}}{\frac{dx}{dt}}$, $\dfrac{dx}{dt} = 0$, the tangent line is perpendicular to the x-axis and parallel to the y-axis: of the form $x = a$.

That is, from $\dfrac{dy}{dx} = \dfrac{\frac{dy}{dt}}{\frac{dx}{dt}}$, $\dfrac{dx}{dt} = 0$ (※ t is a parameter)

Differentiation

Let's look at the following examples.

Example 15

Find the equation of the tangent line to the graph of $y = x^3 + 2$ at $x = 2$.
① Find the slope.
② Use the point of tangency.
③ Find the equation of the line tangent

Answer $y = 12x - 14$

Solution

① $f'(x) = 3x^2$. So, slope is $f'(2) = 3 \cdot 2^2 = 12$

② At $x = 2$, $y = (2)^3 + 2 = 10$. Thus the point of tangency is $(2, 10)$, the equation of the tangent line is $y - 10 = 12(x - 2)$, which gives $y = 12x - 14$

Example 16

Find the equation of the normal line to the graph of $y = \sqrt{2x}$ at $x = 2$.

Answer $y = -2x + 6$

Solution

① $f'(x) = \frac{1}{2}(2x)^{-\frac{1}{2}} \times 2 = \frac{1}{\sqrt{2x}}$. So, tangent line slope is $f'(2) = \frac{1}{\sqrt{2 \cdot 2}} = \frac{1}{2}$.

② Normal line slope is $-\frac{1}{f'(2)} = \frac{1}{-\frac{1}{2}} = -2$

③ At $x = 2$, $y = \sqrt{2 \times 2} = 2$. Thus, the point of tangency is $(2, 2)$, so $y - 2 = -2(x - 2)$, which gives $y = -2x + 6$

AP Calculus AB & BC Rewritten from the Beginning

Example 17

Find the equation of the line that is tangent to the curve $(5t^2+t, 4t^2-2t+2)$ at the point where $t=0$.

Answer

$y=-2x+2$

Solution

$x=5t^2+t$, $y=4t^2-2t+2$, so the slope is $\dfrac{dy}{dx}=\dfrac{\frac{dy}{dt}}{\frac{dx}{dt}}=\dfrac{8t-2}{10t+1}=-\dfrac{2}{1}$.

When $t=0$, $x=5(0)+(0)=0$ and $y=4(0)-2(0)+2=2$.

Thus the point of tangency is $(0,2)$, the corresponding tangent line is $y-2=-2x$, which gives $y=-2x+2$.

Differentiation

● ····· **Problem 1**

(1) Find the slope of the line tangent to the curve $y^3 + xy = 1$ at $(0, 1)$.

(2) Let f be a differentiable function with $f(-2) = 5$ and $f'(-2) = 3$, and let g be the function defined as $g(x) = x^2 f(x)$. Find the equation of the line tangent to the graph of g at the point where $x = -2$.

(3) At what point on the graph $y = x^2$ is the tangent line parallel to the line $2x - y = 5$?
   ⓐ (0, 0)   ⓑ (0, −1)   ⓒ (1, 1)   ⓓ (−1, 2)

● ····· **Answer**   (1) $-\dfrac{1}{3}$ (2) $y = -8x + 4$ (3) ⓒ

● ····· **Solution**

(1) $-\dfrac{1}{3}$

$3y^2 \dfrac{dy}{dx} + y + x \dfrac{dy}{dx} = 0$, so $(3y^2 + x) \dfrac{dy}{dx} = -y$ and thus $\dfrac{dy}{dx} = -\dfrac{y}{3y^2 + x}$.

Therefore, $\dfrac{dy}{dx} = -\dfrac{1}{3}$ at $(0, 1)$. Thus, the slope is $-\dfrac{1}{3}$.

(2) $y = -8x + 4$

The slope of the tangent line is $g'(-2)$ and $g'(x) = 2xf(x) + x^2 f'(x)$, so
$g'(-2) = -4f(-2) + 4f'(-2) = -20 + 12 = -8$.
$g(-2) = 4f(-2) = 20$, so it crosses $(-2, 20)$.
Thus, $y - 20 = -8(x + 2)$, which gives $y = -8x + 4$.

(3) ⓒ

The slope of $y = x^2$ is $y' = 2x$. Parallel lines have the same slope, so if the tangent line at (x_0, y_0) is parallel to $y = 2x - 5$, $2x_0 = 2$.
Thus, $x_0 = 1$ and $y_0 = (1)^2 = 1$. So, the point is $(1, 1)$ and the answer is ⓒ.

AP Calculus AB & BC Rewritten from the Beginning

● ········ **Problem 2**

(1) Find the equation of the line tangent to $(\sin\theta, \cos\theta)$ at the point where $\theta = \dfrac{\pi}{3}$.

(2) A curve P is defined by the parametric equations $x = t^2 - 2t + 3$ and $y = t$. Find the equation of the line tangent to the graph of P at the point $(2, 1)$.

(3) For what values of t does the curve given by the parametric equations $x = \dfrac{1}{3}t^3 - \dfrac{1}{2}t^2 + 5$ and $y = t^4 + 3t^3 + 2t^2 + 5t - 3$ have a vertical tangent?

ⓐ 0 ⓑ 0 and 1 ⓒ 1 ⓓ −1, 0 and 1

● ········ **Answer** (1) $y = -\sqrt{3}\,x + 2$ (2) $x = 2$ (3) ⓑ

● ········ **Solution**

(1) $y = -\sqrt{3}\,x + 2$

$x = \sin\theta, y = \cos\theta$, so $\dfrac{dy}{dx} = \dfrac{\frac{dy}{d\theta}}{\frac{dx}{d\theta}} = -\dfrac{\sin\theta}{\cos\theta} = -\tan\theta$. When $\theta = \dfrac{\pi}{3}$, $\dfrac{dy}{dx} = -\sqrt{3}$. Also, the tangent line passes $(\sin\dfrac{\pi}{3}, \cos\dfrac{\pi}{3})$, that is, $(\dfrac{\sqrt{3}}{2}, \dfrac{1}{2})$. Therefore, the equation of the line is: $y - \dfrac{1}{2} = -\sqrt{3}(x - \dfrac{\sqrt{3}}{2})$. $y = -\sqrt{3}\,x + \dfrac{3}{2} + \dfrac{1}{2}$, which gives $y = -\sqrt{3}\,x + 2$.

(2) $x = 2$

The slope is $\dfrac{dy}{dx} = \dfrac{\frac{dy}{dt}}{\frac{dx}{dt}} = \dfrac{1}{2t - 2}$. $y = 1$, so $t = 1$. When $t = 1$, $\dfrac{dx}{dt} = 0$, so the slope does not exist. Thus, there is a vertical line. Thus, $x = 2$.

(3) ⓑ

$\dfrac{dy}{dx} = \dfrac{\frac{dy}{dt}}{\frac{dx}{dt}}$. Therefore, the graph has a vertical tangent if and only if $\dfrac{dx}{dt} = t^2 - t = 0$, which gives $t = 0, 1$. The answer is ⓑ.

Differentiation

02. Derivatives of Inverse Functions

The graph of the inverse function $y = f^{-1}(x)$ is symmetric to the graph of $y = f(x)$ about the graph of $y = x$. Also, we can only get $y = f^{-1}(x)$ for the interval where $y = f(x)$ is strictly increasing or decreasing.

For example, in the case of the inverse function of $f(x) = 2x$, we exchange x and y to get $f^{-1}(x) = \frac{1}{2}x$. The reason we can find the inverse function easily is because the function $f(x) = 2x$ is increasing on all real numbers. On the other hand, let's think of finding the inverse function of $f(x) = \sin x$. Since this function is not strictly increasing or decreasing on all real numbers, we can only obtain the inverse function on the interval from $-\frac{\pi}{2}$ to $\frac{\pi}{2}$, where the sine function is increasing.

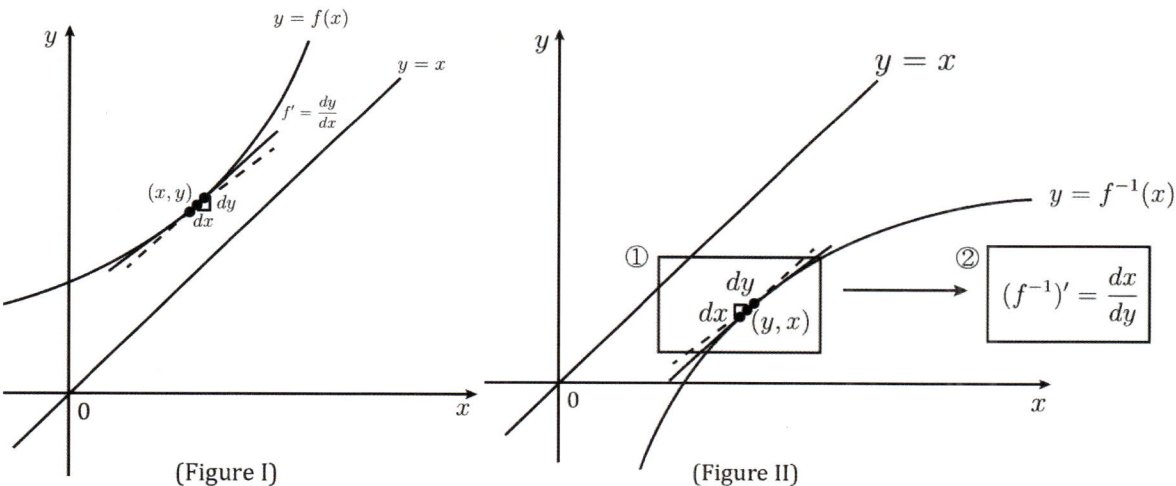

(Figure I)   (Figure II)

In the (Figure I) above, if we reflect the graph of $y = f(x)$ and $y = f'(x) = \frac{dy}{dx}$ about the graph of $y = x$, we get the following (Figure II).

From ① and ② in (Figure II), we can see that the slope of the tangent line of f^{-1} is $\dfrac{dx}{dy}$. We can calculate this using the slope of the tangent line of $y=f(x)$ by $\dfrac{dx}{dy} = \dfrac{1}{\frac{dy}{dx}} = \dfrac{1}{f'(x)}$.

Therefore, the following relation holds, and we must always keep this in mind.

Make Sure to Know the Following!

(x,y) is a point on $y=f(x)$ and the value of y must be used here.

$$(f^{-1})'(\boxed{y}) = \dfrac{dx}{dy} = \dfrac{1}{\frac{dy}{dx}} = \dfrac{1}{f'(\boxed{x})}$$

(x,y) is a point on $y=f(x)$ and we use $y=f(x)$ and the value of y to obtain x.

(x,y) is a point on $y=f(x)$ and the value of x must be used here.

Supplement

Question 1. Which of the following graphs are "functions"?

(A)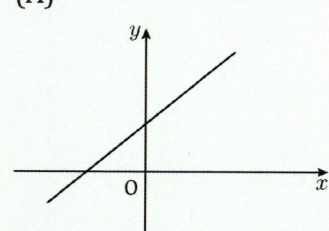
(B)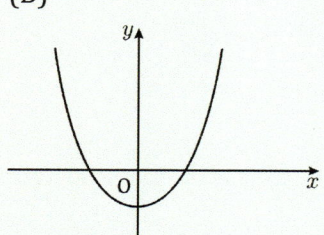
(C)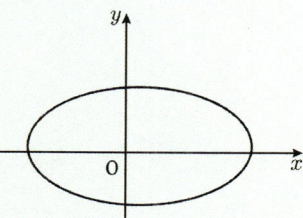

Answer: (A), (B)
A function must have exactly one value of y for each value of x.

Question 2. Which of the following maps are "functions"?

(A)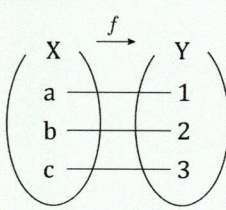
(B)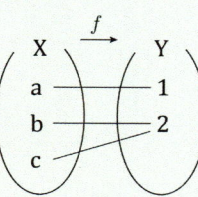
(C)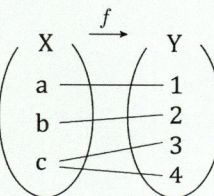

Answer: (A), (B)
A function must have exactly one value of y for each value of x.

Question 3. Which of the following has inverse functions?

(A)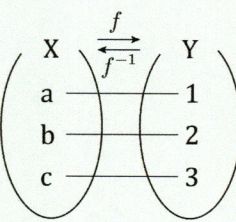
(B)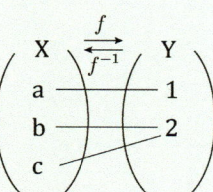
(C)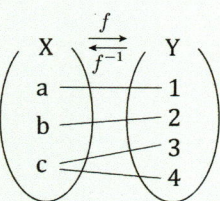

Answer: (A)
In order to have inverse function, not only that each x has exactly one corresponding y but also that each y also has exactly one corresponding x. For (B), $y=2$ has two corresponding values of x; $x=b$ and $x=c$. (C) is not even a function, so there is no inverse function.

Supplement

Question 4. Does every "function" has an inverse function?
Answer is NO! Go back to Question 2. (A) and (B) are functions, but (B) does not have an inverse function.

Question 5. When does inverse function exist?
A function has an inverse function if it gives one-to-one correspondence between x and y.

Question 6. Which graph from Question 1 has an inverse function?
Only (A) has an inverse function. What can we see from the graphs? If a function is one-to-one correspondence, then it must be either strictly increasing or strictly decreasing! (B) is a function but it is not strictly increasing nor strictly decreasing; it is not on-to-one correspondence, and so there is no inverse function.

[Conclusion]
A function f has an inverse function on $[a,b]$ if f is either strictly increasing or strictly decreasing.

Let's look at the following examples to understand this better.

Example 18

If $f(x) = x+2$ and $g(x) = f^{-1}(x)$, then find $g'(3)$.

Answer   1

Solution

Step 1. $f'(x) = (x+2)' = 1$.

Step 2. $g'(3) = (f^{-1})'(3) = (f^{-1})'(y) = \dfrac{1}{f'(x)}$.

Step 3. Now, y is 3. What should be the corresponding x?

$3 = y = x+2$ and so we get $x=1$.

Therefore, $g'(3) = \dfrac{1}{f'(1)} = 1$.

Example 19

Suppose $f(1)=5$, $f'(1)=4$ and $f'(3)=2$, then find $(f^{-1})'(5)$.

Answer $\dfrac{1}{4}$

Solution

Step 1. (Omitted) You don't know what $f'(x)$ is.

For such cases, you replace Step 1 with given information $f(1)=5$, $f'(1)=4$ and $f'(3)=2$.

Step 2. $(f^{-1})'(5) = (f^{-1})'(y) = \dfrac{1}{f'(x)}$.

Step 3. Now, y is 5. What should be the corresponding x?

$5 = y = f(x)$ and $f(1)=5$. So we get $x=1$.

Therefore, $(f^{-1})'(5) = \dfrac{1}{f'(1)} = \dfrac{1}{4}$.

AP Calculus AB & BC Rewritten from the Beginning

Problem 3

(1) If g is the inverse function of f and if $f(x) = x^3 + 1$, then $g'(9) =$

ⓐ 1 ⓑ $\dfrac{1}{12}$ ⓒ 12 ⓓ $\dfrac{1}{243}$

x	$f(x)$	$f'(x)$
1	2	1
2	5	2
3	10	3

(2) The table above gives selected values for a differentiable function f and its derivative. If g is the inverse function of f, what is the value of $g'(5)$?

ⓐ $\dfrac{1}{10}$ ⓑ $\dfrac{1}{3}$ ⓒ $\dfrac{1}{2}$ ⓓ 1

Answer (1) ⓑ (2) ⓒ

Solution

(1) ⓑ

Step 1. $f'(x) = 3x^2$.

Step 2. $g'(9) = (f^{-1})'(9) = (f^{-1})'(y) = \dfrac{1}{f'(x)}$.

Step 3. Now, y is 9. What should be the corresponding x?

$9 = y = x^3 + 1$ and so we get $x = 2$.

Therefore, $(f^{-1})'(9) = \dfrac{1}{f'(2)} = \dfrac{1}{3 \times 2^2} = \dfrac{1}{12}$.

(2) ⓒ

Step 1. (Omitted) You don't know what $f'(x)$ is.
You replace Step 1 with given table.

Step 2. $g'(5) = (f^{-1})'(5) = (f^{-1})'(y) = \dfrac{1}{f'(x)}$.

Step 3. Now, y is 5. What should be the corresponding x?

$5 = y = f(x)$ and $f(2) = 5$. So we get $x = 2$.

Therefore, $(f^{-1})'(5) = \dfrac{1}{f'(2)} = \dfrac{1}{2}$.

Differentiation

03. Mean Value Theorem and Rolle's Theorem

I. Mean Value Theorem(MVT)

When the graph of $y = f(x)$ is continuous and differentiable in a given interval, the following theorem holds.

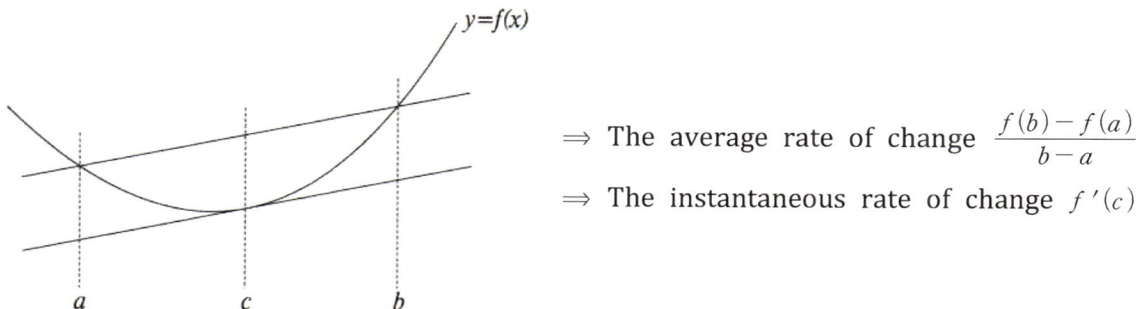

⇒ The average rate of change $\dfrac{f(b)-f(a)}{b-a}$

⇒ The instantaneous rate of change $f'(c)$

If $y = f(x)$ is continuous on a closed interval $[a, b]$ and differentiable on an open interval (a, b), **there exists at least one** c in the open interval (a, b) such that $\dfrac{f(b)-f(a)}{b-a} = f'(c)$; there exists at least one point within the interval such that the instantaneous rate of change at that point is same as the average rate of change over the entire interval.

II. Rolle's Theorem

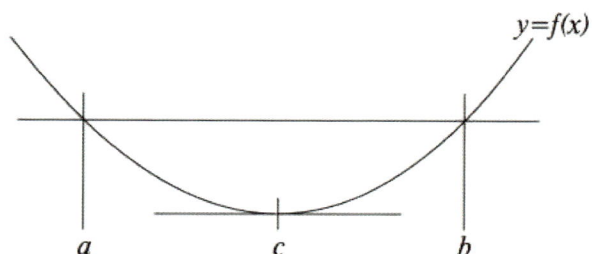

If $y = f(x)$ is **continuous** on a closed interval $[a, b]$ and **differentiable** on an open interval (a, b), and $f(a) = f(b)$, **there exists at least one** c in the open interval (a, b) **such that** $f'(c) = 0$.

III. IVT, Extreme Value Theorem, MVT, Rolle's Theorem.

In this chapter, we will take a look at the Intermediate Value Theorem(IVT), and Extreme Value Theorem, (both of which we briefly learned in the "Limit" chapter) and Mean Value Theorem(MVT) and Rolle's Theorem. These may seem simple, but may be tricky in an actual AP exam.

Let's look at the following.

(1) Extreme Value Theorem

(2) Intermediate Value Theorem ⎤ Must be continuous on a given interval.

(3) Mean Value Theorem

(4) Rolle's Theorem ⎤ Must be differentiable on a given interval.

(1) Extreme Value Theorem

If a function $y = f(x)$ is continuous on a closed interval $[a,b]$, then the function $y = f(x)$ must have a maximum and minimum value within the given interval $[a,b]$.
$f'(x)$ may or may not exist on the given interval.
That is, $f'(x)$ does not have to exist.

Let's look at the following.

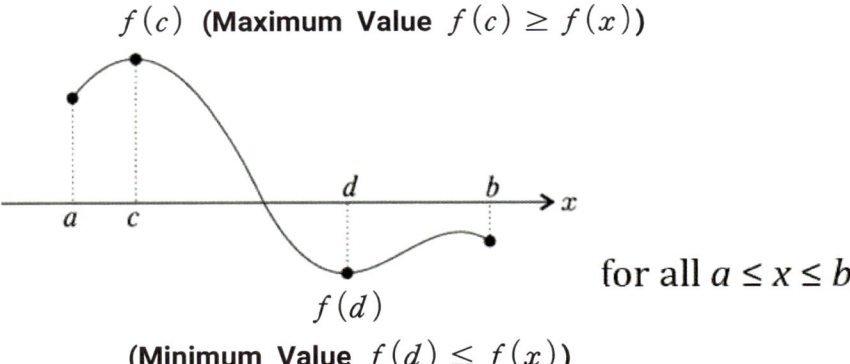

$f(c)$ (**Maximum Value** $f(c) \geq f(x)$)

$f(d)$ (**Minimum Value** $f(d) \leq f(x)$)

for all $a \leq x \leq b$

ⓐ In the above example, $f'(x)$ exists on the given interval $[a,b]$. But remember that this might not hold for other examples since the differentiability is not a necessary condition for the Extreme Value Theorem.

ⓑ However, a maximum and minimum value **MUST** exist within the given interval if the function is continuous.

Differentiation

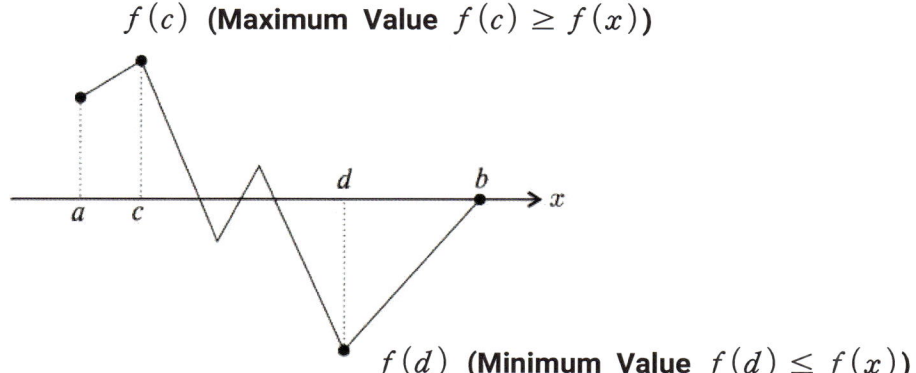

ⓐ In the above example, $f'(x)$ does not exist on the given interval $[a,b]$.
ⓑ However, a maximum and minimum value **MUST** exist within the given interval if the function is continuous. Since the differentiability is not a necessary condition for the Extreme Value Theorem.
ⓒ A value of c such that $\dfrac{f(b)-f(a)}{b-a}=f'(c)$ does not exist.

(2) Intermediate Value Theorem (IVT)

- Can be applied if $y=f(x)$ is continuous on a given interval.
- $y=f(x)$ does not have to be differentiable.
- A theorem where we must know the values of $f(a)$ and $f(b)$ for the given interval $[a,b]$.
- For the given interval $[a,b]$, $f(a)$ and $f(b)$ do not have to be the maximum or minimum values.

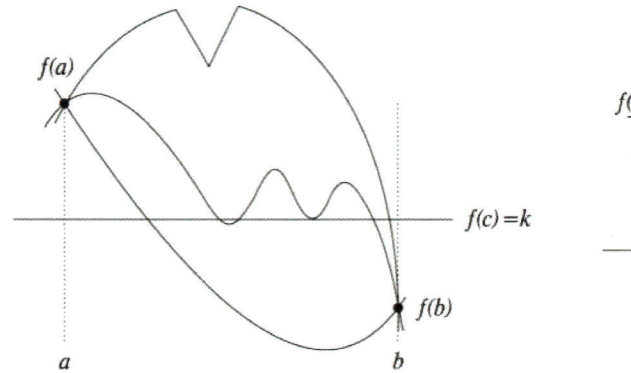 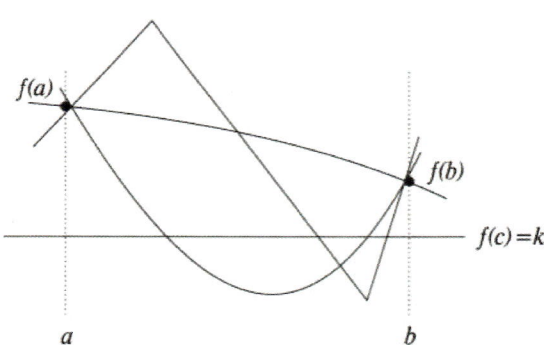

ⓐ If $f(a)>k$ and $f(b)<k$ (or if $f(a)<k$ and $f(b)>k$), there exists at least one c in the open interval (a,b) such that $f(c)=k$.
ⓑ $f'(c)$ does not have to exist in the interval $[a,b]$.
  That is, a value of c such that $\dfrac{f(b)-f(a)}{b-a}=f'(c)$ may or may not exist.

(3) Mean Value Theorem (MVT)

- Can be applied when $y = f(x)$ is **(continuous and) differentiable** on a given interval $[a, b]$.
(If it is differentiable, it must be continuous.)

- There exists at least one c in the given interval such that $\dfrac{f(b) - f(a)}{b - a} = f'(c)$.

(4) Rolle's Theorem

- Can be applied when $y = f(x)$ is **differentiable** on a given interval $[a, b]$ and $f(a) = f(b)$.

- There exists at least one c in the given interval such that $f'(c) = 0$.

- We must know the values of $f(a)$ and $f(b)$ to apply the Rolle's Theorem.

Differentiation

Problem 4

(1) Find the value of c that satisfies the Mean Value Theorem for $f(x) = 3x^2 + 24x + 2$ in the interval $[-2, 2]$.

(2) Find the value of c that satisfies the Rolle's Theorem for $f(x) = 2x^3 - 2x$ in the interval $[-1, 1]$.

Answer

(1) 0 (2) $\pm \dfrac{\sqrt{3}}{3}$

Solution

(1) 0

$f(x) = 3x^2 + 24x + 2$ is continuous and differentiable on the interval $[-2, 2]$.

$f(-2) = 3(-2)^2 + 24(-2) + 2 = -34$, $f(2) = 3(2)^2 + 24(2) + 2 = 62$, and $f'(x) = 6x + 24$.

From $\dfrac{f(2) - f(-2)}{2 - (-2)} = f'(c)$, we get $\dfrac{62 + 34}{4} = 6c + 24$, or $24 = 6c + 24$, so $c = 0$. Since $c = 0$ is included in the interval $[-2, 2]$, so the Mean Value Theorem is satisfied.

(2) $\pm \dfrac{\sqrt{3}}{3}$

$f(x) = 2x^3 - 2x$ is continuous and differentiable on the interval $[-1, 1]$, and $f(-1) = f(1) [\Leftarrow f(-1) = 2(-1)^3 - 2(-1) = 0, f(1) = 2(1)^3 - 2(1) = 0]$, $f'(x) = 6x^2 - 2$, so $f'(c) = 6c^2 - 2$. From $f'(c) = 0$, which is $6c^2 - 2 = 0$, we get $c = \pm \dfrac{1}{\sqrt{3}} = \pm \dfrac{\sqrt{3}}{3}$. $\pm \dfrac{\sqrt{3}}{3}$ are included in the interval $[-1, 1]$, so the Rolle's Theorem is satisfied.

AP Calculus AB & BC Rewritten from the Beginning

Problem 5

If f is a continuous function on the closed interval $[1,5]$, which of the following must be true?

ⓐ There is a number c in the open interval $(1,5)$ such that $f'(c) = \dfrac{f(5)-f(1)}{4}$.

ⓑ There is a number c in the open interval $(1,5)$ such that $f'(c) = 0$.

ⓒ There is a number c in the open interval $(1,5)$ such that $f(c) = 0$.

ⓓ There is a number c in the interval $[1,5]$ such that $f(c) \leq f(x)$ for all x in $[1,5]$.

Answer ⓓ

Solution

ⓐ We cannot apply the MVT, since we do not know if it is "Differentiable..."

ⓑ We do not know if it is "Differentiable", nor the values of $f(1)$ and $f(5)$, so we cannot apply Rolle's Theorem.

ⓒ We don't know the values of $f(1)$ and $f(5)$, so we can not apply Intermediate Value Theorem.

ⓓ f is continuous on the interval $[1,5]$, so maximum and minimum values exist. In this case c is the minimum.

Differentiation

Problem 6

If f is differentiable when $a \leq x \leq b$, which of the following could be false?

ⓐ f has a minimum value on $a \leq x \leq b$.
ⓑ There exists c, where $a < c < b$, such that $f(c) = 0$
ⓒ $f'(c) = \dfrac{f(b)-f(a)}{b-a}$ for some c such that $a < c < b$.
ⓓ If $f(a) = f(b)$, $f'(c) = 0$ for some c such that $a < c < b$.

Answer
ⓑ

Solution

ⓐ If a function is differentiable, it is continuous, so maximum and minimum values exist in the given interval.

ⓑ We need to know $f(a)$ and $f(b)$ to apply the Intermediate Value Theorem (IVT). IVT applies only if $f(a)f(b) < 0$.

ⓒ Differentiable, so we can apply the MVT.

ⓓ $f(a) = f(b)$ and differentiable, so we can apply Rolle's Theorem.

AP Calculus AB & BC Rewritten from the Beginning

04. L'Hopital's Rule

L'Hopital's Rule is a tool to find the limit of a fraction form by using differentiation that would be hard to find otherwise.
In short, it is an easy way to find the limit, or a "trick to calculate the limit"

We can simply follow the steps below!

Make Sure to Know the Following!

For the limits of $\frac{\infty}{\infty}$, and $\frac{0}{0}$ forms, differentiate the denominator and the numerator separately, put them back together and then evaluate the limit! If the new limit is not of the form $\frac{\infty}{\infty}$ or $\frac{0}{0}$, you are done.

What if it is still $\frac{\infty}{\infty}$ or $\frac{0}{0}$?

Then, you repeat the process again! Differentiate once more the denominator and the numerator separately, put them back together and then evaluate.

When do we stop differentiating?
If either the denominator or the numerator is no longer 0 or ∞, we stop.

Let's take a look at the following examples to see what the explanation means.

● ········ **Example 20**

Evaluate $\lim_{x \to \infty} \dfrac{2x^2 - 3}{5x^2 + 3x - 1}$.

● ········ **Answer** $\dfrac{2}{5}$

● ········ **Solution**

Substituting ∞ for x gives a $\dfrac{\infty}{\infty}$ form, so if we keep differentiating the denominator and the numerator, we have

$$\lim_{x \to \infty} \dfrac{(2x^2 - 3)'}{(5x^2 + 3x - 1)'} = \lim_{x \to \infty} \dfrac{(4x)'}{(10x + 3)'} = \lim_{x \to \infty} \dfrac{4}{10} = \dfrac{2}{5}$$

Remember that limit of a fraction we were able to calculate as

$$\lim_{x \to \infty} \dfrac{2x^2 - 3}{5x^2 + 3x - 1} = \lim_{x \to \infty} \dfrac{\dfrac{2x^2 - 3}{x^2}}{\dfrac{5x^2 + 3x - 1}{x^2}} = \lim_{x \to \infty} \dfrac{2 - \dfrac{3}{x^2}}{5 + \dfrac{3}{x} - \dfrac{1}{x^2}} = \dfrac{2 - 0}{5 + 0 - 0} = \dfrac{2}{5}.$$

There is no one fixed way that you should solve limit problems. Both are valid.

AP Calculus AB & BC Rewritten from the Beginning

Example 21

Evaluate $\lim\limits_{x\to 0}\dfrac{\sin 3x}{2x}$.

Answer $\dfrac{3}{2}$

Solution

Substituting 0 for x gives a $\dfrac{0}{0}$ form, so if we keep differentiating the denominator and the numerator, we have

$\lim\limits_{x\to 0}\dfrac{(\sin 3x)'}{(2x)'} \Rightarrow \lim\limits_{x\to 0}\dfrac{3\cos 3x}{2}$ ($\Rightarrow$ Substitute 0 for x and it is no longer $\dfrac{0}{0}$ form!) $= \dfrac{3}{2}$

Example 22

Evaluate $\lim\limits_{x\to\infty}\dfrac{x}{e^x}$.

Answer 0

Solution

Substituting ∞ for x gives a $\dfrac{\infty}{\infty}$ form, so if we keep differentiating the denominator and the numerator, we have $\lim\limits_{x\to\infty}\dfrac{(x)'}{(e^x)'}=\lim\limits_{x\to\infty}\dfrac{1}{e^x}=0$.

※ Now, try to solve Example 22 again, this time WITHOUT using L'Hospital's Rule. Can you solve it? Probably not. Sometimes L'Hospital's rule is the only way that you can quickly compute the given limit problem. Below gives more examples of limits that can be solved quick with L'Hospital but is hard to compute otherwise.

Differentiation

● ······· **Problem 7**

(1) Find $\lim_{x \to 0} \dfrac{5x + \sin 2x}{x}$

(2) Find $\lim_{x \to \frac{\pi}{2}} \dfrac{x - \dfrac{\pi}{2}}{\cos x}$

(3) Find $\lim_{x \to \infty} x e^{-2x}$

(4) Find $\lim_{x \to \infty} e^{-x} \ln x$

● ······· **Answer**   (1) 7   (2) -1 (3) 0   (4) 0

● ······· **Solution**

(1) 7

$\dfrac{0}{0}$ form, so we use L'Hopital's Rule.

$\lim_{x \to 0} \dfrac{(5x + \sin 2x)'}{(x)'} = \lim_{x \to 0} (5 + 2\cos 2x) = 5 + 2 = 7$

(2) -1

$\dfrac{0}{0}$ form, so we use L'Hopital's Rule.

$\lim_{x \to \frac{\pi}{2}} \dfrac{(x - \dfrac{\pi}{2})'}{(\cos x)'} = \lim_{x \to \frac{\pi}{2}} \dfrac{1}{-\sin x} = -1$

(3) 0

$\dfrac{\infty}{\infty}$ form, so we use L'Hopital's Rule.

$\lim_{x \to \infty} \dfrac{(x)'}{(e^{2x})'} = \lim_{x \to \infty} \dfrac{1}{2e^{2x}} = 0$

(4) 0

$\dfrac{\infty}{\infty}$ form, so we use L'Hopital's Rule.

$\lim_{x \to \infty} \dfrac{(\ln x)'}{(e^x)'} = \lim_{x \to \infty} \dfrac{\dfrac{1}{x}}{e^x} = \dfrac{0}{\infty} = 0$

AP Calculus AB & BC Rewritten from the Beginning

Problem 8

(1) Find $\lim\limits_{x\to 0}\dfrac{2\tan x}{e^{5x}-1}$

(2) Find $\lim\limits_{x\to\infty}\dfrac{e^x+5x}{3x}$

(3) Find $\lim\limits_{x\to 0}\dfrac{x^2}{3-3\cos x}$

(4) Find $\lim\limits_{x\to\infty}\dfrac{2x^2}{e^{2x}}$

Answer

(1) $\dfrac{2}{5}$ (2) ∞ (3) $\dfrac{2}{3}$ (4) 0

Solution

(1) $\dfrac{2}{5}$

$\dfrac{0}{0}$ form, so we use L'Hopital's Rule!

$$\lim_{x\to 0}\dfrac{(2\tan x)'}{(e^{5x}-1)'}=\lim_{x\to 0}\dfrac{2\sec^2 x}{5e^{5x}}=\dfrac{2}{5}$$

(2) ∞

$\dfrac{\infty}{\infty}$ form, so we use L'Hopital's Rule!

$$\lim_{x\to\infty}\dfrac{(e^x+5x)'}{(3x)'}\Rightarrow\lim_{x\to\infty}\dfrac{e^x+5}{3}=\dfrac{\infty}{3}=\infty$$

(3) $\dfrac{2}{3}$

$\dfrac{0}{0}$ form, so we use L'Hopital's Rule!

$$\lim_{x\to 0}\dfrac{(x^2)'}{(3-3\cos x)'}\Rightarrow\lim_{x\to 0}\dfrac{(2x)'}{(3\sin x)'}\Rightarrow\lim_{x\to 0}\dfrac{2}{3\cos x}=\dfrac{2}{3}$$

(4) 0

$\dfrac{\infty}{\infty}$ form, so we use L'Hopital's Rule!

$$\lim_{x\to\infty}\dfrac{(2x^2)'}{(e^{2x})'}\Rightarrow\lim_{x\to\infty}\dfrac{(4x)'}{(2e^{2x})'}\Rightarrow\lim_{x\to\infty}\dfrac{4}{4e^{2x}}=\dfrac{4}{\infty}=0$$

Differentiation

Supplement

The calculations of $\frac{0}{0}$ and $\frac{\infty}{\infty}$ in the *Limit* we studied earlier, as well as the calculations in Trigonometric Function Limits, can also be solved using L'Hopital's Rule.

① $\lim\limits_{x \to \infty} \dfrac{9x^3 - 2x^2}{3x^2 + 5x}\ (\dfrac{\infty}{\infty})$

$= \lim\limits_{x \to \infty} \dfrac{(9x^3 - 2x^2)'}{(3x^2 + 5x)'} = \lim\limits_{x \to \infty} \dfrac{27x^2 - 4x}{6x + 5}\ (\dfrac{\infty}{\infty}) = \lim\limits_{x \to \infty} \dfrac{(27x^2 - 4x)'}{(6x + 5)'} = \lim\limits_{x \to \infty} \dfrac{54x - 4}{6(\neq \infty)} = \infty$

② $\lim\limits_{x \to \infty} \dfrac{9x - 1}{3x + 3}\ (\dfrac{\infty}{\infty})$

$= \lim\limits_{x \to \infty} \dfrac{(9x - 1)'}{(3x + 3)'} = \lim\limits_{x \to \infty} \dfrac{9(\neq \infty)}{3(\neq \infty)} = 3$

③ $\lim\limits_{x \to \infty} \dfrac{x}{e^x}\ (\dfrac{\infty}{\infty})$

$= \lim\limits_{x \to \infty} \dfrac{x'}{(e^x)'} = \lim\limits_{x \to \infty} \dfrac{1(\neq \infty)}{e^x} = \dfrac{1}{\infty} = 0$

All of the above ①~③ are of the indeterminate form $\dfrac{\infty}{\infty}$.

In ① and ②, we calculated the limits by dividing both the numerator and the denominator by the highest degree term in the denominator.

However, for ③, there was no straightforward method for calculation.

Nonetheless, it could be solved using L'Hopital's Rule.

④ $\lim\limits_{x \to 0} \dfrac{\sin x}{x}\ (\dfrac{0}{0})$

$= \lim\limits_{x \to 0} \dfrac{(\sin x)'}{x'} = \lim\limits_{x \to 9} \dfrac{\cos x (\neq 0)}{1(\neq 0)} = 1$

⑤ $\lim\limits_{x \to 0} \dfrac{\tan 2x}{5x}\ (\dfrac{0}{0})$

$= \lim\limits_{x \to 0} \dfrac{(\tan 2x)'}{(5x)'} = \lim\limits_{x \to 0} \dfrac{2\sec^2 2x (\neq 0)}{5(\neq 0)} = \dfrac{2}{5}$

Both ④ and ⑤ are of the indeterminate form $\dfrac{0}{0}$. While we have memorized standard limit formulas for trigonometric functions of this type, they can also be solved using L'Hopital's Rule.

07 Exercise

01 Find the equation of the tangent line to the graph of $y=\sqrt{x^2+5}$ at $(2,3)$.

02 Find the equation of the normal line to the graph of $y=(x^2-2)^3$ at $x=1$.

03 Find the values of x where the tangent line to the graph of $y=x^3-5x$ has a slope equal to the slope of $y=x$.

04 A curve in the plane is defined parametrically by the equations $x=2t^2+t$ and $y=5t^4$. Find the equation of the line tangent to the curve at $t=1$.

05 A curve P is defined by the parametric equations $x = t^2 - 6t$ and $y = t^2$. Find the equation of the line tangent to the graph of P at the point $(-9, 9)$.

06 Find the slope of the line tangent to the graph of $\ln(x^2 y^3) = 2y$ at the point where $x = e$ and $y = 1$.

07 If g is the inverse function of f and $f(x) = -x^3$, then $g'(1) =$

ⓐ $-\dfrac{1}{3}$ ⓑ -3 ⓒ 1 ⓓ $\dfrac{1}{3}$

x	$f(x)$	$f'(x)$
1	0	1
2	1	2
3	3	5

08 The table above shows values of function f and its derivative for some values of x. If g is the inverse function of f, what is the value of $g'(1)$?

ⓐ -5 ⓑ -1 ⓒ 0 ⓓ $\dfrac{1}{2}$

AP Calculus AB & BC Rewritten from the Beginning

09 If g is the inverse function of f and if $f(x) = x^3 + x$, then find the slope of the line tangent to the curve $y = g(x)$ at $(2, 1)$.

10 Find the values of c that satisfy the mean value theorem for $f(x) = x^2 + 1$ in the interval $[-1, 2]$.

11 Find the values of c that satisfy the Rolle's Theorem for $f(x) = x^4 + x^2$ in the interval $[-1, 1]$.

x	1	2	3	4	5	6
$f(x)$	5	1	-1	0	-3	5

12 Function f is continuous and differentiable on the closed interval $[1, 6]$. The table above gives the values of f in this interval. Which of the following statements must be true?

ⓐ f is decreasing on the interval $[1, 5]$.
ⓑ The maximum value of f in $[1, 6]$ is 5.
ⓒ There is a number c in the open interval $(1, 6)$ such that $f'(c) = 0$.
ⓓ $f(x) > 0$ for $1 < x < 2$.

13 f is continuous for $1 \leq x \leq 4$ and differentiable for $1 < x < 4$. If $f(1) = -1$ and $f(4) = 8$, which of the following statements could be false?

ⓐ There exists c, where $1 < c < 4$, such that $f(c) = 0$.
ⓑ There exists c, where $1 \leq c \leq 4$, such that $f(c) \leq f(x)$ for all x in the closed interval $1 \leq x \leq 4$.
ⓒ There exists c, where $1 < c < 4$, such that $f'(c) = 3$.
ⓓ There exists c, where $1 < c < 4$, such that $f'(c) = 0$.

14 $\lim\limits_{x \to 0} \dfrac{e^x + \cos x - 2}{x^2 - x}$ is

ⓐ -2 ⓑ -1 ⓒ 0 ⓓ $\dfrac{1}{2}$

15 $\lim\limits_{x \to 0} \dfrac{2\tan x}{e^{5x} - 1}$ is

ⓐ 0 ⓑ $\dfrac{2}{5}$ ⓒ $\dfrac{4}{5}$ ⓓ 2

07   Answers & Solutions

01 $y = \dfrac{2}{3}x + \dfrac{5}{3}$

$y' = \dfrac{1}{2}(x^2+5)^{-\frac{1}{2}} \times 2x = \dfrac{x}{\sqrt{x^2+5}}$, so at $x = 2$, the slope is $\dfrac{2}{3}$ and the point of tangency is $(2, 3)$. Thus, the equation of the tangent line is $y - 3 = \dfrac{2}{3}(x - 2)$, which gives $y = \dfrac{2}{3}x + \dfrac{5}{3}$.

02 $y = -\dfrac{1}{6}x - \dfrac{5}{6}$

$y' = 3(x^2-2)^2 \times 2x = 6x(x^2-2)^2$, so at $x = 1$, the slope of the tangent line is 6, and the slope of the normal line is $-\dfrac{1}{6}$. The point of tangency is $(1, -1)$. So $y + 1 = -\dfrac{1}{6}(x - 1)$, which gives $y = -\dfrac{1}{6}x - \dfrac{5}{6}$.

03 $\pm\sqrt{2}$

The value of $y' = 3x^2 - 5$ has to be the same as the slope of $y = x$, which is 1. So $3x^2 - 5 = 1$, which gives $x^2 = 2$.
Thus, $x = \pm\sqrt{2}$.

04 $y = 4x - 7$

- $\dfrac{dy}{dx} = \dfrac{\frac{dy}{dt}}{\frac{dx}{dt}} = \dfrac{20t^3}{4t+1}$, so at $t = 1$, $\dfrac{dy}{dx} = \dfrac{20}{5} = 4$

- The point of tangency is $(3, 5)$, so $y - 5 = 4(x - 3)$, which gives $y = 4x - 7$.

Differentiation

05 $x = -9$

- $\dfrac{dy}{dx} = \dfrac{\frac{dy}{dt}}{\frac{dx}{dt}} = \dfrac{2t}{2t-6}$.

In order to find $\dfrac{dy}{dx}$, we need to know t. Since $x = -9$, $t^2 - 6t = -9$, and thus $t = 3$.

- When $t = 3$, $\dfrac{dy}{dx}$ does not exist [$\Leftarrow \dfrac{dy}{dx} = \dfrac{2(3)}{2(3)-6} = \dfrac{6}{0}$]. So, the slope does not exist, which means that the tangent line is a vertical line.
- Substituting $t = 3$, we get $x = 9 - 18 = -9$. That is, $x = -9$.

06 $-\dfrac{2}{e}$

Differentiating both sides, we have $\dfrac{1}{x^2 y^3}(2xy^3 + 3x^2 y^2 \dfrac{dy}{dx}) = 2\dfrac{dy}{dx}$.

Substituting $x = e$, and $y = 1$ gives $\dfrac{1}{e^2}(2e + 3e^2 \dfrac{dy}{dx}) = 2\dfrac{dy}{dx}$.

Thus, $\dfrac{dy}{dx} = -\dfrac{2}{e}$. Therefore, the slope of the tangent line is $-\dfrac{2}{e}$.

07 ⓐ

$f(x) = -x^3$, so $f'(x) = -3x^2$.
$f(x) = 1 \Rightarrow -x^3 = 1 \Rightarrow x = -1$ and it implies $f'(-1) = -3$.
Thus, $g'(1) = \dfrac{1}{f'(-1)} = -\dfrac{1}{3}$.

08 ⓓ

When $f(x) = 1$, $x = 2$.   Thus, $g'(1) = (f^{-1})'(1) = \dfrac{1}{f'(2)} = \dfrac{1}{2}$

09 $\dfrac{1}{4}$

$g'(2) = (f^{-1})'(2) = \dfrac{1}{f'(1)}$. $f'(x) = 3x^2 + 1$, so $f'(1) = 4$.

Therefore, the slope of the tangent line is $g'(2) = (f^{-1})'(2) = \dfrac{1}{f'(1)} = \dfrac{1}{4}$.

10 $\frac{1}{2}$

$f'(x) = 2x$

The value(s) of c that satisfy the Mean Value Theorem satisfy $\frac{5-2}{2-(-1)} = f'(c) = 2c$.

So $1 = 2c$ and $c = \frac{1}{2}$. Since $\frac{1}{2}$ is in $[-1, 2]$, it satisfies the Mean Value Theorem.

11 0

From Rolle's Theorem, there exists c satisfying $f'(c) = 4c^3 + 2c = 0$. It is $2c(2c^2 + 1)$, so $c = 0$ and 0 is included in $[-1, 1]$, so it satisfies the Rolle's Theorem.

12 ⓒ

$f(1) = f(6) = 5$ and the function is differentiable on the given interval, so we can apply Rolle's Theorem. That is there is a number c in $(1, 6)$ such that $f'(c) = 0$.

13 ⓓ

The function is differentiable on the given interval, but we do not know if $f(a) = f(b)$, so we cannot apply Rolle's Theorem!

14 ⓑ

$\frac{0}{0}$ form, so apply L'Hopital's Rule: $\lim\limits_{x \to 0} \frac{(e^x + \cos x - 2)'}{(x^2 - x)'} = \lim\limits_{x \to 0} \frac{(e^x - \sin x)}{2x - 1} = -1$.

15 ⓑ

$\frac{0}{0}$ form, so apply L'Hopital's Rule: $\lim\limits_{x \to 0} \frac{(2\tan x)'}{(e^{5x} - 1)'} = \lim\limits_{x \to 0} \frac{(2\sec^2 x)}{5e^{5x}} = \frac{2}{5}$.

Differentiation

AP Calculus AB & BC Rewritten from the Beginning

Differentiation

AP Calculus AB & BC Rewritten from the Beginning

Differentiation

A Brief History of Calculus (Part 2)

As differentiation and integration were further developed, mathematics made great progress and had a significant impact on many fields, including natural and social sciences.

One interesting point is the use of two notations for the derivative of a function

1. $f'(x)$
2. $\dfrac{dy}{dx}$

Why are both used?

Today, it is recognized that both Newton and Leibniz independently developed calculus around the same time. Newton introduced the notation $f'(x)$, while Leibniz introduced the concept of infinitesimals and the notation $\dfrac{dy}{dx}$.

Newton's notation $f'(x)$ is simple and convenient for writing, but Leibniz's notation $\dfrac{dy}{dx}$ is more powerful mathematically, especially in situations like the chain rule, implicit differentiation, and inverse function differentiation.

04 Analyzing Graphs

01. Polynomial Functions
02. Various functions

Graphs are often difficult to draw accurately except for some very simple graphs. Therefore, the "1. Graph Properties and Predictions" part studies the graph of $y=f(x)$ to see where its concavity changes and where it increases or decreases. Although not 100% accurate, the "2. Sketching Graphs" part studies how to roughly draw the graph of $y=f(x)$.

Before we begin

This chapter is very important in learning Calculus. Make sure to practice this chapter again and again until you have mastered it.

01. Polynomial Functions

(1) Polynomial Functions ($y = ax^n + bx^{n-1} + cx^{n-2} + \cdots$)

Polynomial functions are smooth and continuous on all real numbers, which makes them differentiable on all real numbers as well. In addition, their shapes are somehow determined.

If the leading coefficient is positive, then the right end of the graph points upwards and if it is negative, then the right end points downwards. The shapes of the graphs are somewhat determined depending on the highest degree, as shown below.

At $y = ax^n + bx^{n-1} + cx^{n-2} + \cdots$		
	$a > 0$	$a < 0$
$y = ax + b$	/	\
$y = ax^2 + bx + c$	_/	/‾\
$y = ax^3 + bx^2 + \cdots$	⁓ ...	⁓ ...
$y = ax^4 + bx^3 + \cdots$	W ...	M ...

Differentiation

What does the graph of $y=(x-1)^2(x-2)^3(x-3)^4$ roughly look like?

The approximate shape of the graph is as follows.

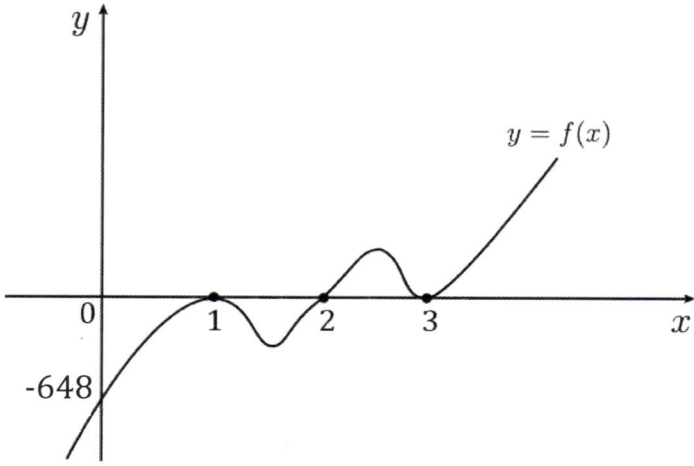

Let's magnify the figure above to analyze it.

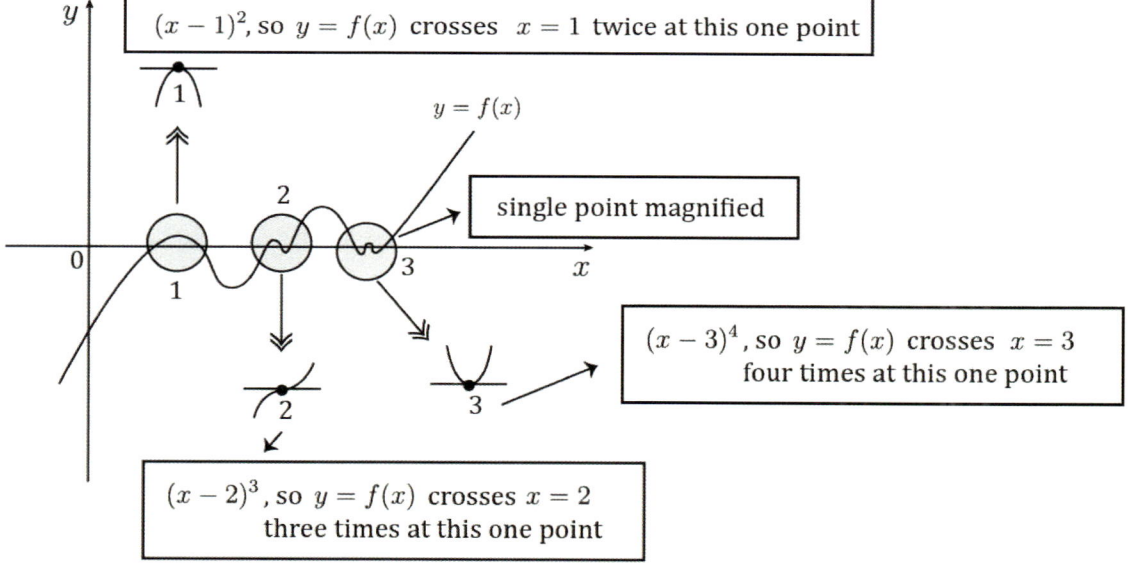

$(x-1)^2$, so $y=f(x)$ crosses $x=1$ twice at this one point

single point magnified

$(x-3)^4$, so $y=f(x)$ crosses $x=3$ four times at this one point

$(x-2)^3$, so $y=f(x)$ crosses $x=2$ three times at this one point

255

Supplement

Sketching Graphs of Polynomial Functions, using its roots

($f(x) = (\ )^n$)

For example, if we magnify the graph of $f(x) = (x-1)(x-2)^2(x-3)^3(x-4)^4$ and take a close look, we would see the following.

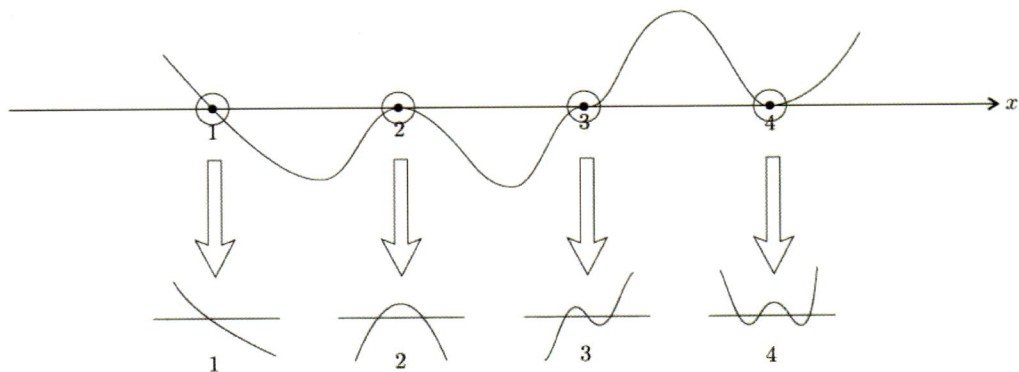

As we can see in the figure above, in $f(x) = (\ )^n$,

if n is even, it is tangent to the x-axis, and if n is odd, it crosses the x-axis.

Differentiation

Example 23

Draw the graphs of the following functions.

(1) $f(x) = (x-1)^2(x+1)(x+2)^3$

(2) $f(x) = -2(x-1)^3(x+3)^2$

Solution

(1)

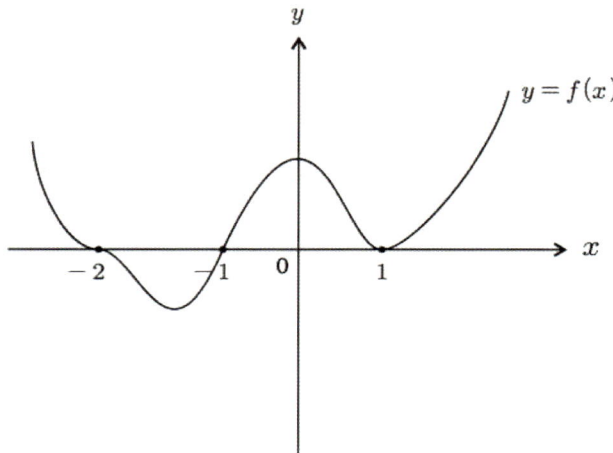

(2)

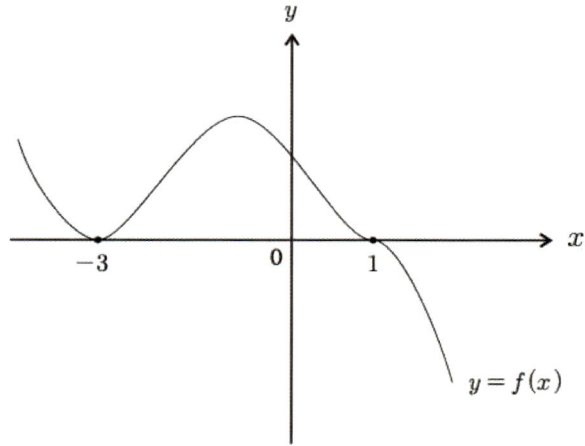

AP Calculus AB & BC Rewritten from the Beginning

(2) Graphing a Polynomial Function

Sketching Graphs of Polynomial Functions

(1) Roughly sketch the graph. If the leading coefficient is positive, then the right end of the graph points upwards and if it is negative, then the right end points downwards.

(2) The shapes of the graphs are somewhat determined depending on the highest degree, as shown below.

	$y = ax^n + bx^{n-1} + cx^{n-2} + \cdots$	
	$a > 0$	$a < 0$
$n = 1$	/	\
$n = 2$	$\cup$	$\cap$
$n = 3$	$\sim$	$\sim$
$n = 4$	W	M

(3) Find the values of x and y such that $f'(x) = 0$ and plot them on the coordinate plane.

Let's explore this in more detail with the following examples.

● ········ **Example 24**

Sketch the graph of the function $f(x) = -x^3 + 9x^2 - 15x + 4$.

● ········ **Solution**

(1) The leading coefficient is negative, so the right end of the graph must point downwards.

(2) The rough shape of the graph of the given function is as follows.

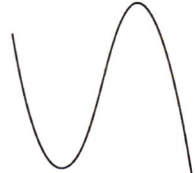

(3) Find the values of x and y such that $f'(x) = 0$.
$f'(x) = -3x^2 + 18x - 15 = 0$, so $x^2 - 6x + 5 = 0$. Therefore, $x = 1, 5$.
$f(1) = -3, f(5) = 29$.

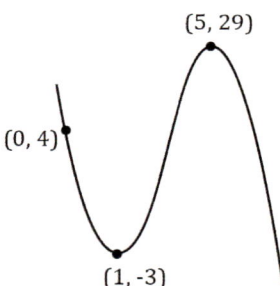

(4) In the coordinate plane, the graph of the function can be plotted as follows.

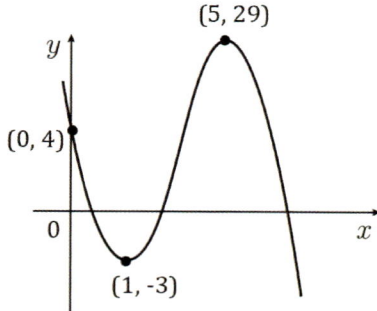

AP Calculus AB & BC Rewritten from the Beginning

Example 25

Roughly sketch the graphs of the following functions.

(1) $y = x^3 - 6x^2 + 9x - 4$

(2) $y = -\dfrac{1}{3}x^3 + x^2 - x + 1$

(3) $y = \dfrac{1}{3}x^3 + \dfrac{1}{2}x^2 + 2x + 1$

(4) $y = -x^2 + 3x + 4$

Solution

(1)

①

The coefficient of x^3 is positive, so the right end of the graph points upwards. Sketch roughly, as shown on the left.

②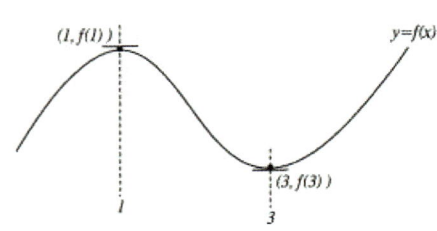

Find the value of x such that $f'(x) = 0$.
$3x^2 - 12x + 9 = 0$,
$3(x-1)(x-3) = 0$
so $x = 1, 3$.
Split the real line into three parts: $x < 1$, $1 < x < 3$, and $3 < x$. On each interval the sign of $f'(x) = 3(x-1)(x-3)$ is positive, negative, and positive.
f increase, decrease, and then increase again.
Therefore, this graph is drawn as shown on the left.

260

Differentiation

● ········ **Solution**

(2)

The coefficient of x^3 is negative, so the right end of the graph points downwards. Sketch roughly as shown on the right.

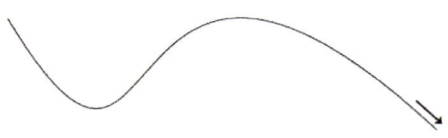

Find the value of x such that $f'(x) = 0$.
$y' = -x^2 + 2x - 1$. $-(x-1)^2 = 0$, so $x = 1$.
Here, something interesting happens. $x = 1$ split the real line into $x < 1$ and $1 < x$ but on both interval $f'(x) = -(x-1)^2$ is negative. f has a point where $f'(x) = 0$ but f decreases the whole time. In such cases, the graph is shaped as shown in the right.

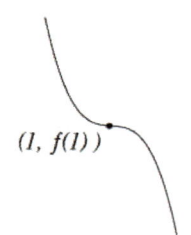

$(1, f(1))$

(3)

The coefficient of x^3 is positive, so the right end of the graph points upwards. Sketch roughly as shown here.

Find the value of x such that $f'(x) = 0$.
$y' = x^2 + x + 2$, $x^2 + x + 2 = 0$, so the value of x is imaginary.
That is, there is no real number that satisfies $f'(x) = 0$.
In fact, $x^2 + x + 2 = (x + \frac{1}{2})^2 + \frac{7}{4} \geq \frac{7}{4} > 0$.

Thus, $y = f(x)$ strictly increases.
In such cases, where $f'(x) = 0$ has no real solution, it is that either $f'(x) > 0$ for all x or $f'(x) < 0$ for all x: in the former case $y = f(x)$ strictly increases and in the latter case $y = f(x)$ strictly decreases.

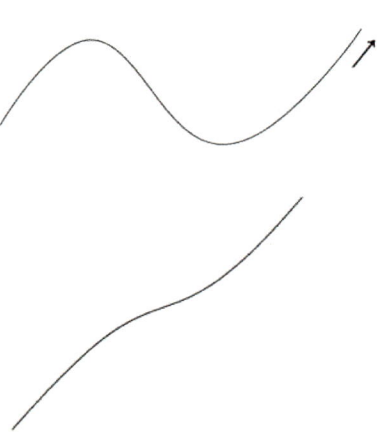

261

AP Calculus AB & BC Rewritten from the Beginning

Solution

(4)

① The coefficient of x^2 is negative, so the right end of the graph points downwards. Sketch roughly as shown here.

② Find the value of x such that $f'(x) = 0$.
$y' = -2x + 3$, so $x = 1.5$.

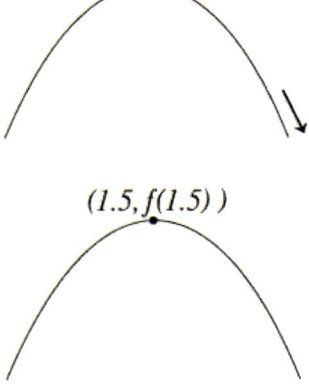

(1.5, f(1.5))

The graphs of quadratic functions can be sketched easily by using differentiation. The graph always comes in the shape of a parabola, with one maximum/minimum.

※ What is the difference between (2) and (3)?
The fact that f is monotone (monotone increasing/monotone decreasing) is the same. However, while in (2) there was a point that $f'(x) = 0$ there is no such point in (3). Would there be any special meaning to the point $x = 1$ (where $f'(x) = 0$) in (2)?
Do you see any difference between the graphs in (2) and (3)?
See how 'rapidly' the shape of the graph changes at $x = 1$ in (2). You can see that in (3) there is no such point. Here we hint out that the points like $x = 1$ in (2) are called "inflection point." This, we will learn more later.

Differentiation

02. Various Functions

(1) Terms in Graphs

Let's remember the following terms.

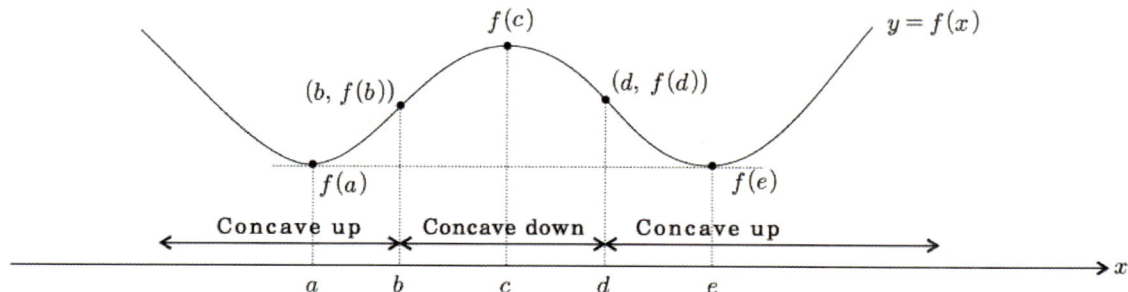

⇒ ① **Relative (Local) Maximum** : $f(c)$
  ② **Relative (Local) Minimum** : $f(a)$, $f(e)$
  ③ **Inflection point**   : $(b, f(b))$, $(d, f(d))$
  ④ **Extreme Value**   : $f(a)$, $f(c)$, $f(e)$

※ • Relative (Local) Maximum or Relative (Local) Minimum does not mean the largest or the smallest value of $y = f(x)$ on the entire domain, respectively.
  • Inflection Point is a point where Concave Downward and Concave Upward interchanges, and the rate of change is fast.

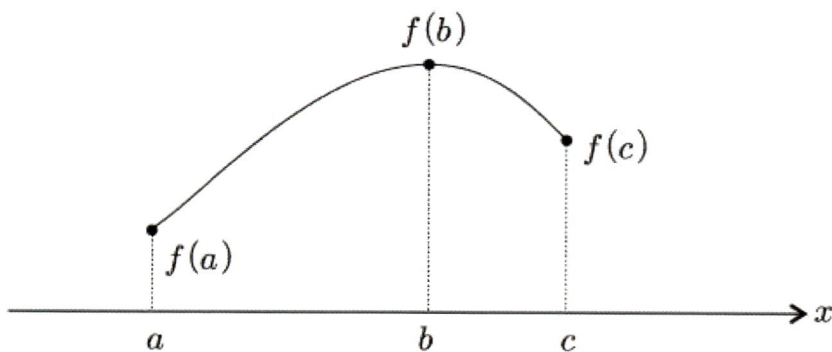

⇒ ① **Absolute Maximum** : $f(b)$
  ② **Absolute Minimum** : $f(a)$

※ Absolute Maximum or Absolute Minimum are the highest and lowest points within the entire domain.

(2) Predicting the Shapes of Graphs (General Case)

We can predict the shape of its graph by using derivative f'. The graph of $y = f(x)$ is increasing when f' is positive and decreasing when f' is negative.

In the following Example, let's use the graph of $y = f(x)$ to predict the shape of the graph of $y = f'(x)$.

Example

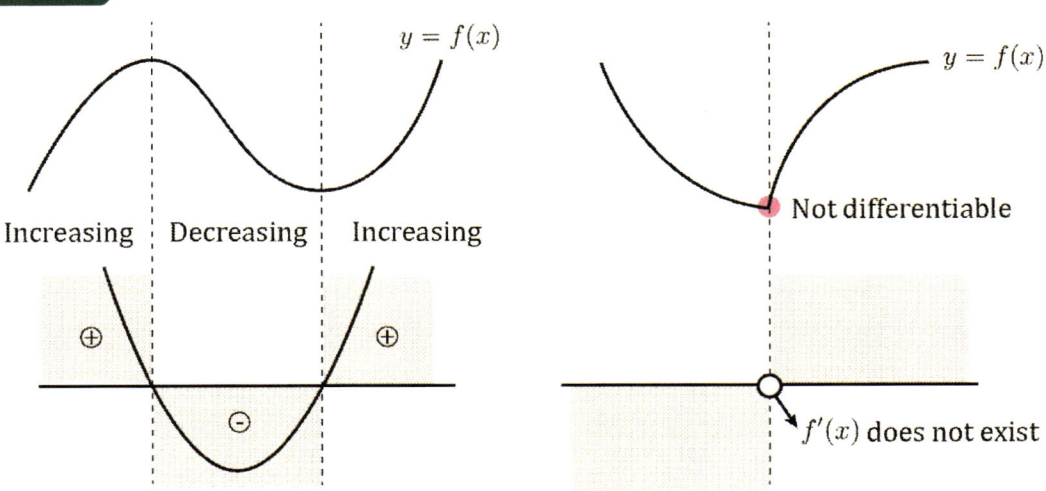

In the following Example, let's use the graph of $y = f'(x)$ to predict the shape of the graph of $y = f(x)$.

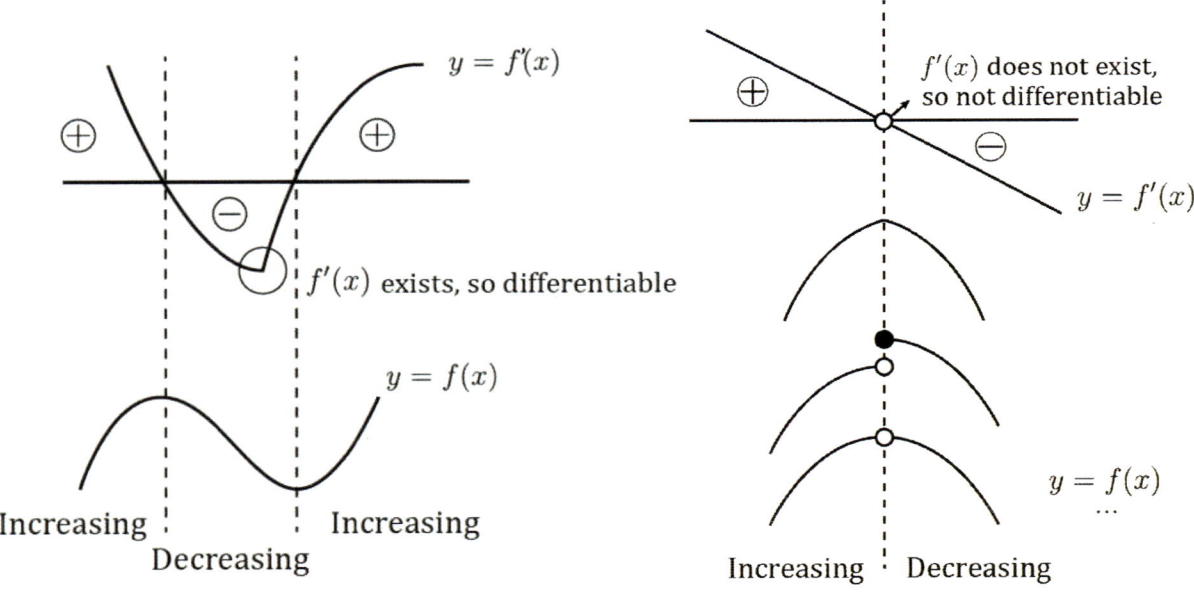

(3) Concave up/Concave down

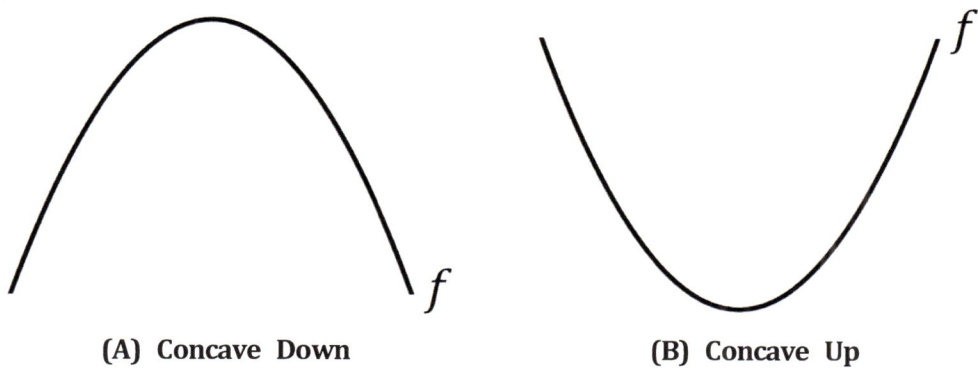

(A) Concave Down   (B) Concave Up

The graph in Figure (A) is concave down. It happens when $f'' < 0$ (f' is decreasing).
The graph in Figure (B) is concave up. It happens when $f'' > 0$ (f' is increasing).

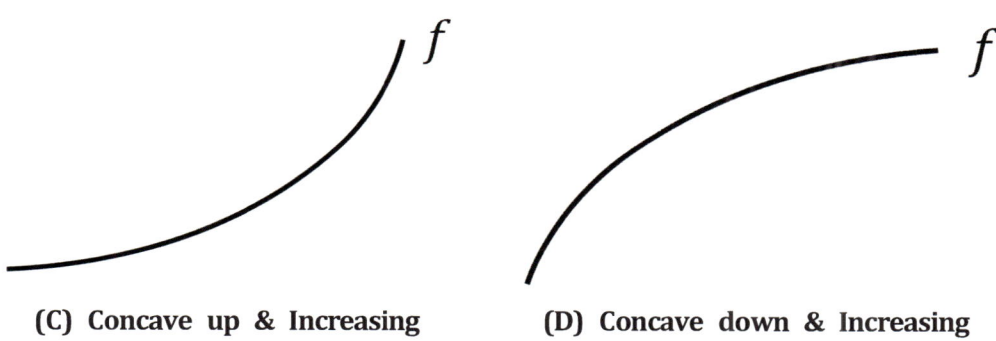

(C) Concave up & Increasing   (D) Concave down & Increasing

The above Figure (C) is the graph of f which is concave up and increasing. Therefore, it satisfies $f' > 0$ and $f'' > 0$ at the same time. Similarly, f described in Figure (D) is concave down and increasing. Therefore, $f' > 0$ and $f'' < 0$ should be satisfied at the same time.

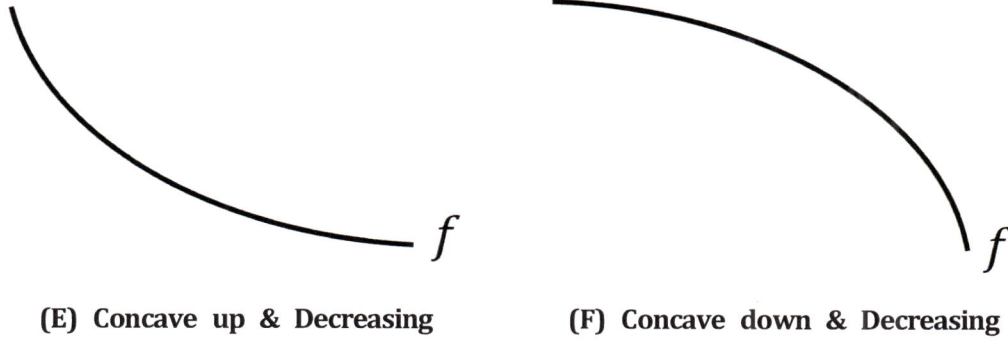

(E) Concave up & Decreasing   (F) Concave down & Decreasing

The above Figure (E) is the graph of f which is concave up and decreasing. Therefore, it satisfies $f' < 0$ and $f'' > 0$ at the same time. Similarly, f described in Figure (F) is concave down and decreasing. Therefore, $f' < 0$ and $f'' < 0$ should be satisfied at the same time.

Here, we used signs of f' and f'' to guess the shape of the graph of f. Then, how can we use the sign of f''' to guess the shape of the graph?

Unfortunately, the answer is "f''' is not being considered to guess the shape of the graph." The reason is that f' and f'' contain enough information to determine the brief shape of the graph.

We now know what does $f''(x) < 0$ and $f''(x) > 0$ means. The former is concave down and the latter is concave up. Then, what are the point x with $f''(x) = 0$? Those x are the inflection point! Point where the graph changes from concave up to concave down, or from concave down to concave up. If $f''(x) = 0$ and the sign of f'' changes at point x, then x is the inflection point.

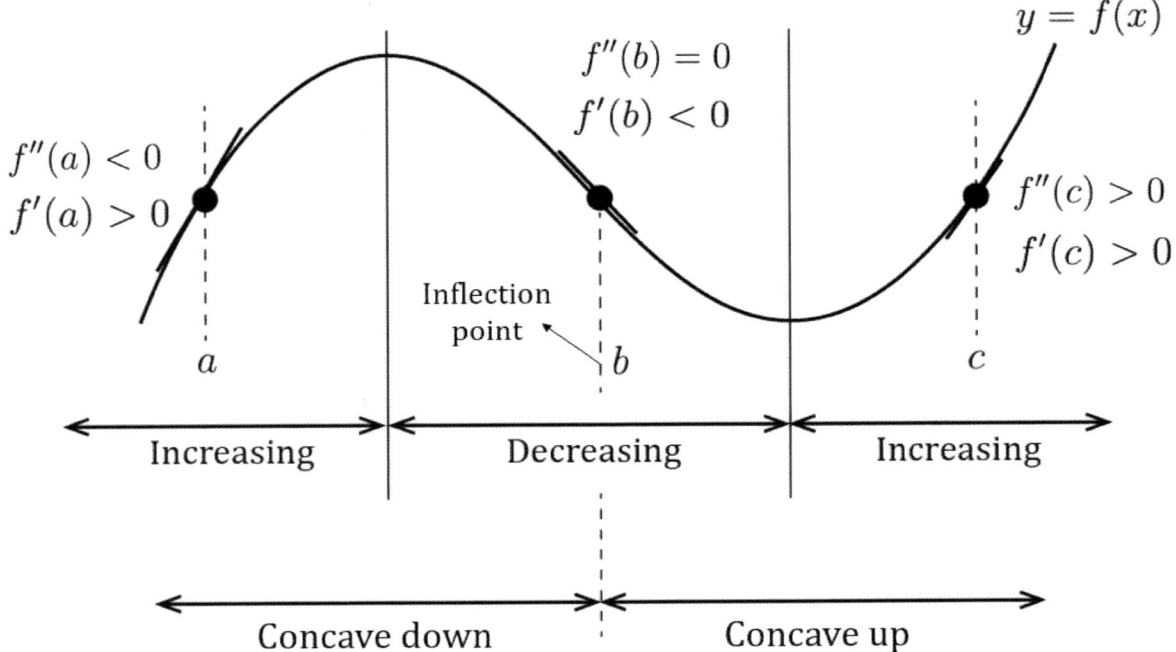

※ Remember that if x is a inflection point then $f''(x)=0$ but the converse is NOT true. Concave up means $f''(x)>0$ and concave down means $f''(x)<0$. So if the graph changes concavity at x then f'' must change sign at x, either from positive to negative or negative to positive! If f'' changes sign at x then clearly, $f''(x)=0$. (What else can be inbetween $f''(x)>0$ and $f''(x)<0$ but $f''(x)=0$?) But $f''(x)=0$ alone does NOT guarantee that the sign of f'' changes at x. This, we will see again very soon. To construct a counter example, consider the graph $f(x)=x^4$. At $(0,0)$ the graph is concave up. However, $f''(0)=0$.

(4) Summary of the Graph of $y = f(x)$

Let's remember the following 7 properties of graphs using the figure below.

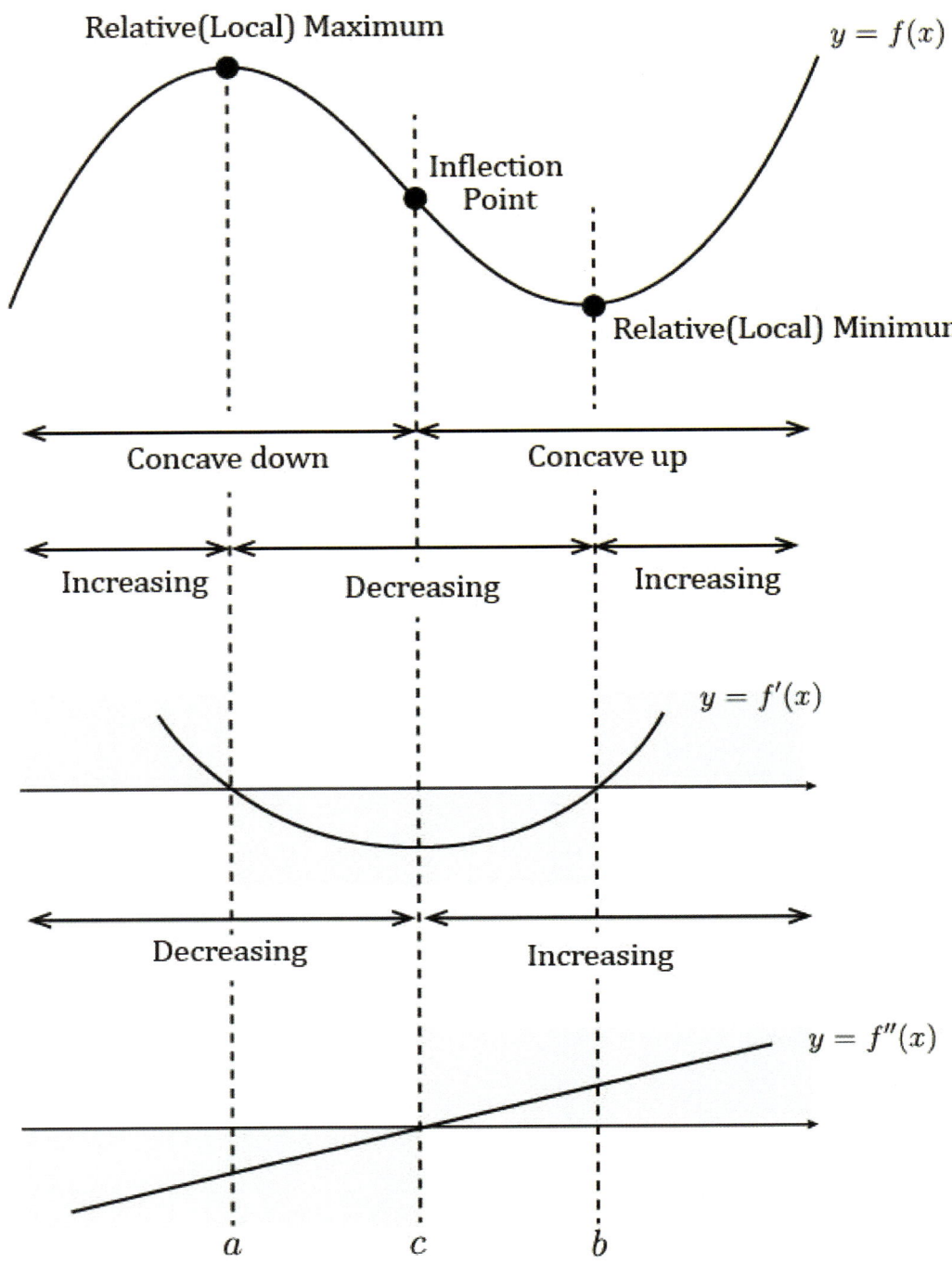

Differentiation

Special Lecture: All About Analyzing Graphs!

(1) Relative Maximum $f(a)$

① The point where $f'(x)$ changes from positive to negative.
② $f'(x)=0$ and $f''(x)<0$.

(2) Relative Minimum $f(b)$

① The point where $f'(x)$ changes from negative to positive.
② $f'(x)=0$ and $f''(x)>0$.

(3) Inflection Point $(c, f(c))$

- The point where the concavity of the graph of $y=f(x)$ changes.
- The point where there is abrupt change in the slope of the tangent line.
- The point where $f'(x)$ changes from decreasing to increasing or from increasing to decreasing.
- The point where $f''(x)=0$ and the sign of $f''(x)$ changes

Example

f has an inflection point at $x=$

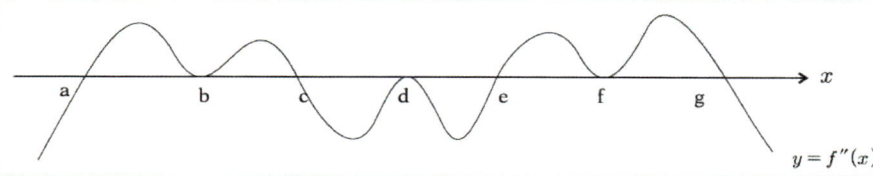

Solution

$x=a, c, e, g$

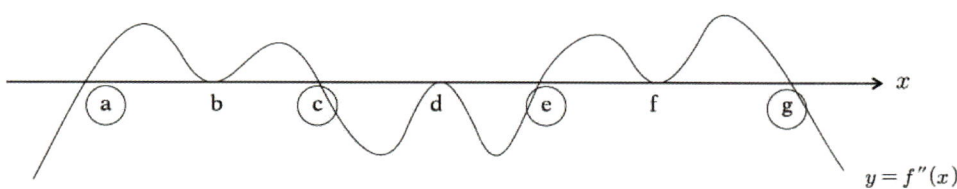

(4) Increasing

The interval where $f'(x)>0$.

(5) Decreasing

The interval where $f'(x)<0$.

(6) Concave upward

The interval where ① $f'(x)$ is increasing and ② $f''(x)>0$. The range of x.

(7) Concave downward

The interval where ① $f'(x)$ is decreasing and ② $f''(x)<0$. The range of x.

(8) Critical point

The value of x such that $f'(x)=0$ or $f'(x)$ is undetermined.

AP Calculus AB & BC Rewritten from the Beginning

(5) Critical Point

A Critical Point is a point $x=a$ such that $f'(a)=0$ or $f'(a)$ is undefined.

Let's take a closer look with the following examples.

Example 26

$f(x)=3x^3-9x$, so $f'(x)=9x^2-9$. $f'(x)$ is defined on the entire domain. Therefore, the critical point occurs when $f'(x)=0$; $9x^2-9=0$ and $x=\pm 1$.
Thus, the critical points are $x=\pm 1$.

Example 27

$f(x)=3x^3+x$, so $f'(x)=9x^2+1$. $f'(x)$ is defined on the entire domain and there is no x such that $f'(x)=0$.
Thus, a critical point does not exist.

Example 28

$f(x)=\sqrt{x-2}$, so $f'(x)=\dfrac{1}{2}(x-2)^{-\frac{1}{2}}=\dfrac{1}{2\sqrt{x-2}}$. There is no x such that $f'(x)=0$.
However, at $x=2$, $f'(x)$ does not exist, so the critical point is $x=2$.

In summary...

Special Lecture About Critical Points..

① All values of x such that $f'(x)=0$ are critical points.

② If $f'(x)$ exists on the entire domain and $f'(x)\neq 0$ for all x, f does not have a critical point.

③ All values of x such that $f'(x)$ is undefined are critical points.

Differentiation

(6) Supplementary about Relative (Local) Maximum and Minimum

Even if the graph of $y = f(x)$ is not differentiable at a certain x value, the graph of $y = f(x)$ can have a Relative (Local) Maximum or Relative (Local) Minimum at this point, as shown in the figure below.

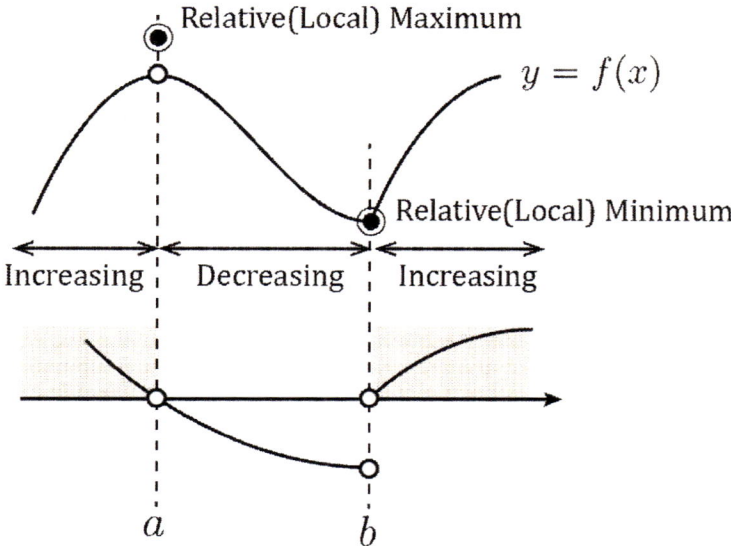

① Even if f' does not exist at a point, Relative (Local) Maximum occurs if f' changes from positive to negative passing that point. ($x = a$ in the figure above)

② Even if f' does not exist at the point, Relative (Local) Minimum occurs if f' changes from negative to positive passing that point. ($x = b$ in the figure above)

(7) Graphing Various Functions (Non-Polynomial Cases)

Polynomial functions have relatively predictable shapes, which makes them easier to graph. However, many non-polynomial functions do not have such clearly defined shapes, making them more difficult to sketch.

Exponential, rational, radical, logarithmic, and trigonometric functions, although non-polynomial, still tend to follow certain recognizable patterns.

However, functions such as $\frac{e^x}{x}$, $x^2 \sin x$, $\frac{x^2}{\ln x}$, ... are often much harder to predict.

Therefore, let's approach the graphing of these functions as follows.

Graphing Various Functions (Non-Polynomial Cases)

(1) First find all values of x such that $f'(x) = 0$.

(2) According to the values found in (1), split the domain into intervals. Select an arbitrary value of x within each interval and investigate the sign of $f'(x)$. $f(x)$ increases in the interval where $f'(x) > 0$ and decreases in the interval where $f'(x) < 0$.

(3) The point where $f'(x)$ changes from positive to negative is local maximum. The point where $f'(x)$ changes from negative to positive is local minimum.

(4) Find all values of x such that $f''(x) = 0$.

(5) According to the values found in (4), split the domain into intervals. Select an arbitrary value of x within each interval and investigate the sign of $f''(x)$. $f(x)$ is concave up in the interval where $f''(x) > 0$ and concave down in the interval where $f''(x) < 0$.

(6) Points where $f''(x)$ changes its sign is inflection point.

Differentiation

Supplement: Additional Step

(7) If the domain of the function is not a closed interval but entire real line, you should also evaluate $\lim_{x \to \infty} f(x)$ and $\lim_{x \to -\infty} f(x)$ too. You need to check what happens if x goes to $+\infty$ and $-\infty$. If the domain is not explicitly mentioned always think of the domain to be the entire real line.

Let's take a closer look through the following example.

Example 29

Sketch the graph of the function $f(x) = \dfrac{x^2 + x + 1}{e^x}$.

AP Calculus AB & BC Rewritten from the Beginning

Solution

(1) Find all values of x such that $f'(x) = 0$.

$$f'(x) = \frac{(2x+1)e^x - (x^2+x+1)e^x}{e^{2x}} = \frac{x - x^2}{e^x} = 0, \text{ so } x = 0, 1.$$

(2) Since the domain is not explicitly given, think of it as the entire real line. Split the real line using $x = 0$ and $x = 1$: $x < 0$, $0 < x < 1$, and $1 < x$. Pick one random number from each interval: -1, $\frac{1}{2}$, and 2.

$$f'(-1) = \frac{(-1) - (-1)^2}{e^{-1}} = -2e < 0: f \text{ is decreasing on } x < 0$$

$$f'\left(\frac{1}{2}\right) = \frac{\left(\frac{1}{2}\right) - \left(\frac{1}{2}\right)^2}{e^{1/2}} = \frac{1}{2\sqrt{e}} > 0: f \text{ is increasing on } 0 < x < 1$$

$$f'(2) = \frac{2 - 2^2}{e^2} = -\frac{2}{e^2} < 0: f \text{ is decreasing on } 1 < x$$

(3) At $x = 0$, $f'(x)$ changes from negative to positive: local minimum.
Local minimum is $(0, 1)$.
At $x = 1$, $f'(x)$ changes from positive to negative: local maximum.
Local maximum is $\left(1, \frac{3}{e}\right)$.

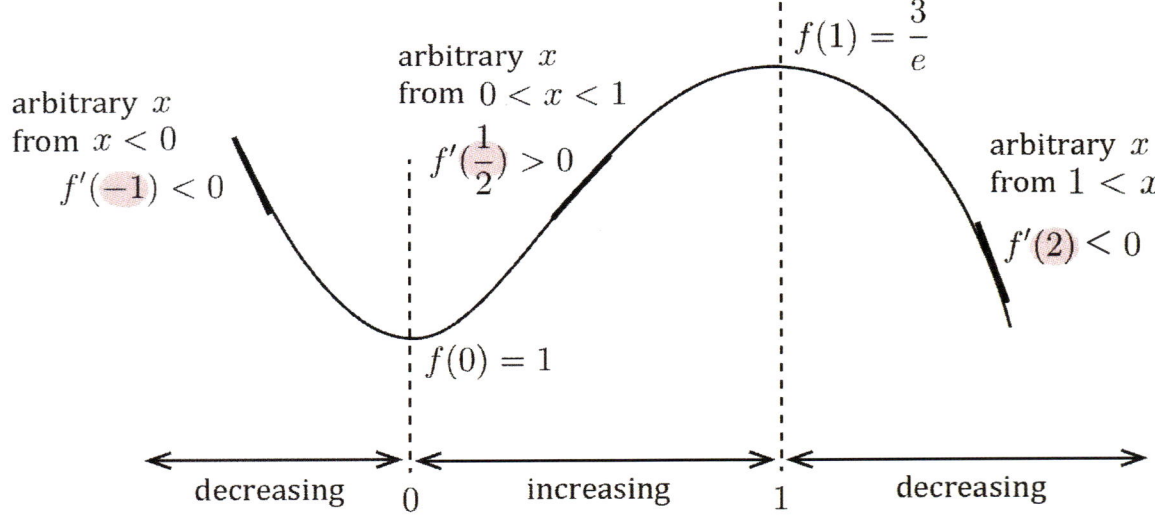

Differentiation

● **Solution**

(4) Find all values of x such that $f''(x)=0$.

$$f''(x) = \frac{(1-2x)\cdot e^x - (x-x^2)e^x}{e^{2x}} = \frac{1-3x+x^2}{e^x} = 0.$$

$1-3x+x^2 = 0$ so $x = \dfrac{3-\sqrt{5}}{2}$, $x = \dfrac{3+\sqrt{5}}{2}$.

(5) Split the real line using $x = \dfrac{3-\sqrt{5}}{2}$ and $x = \dfrac{3+\sqrt{5}}{2}$:

$x < \dfrac{3-\sqrt{5}}{2}$, $\dfrac{3-\sqrt{5}}{2} < x < \dfrac{3+\sqrt{5}}{2}$, and $\dfrac{3+\sqrt{5}}{2} < x$.

Pick one random number from each interval: 0, 1, and 3.

$f''(0) = \dfrac{1}{e^0} > 0$: f is concave up on $x < \dfrac{3-\sqrt{5}}{2}$.

$f''(1) = \dfrac{-1}{e^1} < 0$: f is concave down on $\dfrac{3-\sqrt{5}}{2} < x < \dfrac{3+\sqrt{5}}{2}$.

$f''(3) = \dfrac{1}{e^3} > 0$: f is concave up on $\dfrac{3+\sqrt{5}}{2} < x$.

(6) At both $x = \dfrac{3-\sqrt{5}}{2}$ and $x = \dfrac{3+\sqrt{5}}{2}$, f'' change its sign.

$x = \dfrac{3-\sqrt{5}}{2}$ and $x = \dfrac{3+\sqrt{5}}{2}$ are inflection points.

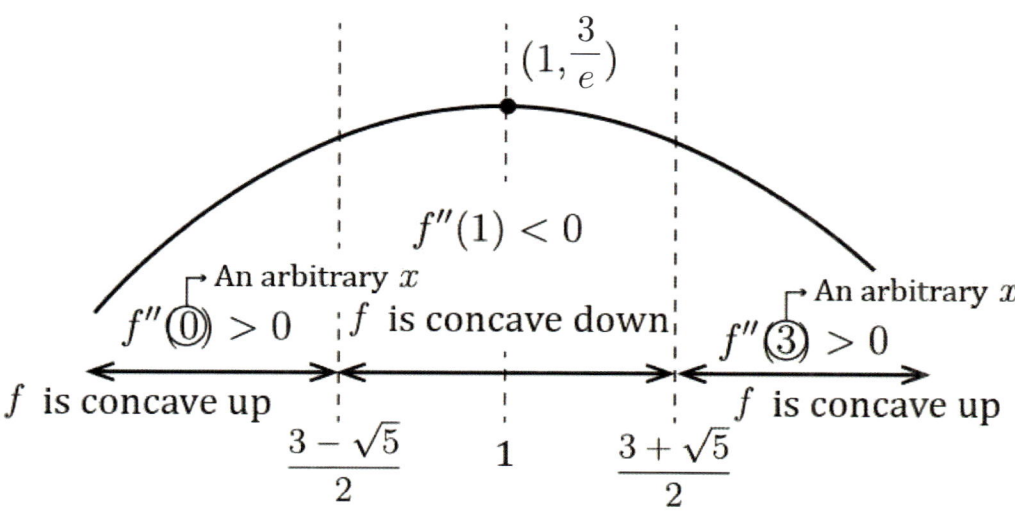

AP Calculus AB & BC Rewritten from the Beginning

Solution

(7) Since the domain is the entire real line, evaluate $\lim\limits_{x \to \infty} f(x)$ and $\lim\limits_{x \to -\infty} f(x)$ too.

- $\lim\limits_{x \to \infty} f(x) = \lim\limits_{x \to \infty} \dfrac{x^2 + x + 1}{e^x}$.

  Use L'Hôpital's rule: $\lim\limits_{x \to \infty} \dfrac{x^2 + x + 1}{e^x} = \lim\limits_{x \to \infty} \dfrac{2x+1}{e^x} = \lim\limits_{x \to \infty} \dfrac{2}{e^x} = 0$

- $\lim\limits_{x \to -\infty} f(x) = \lim\limits_{x \to -\infty} \dfrac{x^2 + x + 1}{e^x}$

  $\lim\limits_{x \to -\infty} \dfrac{x^2 + x + 1}{e^x} = \lim\limits_{t \to \infty} \dfrac{(-t)^2 + (-t) + 1}{e^{-t}} = \lim\limits_{t \to \infty} \dfrac{t^2 - t + 1}{e^{-t}}$

  As $t \to \infty$, $e^{-t} \to 0$ and $t^2 - t + 1 \to +\infty$

  $\lim\limits_{t \to \infty} \dfrac{t^2 - t + 1}{e^{-t}} = +\infty$

Plot the graph on the coordinate plane and your final graph is

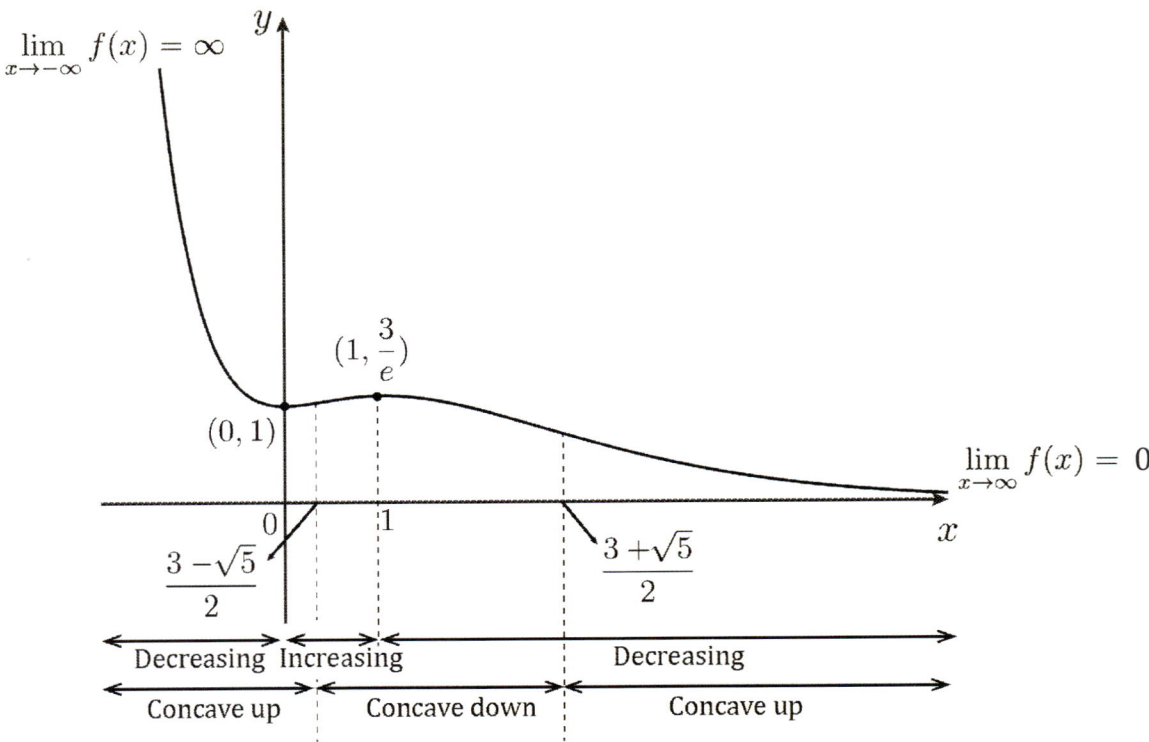

This is 'fully extended' version of how you can plot the graph of a given function. However, not always this extent is required. We will consider more examples.

Differentiation

● **Problem 1**

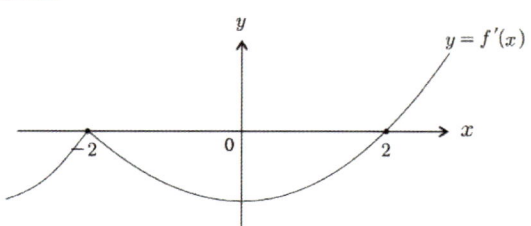

The graph of the derivative of f is shown in the figure above. Which of the following could be the graph of f?

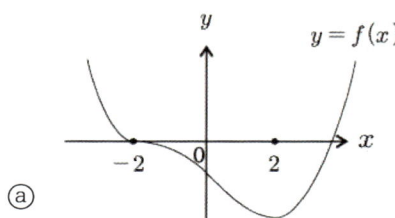
ⓐ

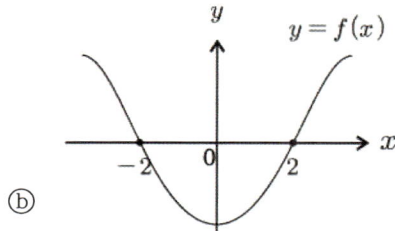
ⓑ

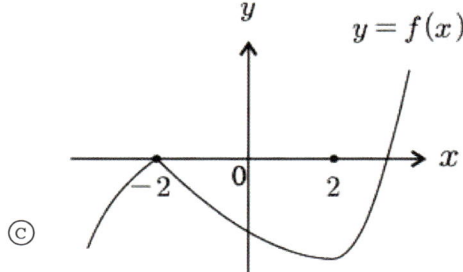
ⓒ

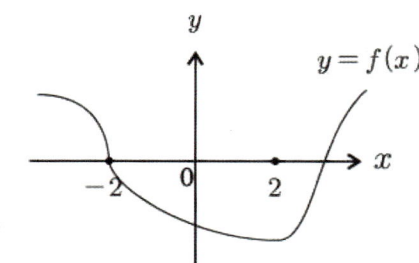
ⓓ

● **Answer** ⓐ

● **Solution**

For $x < -2$, $f'(x) < 0$, so $f(x)$ is decreasing.
For $-2 \leq x < 2$, $f'(x) < 0$, so $f(x)$ is decreasing.
For $x > 2$, $f'(x) > 0$, so $f(x)$ is increasing. ⓐ, ⓓ can be the answer.
For $x < -2$, $f'(x)$ is increasing, so $f(x)$ is concave upwards.
For $-2 \leq x < 0$, $f'(x)$ is decreasing, so $f(x)$ is concave downwards.
For $x \geq 0$, $f'(x)$ is increasing, so $f(x)$ is concave upwards. Thus, the answer is ⓐ.

AP Calculus AB & BC Rewritten from the Beginning

● ········ **Problem 2**

(1) If $f''(x) = (x-1)^2(x+1)(x+3)^3$, then the graph of $f(x)$ has inflection point(s) when $x =$

ⓐ -3 ⓑ -1 ⓒ 1 ⓓ $-3, -1$

(2) The graph of the function $y = \dfrac{1}{3}x^3 + 3x^2 + 3$ changes concavity at $x =$

ⓐ -3 ⓑ -2 ⓒ 0 ⓓ 1

(3) 🖩 The function f has a second derivative given by $f''(x) = \sqrt{x}\cos x - e^x + 3$, what is the x-coordinate of the inflection point of the graph of f?

ⓐ 0.87 ⓑ 0.98 ⓒ 1.22 ⓓ 1.38

● ········ **Answer**   (1) ⓓ   (2) ⓐ   (3) ⓒ

● ········ **Solution**

(1) When f'' is 0 and the sign changes, it is an inflection point, so $x = -3, -1$. (Check left and right to the points where f'' is 0 to see if sign changes.)

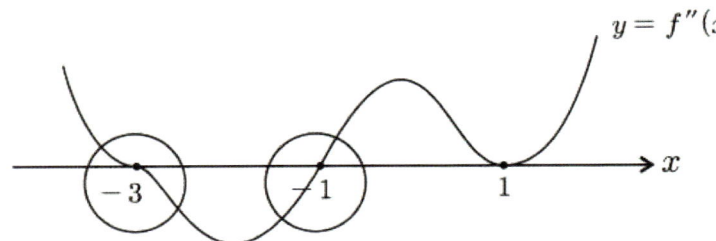

Thus, the answer is ⓓ.

(2) Change concavity $\Rightarrow$ Inflection Point!
$y' = x^2 + 6x$, $y'' = 2x + 6$. The sign of y'' changes at $x = -3$. So the answer is ⓐ.

(3) The graph of $y = f''(x)$ passes the x-axis at $x = 1.22$. That is, at $x = 1.22$, $f''(x) = 0$ and the sign changes, so this is an inflection point.
Therefore, the answer is ⓒ.

Problem 3

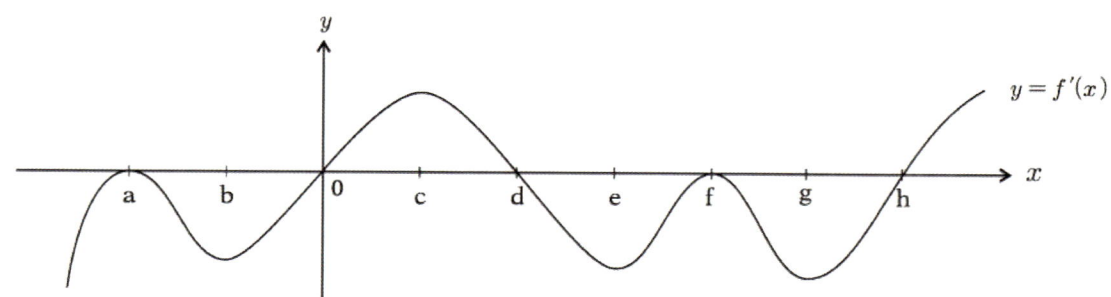

The graph of the derivative of f is shown in the figure above. For what values of x does the graph of f have a point of inflection?

ⓐ $a, 0, d, f, h$　　　ⓑ b, c, e, f　　　ⓒ a, b, c, e, f, g　　　ⓓ $a, 0, h$

Answer ⓒ

Solution

$y = f(x)$ has an inflection point when f' changes from increasing to decreasing or from decreasing to increasing. Therefore, the answer is ⓒ.

AP Calculus AB & BC Rewritten from the Beginning

Problem 4

(1) The function f given by $f(x) = -2x^3 + 9x^2 - 12x + 6$ has a relative maximum at $x =$

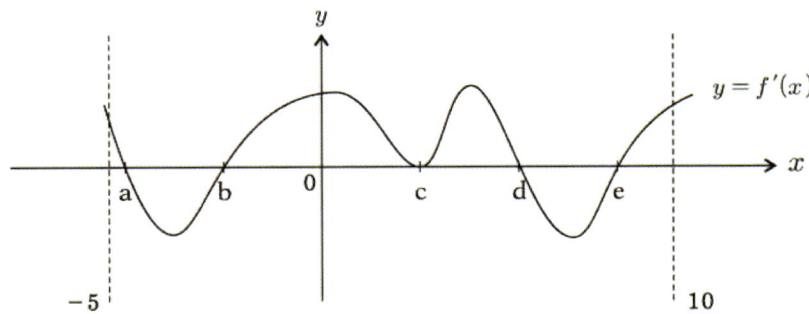

(2) The graph of f', the derivative of f, is shown in the figure above. Which of the following describe all relative extremes of f on the open interval $(-5, 10)$?

ⓐ f has relative maxima at $x = a, c$
ⓑ f has two relative maxima and three relative minima.
ⓒ f has two relative maxima and two relative minima.
ⓓ f has three critical points.

Answer (1) $x = 2$ (2) ⓒ

Solution

(1) • $f'(x) = -6x^2 + 18x - 12$.
The values of x that satisfy $-6x^2 + 18x - 12 = 0$ are $1, 2$.
• $f''(x) = -12x + 18$. $f''(1) = 6 > 0$, $f''(2) = -6 < 0$,
so $f(x)$ has a relative maximum at $x = 2$. Therefore, the answer is $x = 2$.

(2) When f' changes from positive to negative, the function has a relative maximum $(x = a, d)$ and when it changes from negative to positive, it has a relative minimum $(x = b, e)$.
Therefore, the answer is ⓒ.

Differentiation

Problem 5

(1) The function f is given by $f(x) = x^3 - 3x - 2$. On which of the following intervals is f decreasing?

ⓐ $(-1, 1)$ ⓑ $(-1, 2)$ ⓒ $(1, 2)$ ⓓ $(-\infty, \infty)$

(2)

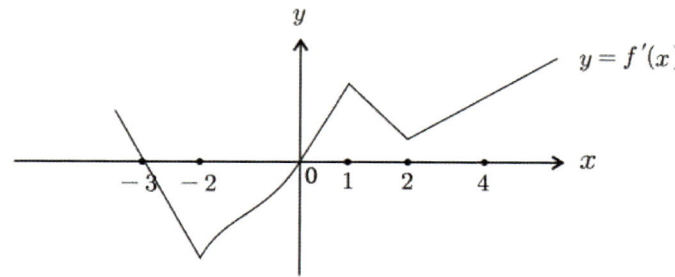

The graph of f', the derivative of a function f, is shown above.
Which of the following statements is true about f?

ⓐ f has a relative maximum at $x = 1$.
ⓑ f is decreasing in the interval $1 \leq x \leq 2$.
ⓒ f is increasing in the interval $0 \leq x \leq 4$.
ⓓ f is not differentiable at $x = -2, 1$, and 2.

Answer   (1) ⓐ (2) ⓒ

Solution

(1) Find the range of x such that $f'(x) < 0$.
If $f'(x) = 3x^2 - 3 < 0$, then $x^2 - 1 < 0$. That is, $(x-1)(x+1) < 0$, $-1 < x < 1$, so the answer is ⓐ.

(2) When $f'(x) > 0$, f is increasing, so ⓒ is correct and ⓑ is not correct.
$f'(-2)$, $f'(1)$, $f'(2)$ all exist, so ⓓ is not correct.
(*If the graph of f is as shown above, ⓓ would be correct.)
f has a relative maximum at $x = -3$ and a relative minimum at $x = 0$.
Therefore, ⓐ is not correct. The answer is ⓒ.

AP Calculus AB & BC Rewritten from the Beginning

Problem 6

(1) The graph of $y = \dfrac{1}{12}x^4 - \dfrac{1}{3}x^3 - \dfrac{3}{2}x^2 + 5x + 1$ is concave downwards for

ⓐ $-1 < x < 0$ ⓑ $0 < x < 3$ ⓒ $-3 < x < 1$ ⓓ $-1 < x < 3$

(2)

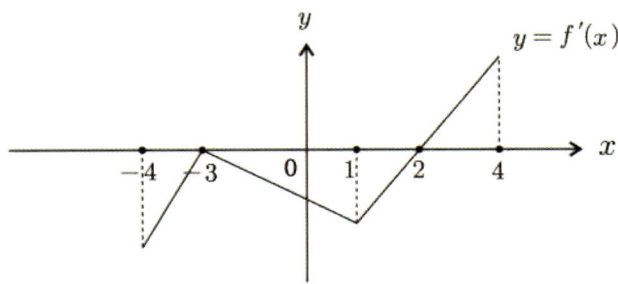

The graph of f', the derivative of a function f, is shown above. Which of the following statements about f are true?

| I. f is concave down for $-3 < x < 1$. |
| II. f is concave up for $1 < x < 4$. |
| III. f is increasing for $1 < x < 4$. |

ⓐ I ⓑ II ⓒ I, II ⓓ I, III

Answer (1) ⓓ (2) ⓒ

Solution

(1) Find the range of x such that $f''(x) < 0$.

$y' = \dfrac{1}{3}x^3 - x^2 - 3x + 5$, $y'' = x^2 - 2x - 3$. If $x^2 - 2x - 3 < 0$, $(x-3)(x+1) < 0$, and so $-1 < x < 3$. Therefore, the answer is ⓓ.

(2) When $f'(x) > 0$, f is increasing and when $f'(x) < 0$, f is decreasing. When $f'(x)$ is increasing, f is concave upwards and when $f'(x)$ is decreasing, it is concave downwards. Therefore, only I and II are correct and the answer is ⓒ.

Differentiation

● **Problem 7**

The function f has the property that $f(x) > 0$, $f'(x) < 0$, and $f''(x) > 0$ for all real values of x. Which of the following could be the graph of f?

ⓐ
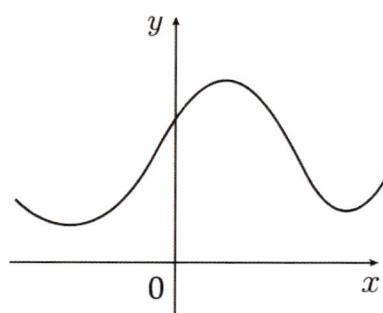

ⓑ
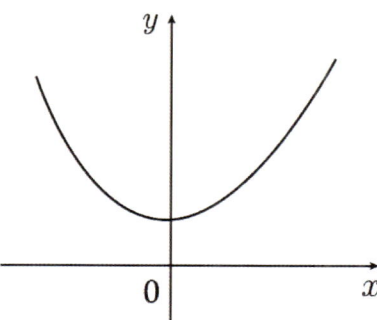

ⓒ
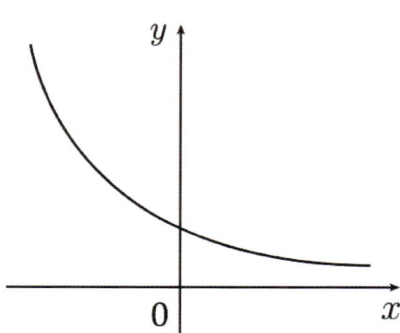

ⓓ
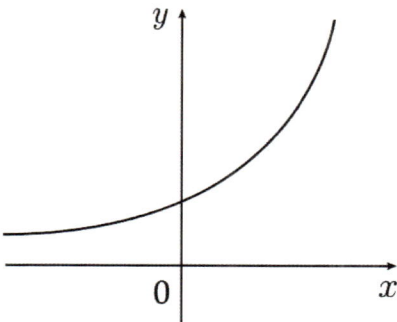

● **Answer** ⓒ

● **Solution**

$f(x) > 0$, so the graph is above the x-axis, and since $f'(x) < 0$, the function is decreasing for all real values for x. $f''(x) > 0$, so it is concave upwards.
Therefore, the answer is ⓒ.

AP Calculus AB & BC Rewritten from the Beginning

Problem 8

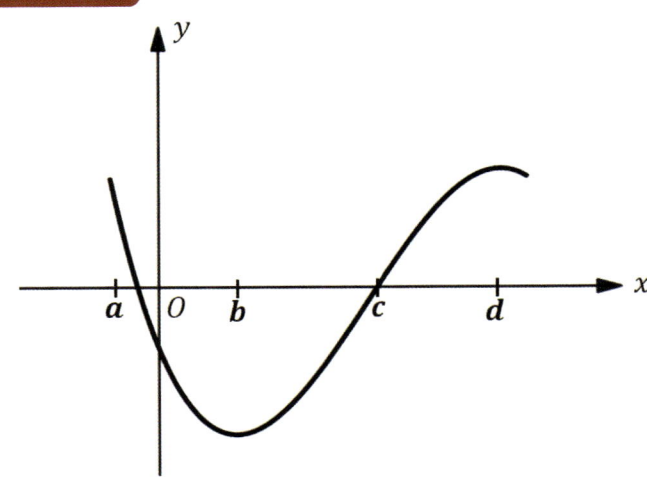

The graph of a twice-differentiable function f is shown in the figure above. Which of the following is true?

ⓐ $f''(a) < f(a) < f'(a)$
ⓑ $f(b) < f'(b) < f''(b)$
ⓒ $f'(c) < f(c) < f''(c)$
ⓓ $f''(d) < f(d) < f'(d)$

Answer ⓑ

Solution

For some constant k,
① If $f(k) > 0$, $f(k) = 0$, or $f(k) < 0$, the value is above, on, or below the x-axis, respectively.
② At $x = k$, if $f'(k) > 0$, $f(x)$ is increasing and if $f'(k) < 0$, it is decreasing
③ At $x = k$, if $f''(k) > 0$ $f(x)$ is concave upwards and if $f''(k) < 0$, it is concave downwards.

ⓐ We have $f(a) > 0$, $f'(a) < 0$ and $f''(a) > 0$. Therefore, either $f'(a) < f(a) < f''(a)$ or $f'(a) < f''(a) < f(a)$. But we cannot compare the sizes of $f''(a)$ and $f(a)$.
ⓑ We have $f(b) < 0$, $f'(b) = 0$ and $f''(b) > 0$. Therefore, $f(b) < f'(b) < f''(b)$.
ⓒ We have $f(c) = 0$, $f'(c) > 0$ and $f''(c) < 0$. Therefore, $f''(c) < f(c) < f'(c)$.
ⓓ We have $f(d) > 0$, $f'(d) = 0$ and $f''(d) < 0$. Therefore, $f''(d) < f'(d) < f(d)$.

Differentiation

Problem 9

The function f has the property that $f'(x) < 0$ and $f''(x) > 0$ for all x in the closed interval $[1, 4]$. Which of the following could be the table of values for f?

ⓐ
x	$f(x)$
1	10
2	5
3	3
4	2

ⓑ
x	$f(x)$
1	10
2	9
3	7
4	2

ⓒ
x	$f(x)$
1	10
2	11
3	12
4	13

ⓓ
x	$f(x)$
1	2
2	7
3	9
4	10

Answer

ⓐ

Solution

$f'(x) < 0$, so the function is decreasing on $[1, 4]$. $f''(x) > 0$, so it is concave upwards on $[1, 4]$. Therefore, the graph of $f(x)$ should be of the shape as shown below.

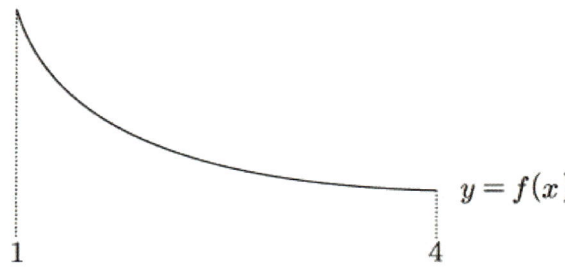

That is, the function decreases significantly in the beginning and decreases slowly later.

Within the given options, the only table that satisfies this is ⓐ. Therefore, the answer is ⓐ.

AP Calculus AB & BC Rewritten from the Beginning

Problem 10

(1) Let f be the function with the derivative given by $f'(x) = \cos(2x^2)$. How many relative extremes does f have in the interval $0 < x < 3$?
ⓐ Three   ⓑ Four   ⓒ Five   ⓓ Six

(2) Let f be the function with the derivative given by $f'(x) = \sin(x^2)$ in the interval $0 < x < 4$. How many points of inflection does the graph of f have in this interval?
ⓐ Two   ⓑ Three   ⓒ Four   ⓓ Five

(3) The first derivative of a function f is given by $f'(x) = \ln(2x) + \cos^2(5x) - 2$. How many critical values does f have in the open interval $(3, 7)$?
ⓐ One   ⓑ Two   ⓒ Three   ⓓ Four

Answer

(1) ⓓ  (2) ⓓ   (3) ⓑ

Solution

(1) ⓓ

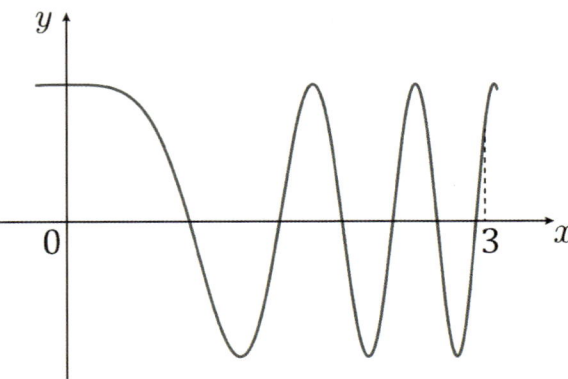

The graph of $f'(x)$ crosses the x-axis in the interval $(0, 3)$ six times. That is, the sign of $f'(x)$ changes six times, so there are 6 relative maxima or minima in the given interval. Therefore, the answer is ⓓ.

Differentiation

● ········ Solution

(2) ⓓ

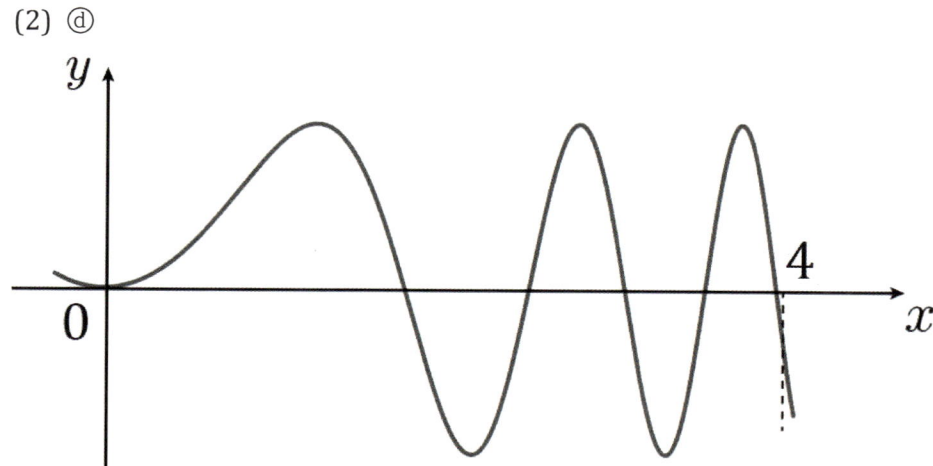

When we draw the graph of $f'(x) = \sin(x^2)$ with a calculator, we see that there are 5 points where it changes from increasing to decreasing or from decreasing to increasing in the interval $(0, 4)$. Therefore, the answer is ⓓ.

(3) ⓑ

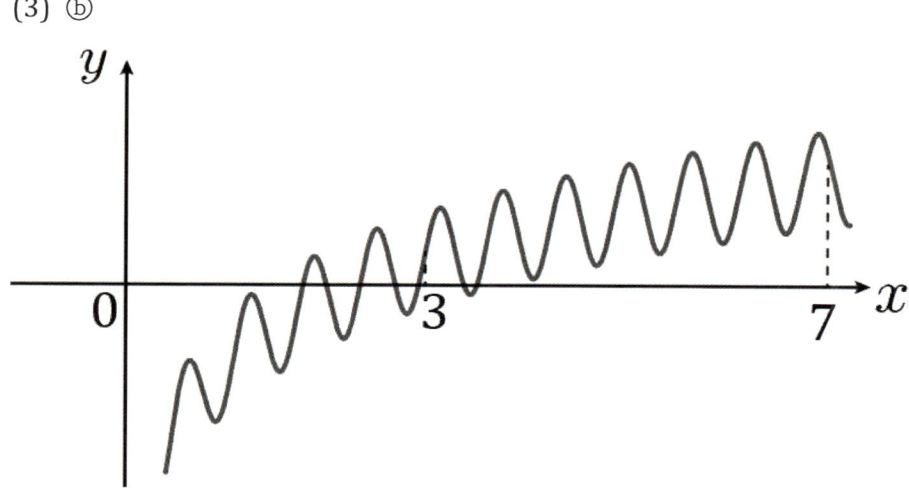

When we draw the graph of $f'(x)$ with a calculator, we see that there are 2 points such that $f'(x) = 0$ in the given interval.
Therefore, the answer is ⓑ.
(x is a critical value: $f'(x) = 0$ or $f'(x)$ is undefined)

AP Calculus AB & BC Rewritten from the Beginning

Problem 11

(1) What are the values of x for which the function f defined by $f(x) = (2x^2 + 3)e^x$ is increasing?

ⓐ $(2, \infty)$ ⓑ $(-2, 1)$ ⓒ $(-1, 3)$ ⓓ $(-\infty, \infty)$

(2) Let f be the function given by $f(x) = 4xe^{-x}$. The graph of f is concave down when

ⓐ $x < -2$ ⓑ $x < 2$ ⓒ $0 < x < 2$ ⓓ $-2 < x < 0$

Answer

(1) ⓓ (2) ⓑ

Solution

(1) ⓓ

$f'(x) = (4x)e^x + (2x^2 + 3)e^x = e^x(2x^2 + 4x + 3)$, and $e^x > 0$, we get
$$2x^2 + 4x + 3 = 2(x+1)^2 + 1 > 0.$$
Therefore, $f'(x) > 0$; the function is increasing for all real values.
The answer is ⓓ $(-\infty, \infty)$.

(2) ⓑ

$f(x)$ is concave downwards where $f''(x) < 0$.
$f'(x) = 4e^{-x} - 4xe^{-x} = (4 - 4x)e^{-x}$, $f''(x) = -4e^{-x} - (4 - 4x)e^{-x} = e^{-x}(-8 + 4x)$.
$e^{-x} > 0$ for all x. Therefore, $f''(x) < 0$ where $-8 + 4x < 0$. Thus, $x < 2$.
The answer is ⓑ.

Differentiation

Problem 12

Let f be the function defined by $f(x) = -\dfrac{1}{3}x^3 + \dfrac{7}{2}x^2 - 10x + 1$. Find the intervals where f is both increasing and concave down.

Answer

$\dfrac{7}{2} < x < 5$

Solution

① f is increasing $\Leftrightarrow f'(x) > 0 \Leftrightarrow -x^2 + 7x - 10 > 0 \Leftrightarrow x^2 - 7x + 10 < 0$.
The function is increasing on $2 < x < 5$.

② f is concave downwards $\Leftrightarrow f''(x) < 0 \Leftrightarrow -2x + 7 < 0 \Leftrightarrow x > \dfrac{7}{2}$.

The function is concave downwards on $x > \dfrac{7}{2}$. Therefore, $\dfrac{7}{2} < x < 5$.

Problem 13

x	1	2	3	4	5
$f'(x)$	2	-3	0	2	-2

A polynomial function f is given. Some values of its first derivative f' are given in the table above. Which of the following statements must be true?
ⓐ f has a relative maximum at $x = 4$.
ⓑ f has a point of inflection at $x = 3$.
ⓒ f has at least one local maximum on the interval $(1, 2)$.
ⓓ f is decreasing on the interval $(4, 5)$.

Answer

ⓒ

Solution

f' changes from positive to negative at least once on $(1, 2)$, so the answer is ⓒ.

AP Calculus AB & BC Rewritten from the Beginning

Problem 14

The function f is continuous on the closed interval $[1,3]$ and differentiable on the open interval $(1,3)$. If $f'(2) = -1$ and $f''(x) > 0$ on the entire open interval $(1,3)$, which of the following could be a table of values for f?

ⓐ
x	$f(x)$
1	3
2	2
3	1.5

ⓑ
x	$f(x)$
1	3.5
2	2
3	1.5

ⓒ
x	$f(x)$
1	4
2	2
3	1

ⓓ
x	$f(x)$
1	2
2	2.5
3	3.5

Answer
ⓑ

Solution

$f''(x) > 0$ on the entire open interval $(1,3)$ means that f is concave upwards on the open interval $(1,3)$. Using that $f'(2) = -1$ and f is concave up, we get the following plotting of f.

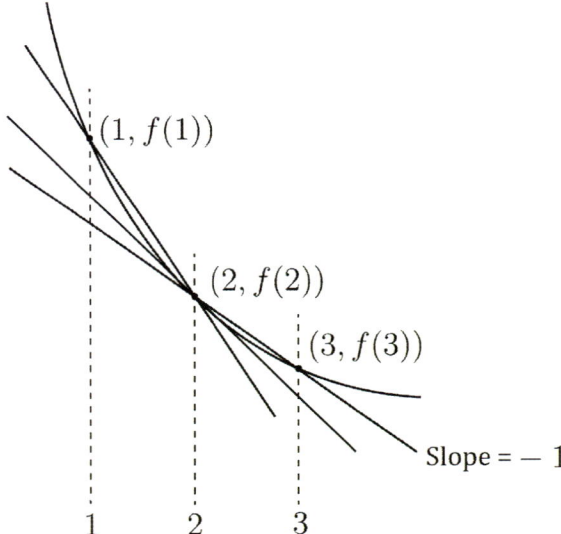

As shown above, if f is concave up, average slope between 1 and 2 ($\frac{f(2)-f(1)}{2-1}$) should be smaller than $f'(2) = -1$ and the average slope between 2 and 3 $\frac{f(3)-f(2)}{3-2}$ is greater than -1. The only table that satisfies this is ⓑ.

Differentiation

●········· **Problem 15**

The function f is twice differentiable, and the graph of f has no points of inflection. If $f(2)=2$, $f'(2)=-1$, and $f''(2)=-3$, which of the following could be the value of $f(3)$?

ⓐ 4 ⓑ 3 ⓒ 2 ⓓ 0.5

●········· **Answer** ⓓ

Solution

$f'(2) = -1 < 0 \Rightarrow$ Decreasing!

$f''(2) = -3 < 0 \Rightarrow$ Concave Down!

"... has no points of inflection···" $\Rightarrow$ concavity doesn't change!

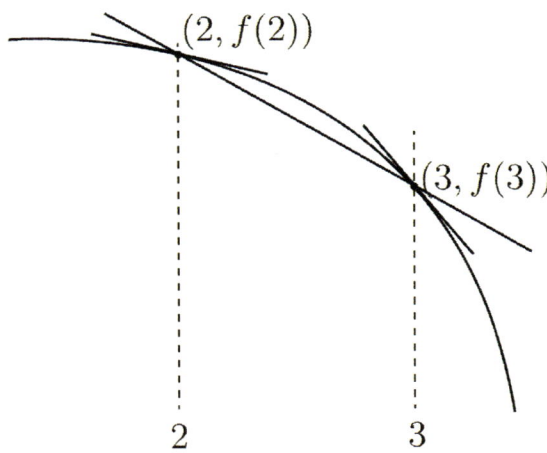

Thus, as in the figure above, the slope between 2 and 3 should be smaller than −1 $\Rightarrow \dfrac{f(3)-f(2)}{3-2} < -1$ **and thus,** $f(3) < 1$.

Therefore, the only possible answer is ⓓ.

Problem 16

The function f given by $f(x) = 3x^{\frac{2}{3}} + x - 1$ has a relative minimum at $x =$

ⓐ −8   ⓑ −4   ⓒ −21   ⓓ 0

Differentiation

● ········ **Answer**　ⓓ

● ········ **Solution**

Possible candidates of the values of x where f has a relative minimum are the values of x such that $f'(x)=0$ or $f'(x)$ is undefined.

If $f'(x)=3\times\dfrac{2}{3}x^{-\frac{1}{3}}+1=0$, then $x=-8$. However, at $x=-8$, f' changes from positive to negative ($f(-9)>0$, $f(-7)<0$). Thus, $f(-8)$ is a relative maximum not a relative minimum.

Now, we look for the values of x such that $f'(x)$ is undefined: $f'(x)$ is undefined at a single point $x=0$.
$f'(0)$ is undefined and f' changes from negative to positive at $x=0$.
Therefore, $f(0)$ is a relative minimum.

AP Calculus AB & BC Rewritten from the Beginning

Problem 17

Sketch the graphs of the following functions.
(1) $f(x) = (x-1)^3(x-2)^2(x-3)$
(2) $f(x) = x^3 - 3x^2 + 3x + 1$
(3) $f(x) = -x^4 + 2x^2 - 1$

Solution

(1)
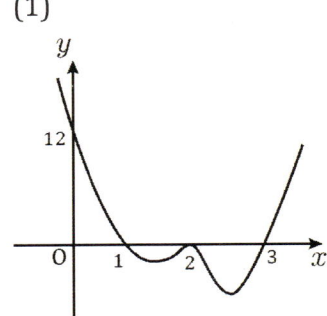

(2) ① The coefficient of x^3 is positive, so the right end of the graph points upwards.

Roughly sketch the graph.

② Find values of x such that $f'(x) = 0$.

$f'(x) = 3x^2 - 6x + 3 = 0$, so $x = 1$. Moreover, $f'(x) = 3(x-1)^2 \geq 0$.

So even though $f'(x) = 0$ at $x = 1$, f is constantly increasing.

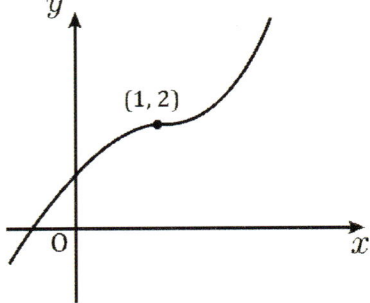

Differentiation

Solution

(3) ① The coefficient of x^4 is negative, so the right end of the graph points downwards. Roughly sketch the graph.

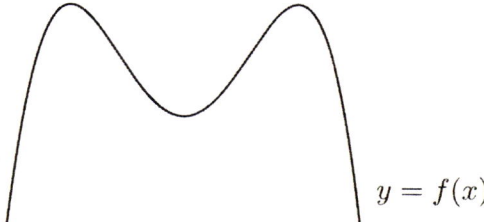

② Find values of x such that $f'(x) = 0$. $f'(x) = -4x^3 + 4x = 0$, so $x = -1, 0, 1$.

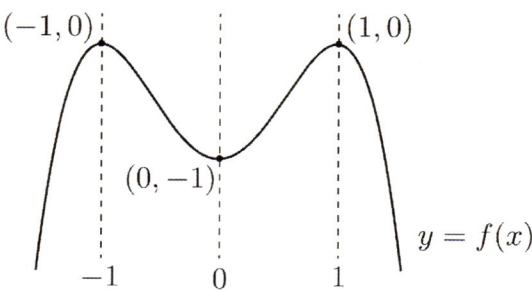

③ In the coordinate plane, the graph of the function can be plotted as follows.

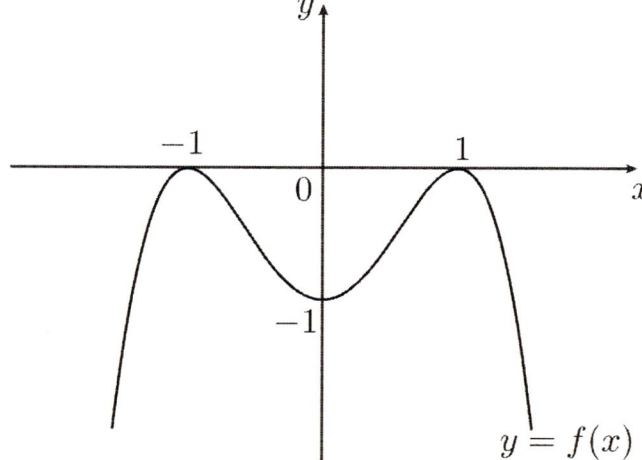

AP Calculus AB & BC Rewritten from the Beginning

● ········ **Problem 18**

Draw the graphs of the following functions. However, you do not have to investigate $f''(x)$.

1. $f(x) = e^{-x^2}$

2. $f(x) = \dfrac{x}{e^x}$

● ········ **Solution**

1. $f(x) = e^{-x^2}$

① Find values of x such that $f'(x) = 0$. If $f'(x) = -2xe^{-x^2} = 0$, then $x = 0$.

② Split the domain (not stated otherwise so we take it to be the real line) according to $x = 0$: $x < 0$ and $0 < x$.

Pick a point each from each interval: -1 and 1.

Determine the sign: $f'(-1) > 0$ and $f'(1) < 0$.

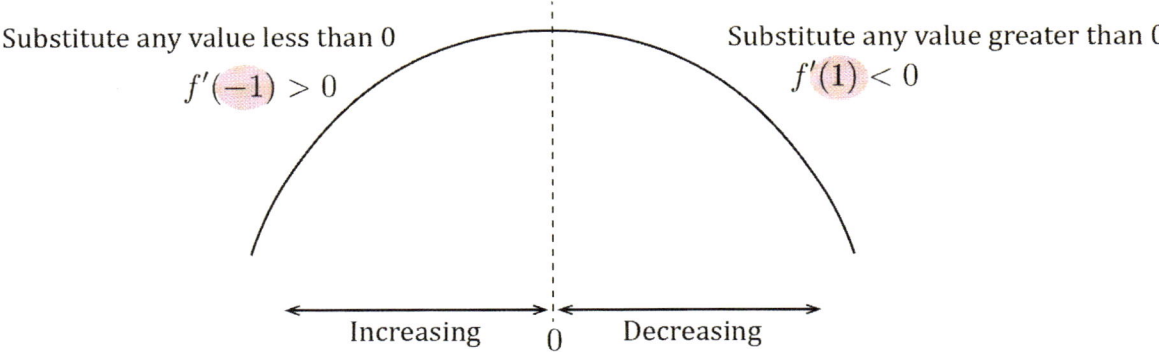

③ $\lim\limits_{x \to \infty} e^{-x^2} = 0$, $\lim\limits_{x \to -\infty} e^{-x^2} = 0$

④ Draw this on the coordinate plane.

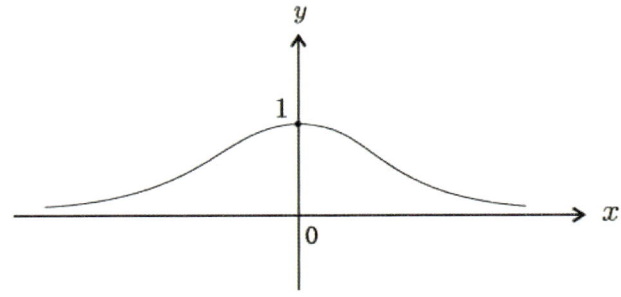

Differentiation

● ······· **Solution**

2. $f(x) = \dfrac{x}{e^x}$

① Find values of x such that $f'(x)=0$.

$f'(x) = \dfrac{x' \times e^x - x(e^x)'}{(e^x)^2} \Rightarrow f'(x) = \dfrac{e^x - xe^x}{e^{2x}} \Rightarrow f'(x) = \dfrac{e^x(1-x)}{e^{2x}} = \dfrac{1-x}{e^x}$.

Therefore, if $f'(x)=0$, then $x=1$.

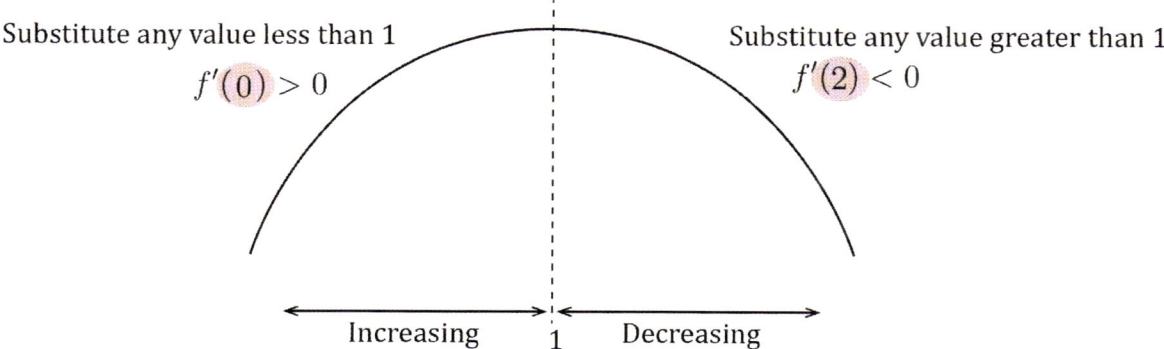

Substitute any value less than 1   Substitute any value greater than 1
$f'(0) > 0$ $f'(2) < 0$

Increasing   1   Decreasing

② Split the domain (not stated otherwise so we take it to be the real line) according to $x=1$: $x<1$ and $1<x$. Pick a point each from each interval: 0 and 2. Determine the sign: $f'(0)>0$ and $f'(2)<0$.

③ The domain is not given, so we think of the domain as the entire real line and find $\lim\limits_{x \to \infty} f(x)$ and $\lim\limits_{x \to -\infty} f(x)$.

$\lim\limits_{x \to \infty} \dfrac{x}{e^x} \Rightarrow \dfrac{\infty}{\infty}$ form, so apply L'Hopital's Rule!

$\lim\limits_{x \to \infty} \dfrac{(x)'}{(e^x)'} \Rightarrow \lim\limits_{x \to \infty} \dfrac{1}{e^x} = \dfrac{1}{\infty} = 0$

• $\lim\limits_{x \to -\infty} \dfrac{x}{e^x}$ is not of $\dfrac{\infty}{\infty}$ form, so just directly substitute $-\infty$ for x!

$\lim\limits_{x \to -\infty} \dfrac{x}{e^x} \Rightarrow \dfrac{-\infty}{e^{-\infty}} = -\infty \times e^{\infty} = -\infty$

AP Calculus AB & BC Rewritten from the Beginning

Solution

④ Draw this on the coordinate plane.

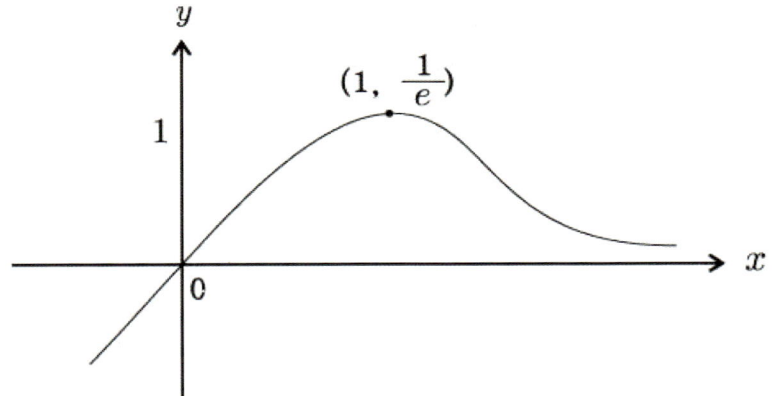

If we determine the concavity with $f''(x)$, we can draw a more precise graph but that is not asked to be done for this problem. Sometimes, only knowing where the function increases and where the function decreases is enough for our practical purposes.

Differentiation

Problem 19

Sketch the graphs of the functions given below. (※ For problem (3), plot the inflection points)

(1) $f(x) = \dfrac{1}{3}x^3 - 2x^2 + 3x + 1$

(2) $f(x) = -x^3 + 6x^2 - 12x - 2$

(3) $f(x) = \dfrac{\ln x}{x^3}$ $(x > 0)$

(4) $f(x) = \sin x + \dfrac{1}{2}\sin 2x$ $(0 \leq x \leq 2\pi)$

Solution

(1) A. The leading coefficient is positive, so the right end of the graph points upwards.

B. The rough shape of the graph is as follows.

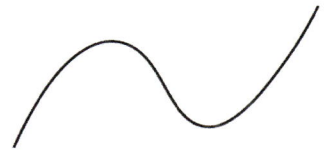

C. Find the values of x and y such that $f'(x) = 0$.
$f'(x) = x^2 - 4x + 3 = 0$, so $x = 1, 3$.
$f(1) = \dfrac{7}{3}$ and $f(3) = 1$.

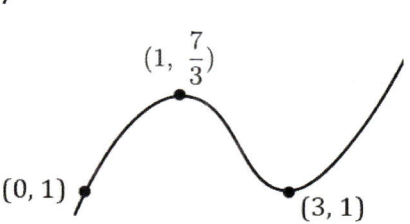

D. Let's plot the graph on the coordinate plane.

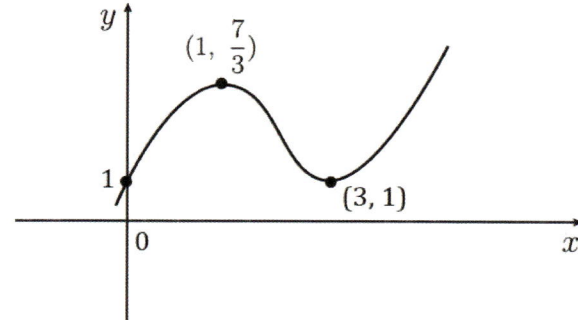

AP Calculus AB & BC Rewritten from the Beginning

Solution

(2) A. The leading coefficient is negative, so the right end of the graph points downwards.

B. The rough shape of the graph is as follows.

C. Find the values of x and y such that $f'(x) = 0$.
$f'(x) = -3x^2 + 12x - 12 = 0$, so $x^2 - 4x + 4 = 0$.
Thus, $x = 2$. $f(2) = -10$.
There is only one value of x such that $f'(x) = 0$, so the graph can be roughly drawn as follows.

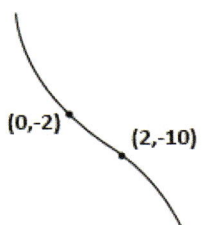

D. Let's plot the graph on the coordinate plane.

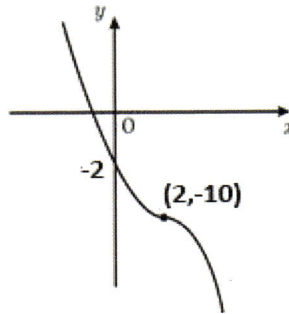

(3) A. Find all values of x such that $f'(x) = 0$.
$f(x) = \dfrac{\ln x}{x^3}$, so $f'(x) = \dfrac{1 - 3 \cdot \ln x}{x^4}$. Therefore, $x = \sqrt[3]{e}$.

B.

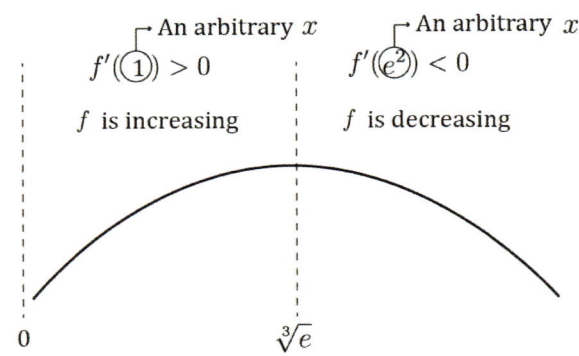

Differentiation

Solution

C. $f'(x) = \dfrac{-\dfrac{3}{x} \cdot x^4 - (1 - 3\ln x) \cdot 4x^3}{x^8} = 0$, which gives $f''(x) = \dfrac{-7 + 12 \cdot \ln x}{x^5} = 0$, so $x = e^{\frac{7}{12}}$.

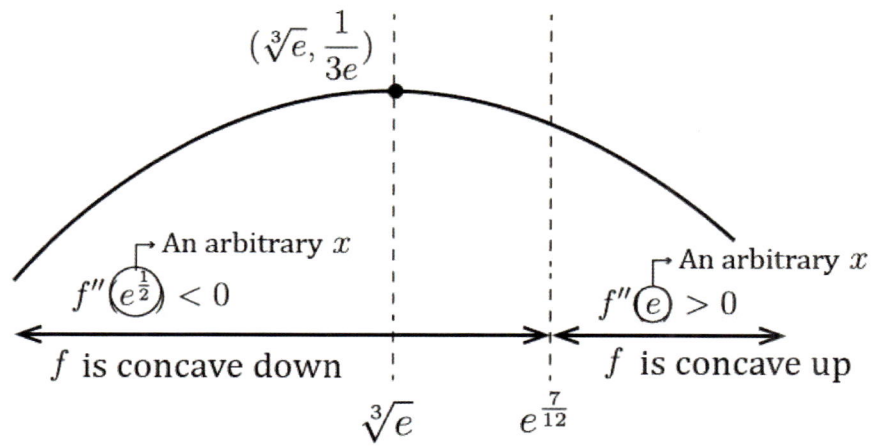

D. $\lim\limits_{x \to \infty} f(x) = \lim\limits_{x \to \infty} \dfrac{\ln x}{x^3}$. Using L'Hôpital's rule, we get $\lim\limits_{x \to \infty} \dfrac{\dfrac{1}{x}}{3x^2} = 0$.

$\lim\limits_{x \to -\infty} f(x) = \lim\limits_{x \to -\infty} \dfrac{\ln x}{x^3} = -\infty$

E. Let's plot the graph on the coordinate plane.

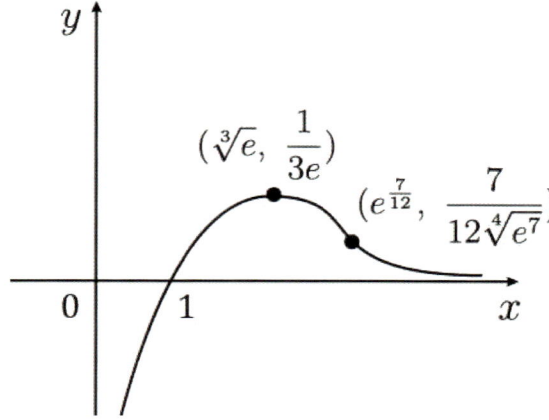

Solution

(4) A. Find all values of x such that $f'(x) = 0$.

$\sin 2x = 2\sin x \cdot \cos x$, so $f(x) = \sin x + \sin x \cdot \cos x$.

Therefore, $f'(x) = -\sin^2 x + \cos x + \cos^2 x = 2\cos^2 x + \cos x - 1 = (2\cos x - 1)(\cos x + 1)$.

$2\cos x - 1 = 0$ gives $x = \dfrac{\pi}{3}, \dfrac{5}{3}\pi$ and $\cos x + 1 = 0$ gives $x = \pi$.

B.

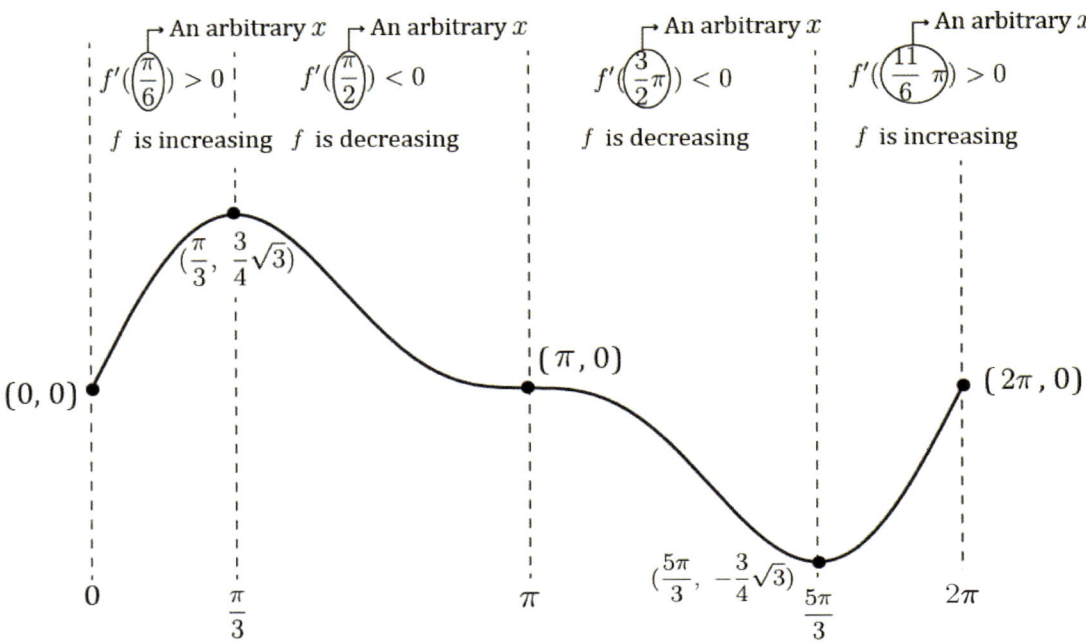

C. Let's plot the graph on the coordinate plane.

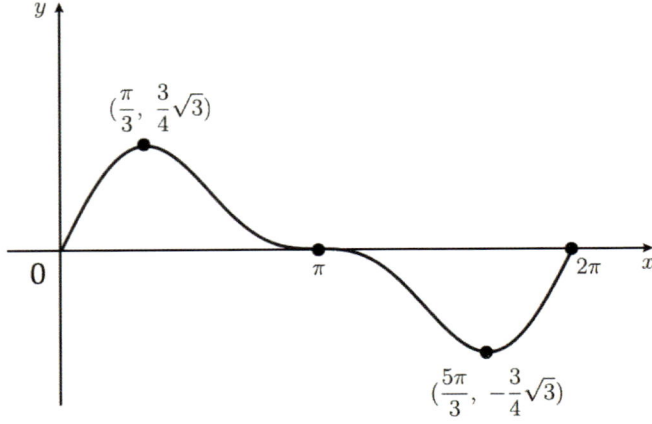

08 Exercise

01 Graph $y = -\dfrac{1}{3}x^3 + x^2 - x + 1$.

02 Sketch the graph of the following equation

(1) $y = -x^2 + 3x + 4$

(2) $y = \dfrac{2x}{x^2 + 1}$

03 Graph $y = (x-1)^2(x+1)(x+3)^4$.

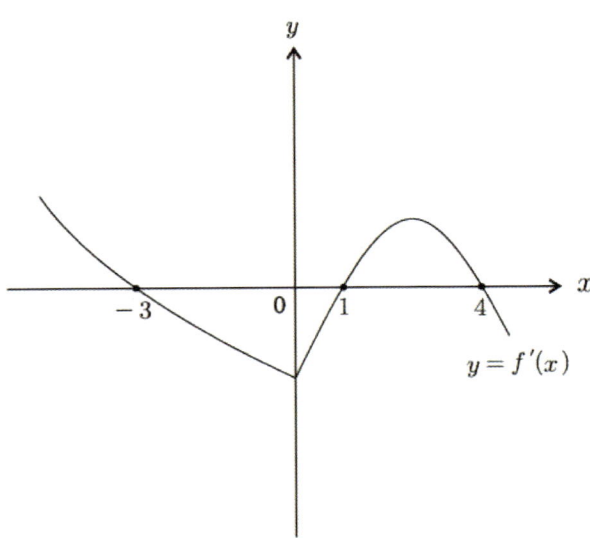

04 The graph of the derivative of f is shown in the figure above. Which of the following could be the graph of f?

ⓐ
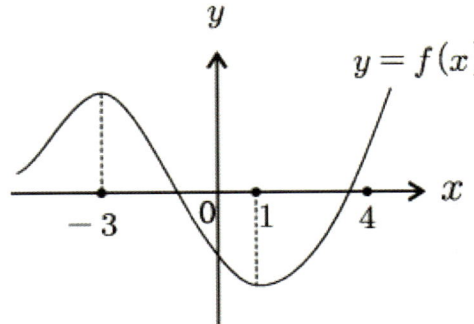

ⓑ
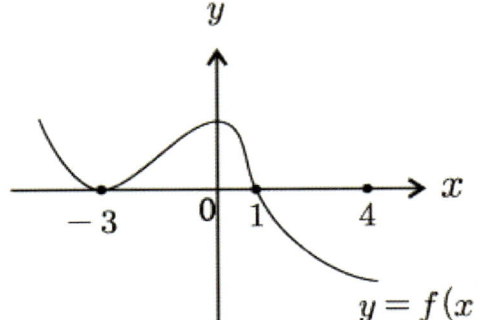

ⓒ
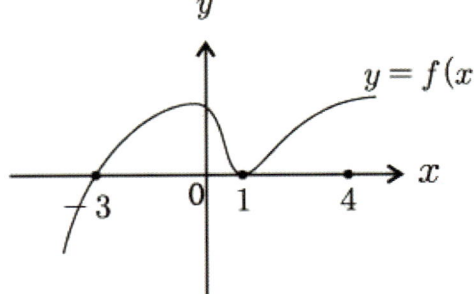

ⓓ
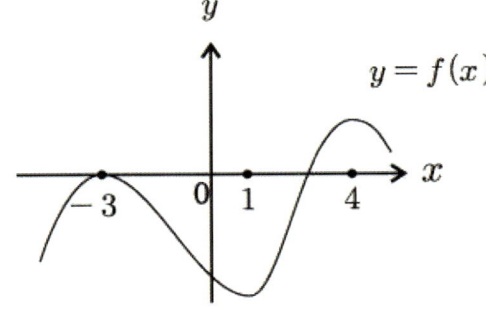

05 If $f''(x)=(x+1)^2(x+2)^4(x+3)^5$, then the graph of $f(x)$ has inflection point(s) when $x=$

ⓐ -3 ⓑ -2 ⓒ -1 ⓓ $-3,\,-1$

06 What is the x-coordinate of the point of inflection on the graph of $y=\dfrac{1}{3}x^3-3x^2+1$?

ⓐ -3 ⓑ -2 ⓒ 0 ⓓ 3

07 The function f has second derivative given by $f''(x)=(x-1)\sin(2x)$, $\dfrac{\pi}{4}\le x\le\dfrac{3\pi}{4}$. What is the x-coordinate(s) of the inflection point of f?

ⓐ $-1,\,-1.57$ ⓑ -1 ⓒ 1.57 ⓓ $1,\,1.57$

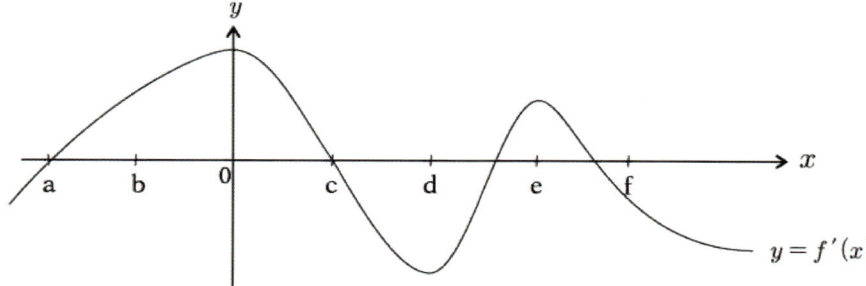

08 The graph of $y=f'(x)$ is shown above. Find all the x-coordinates of points of inflection for the graph of f.

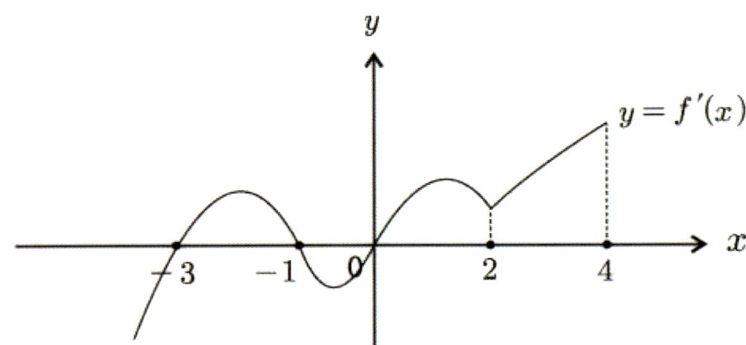

09 The graph of f', the derivative of the function f, is shown above. Which of the following statements is true about f?

ⓐ f is increasing for $-3 \leq x \leq 0$ and $2 \leq x \leq 4$.
ⓑ f has three inflection points.
ⓒ f has relative minimum at $x = -1$.
ⓓ f is decreasing for $-1 \leq x \leq 0$.

10 The graph of $y = x^3 - 4x^2 + 3x + 2$ is concave up for

ⓐ $x > \dfrac{4}{3}$ ⓑ $x < \dfrac{4}{3}$ ⓒ $0 < x < \dfrac{4}{3}$ ⓓ $x > -\dfrac{4}{3}$

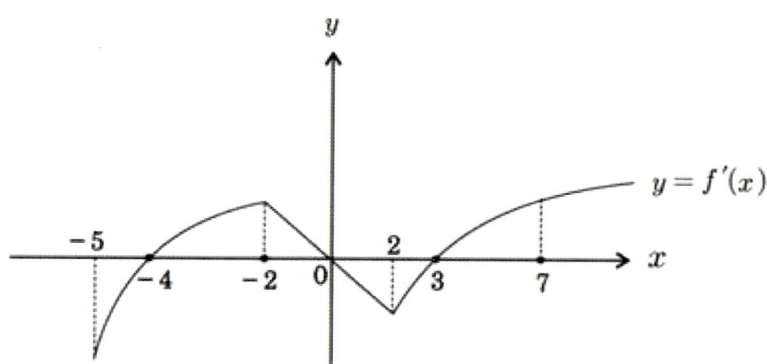

11 The graph of f', the derivative of the function f, is shown above. Which of the following statements about f are true?

> I. f is concave up for $-4 < x < 0$
> II. f is concave down for $-2 < x < 2$
> III. f has a relative maximum at $x = 3$
> IV. f has two inflection points

ⓐ I, III   ⓑ II, IV   ⓒ II, III, and IV   ⓓ I, II, and III

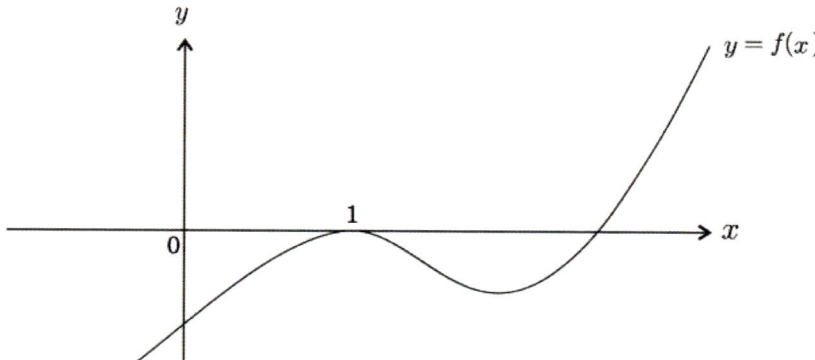

12 The graph of a twice-differentiable function f is shown in the figure above. Which of the following is true?

ⓐ $f(1) < f'(1) < f''(1)$ ⓑ $f''(1) < f'(1) = f(1)$
ⓒ $f'(1) = f''(1) < f(1)$ ⓓ $f(1) < f''(1) < f'(1)$

13 The function f has the property that $f'(x) > 0$ and $f''(x) < 0$ for all x in the closed interval $[1, 4]$. Which of the following could be a table of values for f?

ⓐ
x	$f(x)$
1	10
2	5
3	3
4	2

ⓑ
x	$f(x)$
1	10
2	9
3	7
4	2

ⓒ
x	$f(x)$
1	10
2	11
3	12
4	13

ⓓ
x	$f(x)$
1	2
2	7
3	9
4	10

(14~16) 🖩

Let f be the function with derivative given by $f'(x) = \sin(2x + 1)$ on the interval $\frac{1}{2} < x < 7$.

14 How many relative extrema does f have on this interval?
ⓐ Three ⓑ Four ⓒ Five ⓓ Six

15 How many points of inflection does the graph of f have on this interval?
ⓐ Three ⓑ Four ⓒ Five ⓓ Six

16 How many critical value does f have on this interval?
ⓐ Three ⓑ Four ⓒ Five ⓓ Six

(17~18) Let f be the function given by $f(x)=x+2\sin x$ on the interval $0<x<2\pi$.

17 What are all values of x for which the function f is decreasing?

ⓐ $\dfrac{2}{3}\pi < x < \dfrac{4}{3}\pi$ ⓑ $\pi < x < 2\pi$

ⓒ $\dfrac{2}{3}\pi < x < 2\pi$ ⓓ $0 < x < \pi$

18 What are all value of x for which the function f is concave up?

ⓐ $\dfrac{2}{3}\pi < x < \dfrac{4}{3}\pi$ ⓑ $\pi < x < 2\pi$

ⓒ $\dfrac{2}{3}\pi < x < 2\pi$ ⓓ $0 < x < \pi$

(19~21)

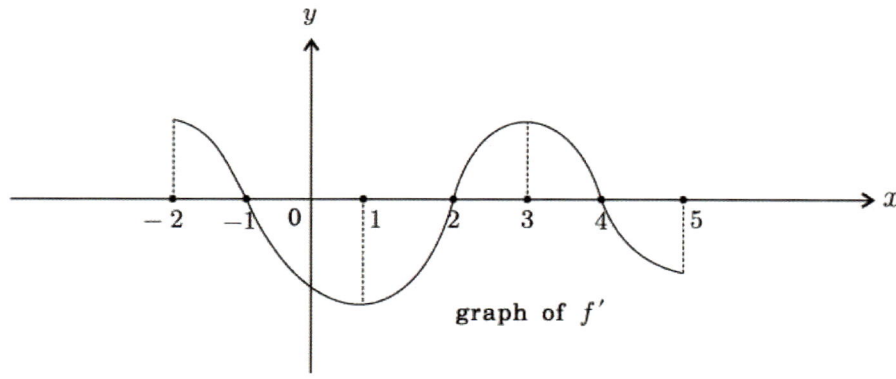

graph of f'

The graph of f', the derivative of f, is shown above. Let g be the function given by $g(x)=e^{-f(x)}$.

19 For $-2<x<5$, find all values of x at which g has a relative minimum. Justify your answer.

AP Calculus AB & BC Rewritten from the Beginning

20 For $-2 < x < 5$, find all values of x at which f has an inflection point. Justify your answer.

21 For $-2 < x < 5$, find all the critical points.

22 Given f' as graphed, which could be the graph of f?

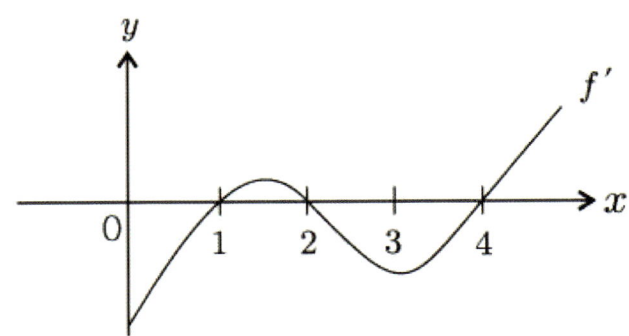

ⓐ

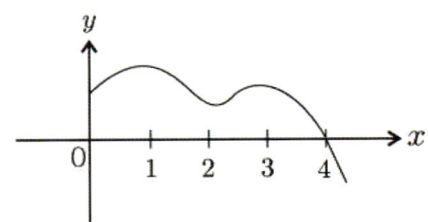

ⓑ

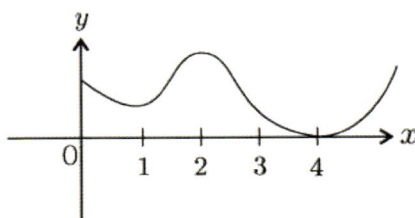

ⓒ

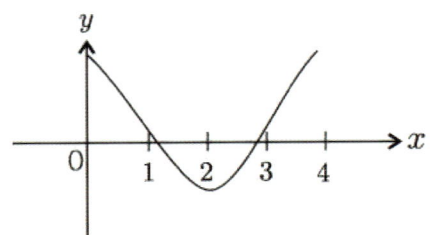

ⓓ

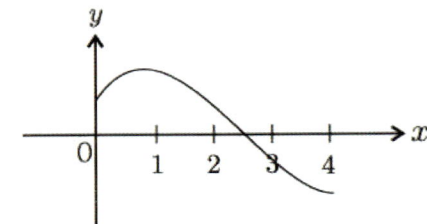

23 Let $f(x)=2x^3-27x^2+48x+4$. Find intervals of x where f is both decreasing and concave down.

24 A polynomial function f is given. Some values of its second derivative f'' are given in the table below. Which of the following statements must be true?

x	1	2	3	4	5
$f''(x)$	2	1	−1	5	2

ⓐ f has local maximum at $x=4$.
ⓑ f has local minimum at $x=3$.
ⓒ f is concave upward on the interval $(1,2)$.
ⓓ f has at least one inflection point on the interval $(3,4)$.

25 The function f is continuous on the closed interval $[2,4]$ and differentiable on the open interval $(2,4)$. If $f'(3)=2$ and $f''(x)<0$ on the entire open interval $(2,4)$, which of the following could be a table of values for f?

ⓐ
x	$f(x)$
2	0
3	2
4	4

ⓑ
x	$f(x)$
2	3
3	2
4	0

ⓒ
x	$f(x)$
2	1
3	2
4	4

ⓓ
x	$f(x)$
2	−2
3	3
4	4

26 The function f given by $f(x) = 6x^{\frac{2}{3}} + 2x + 2$ has relative minimum at $x =$

ⓐ -8

ⓑ -4

ⓒ -2

ⓓ 0

27 Sketch the graphs of the functions given below. As for (1) and (3), indicate where the graph increases/decreases. Plot the relative extrema, if any. As for (2), also indicate where the graph is concave up/concave down. Plot the inflection points, if any.

(1) $f(x) = x^3 + \dfrac{3}{2}x^2 + 6x + 3$

(2) $f(x) = e^{-x^2}$

(3) $f(x) = \dfrac{x}{x^2 + 1}$

28 Sketch the graph.

$f(x) = x - 2\cos x \ (0 \leq x < 2\pi)$

Differentiation

08   Answers & Solutions

01

① The coefficient of x^3 is negative, so the right end points downwards.
Roughly sketch the graph as shown on the right.

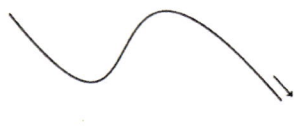

② Find the value of x such that $f'(x)=0$.
$f'(x)=-x^2+2x-1$ so $f'(x)=0$ when $x=1$.
Moreover, $f'(x)\leq 0$ for all x so the function is always decreasing. The graph is as shown on the right.

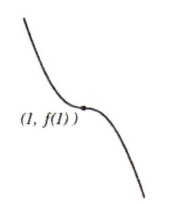

02

(1) ① The coefficient of x^2 is negative, so the right end points downwards.
Roughly sketch the graph as shown on the right.

② Find the value of x such that $f'(x)=0$.
$f'(x)=-2x+3$, so $f'(x)=0$ when $x=1.5$.

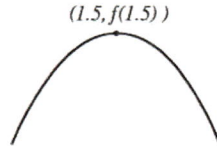

(2) ① $y'=\dfrac{-2(x+1)(x-1)}{(x^2+1)^2}$, so the value of x such that $y'=0$ are $-1, 1$.

② $f'(-2)<0,\ f'(0)>0,\ f'(2)<0$

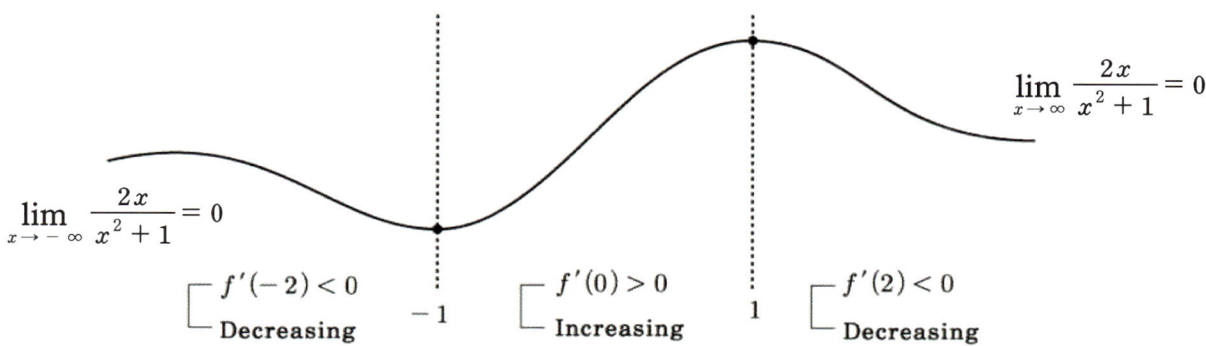

313

03

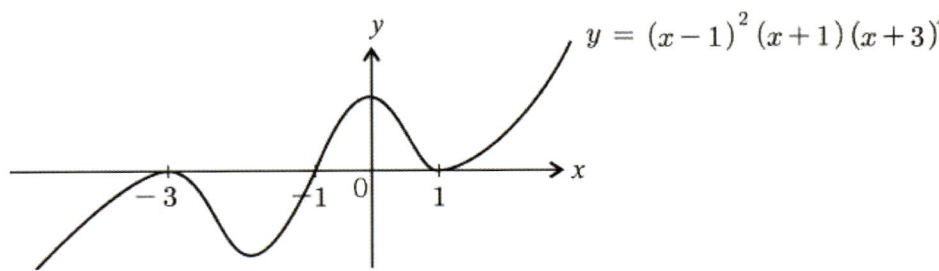

04 ⓓ

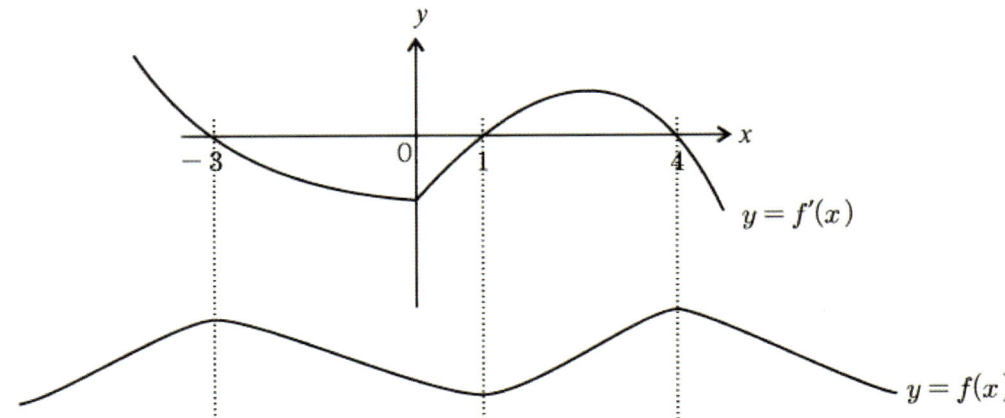

At $x < -3$, $f'(x) > 0$, so f is increasing.
At $-3 < x < 1$, $f'(x) < 0$, so f is decreasing.
At $1 < x < 4$, $f'(x) > 0$, so f is increasing.
At $4 < x$, $f'(x) < 0$, so f is decreasing.

05 ⓐ

The graph of $y = f''(x)$ is...

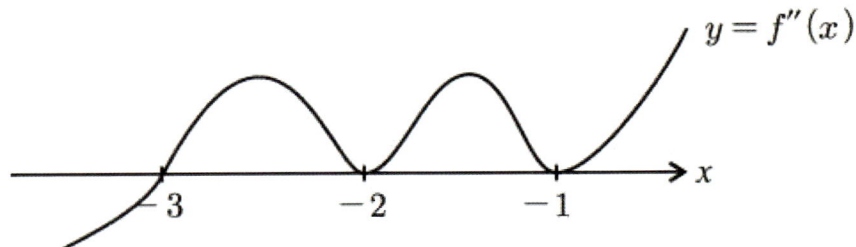

That is, at $x = -3$, f'' is 0 and the sign changes.

06 ⓓ

$y' = x^2 - 6x$, $y'' = 2x - 6$

That is,

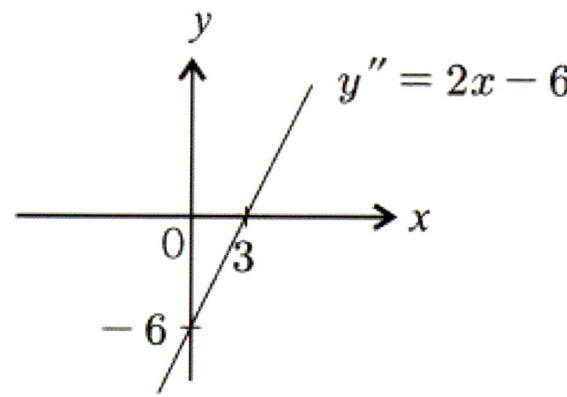

y'' becomes 0 at $x = 3$ and the sign changes,
so $y = f(x)$ has an inflection point at $x = 3$.

07 ⓓ

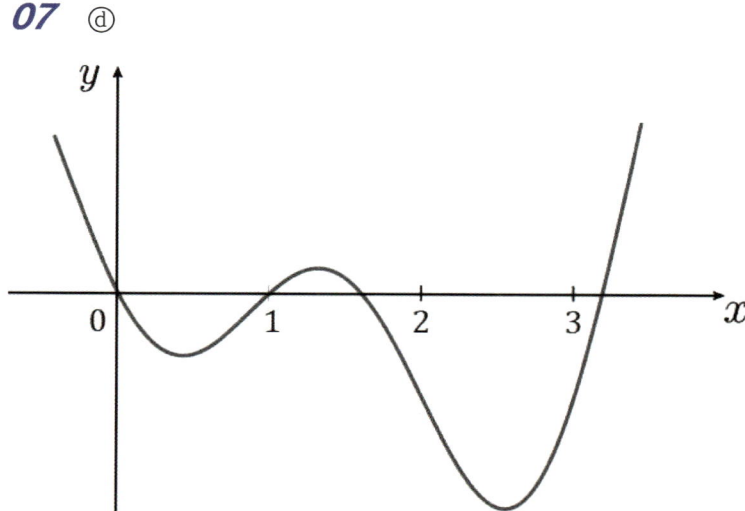

When we draw the graph of $f''(x) = (x-1)\sin(2x)$ using a calculator, we can see that it crosses the x-axis ($f''(x) = 0$) at $x = 1$ and $x = 1.57$.
Also, at these two points the sign of $f''(x)$ changes: the x coordinates of the inflection points are 1 and 1.57.

AP Calculus AB & BC Rewritten from the Beginning

08 ⓑ, ⓓ, ⓔ

When $f'(x)$ changes from increasing to decreasing or from decreasing to increasing, the function has an inflection point.

09 ⓓ

f is increasing when $f'(x) > 0$, however, $f'(x) < 0$ at $-1 < x < 0$, so ⓐ is not correct.
f has inflection points when $f'(x)$ changes from decreasing to increasing or from increasing to decreasing. So, f has 4 inflection points. So, ⓑ is not correct.
f has a relative minimum when $f'(x) = 0$ and is increasing. At $x = -1$, $f'(x)$ is decreasing, so ⓒ is not correct.

$f(x)$ is decreasing where $f'(x) \leq 0$, so the answer is ⓓ.

10 ⓐ

$y' = 3x^2 - 8x + 3$, $y'' = 6x - 8$.
The function is concave up where $y'' > 0$: $6x - 8 > 0$.
That is, $x > \dfrac{4}{3}$.

11 ⓑ

If $f'(x)$ is decreasing, $f(x)$ is concave down, and if it is increasing, $f(x)$ is concave up. So, $f(x)$ is concave down for $-2 < x < 2$, and concave up for $-5 < x < -2$ and $x > 2$.
When $f'(x)$ changes from increasing to decreasing or from decreasing to increasing, the function has an inflection point, so f has two inflection points at $x = -2$ and $x = 2$.
f has a relative maximum when $f'(x) = 0$ and $f'(x)$ changes from positive to negative. $f'(x) = 0$ and f is decreasing at $x = 0$.

12 ⓑ

$f(1)=0$, $f'(1)=0$, $f''(1)<0$, so $f''(1)<f'(1)=f(1)$, and the answer is ⓑ.

13 ⓓ

$f'(x)>0$ and $f''(x)<0$, so $f(x)$ is increasing and concave down. Therefore, the graph should be of the shape as shown below.

It increases significantly in the beginning and increases slowly later.

Among (a), (b), (c), and (d), only (d) is in this shape.

14 ⓑ

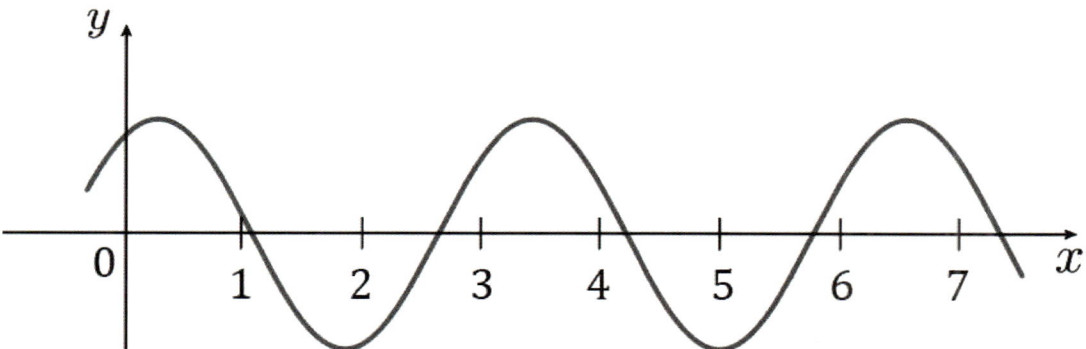

When we draw the graph of $f'(x)=\sin(2x+1)$ using a calculator, we can see that it crosses the x-axis at 4 different points within the given interval. That is, the sign of $f'(x)$ changes 4 times, so the function has 4 extreme values.

15 ⓑ

There are 4 points where the graph of $f'(x)$ changes from increasing to decreasing or from decreasing to increasing, so the function has 4 inflection points.

16 ⓑ

Critical values are values of c such that $f'(c)=0$ or $f'(c)$ is undefined. $f'(c)$ is defined on the entire domain and there are 4 values of c such that $f'(c)=0$. Therefore, there are 4 critical values.

17 ⓐ

f is decreasing when $f'(x)<0$. $f'(x)=1+2\cos x$.

$1+2\cos x<0 \Leftrightarrow \cos x<-\dfrac{1}{2} \Leftrightarrow \dfrac{2}{3}\pi<x<\dfrac{4}{3}\pi$.

18 ⓑ

The function is concave up where $f''(x)>0$. $f''(x)=-2\sin x$.

$-2\sin x>0 \Leftrightarrow \sin x<0 \Leftrightarrow \pi<x<2\pi$.

19 $x=-1, 4$

Where $g'(x)$ changes from negative to positive, there is a relative minimum. $e^{-f(x)}$ is always positive (for any value of $f(x)$), so $g(x)$ has a relative minimum where $-f'(x)$ changes from negative to positive. Therefore, g has relative minimum at $x=-1$ and $x=4$.

(*Note that the graph of $-f'(x)$ is a reflection of the graph of $f'(x)$ about the x-axis.)

20 $x=1, 3$

f has an inflection point where f' changes from increasing to decreasing, or from decreasing to increasing.

The function f' changes from decreasing to increasing at $x=1$, and changes from increasing to decreasing at $x=3$.

Differentiation

21 $x = -1, 2,$ and 4

The values of c such that $f'(c) = 0$ or $f'(c)$ is undefined are the critical values.
In this graph, the values of c such that $f'(c) = 0$ are $-1, 2, 4$.

22 ⓑ

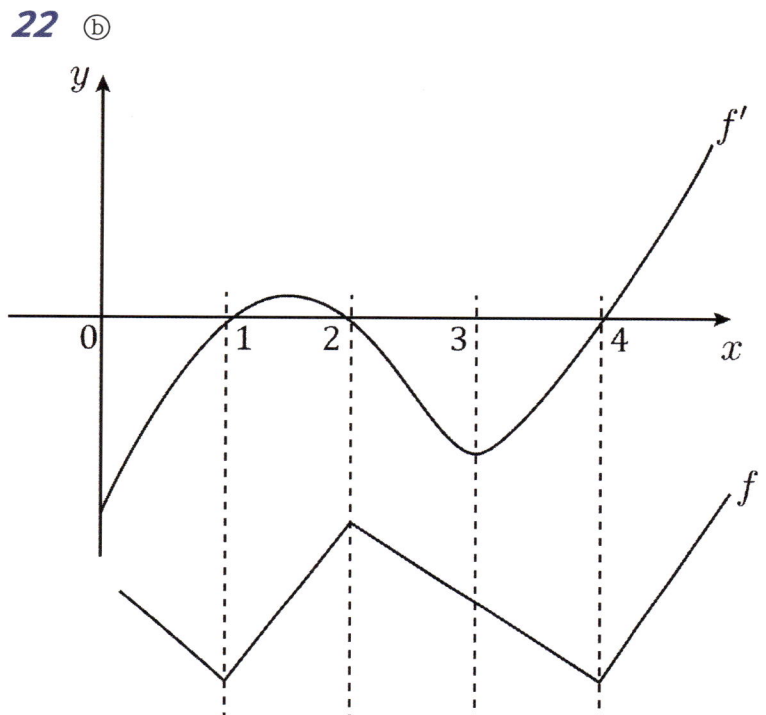

f' is negative at $0 \leq x < 1$, so f is decreasing at $0 \leq x < 1$.
f' is positive at $1 < x < 2$, so f is increasing at $1 < x < 2$.
f' is negative at $2 < x < 4$, so f is decreasing at $2 < x < 4$.
f' is positive at $4 < x$, so f is increasing at $4 < x$.

23 $1 < x < \dfrac{9}{2}$

- f is decreasing $\Leftrightarrow f' < 0$
$\Rightarrow f'(x) = 6x^2 - 54x + 48 < 0$, so $x^2 - 9x + 8 < 0$. $1 < x < 8$
- f is concave down $\Leftrightarrow f'' < 0$
$\Rightarrow f''(x) = 12x - 54 < 0$. $x < \dfrac{54}{12}$, so $x < \dfrac{9}{2}$.

Therefore, the interval of x where f is both decreasing and concave down is $1 < x < \dfrac{9}{2}$.

24 ⓓ

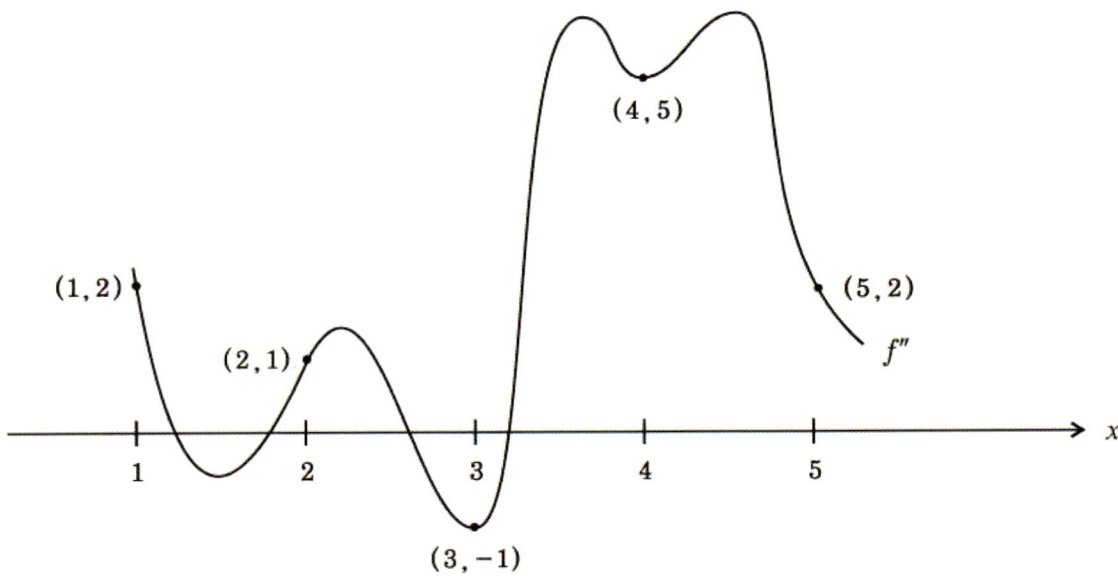

Many different graphs can be drawn from the information given in the table. The graph above shows one possible graph. We know that the sign of f'' must change in the open interval $(3, 4)$ (this is due to the Intermediate Value Theorem!), so the graph of f has at least one inflection point.

Local maximum and minimum information is obtained from the graph of f'. That is, when $f' = 0$. So, we can not conclude about (a) and (b) with the given information.

f is concave upwards when $f'' > 0$, and concave downwards when $f'' < 0$, however, because this is a table and not a graph, we can not conclude whether there is no value of $f'' < 0$ in interval $(1, 2)$.

f has an inflection point when $f'' = 0$ and sign changes. From the given table, since there is a change in sign in interval $(3, 4)$, we can conclude that there is at least a point in the interval when $f'' = 0$ and the sign changes.

25 ⓓ

Since $f''(x) < 0$ on the entire interval $(2, 4)$, the function is concave down. Also, since $f'(3) = 2 > 0$, f is increasing at $x = 3$.

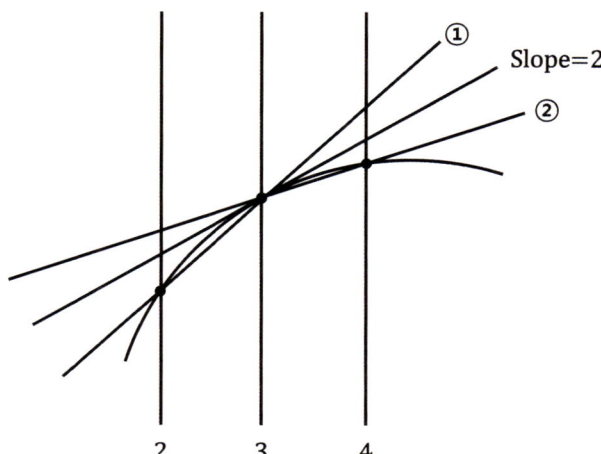

That is, the slope of ① ($\frac{f(3) - f(2)}{3 - 2}$) must be greater than 2, and the slope of ② ($\frac{f(4) - f(3)}{4 - 3}$) must be smaller than 2. The only choice that satisfies this is ⓓ.

26 ⓓ

$f'(x) = 4x^{-\frac{1}{3}} + 2 = \frac{4}{\sqrt[3]{x}} + 2$.

Possible candidates of the values of x where f has a relative minimum are the values of x such that $f'(x) = 0$ or $f'(x)$ is undefined.

At $x = -8$, $f'(x) = 0$.

When we substitute -8 in x in $f''(x) = -\frac{4}{3}x^{-\frac{4}{3}}$, we get $f'' = -\frac{4}{3}\frac{1}{\sqrt[3]{(-8)^4}} < 0$.

Therefore, the function has a relative maximum at $x = -8$.

At $x = 0$, $f'(x)$ does not exist.

Also, $\lim\limits_{x \to 0^-} f'(x) = \lim\limits_{x \to 0^-} (\frac{4}{\sqrt[3]{x}} + 2) < 0$ and $\lim\limits_{x \to 0^+} f'(x) = \lim\limits_{x \to 0^+} (\frac{4}{\sqrt[3]{x}} + 2) > 0$,

so f' changes from negative to positive at $x = 0$.
Therefore, f has a relative minimum at $x = 0$.

27

(1)

A. The leading coefficient is positive, so the right end of the graph points upwards.

B. The rough shape of the graph is as follows.

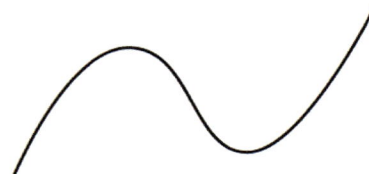

C. Find the values of x such that $f'(x) = 0$.

$$f'(x) = 3x^2 + 3x + 6 = 3(x + \frac{1}{2})^2 + \frac{21}{4} > 0.$$

That is, there is no point on the graph of $y = f(x)$ such that the slope of the tangent line is 0. $f'(x) > 0$ on the entire real line. Therefore, the graph is increasing on all real numbers as follows.

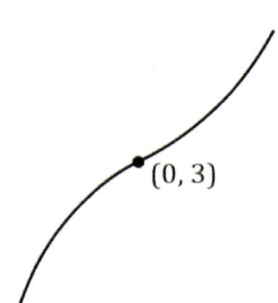
(0, 3)

D. Plot the graph on the coordinate plane.

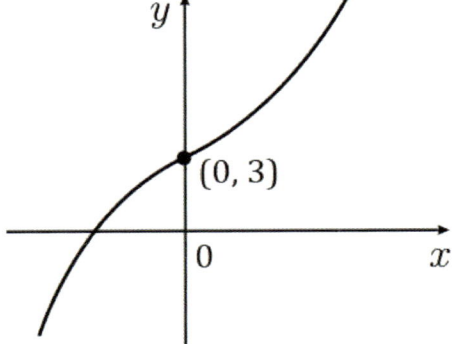
(0, 3)

(2)
A. Find all values of x such that $f'(x)=0$.

$f(x)=e^{-x^2}$, so $f'(x)=-2xe^{-x^2}=0$. Therefore, $x=0$.

B.

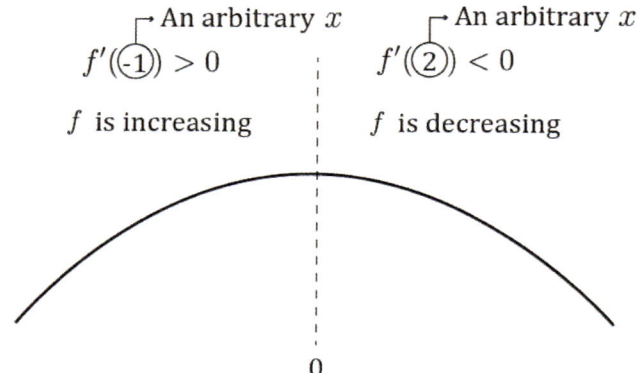

C. Find all values of x such that $f''(x)=0$.

$f''(x)=-2e^{-x^2}+(-2x)\cdot e^{-x^2}\cdot(-2x)=-2e^{-x^2}+4x^2e^{-x^2}=(4x^2-2)e^{-x^2}=0$.

Therefore, $x=\pm\dfrac{\sqrt{2}}{2}$.

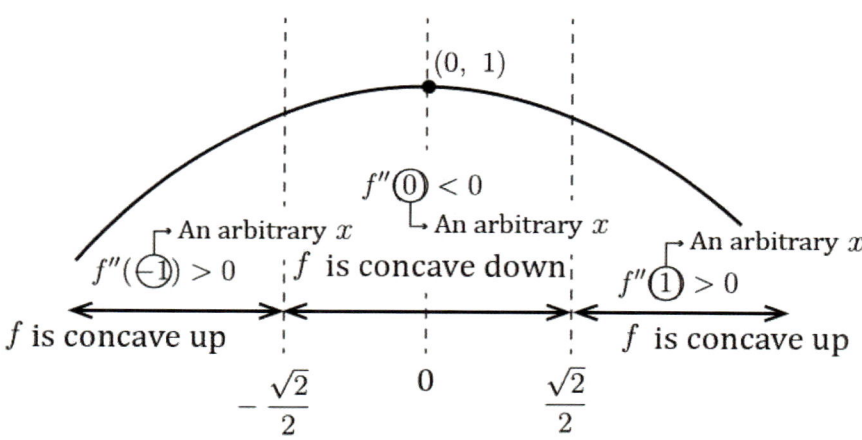

D. $\lim\limits_{x\to\infty}f(x)=\lim\limits_{x\to\infty}\dfrac{1}{e^{x^2}}=0$, $\lim\limits_{x\to-\infty}f(x)=\lim\limits_{x\to-\infty}\dfrac{1}{e^{x^2}}=0$

E. Plot the graph on the coordinate plane.

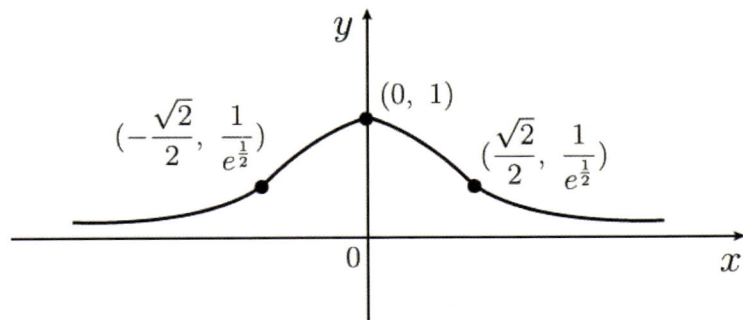

(3)
A. Find all values of x such that $f'(x) = 0$.
$f'(x) = \dfrac{x^2+1 - x \cdot 2x}{(x^2+1)^2} = \dfrac{1-x^2}{(x^2+1)^2} = 0$, so $x = \pm 1$.

B.
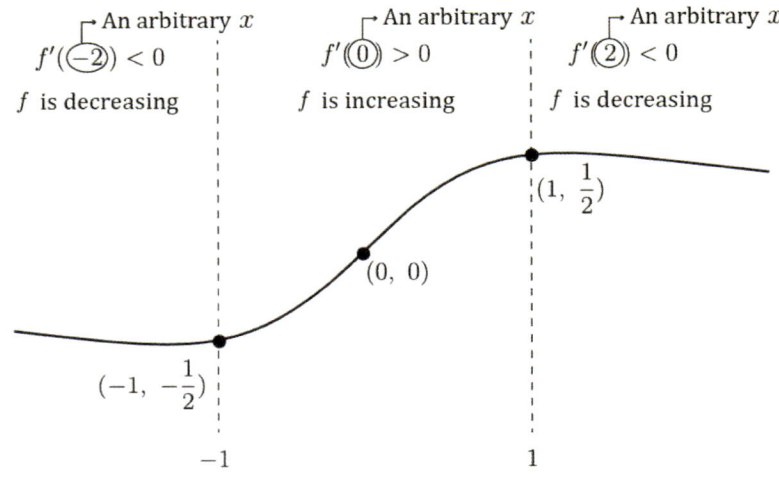

C. $\lim\limits_{x \to \infty} f(x) = \lim\limits_{x \to \infty} \dfrac{x}{x^2+1} = 0$, $\lim\limits_{x \to -\infty} f(x) = \lim\limits_{x \to -\infty} \dfrac{x}{x^2+1} = 0$

D. Plot the graph on the coordinate plane.

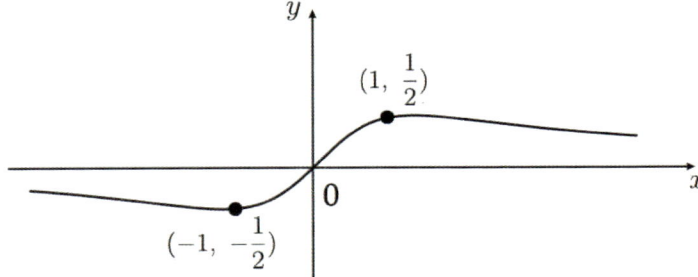

Differentiation

28

The domain of x is determined, so we do not need to find $\lim\limits_{x \to \pm\infty} f(x)$.

① Find values of x such that $f'(x) = 0$ and determine the sign of $f'(x)$ in each interval.

If $f'(x) = 1 + 2\sin x = 0$, then $\sin x = -\dfrac{1}{2}$ and thus, $x = \dfrac{7}{6}\pi, \dfrac{11}{6}\pi$.

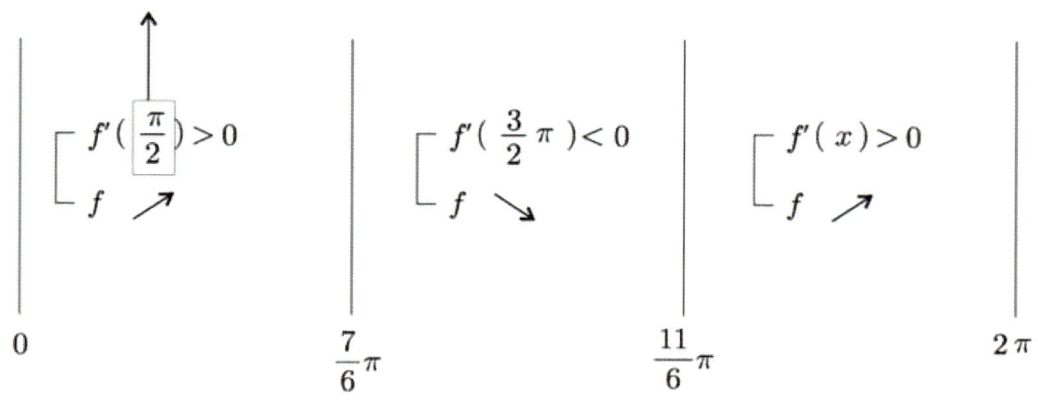

② $f(0) = -2$, $f(\dfrac{7}{6}\pi) = \dfrac{7}{6}\pi + \sqrt{3}$, $f(\dfrac{11}{6}\pi) = \dfrac{11}{6}\pi - \sqrt{3}$, $f(2\pi) = 2\pi - 2$

③ Move this to the coordinate plane.

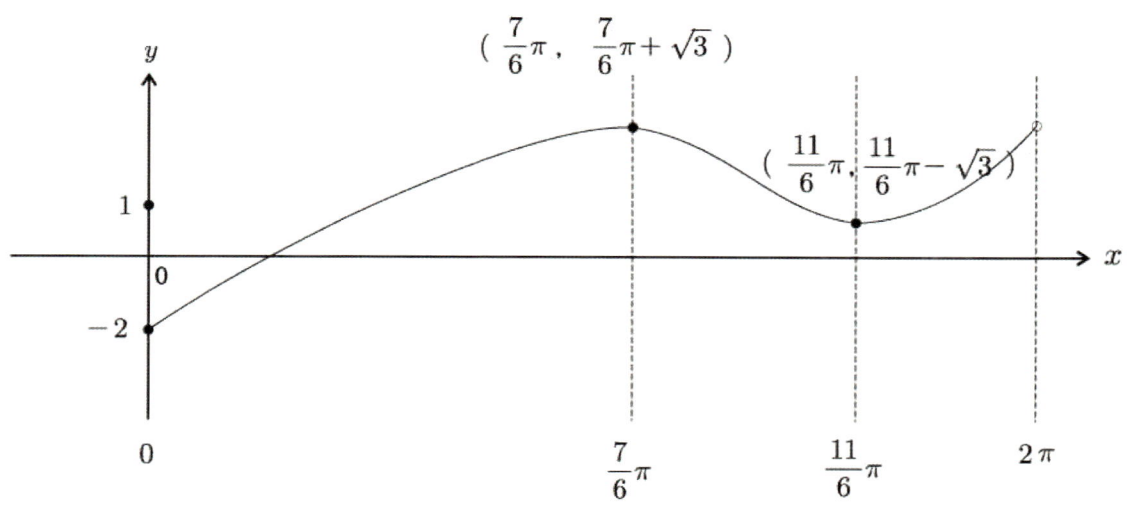

AP Calculus AB & BC Rewritten from the Beginning

Supplement

How can we determine the sign of $f'(x)$ between $\dfrac{11\pi}{6}$ and 2π? We use

$$\sin(\alpha + \beta) = \sin\alpha \cos\beta + \cos\alpha \sin\beta.$$

Then, we have

$$\sin(345°) = \sin(300° + 45°) = \sin 300° \cos 45° + \cos 300° \sin 45° = \dfrac{-\sqrt{6}+\sqrt{2}}{4},$$

and $f'(x) = 1 + 2\sin x$. We get $f'(345°) = 1 + 2 \times \dfrac{-\sqrt{6}+\sqrt{2}}{4} > 0$. Therefore, $f'(345°) > 0$.

Differentiation

Why didn't Leibniz explain why dy/dx can be used like a fraction?

Gottfried Wilhelm Leibniz, one of the founders of calculus, introduced the notation $\frac{dy}{dx}$. However, he did not provide a mathematically rigorous explanation for why this symbol behaves like a fraction.

To be more specific:

Leibniz used $\frac{dy}{dx}$ as a symbol for the rate of change and intuitively manipulated it as if it were a fraction. He recognized that it could be treated in that way, but did not offer a formal justification for why such manipulations were valid.

In fact, he considered dy and dx to be infinitesimally small quantities and treated them accordingly. But since the concept of limits had not yet been fully developed in his time, he was unable to clearly explain this behavior using precise mathematics.

In conclusion, while Leibniz intuitively used $\frac{dy}{dx}$ as if it were a fraction, he did not provide a rigorous mathematical proof—by modern standards—for why such usage is valid.

Leibniz

AP Calculus AB & BC Rewritten from the Beginning

05 Related Rates

This is a chapter related to finding the rate of change. The questions are longer than other chapters, but they are actually quite easy.

What is the rate of change?
"The rate of change in volume, length, radius, ... in a short period of time"

In summary, this chapter is about
The Rate of Change in

- Volume: $\dfrac{dV}{dt}$
- Length: $\dfrac{dL}{dt}$
- Area: $\dfrac{dA}{dt}$
- Radius: $\dfrac{dr}{dt}$

Special Lecture: Methods of Solving Related Rates Problems

① Clarify what we need to find.
(This generally appears at the end of the problem.
The rate of change in length, volume, ...)

② Derive an equation about the variable we want to find.
(e.g. The area of a circle is $A = \pi r^2$, the volume of a sphere is $V = \dfrac{4}{3}\pi r^3$, ... etc)

③ Differentiate each side of the equation with respect to t. That is, take $\dfrac{d}{dt}$ of both sides.

④ All the values and information required to solve the question are already provided in the problem, so don't worry.

Differentiation

●········ **Problem 1**

The radius of a circle is increasing at a constant rate of 0.03 inches per second. In terms of the circumference P, what is the rate of change of the area of the circle in square inches per second?

ⓐ $0.03P$ ⓑ $(0.03)2\pi P$ ⓒ $\dfrac{0.03}{2\pi}P$ ⓓ $\dfrac{2\pi}{0.03}P$

●········ **Answer**   ⓐ

●········ **Solution**

① Let's denote the area of the circle as A. Then, what we want to find is $\dfrac{dA}{dt}$.

② Set an equation: $A = \pi r^2$.

③ Take $\dfrac{d}{dt}$ of both sides! (Differentiate each side with respect to t)

$$\dfrac{dA}{dt} = (2\pi r)\dfrac{dr}{dt}$$

④ "All values we need are provided!. $\dfrac{dr}{dt} = 0.03$ and the circumference of a circle is $P = 2\pi r$, so $\dfrac{dA}{dt} = 0.03P$.

AP Calculus AB & BC Rewritten from the Beginning

Problem 2

(1) A circle is increasing in area at a constant rate of $12\pi\ (in^2/\text{sec})$. When the radius of the circle is 4 inches, how fast does the radius of this circle increases?

(2) The radius of a circle is increasing at a constant rate of 0.5 meters per second. What is the rate of increase in the area of the circle at the instant when the circumference of the circle is 40π meters?

ⓐ $0.2\pi m^2/\text{sec}$ ⓑ $10\pi m^2/\text{sec}$ ⓒ $20\pi m^2/\text{sec}$ ⓓ $40\pi m^2/\text{sec}$

Answer   (1) $\frac{3}{2} in/\text{sec}$ (2) ⓒ

Solution

(1) ① What we want to find $\Rightarrow$ How fast does the radius change $= \dfrac{dr}{dt}$

② Since this problem is related to the area of a circle, we set the following: $A = \pi r^2$

③ Differentiate each side with respect to t.

$$\frac{d}{dt}A = \frac{d}{dt}(\pi r^2) \Rightarrow \frac{dA}{dt}\frac{d}{dA}(A) = \frac{dr}{dt}\frac{d}{dr}(\pi \cdot r^2) \Rightarrow \frac{dA}{dt} = \frac{dr}{dt}(2\pi r)$$

④ The problem says "increasing in area at a constant rate of $12\pi in^2/\text{sec}$"; $\dfrac{dA}{dt} = 12\pi\ (in^2/\text{sec})$. Therefore, $12\pi\ (in^2/\text{sec}) = 2\pi \cdot 4(in) \cdot \dfrac{dr}{dt}$, so $\dfrac{dr}{dt} = \dfrac{3}{2}(in/\text{sec})$.

(2) ① Denote the area of the circle as A. Then, what we want to find is $\dfrac{dA}{dt}$.

② Set an equation: $A = \pi r^2$

③ Take $\dfrac{d}{dt}$ of both sides! $\dfrac{dA}{dt} = (2\pi r)\dfrac{dr}{dt}$

④ All values we need are provided! $\dfrac{dr}{dt} = 0.5$ and $2\pi r = 40\pi$, so $r = 20$.

Therefore, $\dfrac{dA}{dt} = 2\pi \cdot 20 \times 0.5 = 20\pi\ (m^2/\text{sec})$

Differentiation

 **Problem 3**

Sally who is 1.7 meters tall walks directly away from a streetlight that is 8.5 meters above the ground. If Sally is walking at a constant rate and her shadow is lengthening at the rate of 0.4 meters per second, at what rate, in meters per second, is Sally walking?

ⓐ 0.6 ⓑ 0.9 ⓒ 1.2 ⓓ 1.6

 **Answer** ⓓ

Solution

① Let's draw the following figure to determine what we need to find.

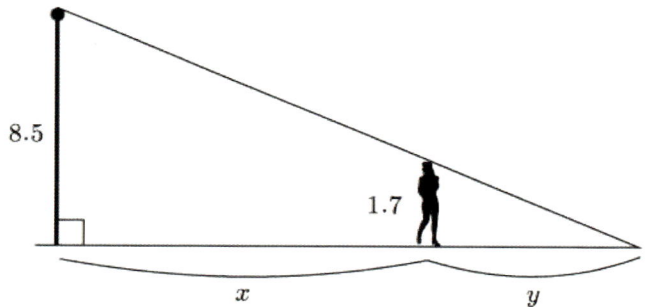

② Set an equation: $1.7 : 8.5 = y : x+y$, so $8.5y = 1.7x + 1.7y$. Therefore, $6.8y = 1.7x$

③ Differentiate each side with respect to t.

$$6.8\frac{dy}{dt} = 1.7\frac{dx}{dt}$$

④ $\frac{dy}{dt} = 0.4 (m/\sec)$, so $\frac{dx}{dt} = 1.6 (m/\sec)$.

Problem 4

(1) A balloon is being filled with air at a constant rate of $2in^3/\text{sec}$. The rate, in square inch per second, at which the surface area is increasing when the volume is $\frac{32}{3}\pi in^3$ is

ⓐ $0.5in^2/\text{sec}$ ⓑ $1in^2/\text{sec}$ ⓒ $1.5in^2/\text{sec}$ ⓓ $2in^2/\text{sec}$

(2)

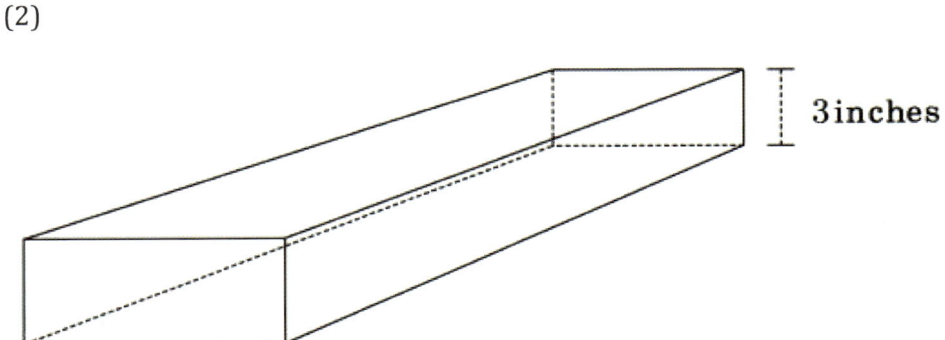

In the rectangular prism above, the height is 3 inches. Its length increases at a constant rate of $0.5in/\text{sec}$, and its width increases at a constant of $1.5in/\text{sec}$. When the length is 4 inches and the width is 8 inches, the rate, in cubic inches per second, at which the volume of the rectangular prism is changing is

ⓐ $6in^3/\text{sec}$ ⓑ $18in^3/\text{sec}$ ⓒ $20in^3/\text{sec}$ ⓓ $30in^3/\text{sec}$

Differentiation

● **Answer**   (1) ⓓ   (2) ⓓ

● **Solution**

(1)

① Denote the surface area as A. Then, what we need to find is $\dfrac{dA}{dt}$.

② "Set an equation": $A = 4\pi r^2$

③ "Differentiate each side with respect to t"

$\dfrac{dA}{dt} = (8\pi r)\dfrac{dr}{dt}$

④ All values we need are provided!

- $V = \dfrac{32}{3}\pi = \dfrac{4}{3}\pi r^3$, so $r = 2$.

- $\dfrac{dV}{dt} = 2$. From $V = \dfrac{4}{3}\pi r^3$, we get $\dfrac{dV}{dt} = (4\pi r^2)\dfrac{dr}{dt}$ and when $r = 2$, $2 = (16\pi)\dfrac{dr}{dt}$.

Thus, $\dfrac{dr}{dt} = \dfrac{1}{8\pi}$.

Therefore, $\dfrac{dA}{dt} = (8\pi \cdot 2)\dfrac{1}{8\pi} = 2 \, (in^2/\sec)$.

(2)

① "Determine what we need to find" : $\dfrac{dV}{dt}$

② "Set an equation": Let the length be x, and the width be y.
Then, $V = 3xy$

③ "Differentiate each side with respect to t."

$\dfrac{dV}{dt} = (3y)\dfrac{dx}{dt} + (3x)\dfrac{dy}{dt}$

④ All values we need are provided!

$x = 4$, $y = 8$, $\dfrac{dx}{dt} = 0.5$, $\dfrac{dy}{dt} = 1.5$, so $\dfrac{dV}{dt} = 3 \cdot 8 \cdot (0.5) + 3 \cdot 4 \cdot (1.5) = 30 \, (in^3/\sec)$.

AP Calculus AB & BC Rewritten from the Beginning

● **Problem 5**

A water tank is in the shape of an inverted cone. Water is leaking out from the bottom of the inverted cone such that the water level is falling at a constant rate of $\frac{1}{4}$ m/sec. If the tank has a height of 10 meters and a radius of 3 meters, at what rate is the water leaking, in terms of cubic meters per second, when the water level is 3 meters in depth?

● **Answer** $\quad -\dfrac{81}{400}\pi\, m^3/\sec$

● **Solution**

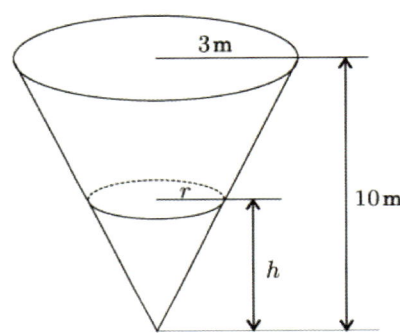

① "Determine what we need to find": $\dfrac{dV}{dt}$

② "Set an equation"

$$V = \frac{1}{3}\pi r^2 h$$

Moreover, since $3 : r = 10 : h$, $r = \dfrac{3}{10}h$, and thus $V = \dfrac{1}{3}\pi \times \dfrac{9}{100}h^3 = \dfrac{3}{100}\pi h^3$.

③ "Differentiate each side with respect to t."

$$V = \frac{3}{100}\pi h^3 \Rightarrow \frac{dV}{dt} = \frac{3}{100}\pi (3h^2)\frac{dh}{dt}$$

④ All the values we need are provided!

$\dfrac{dh}{dt} = -\dfrac{1}{4}$, $h = 3$, so $\dfrac{dV}{dt} = \dfrac{3}{100} \times \pi \times 3^3 \times \left(-\dfrac{1}{4}\right) = -\dfrac{81}{400}\pi\ (m^3/\sec)$.

Differentiation

● ········ **Problem 6**

A student stands on the road 50 meters north of the crossing and watches an westbound car traveling at a speed of 12 meters per second. At how many meters per second is the car moving away from the student 10 seconds after it passes through the intersection? (A road track and a road cross is at right angles.)

● ········ **Answer** $11.077(m/\sec)$

● ········ **Solution**

① Let's draw the following figure to determine what we need to find.

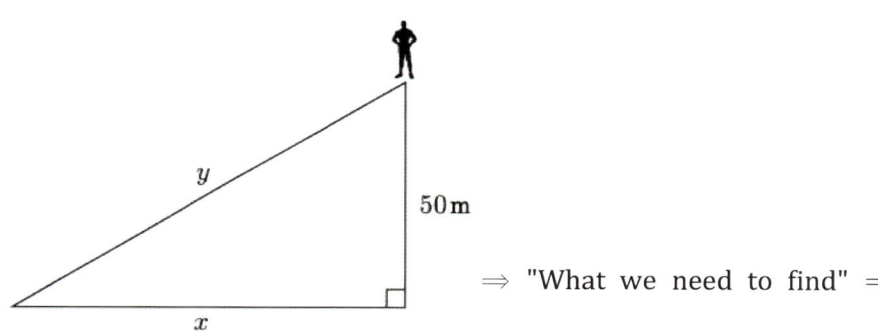

$\Rightarrow$ "What we need to find" $= \dfrac{dy}{dt}$

② Set an equation. $y^2 = x^2 + 50^2$

③ Differentiate each side with respect to t.

$(2y)\dfrac{dy}{dt} = (2x)\dfrac{dx}{dt}$, so $\dfrac{dy}{dt} = \dfrac{x}{y}\dfrac{dx}{dt}$

④ All the values we need are provided!

$t = 10$, so $x = speed \times time\, s = 12 \times 10 = 120$ and from $y^2 = 120^2 + 50^2$, $y = 130$. Since $\dfrac{dx}{dt} = 12$, $\dfrac{dy}{dt} = \dfrac{120}{130} \times 12 \approx 11.077(m/\sec)$.

AP Calculus AB & BC Rewritten from the Beginning

Problem 7

The top of a 13 foot ladder is sliding down a vertical wall at a constant rate of 0.2 feet per second. When the top of the ladder is 5 feet from the ground, find the rate of change of the distance between the bottom of the ladder and the wall.

Answer

$\frac{1}{12} ft/\sec$

Solution

① Let's draw the following figure to determine what we need to find.

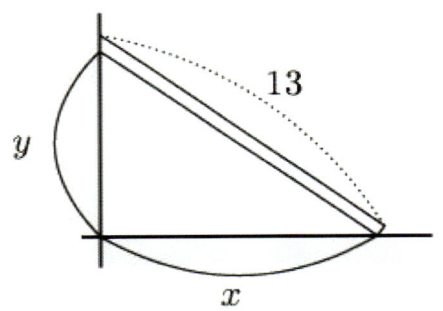

$\Rightarrow$ "What we need to find" $= \frac{dx}{dt}$

② Set an equation. $x^2 + y^2 = 13^2$

③ Differentiate each side with respect to t.

$$(2x)\frac{dx}{dt} + (2y)\frac{dy}{dt} = 0$$

④ All the values we need are provided!

$\frac{dy}{dt} = -0.2$. If $y = 5$, from $x^2 + y^2 = 13^2$, we get $x = 12$.

Therefore, $(24)\frac{dx}{dt} + 10(-0.2) = 0$ and $\frac{dx}{dt} = \frac{1}{12} (ft/\sec)$.

Problem 8

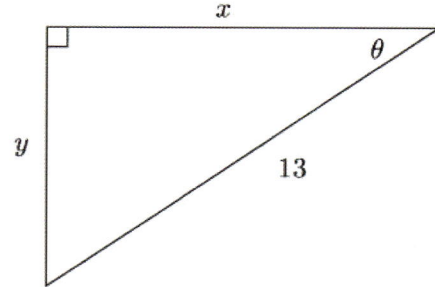

(1) In the triangle shown above, if θ increases at a constant rate of 2 radians per second, at what rate is y increasing in units per second when y equals 5 units? (Suppose that x remains constant throughout time.)

ⓐ 2   ⓑ 4   ⓒ 12   ⓓ 24

(2) A hot air balloon is rising vertically at a rate of 30 meters per second. A student on the ground is standing 100 meters away from the hot air balloon's launching point. At what rate does the angle between the ground and the hot air balloon increases when the hot air balloon is 50 meters away from the ground? (Disregard the student's height.)

AP Calculus AB & BC Rewritten from the Beginning

Answer (1) ⓓ   (2) $\dfrac{6}{25} rad/sec$

Solution

(1)

① What we need to find: $\dfrac{dy}{dt}$.

② Set an equation. $\sin\theta = \dfrac{y}{13}$

③ Differentiate each side with respect to t. $\cos\theta \dfrac{d\theta}{dt} = \dfrac{1}{13}\dfrac{dy}{dt}$

④ All values we need are provided! $\dfrac{d\theta}{dt} = 2$.

Also, when $y = 5$, from $13^2 = x^2 + y^2$ we get $x = 12$ and therefore $\cos\theta = \dfrac{12}{13}$.

Therefore, $\dfrac{12}{13} \times 2 = \dfrac{1}{13}\dfrac{dy}{dt}$ and $\dfrac{dy}{dt} = 24$.

(2)

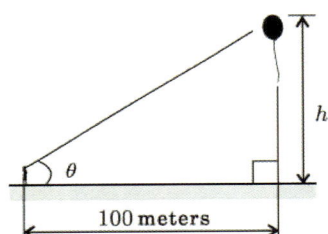

① What we need to find ⇒ "At what rate does the angle…" = $\dfrac{d\theta}{dt}$

② This problem is about an angle, so we use trigonometric functions. $\tan\theta = \dfrac{h}{100}$

③ Differentiate each side with respect to t.
$\sec^2\theta \dfrac{d\theta}{dt} = \dfrac{1}{100}\dfrac{dh}{dt}$,

④ All values we need are provided!

$\dfrac{dh}{dt} = 30\,(m/sec)$ and $\sec^2\theta$ can be calculated from $1 + \tan^2\theta = \sec^2\theta$.

If $h = 50$, $\tan\theta = \dfrac{50}{100} = \dfrac{1}{2}$ and $\sec^2\theta = 1 + \dfrac{1}{4} = \dfrac{5}{4}$.

Therefore, $\dfrac{5}{4}\dfrac{d\theta}{dt} = \dfrac{1}{100} \times 30$, so $\dfrac{d\theta}{dt} = \dfrac{6}{25}(rad/sec)$.

09 Exercise

01 A circular pool is expanding at a constant rate of $5\pi\ m^2/\text{sec}$. At what rate does the radius of this pool expand when the radius is 10 m?

02 A spherical balloon is expanding at a constant rate of $10\pi\ in^3/\text{sec}$. How fast does the surface area of the balloon expand when the radius of the balloon is 2 inches?

03 A water tank is in the shape of an inverted cone. This water tank is being filled up with water at a constant rate of $10\pi\ m^3/\text{sec}$. If the tank has a height of 20 meters and a radius of 5 meters, at what rate does the water level rise when the water level is 4 meters?

04 John is a 2 meter-tall man, walks directly away from a streetlight that is 6 meters above the ground. If John is walking at a constant rate and his shadow is lengthening at the rate of 0.5 meters per second, at what rate, in meters per second, is John walking?

05 Air is being pumped into a spherical balloon at the rate of $25\pi\,in^3/\sec$. How fast does the radius increase when the radius of this balloon is 2 inches?

06 An observer, on the ground, is standing 100 meters away from a rocket's launching point. The rocket is rising vertically at a constant rate of $5m/\sec$. How fast does the angle of elevation between the ground and the observer's line of sight to the rocket increase when the rocket is at an elevation of 100 meters? (Disregard the observer's height.)

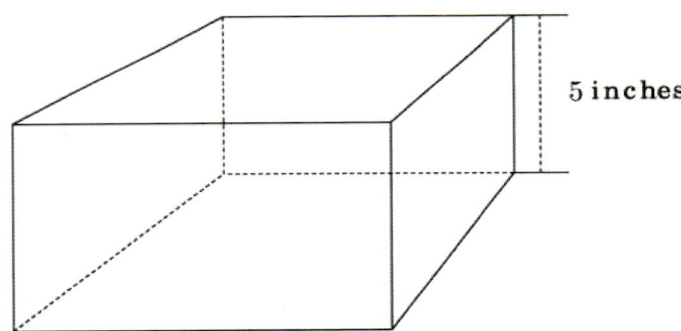

5 inches

07 In the rectangular box above, the height is 5 inches. Its length increases at the rate of $2in/\sec$, and its width increases at the rate of $3in/\sec$. When the length is 7 inches and the width is 6 inches, the rate, in cubic inches per second, at which the volume of the rectangular box is changing is

ⓐ 30 ⓑ 75 ⓒ 100 ⓓ 165

09 Answers & Solutions

Differentiation

01 $0.25 m/\sec$

Let r be the radius of the pool and A be the area of the pool.

① What we need to find : $\dfrac{dr}{dt}$.

② $A = \pi r^2$

③ Differentiating each side with respect to t, we get $\dfrac{dA}{dt} = 2\pi r \dfrac{dr}{dt}$.

④ "… at the rate of $5\pi cm^2/\sec$ …" : $\dfrac{dA}{dt} = 5\pi$

Since $r = 10$, $5\pi = 20\pi \dfrac{dr}{dt}$. Therefore, $\dfrac{dr}{dt} = 0.25 (m/\sec)$.

02 $10\pi in^2/\sec$

Let r be the radius of the balloon, A be the surface area of the balloon, and S be the volume of the balloon.

① What we need to find : $\dfrac{dA}{dt}$.

② $A = 4\pi r^2$

③ Differentiating each side with respect to t, we get $\dfrac{dA}{dt} = 8\pi r \dfrac{dr}{dt}$.

④ We know that $r = 2$ but we do not know $\dfrac{dr}{dt}$ yet.

We also know:

"… at the rate of $10\pi in^3/\sec$ …" : $\dfrac{dV}{dt} = 10\pi$

$V = \dfrac{4}{3}\pi r^3$, so differentiating each side with respect to t, we get $\dfrac{dV}{dt} = 4\pi r^2 \dfrac{dr}{dt}$.

When $r = 2$, $10\pi = 16\pi \dfrac{dr}{dt}$ and $\dfrac{dr}{dt} = \dfrac{10}{16} = \dfrac{5}{8} (in/\sec)$.

Therefore, $\dfrac{dA}{dt} = 8\pi \times 2 \times \dfrac{5}{8} = 10\pi (in^2/\sec)$.

AP Calculus AB & BC Rewritten from the Beginning

03 $10m/\sec$

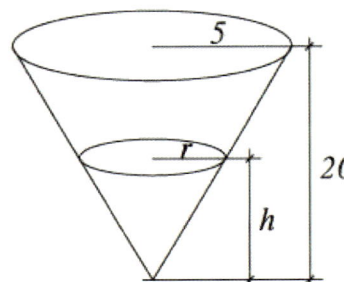

Let h, r, and V be the height, the radius and the volume of the water.

① What we need to find : $\dfrac{dh}{dt}$.

② $5:r=20:h$, so $h=4r$.

$V=\dfrac{1}{3}\pi r^2 h$ and $r=\dfrac{h}{4}$, so $V=\dfrac{1}{3}\pi(\dfrac{h}{4})^2 h$, which gives $V=\dfrac{1}{48}\pi h^3$.

③ Differentiating each side with respect to t, we get $\dfrac{dV}{dt}=\dfrac{1}{16}\pi h^2 \dfrac{dh}{dt}$.

④ "··· at the rate of $10\pi m^3/\sec$ ···" : $\dfrac{dV}{dt}=10\pi(m^3/\sec)$

$h=4$, so $10\pi=(\dfrac{1}{16}\pi\times 16)\dfrac{dh}{dt}$ and $\dfrac{dh}{dt}=10(m/\sec)$.

04 $1m/\sec$

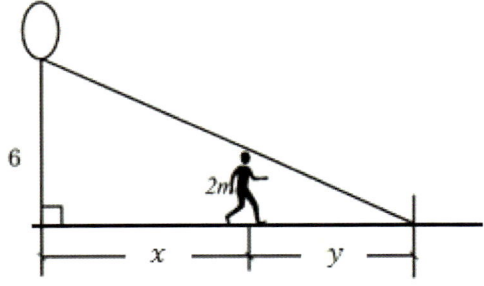

Let x and y denote the lengths as in the figure above.

① We need to find : $\dfrac{dx}{dt}$.

② $2:6=y:x+y$, so $6y=2x+2y$. This gives $y=\dfrac{1}{2}x$.

③ Differentiating each side with respect to t, we get $\dfrac{dy}{dt}=\dfrac{1}{2}\dfrac{dx}{dt}$.

④ $\dfrac{dy}{dt}=0.5$, so $\dfrac{dx}{dt}=1$. Therefore, the answer is $1m/\sec$.

Differentiation

05 $\dfrac{25}{16} in/\sec$

Let r be the radius of the balloon and V be the volume of the balloon.

① What we need to find : $\dfrac{dV}{dt}$.

② $V = \dfrac{4}{3}\pi r^3$

③ Differentiating each side with respect to t, we get $\dfrac{dV}{dt} = 4\pi r^2 \dfrac{dr}{dt}$.

④ "⋯ at the rate of $25\pi in^3/\sec$ ⋯" : $\dfrac{dV}{dt} = 25\pi \, (in^3/\sec)$

When $r = 2$, $25\pi = 4\pi 4 \dfrac{dr}{dt}$, so $\dfrac{dr}{dt} = \dfrac{25}{16} (in/\sec)$.

06 0.025 radians per second

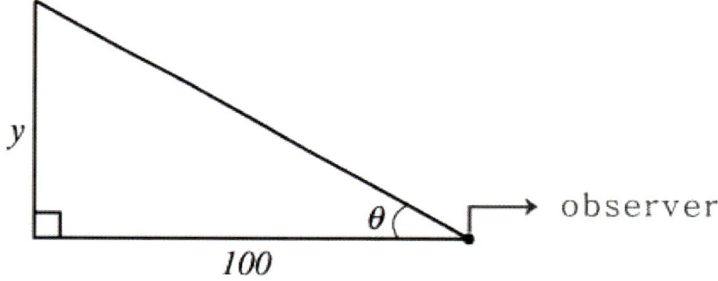

① What we need to find : $\dfrac{d\theta}{dt}$ (when $y = 100$).

② $\tan\theta = \dfrac{y}{100}$

③ Differentiating each side with respect to t, we get $\sec^2\theta \dfrac{d\theta}{dt} = \dfrac{1}{100}\dfrac{dy}{dt}$.

④ "⋯ at the constant rate of $5m/\sec$ ⋯" : $\dfrac{dy}{dt} = 5(m/\sec)$.

Also, when $y = 100$, $\tan\theta = 1$. Therefore, from $1 + \tan^2\theta = \sec^2\theta$, $\sec^2\theta = 2$.

$2\dfrac{d\theta}{dt} = \dfrac{1}{100} \times 5$, so $\dfrac{d\theta}{dt} = \dfrac{1}{40} = 0.025$ (radians per second).

07 ⓓ

Let x be the length of the cube, y be the width of the cube and V be the volume of the cube.

① What we need to find : $\dfrac{dV}{dt}$.

② $V = 5xy$.

③ Differentiate each side with respect to t.

$\dfrac{dV}{dt} = (5y)\dfrac{dx}{dt} + (5x)\dfrac{dy}{dt}$

④ $\dfrac{dx}{dt} = 2$, $\dfrac{dy}{dt} = 3$, $x = 7$, $y = 6$, so $\dfrac{dV}{dt} = 30 \times 2 + 35 \times 3 = 165\,(in^3/\sec)$.

Differentiation

Which version of calculus is more practical —Newton's or Leibniz's?

Newton and Leibniz both developed calculus independently, but their approaches and goals were quite different. In terms of practicality, Leibniz's version has proven to be more useful in the long run.

To put it simply, Leibniz's calculus is more practical. His notation — $\dfrac{dy}{dx}$ for derivatives and $\int$ for integrals — is highly general and versatile. It has become the standard in modern calculus textbooks, academic papers, and engineering calculations across nearly every field.

While Newton's method of fluxions was primarily suited for describing motion and changes over time, Leibniz's approach could be applied to a much broader range of mathematical contexts, such as functions, geometry, optimization, probability, and more.

Today, the notation and conceptual framework used in calculus around the world are almost entirely based on Leibniz's system.

06 Applied Maximum and Minimum Problems

Special Lecture: Applied Maximum and Minimum Problems

This chapter is about finding the absolute maximum or minimum in a given situation.

Let's look at the following method.

① Clarify what we need to find.
   (Area, Volume...).
② Set an equation and rearrange it to make it as a function of a single variable.
③ Determine the domain
   · x, y are lengths $\Rightarrow x > 0$, $y > 0$

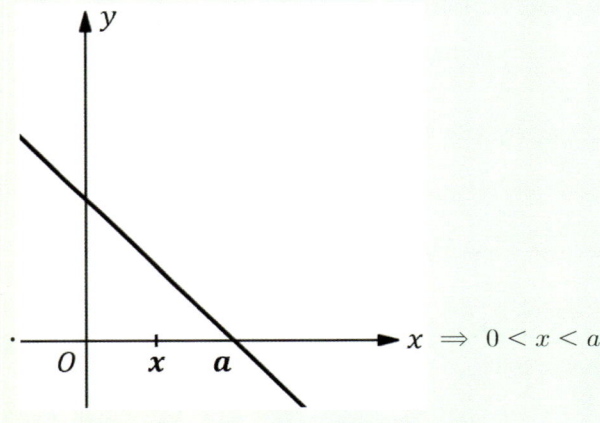

$\quad x \Rightarrow 0 < x < a$

· $t = \sin x$ $\quad\Rightarrow\quad -1 \leq t \leq 1$
  (or $t = \cos x$)

④ Use a graph to find the maximum or minimum value within the domain.

Differentiation

● **Problem 1**

If $f(x)=\sin^3 x+3\cos^2 x-2$, what is the difference between the maximum and the minimum values of f?

ⓐ 1 ⓑ 2 ⓒ 3 ⓓ 4

● **Answer** ⓓ

● **Solution**

① What we need to find is clear:
   maximum and minimum value of $f(x)=\sin^3 x+3\cos^2 x-2$.

② We want to express $f(x)$ as a function of $\sin x$ (in other words, we want to eliminate $\cos x$). $\cos^2 x=1-\sin^2 x$, so $f(x)=\sin^3 x+3-3\sin^2 x-2$ and thus, $f(x)=\sin^3 x-3\sin^2 x+1$.
   Let $\sin x=t$. Then, $f(t)=t^3-3t^2+1$.

③ Since the value of sine is given between -1 and 1, inclusive, $-1 \leq t \leq 1$.

④ $f'(t)=3t^2-6t$, so $f'(t)=0$ when $t=0, 2$. Only $t=0$ is in the required range. $f''(t)=6t-6$, and $f''(0)=-6<0$. So, $f(0)$ is a maximum point.

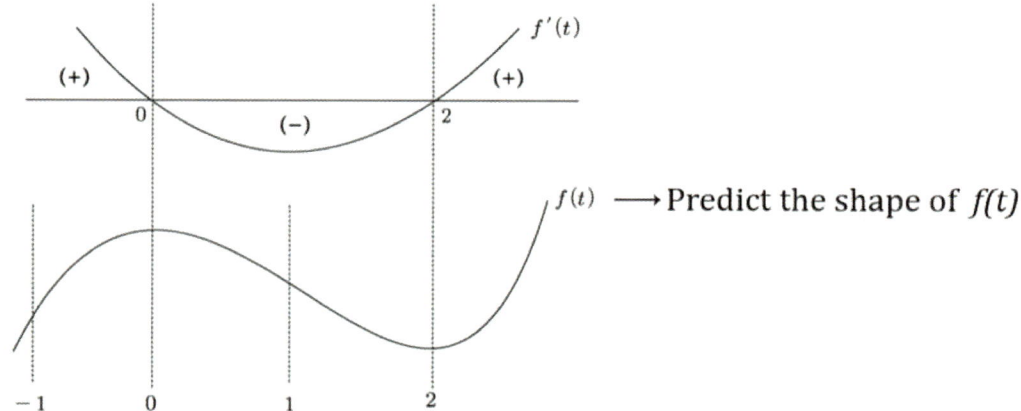

→ Predict the shape of *f(t)*

Thus, the maximum value is $f(0)=(0)^3-3(0)^2+1=1$, and the minimum value will be in one of the endpoints, since there is only one turning point in the interval.
Since $f(1)=-1$ and $f(-1)=-3$, the minimum value is $f(-1)=-3$.
Therefore, the answer is $1-(-3)=4$.

AP Calculus AB & BC Rewritten from the Beginning

Problem 2

The graph of $y = -2x + 4$ encloses a region with the x-axis and y-axis in the first quadrant. A rectangle in the enclosed region has a vertex at the origin and the opposite vertex on the graph of $y = -2x + 4$. Find the maximum area of the rectangle.

Answer

2

Solution

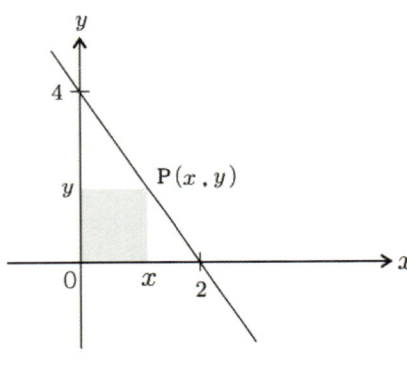

① Let A be the area of the rectangle. Then, what we want to find is the maximum of A.

② $A = xy$ and $y = -2x + 4$.
So $A = x(-2x + 4) = -2x^2 + 4x$.

③ Since the rectangle is within the enclosed region, $0 < x < 2$.

④ $\dfrac{dA}{dx} = -4x + 4$, so $\dfrac{dA}{dx} = 0$ at $x = 1$.

A has its maximum value at $x = 1$. Therefore, the answer is $1 \times (-2 \times 1 + 4) = 2$.

Differentiation

● ········ **Problem 3**

A man wants to design an open box with a square base and a surface area of 64 square inches. What dimensions will produce a box with the maximum volume?

● ········ **Answer**   Width : $\dfrac{8}{\sqrt{3}}$ (inches), Height : $\dfrac{4}{3}\sqrt{3}$ (inches).

● ········ **Solution**

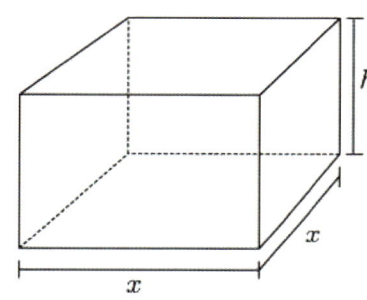
$\Rightarrow$ ┌ Volume $= x^2 h$
└ Surface Area $= x^2 + 4xh = 64$

① What we need to find : the value of x and h when V is at its maximum.

② From the surface area, $h = \dfrac{64 - x^2}{4x}$. Thus, $V = x^2 \left(\dfrac{64 - x^2}{4x}\right) = 16x - \dfrac{1}{4}x^3$.

③ x and h represent lengths, so $x > 0$ and $h = \dfrac{64 - x^2}{4x} > 0$.

Therefore, $0 < x < 8$.

④ $\dfrac{dV}{dx} = 16 - \dfrac{3}{4}x^2$, so $\dfrac{dV}{dx} = 0$ where $x = \pm \dfrac{8}{\sqrt{3}}$.

Therefore, the graph of V, roughly, is :

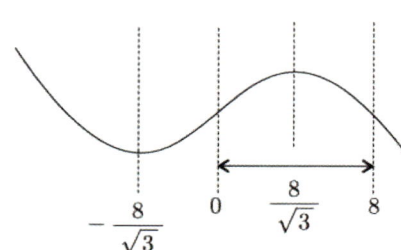

- Volume has its maximum value at $x = \dfrac{8}{\sqrt{3}}$.
- When $x = \dfrac{8}{\sqrt{3}}$, $h = \dfrac{64 - x^2}{4x} = \dfrac{4}{3}\sqrt{3}$.

Therefore, the maximum volume is,

$\dfrac{8}{3}\sqrt{3} \times \dfrac{8}{3}\sqrt{3} \times \dfrac{4}{3}\sqrt{3}$.

AP Calculus AB & BC Rewritten from the Beginning

Problem 4

Albert has 48 meters of wire fence with which he plans to build two identical rectangular adjacent fences. What are the dimensions of the enclosure that has the maximum area?

Answer
Width : 8 (meters), Length : 12 (meters)

Solution

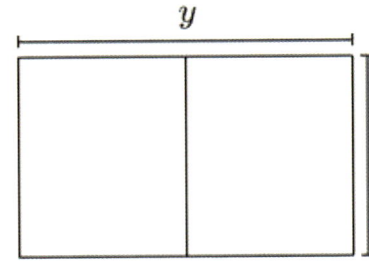

- $3x + 2y = 48$
- Denote the total area as A.

$\Rightarrow$ Then, $A = xy$.

① What we need to find : the value of x and y when A is at its maximum.

② From $3x + 2y = 48$, $y = 24 - \frac{3}{2}x$, so $A = x(24 - \frac{3}{2}x) = 24x - \frac{3}{2}x^2$.

③ x and y represent lengths, so $x > 0$ and $y = 24 - \frac{3}{2}x > 0$. Therefore, $0 < x < 16$.

④ $\frac{dA}{dx} = 24 - 3x$, so $\frac{dA}{dx} = 0$ where $x = 8$.

Therefore, the graph of total area $A = 24x - \frac{3}{2}x^2$, roughly, is :

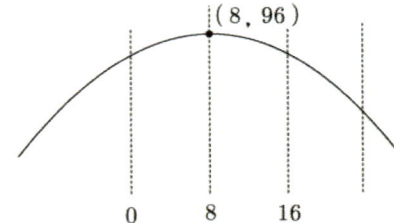

Thus, the total area has its maximum value at $x = 8$.

When $x = 8$, $y = 24 - \frac{3}{2}x = 24 - \frac{3}{2}(8) = 12$.

Differentiation

● ········ **Problem 5**

A cone with an altitude of 9 and the radius of 3 is given. Find the greatest volume of the right circular cylinder that can be inscribed in this cone.

● ········ **Answer** 12π

● ········ **Solution**

① Let V be the volume of the right cylinder. Then, what we need to find is the maximum of V.

②

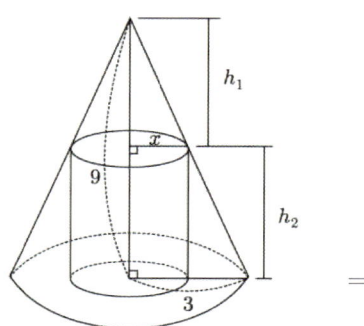

- $x : 3 = h_1 : 9$, so $h_1 = 3x$
- Let h_2 be the height of the right cylinder. Then, $h_2 = 9 - 3x$.
- Thus, $V = \pi x^2 h_2 = \pi x^2 (9 - 3x)$.

③ $0 < x < 3$

④ $\dfrac{dV}{dx} = 18\pi x - 9\pi x^2 = 9\pi x (2 - x)$

Therefore, $\dfrac{dV}{dx} = 0$ when $x = 0, 2$. Since $0 < x < 3$, $x = 2$.

Also, $\dfrac{d^2 V}{dx^2} = 18\pi - 18\pi x$. And at $x = 2$, $\dfrac{d^2 V}{dx^2} = -18\pi < 0$, so V is maximum.

- The graph of volume $= 9\pi x^2 - 3\pi x^3$ is, roughly,

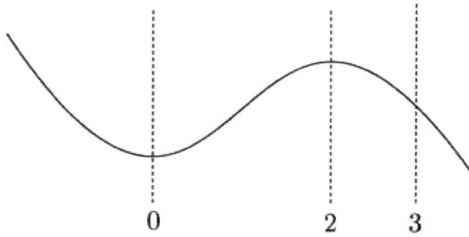

Thus, the volume of the right cylinder has its maximum volume is achieved at $x = 2$:
$V(2) = 9\pi \times (2)^2 - 3\pi \times (2)^3 = 36\pi - 24\pi = 12\pi$.

10 Exercise

01 If $f(x) = \sin x \cos^2 x$, what is the difference between the maximum and the minimum values of f?

ⓐ $\dfrac{2}{9}$ ⓑ $\dfrac{2\sqrt{3}}{9}$ ⓒ $\dfrac{4\sqrt{3}}{9}$ ⓓ $\dfrac{4}{9}$

02 A rectangle with its base on the positive x-axis is within the parabola $y = 12 - x^2$ and is located on the first quadrant. What is the largest possible area of the rectangle?

03 Joseph has 384 meters of wire fence with which he plans to build two identical adjacent rectangular fences. What are the width and length of the entire fence when the fence has the largest area?

04 A rectangular box is to be made from a piece of plank 14 inches long and 7 inches wide by cutting out identical squares from the four corners and turning up the sides. Find the maximum volume of the box.

05 If the altitude of a cone is 12 and the radius of its base is 4, find the greatest volume of the right circular cylinder that can be inscribed in the cone.

10   Answers & Solutions

01 ⓒ

① What we need to find : maximum and minimum of $f(x)=\sin x\cos^2 x$.

② We want to express $f(x)$ as a function of $\sin x$ (in other words, we want to eliminate $\cos x$). $\cos^2 x=1-\sin^2 x$, so $f(x)=\sin x(1-\sin^2 x)$.
Let $\sin x=t$. Then, $f(t)=t(1-t^2)=t-t^3$.

③ Since the value of sine is given between -1 and 1, inclusive, $-1\le t\le 1$.

④ $f'(t)=1-3t^2$, so $f'(t)=0$ when $t=\pm\dfrac{1}{\sqrt{3}}$.

The graph of $f(t)$, roughly, is

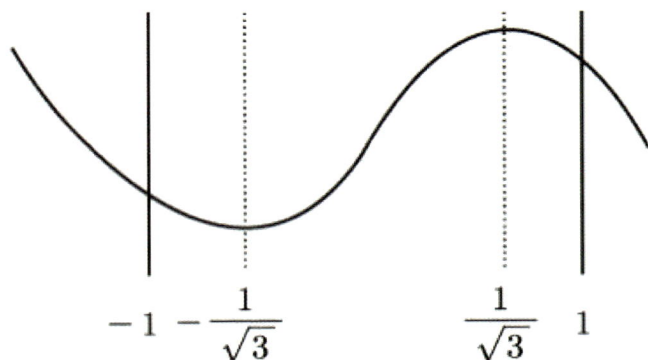

- Maximum Value: $f(1)=0$ and $f(\dfrac{1}{\sqrt{3}})=\dfrac{2\sqrt{3}}{9}$, so the maximum is $\dfrac{2\sqrt{3}}{9}$.

- Minimum Value: $f(-1)=0$ and $f(-\dfrac{1}{\sqrt{3}})=-\dfrac{2\sqrt{3}}{9}$, so the minimum is $-\dfrac{2\sqrt{3}}{9}$.

Therefore, the answer is $\dfrac{2\sqrt{3}}{9}-(-\dfrac{2\sqrt{3}}{9})=\dfrac{4\sqrt{3}}{9}$.

02 16

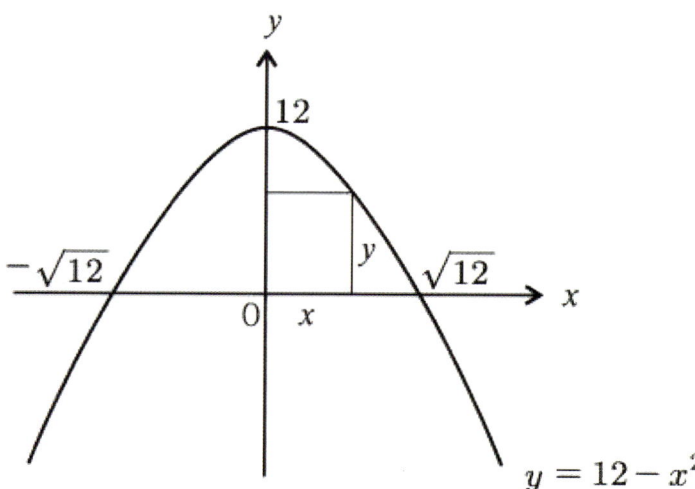

① Let A be the area of the rectangle.
Then, what we want to find is the maximum of A.

② $A = xy$ and $y = 12 - x^2$. So $A = x(12 - x^2) = 12x - x^3$.

③ Since the rectangle is within the first quadrant and under the parabola, $0 < x < \sqrt{12}$.

④ $\dfrac{dA}{dx} = 12 - 3x^2$, so $\dfrac{dA}{dx} = 0$ at $x = \pm 2$.

Since x is in the first quadrant, $x = 2$. Also, $\dfrac{d^2A}{dx^2} = -6x$, and at $x = 2$, $\dfrac{d^2A}{dx^2} = -12 < 0$, so A is maximum.

The graph of $A = 12x - x^3$, roughly, is ...

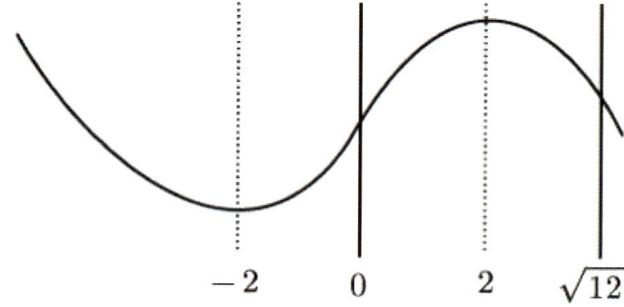

That is, A has its maximum at $x = 2$; $12 \times 2 - 2^3 = 16$.

03 Length : 64, Width : 96

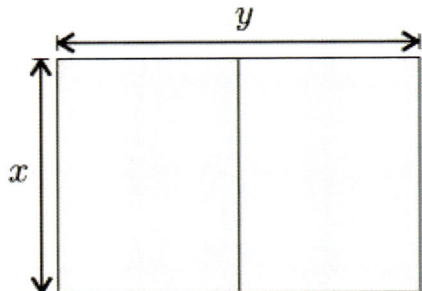

As in the figure above, let x be the length of the fence and let y be the width of the fence. Also, let us let A denote the area of the fence.

① What we need to find : the value of x and y when A is at its maximum.
② Express A in terms of x and y.
- $3x + 2y = 384$
- $A = xy$
- $A(x) = x\left(192 - \dfrac{3}{2}x\right) = 192x - \dfrac{3}{2}x^2$

③ Since x and y represent lengths, $x > 0$ and $y = 192 - \dfrac{3}{2}x > 0$. Therefore, $0 < x < 128$.

④ $\dfrac{dA}{dx} = 192 - 3x = 0$, so $x = 64$.

Therefore, the graph of $A = 192x - \dfrac{3}{2}x^2$, roughly, is...

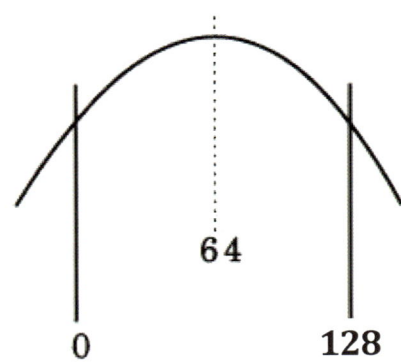

Thus, A has its maximum at $x = 64$.
When $x = 64$, $y = 192 - \dfrac{3}{2}x = 96$.

04 66.01

① Let V be the volume of the box. Then, what we need to find is the maximum of V.

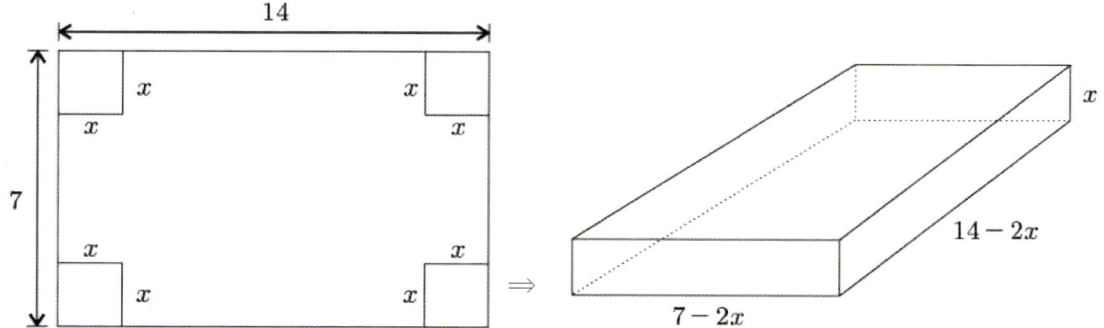

② As in the figure above, let x denote the side length of a square that will be cut out. Then, we can express V as a function of x; $V(x) = x(7-2x)(14-2x) = 98x - 42x^2 + 4x^3$.

③ Since $7-2x > 0$, $14-2x > 0$, and $x > 0$, the range of x is $0 < x < 3.5$.

④ $V'(x) = 98 - 84x + 12x^2$, so $V'(x) = 0$ at $x \approx 1.479, 5.521$. Since $0 < x < 3.5$, $x \approx 1.479$. Also, $V''(x) = 24x - 84$, and $V''(1.479) = -48.504 < 0$, so V is maximum.

The graph of $V(x) = 98x - 42x^2 + 4x^3$ is roughly,

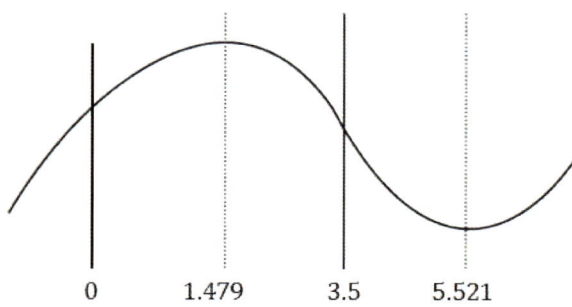

Therefore, the box has its maximum volume at $x = 1.479$; $V(1.479) \approx 66.010$.

05 $\dfrac{256}{9}\pi$

① Let V be the volume of the right cylinder. Then, what we need to find is the maximum of V.

② We want to express V in terms of x, where x is the radius of the cylinder,

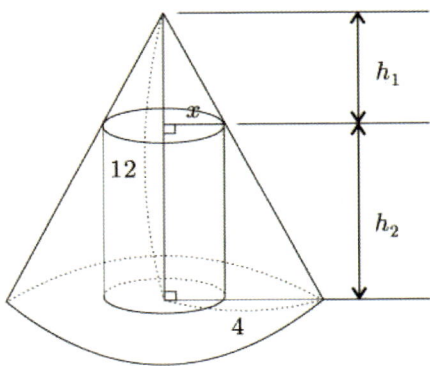

- $x : 4 = h_1 : 12$, so $h_1 = 3x$.
- Let the height of the right cylinder be h_2. Then, $h_2 = 12 - 3x$.
- (the volume of the right cylinder) $= \pi x^2 h_2$, so $V(x) = \pi x^2 (12 - 3x) = 12\pi x^2 - 3\pi x^3$.

③ The domain of x is : $0 < x < 4$.

④ $\dfrac{dV}{dx} = 24\pi x - 9\pi x^2$, so $\dfrac{dV}{dx} = 0$ when $x = 0, \dfrac{8}{3}$.

Since $0 < x < 4$, $x = \dfrac{8}{3}$.

Also, $\dfrac{d^2 V}{dx^2} = 24\pi - 18\pi x$. At $x = \dfrac{8}{3}$, $\dfrac{d^2 V}{dx^2} = 24\pi - 48\pi = -24\pi < 0$, so V is maximum.

The graph of $V(x) = 12\pi x^2 - 3\pi x^3$, roughly, is

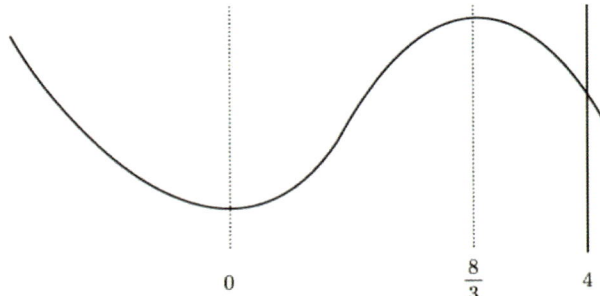

Therefore, the right cylinder has its maximum volume at $x = \dfrac{8}{3}$:

$V(\dfrac{8}{3}) = 12\pi (\dfrac{8}{3})^2 - 3\pi (\dfrac{8}{3})^3 = \dfrac{256}{9}\pi$.

Differentiation

Lesser-Known Mathematicians Who Contributed to Calculus

Historically, Leibniz and Newton are recognized as the main figures behind the development of calculus. However, there were other lesser-known mathematicians who also made significant contributions to its foundation.

Bhāskara II (1114-1185, India)
Long before Europe's development of calculus, Bhāskara II explored quasi-differential-like methods in the 12th century, particularly involving the concept of tangents to curves.
In his work *Siddhānta Śiromaṇi*, he dealt with ideas related to rates of change and applied early differential thinking to geometric problems.

Isaac Barrow (1630-1677, England)
Barrow, the teacher of Newton, was the first to clearly articulate the relationship between differentiation and integration.
He laid out the foundational idea of what would later be called the Fundamental Theorem of Calculus.
Even before Newton systematized this theory, Barrow's lecture notes already contained the essential concepts of modern calculus.

Bhaskara II

Isaac Barrow

07 Differential Approximation

Differentials and Approximations

Recall that the definition of the derivative is as follows.

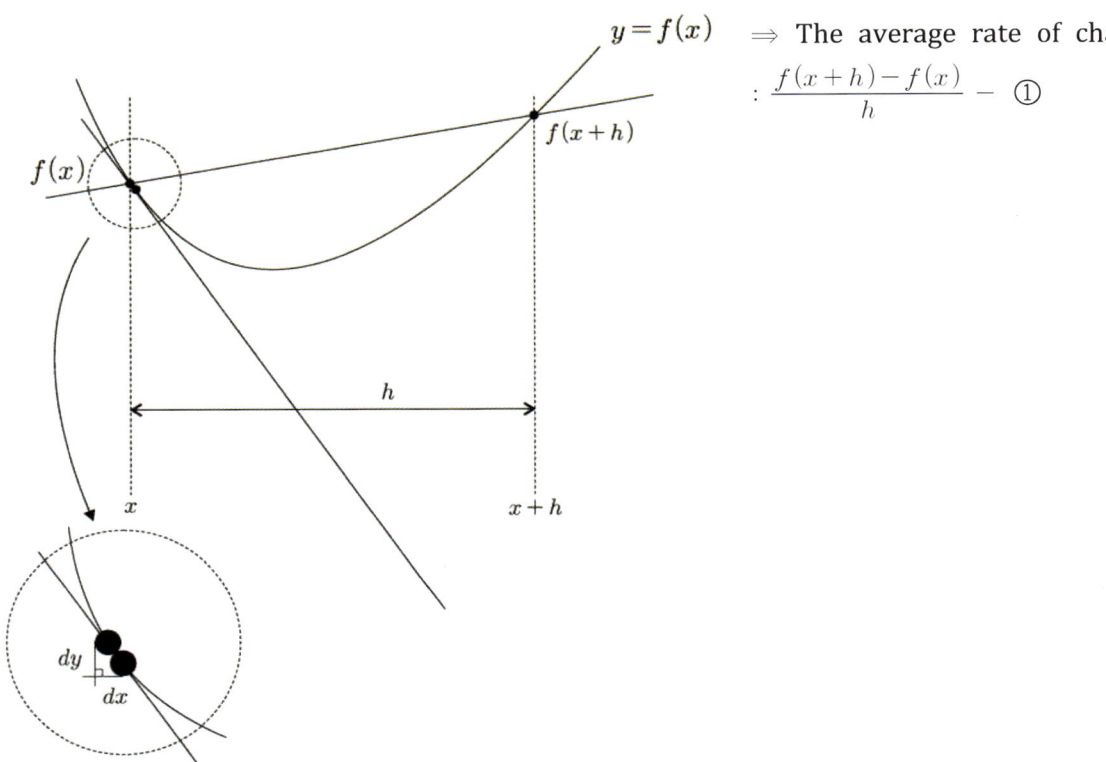

⇒ The average rate of change

$$: \frac{f(x+h)-f(x)}{h} \quad \text{①}$$

⇒ The instantaneous rate of change

$$\lim_{h \to 0} \frac{f(x+h)-f(x)}{h} = f'(x) = \frac{dy}{dx} \quad \text{②}$$

The ② above is the definition of the derivative.

$\lim_{h \to 0} \frac{f(x+h)-f(x)}{h} = f'(x)$, and $\lim_{h \to 0} h$ is a very small change in x, that is, dx.

Differentiation

Let's rewrite the above definition of the derivative.

$$\underbrace{f(x+h) - f(x)}_{\text{Change in } y\ (\Delta y)} = f'(x)\underbrace{\underbrace{\lim_{h \to 0} h}_{= dx}}_{\text{Minute change in } y\ (dy)}$$

($\ast\ f'(x)dx = dy \to f'(x) = \dfrac{dy}{dx}$)

From the above, we can learn the following.

Make Sure to Know the Following!

$$f(x+dx) \approx f(x) + dy = f(x) + f'(x)dx$$

Let's look at the following examples.

●······ **Example 30**

Using differentials :
(1) Approximate : $\sqrt{4.2}$ (2) Approximate : $\sqrt{8.2}$

●······ **Answer** (1) 2.05 (2) 2.867

●······ **Solution**

(1) Let $f(x) = \sqrt{x}$. $f(4+0.2) \approx f(4) + dy$, so $f'(x) = \dfrac{dy}{dx} = \dfrac{1}{2\sqrt{x}}$ and $dy = \dfrac{1}{2\sqrt{x}}dx$. If $x = 4$ and $dx = 0.2$, then, $dy = \dfrac{1}{2\sqrt{4}}(0.2) = \dfrac{0.2}{4} = 0.05$

Therefore, $\sqrt{4.2} \approx \sqrt{4} + 0.05 = 2.05$.

(2) Let $f(x) = \sqrt{x}$. $f(9-0.8) \approx f(9) + dy$
$dy = \dfrac{1}{2\sqrt{x}}dx$. If $x = 9$, and $dx = -0.8$, then, $dy = \dfrac{1}{2\sqrt{9}}(-0.8) = \dfrac{-0.8}{6} \approx -0.133$

Therefore, $\sqrt{8.2} \approx \sqrt{9} - 0.133 = 2.867$.

AP Calculus AB & BC Rewritten from the Beginning

Example 31

The side of a cube is measured to be 6 in with an error of ± 0.2 inches. Estimate the error in the volume of the cube.

Answer

Absolute Error : 21.6   Relative Error : 0.1

Solution

The approximate volume of the cube is $6^3 = 216$.

Let the side of the cube be x and the volume of the cube be V. Then, $V = x^3$ and $\dfrac{dV}{dx} = 3x^2 \Rightarrow dV = 3x^2 dx$. If $x = 6$ and $dx = 0.2$, then $\Delta V \approx dV = 3(6)^2(0.2) = 21.6$.

Therefore, (the volume of the cube) $= 216 \pm 21.6$ (cubic inches).

※ Here 21.6 is the "Absolute Error".

From $\dfrac{\Delta V}{V} \approx \dfrac{dV}{V} \approx \dfrac{21.6}{216} = 0.1$ we call 0.1 the "Relative Error".

Therefore, the relative error is 0.1.

Differentiation

Problem 1

Use differentials to approximate the given number.

(1) $\sqrt{35.7}$ (2) $\sqrt[3]{63.91}$

Answer

(1) 5.975 (2) 3.998125

Solution

(1) $f(36-0.3) \approx f(36)+dy$ where $f(x)=\sqrt{x}$. Then, from $\dfrac{dy}{dx}=\dfrac{1}{2\sqrt{x}}$, we have $dy=\dfrac{1}{2\sqrt{x}}dx$.

If $x=36$ and $dx=-0.3$, we have $dy=\dfrac{1}{2\sqrt{36}}(-0.3)=\dfrac{-0.3}{12}=-0.025$.

Therefore, $\sqrt{35.7}=\sqrt{36}-0.025=5.975$.

(2) $f(64-0.09) \approx f(64)+dy$ where $f(x)=\sqrt[3]{x}=x^{\frac{1}{3}}$.

Then, from $\dfrac{dy}{dx}=\dfrac{1}{3}x^{-\frac{2}{3}}$, we have $dy=\dfrac{1}{3}x^{-\frac{2}{3}}dx$.

If $x=64$ and $dx=-0.09$, we have $dy=\dfrac{1}{3}(64)^{-\frac{2}{3}}(-0.09)=-\dfrac{0.09}{48}\approx-0.001875$.

Thus, $\sqrt[3]{63.91} \approx \sqrt[3]{64}-0.001875=3.998125$.

Therefore, the answer is 3.998125.

AP Calculus AB & BC Rewritten from the Beginning

Problem 2

Use differentials to approximate the increase in the area of a sphere when its radius increases from 3 inches to 3.02 inches.

Answer 0.48π square inches

Solution

The surface area of a sphere is $A = 4\pi r^2$, and from $\dfrac{dA}{dr} = 8\pi r$, we get $dA = 8\pi r\, dr$. If $r = 3$ and $dr = 0.02$, then $\Delta A \approx dA = 8\pi(3)(0.02) = 0.48\pi$ (square inches).

11　Exercise

01 Use differentials to approximate the given numbers.
(1) $\sqrt{100.03}$
(2) $\sqrt[3]{8.2}$

02 The sides of a cube are measured to be 3 inches with an error of ± 0.03 inches. Estimate the error in the volume of the cube.

11 Answers & Solutions

01 (1) 10.0015 (2) 2.0167

(1) $f(100.03) \approx f(100) + dy$ where $f(x) = \sqrt{x}$. $\dfrac{dy}{dx} = \dfrac{1}{2\sqrt{x}}$, so $dy = \dfrac{1}{2\sqrt{x}} dx$.

If $x = 100$ and $dx = 0.03$, then $dy = \dfrac{0.03}{2\sqrt{100}} = \dfrac{0.03}{20} = 0.0015$.

Therefore, $\sqrt{100.03} \approx \sqrt{100} + 0.0015 = 10.0015$.

(2) $f(8.2) \approx f(8) + dy$ where $f(x) = \sqrt[3]{x}$. $\dfrac{dy}{dx} = \dfrac{1}{3} x^{-\frac{2}{3}}$, so $dy = \dfrac{1}{3} x^{-\frac{2}{3}} dx$.

If $x = 8$ and $dx = 0.2$, then $dy = \dfrac{1}{3} (\dfrac{1}{4})(0.2) = 0.0167$.

Therefore, $\sqrt[3]{8.2} \approx \sqrt[3]{8} + 0.0167 = 2.0167$.

02 Absolute Error $= 0.81$, Relative Error $= 0.03$

The approximate volume of the cube is $3^3 = 27$.

If we denote the side of the cube as x, and the volume of the cube as V,

$V = x^3$, so $\dfrac{dV}{dx} = 3x^2 \Rightarrow dV = 3x^2 dx$.

If $x = 3$ and $dx = 0.03$, then $\Delta V \approx dV = 3(3)^2(0.03) = 0.81$.

Thus, (the volume of the cube) $= 27 \pm 0.81$ (cubic inches).

Absolute Error $= 0.81$

Relative Error $= \dfrac{\Delta V}{V} \approx \dfrac{dV}{V} \approx \dfrac{0.81}{27} \approx 0.03$

7th Edition

AP Calculus
AB&BC Rewritten from the Beginning
Vol.1

A Whole New Way to Understand Calculus
Hyunsung Shim (Albert Shim)

Copyright © 2025 by Mastering Math
All rights reserved. No part of this book may be reproduced in any form without permission of the publisher. In order to use it as educational material in schools or organizations, it is necessary to have a contact with the author first.

America Math Lab(Mastering Math)
One Samsone Street, Suite 3500, San Francisco, CA94104

Room 403, Sky Plaza, 322 Byeollae 3-ro, Namyangju-si, Gyeonggi-do, Republic of Korea

Email address : albertmath11@gmail.com